CONTENTS

SPSS FOR WINDOWS MADE SIMPLE

(Second Edition)

Paul R. Kinnear

Colin D. Gray

Department of Psychology,

University of Aberdeen

Psychology Press
a member of the Taylor & Francis group

Psychology Press, Publishers
27 Church Road
Hove
East Sussex, BN3 2FA
UK

British Library Cataloguing in Publication Data

A catalogue record for this book is available from the British Library

ISBN 0-86377-827-5

Printed and bound by Redwood Books, Trowbridge, Wiltshire, UK
from camera-ready copy supplied by the authors

PREFACE TO SECOND EDITION

This book is an introduction to the use of SPSS for Windows. Some years ago it became evident, from our own extensive experience of teaching university students, that an introductory book on SPSS was needed, particularly one specially tailored to the requirements of researchers in the social and biological sciences. We thought then that an informal text would not only help readers to get started with SPSS, but also serve as a preparation for the more comprehensive texts already available. The gratifyingly favourable response to *SPSS for Windows Made Simple* exceeded all expectation and encouraged us to produce a Second Edition which, as well as describing the inevitable software updates, also incorporates the fruits of the experience and advice gained over the intervening period.

The First Edition described the use of Release 5 of SPSS in the Windows 3.1 environment. Subsequently, Windows 3.1 was succeeded by Windows 3.11 and Windows 95; and SPSS Release 5 was followed by 6.1 and 6.1.3 (for Windows 3.1 and 3.11, respectively) and 7.0 (for Windows 95). Releases 6.1 and 6.1.3 were very similar to Release 5, but Release 7 has brought some major changes, including the Output Navigator, which offers a much higher quality of output and gives the user greater editorial control over SPSS output than ever before.

The Second Edition of *SPSS for Windows Made Simple* has benefited not only from the queries and comments of our own students, but also from the correspondence and queries of readers from a surprisingly wide range of disciplines. As a result, some topics, such as the choice of a statistical test, are now given a fuller treatment; although it is stressed that this is not a statistical text as such, and the reader is referred to the appropriate authorities. Since readers welcomed the illustrative material in the First Edition, the Second Edition has an abundance of worked examples using both SPSS 6 and SPSS 7. As before, there are screen images of menus and dialog boxes, as well as annotated output listings. These are accompanied by clarification of the points that have arisen most frequently from readers' comments and students' queries during practical classes. While, as the title suggests, the emphasis is upon simplicity rather than comprehensiveness, the range of problems and techniques covered is considerably wider than in other comparable introductory texts.

We anticipate that readers will have had varied experience of computing and the use of computing packages. Accordingly, Chapters 1 to 4 introduce the reader to the PC, the Windows operating system (including Windows 95), and the preparation and exploration of data sets. At various points, the reader is informed of the material that is about to be presented, so that the experienced user can skip the section (or even the chapter) concerned. Chapter 5, which gives advice on choosing a statistical test, has been greatly expanded to give closer consideration to those aspects of the research situation that govern the choice of a statistical test. There are also much fuller tabular summaries of tests for one-sample, two-sample and multi-sample designs. There is also coverage of regression, and of multivariate methods such as MANOVA, discriminant analysis and factor analysis. The remaining chapters are fairly self-contained, each dealing with a particular test or procedure, with preliminary comments about its use and specification of the conditions that must be satisfied for its correct application.

The book concludes with a course of twenty-four Exercises, the first eight being concerned mainly with data exploration and manipulation, the remainder with topics from Chapters 6 - 15. Wherever possible, the opportunity has been taken to amplify and illustrate important points that could only be touched upon in the body of the text. There is also a comprehensive Index.

Instructors familiar with the First Edition will find that Chapter 3 has been expanded to cover more fully the inputting of data from experiments with between subjects and within subjects factors. Chapter 4 has been expanded to include graphical procedures. Chapter 5 has been rewritten as described earlier. The remaining chapters have been revised to improve clarity. Where appropriate, all chapters now include output listings from both SPSS 6 and SPSS 7. Additional exercises have been added; in fact, instructors may wish to use the first eleven Exercises (up to one-way ANOVA) for an introductory course and the remainder for a more advanced course.

The authors are most grateful to those who have helped in the production of this book. Our chief debts are to John Lemon, Senior Computing Adviser at the Computing Centre at Aberdeen University, whose comments and help have been invaluable, and to Caroline Green of the Department of Psychology who, as our students' principal tutor in the Department in recent years, has suggested many improvements upon the original text and been mainly responsible for preparing the new Exercises on data exploration and manipulation in this Second Edition. Finally, we would like to thank all those who, though too numerous to mention individually, have contributed advice or comments, or have helped to maintain the smooth operation of the hardware and software.

Paul R. Kinnear and Colin D. Gray.
May 1997.

[illegible]

CHAPTER 1

THE PERSONAL COMPUTER

1.1 INTRODUCTION

1.1.1 To The Reader

We anticipate that our readers will vary considerably in their computing background. Some will certainly be experienced in the use of computing systems and packages; but others, just as certainly, will be newcomers to computing. Should you be in the former category, you will probably wish to skip the remainder of this chapter, which is about computer basics, and move directly to Chapter 2; indeed, if you are already a **Windows** expert, Chapter 3 might be your best starting point. But if you are not an experienced user, we suggest you begin with this chapter, and familiarise yourself with some computing terminology, with the layout of the PC computer keyboard, with the nature and functions of an operating system, and with the organisation of files and directories. If any of these terms are unfamiliar to you, they will be explained in the following sections.

1.1.2 Computers in general

A computer is a device for **processing information**. This processing has three aspects:

(1) the **inputting** of information;

(2) the **central processing** of the input;

(3) the **output** of the results.

Computers are designed to follow sets of instructions known as **programs**, or **software**, the computer itself (together with additional 'peripheral' items of machinery, such as printers) being known as **hardware**.

There are several ways of inputting information to a computer. One way is by typing at a **keyboard** resembling that on a typewriter; but information can also be retrieved from storage and entered, or input from a network.

The computer's responses to commands can be viewed on a monitor **screen**. Commands can be given by using a **mouse** and variants such as the **trackball**, a device which controls the position of a **screen pointer**. (There are now many analogues, such as **trackpads**, which respond to the touch of a finger, and **light pens**, which the user applies to the screen; but the principle is always the same.) The mouse (we shall retain this as a generic term for all such analogues) is one of the mainstays of modern computing.

The inputting of information, the giving of commands and the inspection of computer output can all be implemented with the mouse and monitored on the screen. It is often useful, however, to have a permanent record of the work the computer has done. A permanent print-out, or **hard copy**, of computer output is obtained by the use of a piece of peripheral hardware known as a **printer**.

An important aspect of computing is the retention of information in memory, both in the **short term** (that is, for the duration of a computing session) and in the **long term** (indefinitely). Information is stored in units called **files**, which are patterns of electromagnetic disturbance on the surfaces of structures known as **disks**, the latter being driven by hardware called **disk drives**. (For additional back-up storage, particularly in mainframes, electronic **recording tape** is used.)

By the operation of a disk drive, information is stored in and read from files on disk. Until quite recently, there have been two main types of disks:

(1) **floppy disks**, which are physically accessible to the user and hence portable;

(2) **hard disks**, which are an integral part of the hardware and cannot be withdrawn by the user.

Modern machines, however, may also have **compact disk (CD) drives**, which can store large amounts of information.

In the early days of desktop computers, floppy disks (and hard disks too) could only too easily be damaged, or **corrupted**, so that the information they contained was lost, a sickening experience when a file has taken many hours to build. Since then, floppy disks (and files stored on them) have certainly become more robust. Corruption, however, can still occur, and it is still very sound practice to **duplicate and store all important files, preferably on hard disk.** The resulting peace of mind is well worth the trouble.

Before a new floppy disk can be used to record material, it must be **formatted** (i.e. prepared for use with a specific **operating system** - see below). Until recently, it was standard practice for users to format their own disks, but now disks intended for a particular computer platform usually come ready-formatted from the manufacturer.

Some PCs are **stand-alone** machines, intended for independent use; others are part of a **computer network**, in which the user's PC is one of several that are linked to a central machine known as a **file server**. In either case, however, the procedure for operating SPSS for Windows is basically the same, barring a few minor details, such as the manner in which one enters and leaves the system, and how one prints the output.

1.1.3 Programs, programming and operating systems

There are many programming languages, and expertise in programming takes some time to acquire. Fortunately, there are available sets, or **packages**, of pre-written programs, which can be used effectively by those with little or no programming experience. The **Statistical Package for the Social Sciences (SPSS)** is an example of a computing package which, over the years, has developed and changed with the latest advances in computing technology.

The software and hardware themselves, however, are insufficient to make an effective computing **system** which, as an integrated functional whole, is more than the sum of its parts. In order that the elements of a computing system can contribute effectively to the work of the system, the elements must be able to communicate, or **interface**, effectively to ensure that the chain of information transfer remains unbroken. There are several important interfaces in a computing system. From our point of view, the most important is between the software and the user. To be accessed and used, a program must be set within an appropriate **environment**, within which the user operates by giving commands, making choices and monitoring the results of the computer's response.

In this context, there are two kinds of programs:

(1) **applications**, such as SPSS, which are designed to carry out the user's assignments (word processors also come into this category);

(2) **operating systems**, which create the computing environment within which the application programs are used. An operating system controls basic functions which are common to the use of all programs, and in this sense can be thought of as a program manager, or metaprogram.

An operating system, however, also has several functions with which the user is directly concerned. These include disk formatting, file management and the running of programs. The **Windows** operating system was designed for PCs by the Microsoft company. Microsoft also devised the **Microsoft Disk Operating System (MS-DOS**, or **DOS** for short). While in this book the emphasis will be upon Windows, some consideration of DOS is also essential, especially the notation for storage units and the manner in which these are organised.

A PC system can be set up, or **configured**, so that the user works entirely in a Windows environment. It is also possible, however, to access Windows from DOS. A third possibility is that, especially if the user is on a PC network, a menu will appear which offers Windows as one of several possible choices.

1.1.4 Files and directories

The manner in which information is stored by a computing system may be clarified by analogy with an office filing system, in which an individual item (a document, such as a letter or a bill) is contained in a labelled folder which, in turn, is stored in one of the shelves of the cabinet which, in turn, may be just one of several such units in the office.

We have seen that, in a computing system, information is stored in units called **files**. Files can usefully be thought of as individual documents, like letters, or manuscripts. Files are stored in larger units called **directories**, which are like the labelled folders in a filing cabinet. Since there may be several directories on a disk, they correspond to the shelves in the cabinet. Finally, the files and directories can be located in different disk drives, that is, in different filing cabinets.

Each disk drive is labelled with a letter. Often the PC's own hard disk is known as **Drive c** (it is immaterial whether upper or lower case is used), and the floppy disk drives as **Drive a, Drive b** and so on. If the PC is part of a network, the hard disk of the file server may be labelled **f**. In **DOS notation** (which is used both in MS-DOS and in Windows), a drive's letter label is followed by a colon thus: **c:**, **a:**, **f:**.

1.1.5 The naming of files and directories

A **file name** (two words) can have two components:

(1) a **filename**, which can be up to eight characters (with no gaps);

(2) an optional three-character **extension**, separated from the filename by a period.

For example, in the file name **ttest.sav,** the filename is **ttest** and the extension is **sav.**

The writing of file names is subject to strict rules. The filename component must not exceed eight characters and must have no spaces between its first and last characters. Also, a file name, whether or not there is an extension, **must not end with a full stop.** So **data** is a possible file name; but **data.** is not. The full stop, however, is the only acceptable separator of a filename from its extension: neither a semicolon nor a comma will do. Like a file, a directory has a name of up to eight characters in length; but directory names rarely have extensions.

1.1.6 The organisation of files and directories

The information on a disk is organised hierarchically: files are contained within directories, which themselves can be organised at several levels. At the top of the hierarchy is the **root directory**, which is created by the system itself. In DOS operating system notation, a directory is denoted by the **backslash character** (\): so the notation **a:** locates control in the root directory of the disk in drive **a**. If a file named **survey.sav** is stored on a floppy disk in drive **a**, in a directory named **research,** the **path name** of the file, that is, its position in the hierarchy, is **a:\research\survey.sav**, the second backslash indicating that the directory named **research** is a **subdirectory** of the root directory (which is represented by the first backslash).

Since subdirectories of the root directory can themselves contain subdirectories, the path name of a file can be quite complex if it is buried deeply in the hierarchy. If a draft of a chapter (say Chapter 3) in a book has been stored on a floppy disk in drive **a**, in a file named **chapt3.doc**, in a directory named **section1**, within another directory called **book,** the file's path name would then be **a:\book\section1\chapt3.doc** (no period at the end).

1.2 THE PC COMPUTER KEYBOARD

To use a computer effectively, the user must become accustomed to the layout of the keyboard. Ideally, this section should be read at a real PC keyboard, where the various items can be identified with the descriptions in the text. The reader should access a word-processing package such as Word 6, write a few lines of text and work through this section to learn the effects of various key-pressing sequences and combinations.

1.2.1 Arrangement of the keys on a PC keyboard

To the proficient typist, the PC keyboard will look very familiar. The letter keys are arranged exactly as they are on an ordinary typewriter and there is a **space bar** running along the bottom of the keyboard, a single press of which moves the **cursor**, a blinking image on the screen of the VDU, one space to the right, without any character appearing. Some of the other features of a computer keyboard are shown in Figure 1.

Figure 1.

A typical computer keyboard

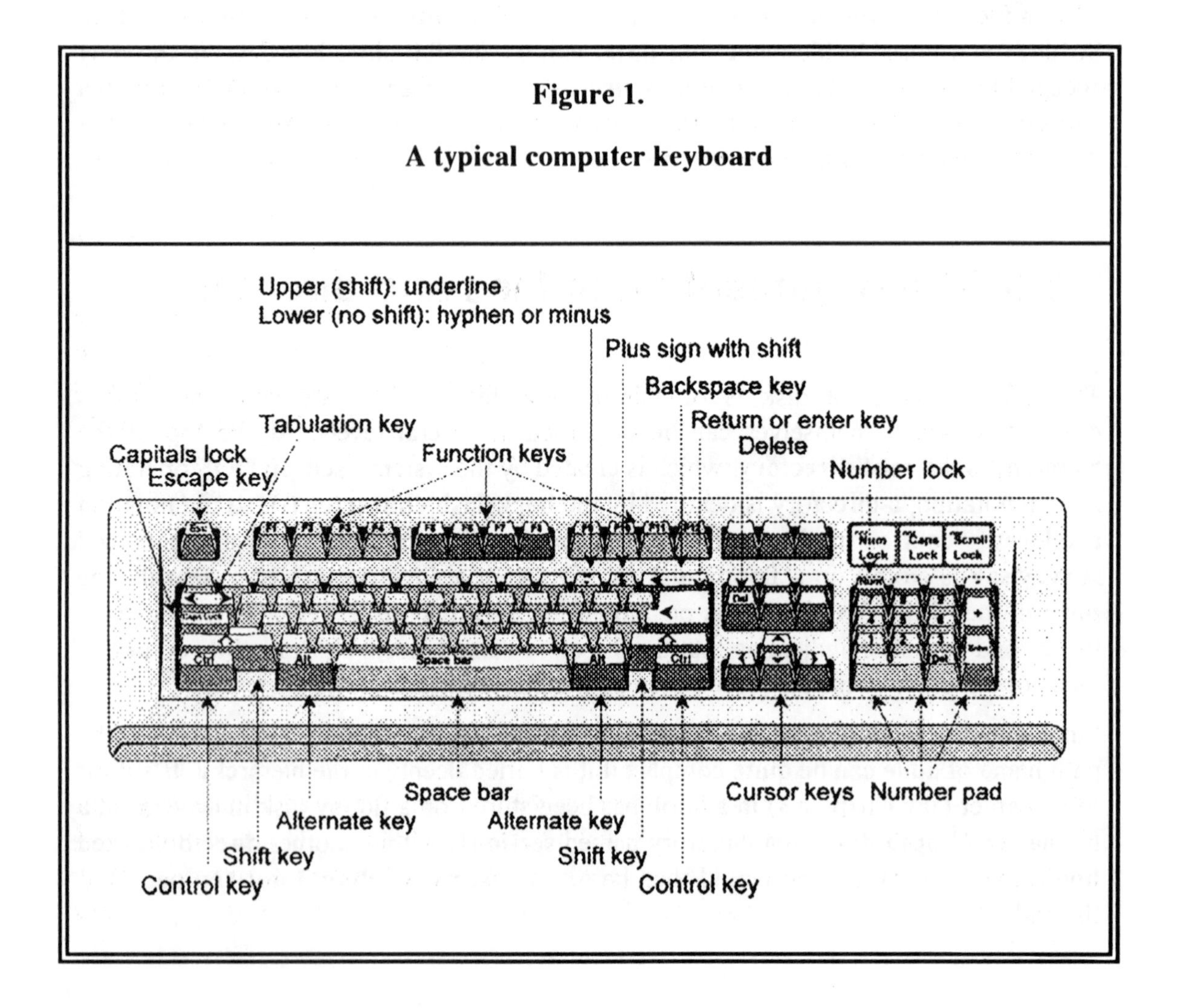

Like an ordinary typewriter, the PC keyboard has two **shift** keys, which in some machines are identically marked with wide upward-pointing arrows ⇑ (Figure 1). When a shift key is pressed and held down, pressing a double-character key will give the upper character. For example, if, while holding down the shift key, you press the key bearing the characters 8 and *, you will obtain the asterisk.

The shift keys also control whether letters are printed in **lower** or **UPPER** case. In the original, or **default**, set-up, pressing a letter key (say that marked E) will show that letter on the screen in lower case (e). But if the same letter key is pressed after a shift key has been pressed and held down, the same letter will appear in upper case (E). Should the user wish to type several letters in upper case, a single press of the **Capitals Lock** key (abbreviated to **Caps Lock** on the key - see below) will achieve this; lower case is restored by another press of Capitals Lock. The Capitals Lock key thus functions as a **toggle switch**: one press produces a change in state, which is reversed when the key is pressed again. Most toggle keys have an indicator light on the keyboard to show their state.

In this book, to make it clear that a key is to be pressed, rather than a sequence of letters typed, the key will be referred to by its name (or a shortened form of this) or its symbol, as in the instruction: **Press Shift**, meaning 'Press the shift key'.

Holding down one key (such as **Shift**) and then pressing another will be represented by using the **slash character (/)** thus: **Shift/E**, which means 'Hold down the Shift key, then press and release E'.

Sometimes, two or more keys are held down together. This will be indicated by separating the names of the keys by hyphens within a single set of square brackets: thus **Ctrl-Alt-Del** means that three keys are to be pressed and held down simultaneously. Be sure to make a clear distinction between the **zero** (0) key (which is one of the number keys above the top row of letters) and the **letter O** (O) key, which is in the top row of letters. They may look similar on the keyboard, but a computer does not interpret the letter O as a zero.

On a computer keyboard, there are several additional keys with functions specific to computing (see Figure 1). For example, in a rectangular area to the right of the main keyboard, there is an extra set of number keys, known as the **number pad**, which is useful when one is typing in a succession of numerical values. Most of the keys on the number pad are labelled with a number plus another character. The numbers are obtained when the **Num Lock** function is active. (To ensure this, it may be necessary to press **Num Lock** - see below.)

1.2.2 A glossary of keys for future reference

The following, for your future reference as you work through this book, is a list of the keys on a typical PC keyboard (newer keyboards may have additional keys for Windows 95 users). At this point, they will be described briefly, and you should try to identify them on a real computer keyboard at the earliest opportunity. With experience, the user may find alternative ways of carrying out some of the operations accessed by these keys.

Alternate (Alt)

This, the bottom left key on the keyboard, is used like the **Shift** key: it works only in combination with other keys, being held down while the latter are pressed. For example, one might hold down the **Alternate** key while pressing E, an operation for which our notation is **Alt /E** .

Backspace (🡐)

The long horizontal key with the left-pointing arrow is the **Backspace** key. When you are typing from a computer keyboard, the current entry point on the screen is indicated by the **cursor**, a small blinking image. Should the user type a letter or a number key, that character will appear at the cursor point. If you press **Backspace**, the cursor will move one space to the left and delete any character that happens to be in that space.

Capitals Lock (Caps Lock)

As explained earlier, the **Capitals Lock** or **Caps Lock** key is a **toggle switch**, determining whether letters are shown in upper or in lower case. The **Caps Lock** key affects only the letter keys.

The cursor keys (←, ↑, →, ↓)

The four keys with thin arrows pointing up, down, left and right are known as the **cursor** keys, because they move the cursor in the directions indicated.

Delete (Del)

A single press of the **Delete** key erases the character at the position of the cursor and replaces it with the next character on the right. The position of the cursor on the screen, however, is unchanged. The effect of continuing to press **Del** has the effect of 'sucking in' text from the right and deleting it, while the cursor remains stationary.

Escape (Esc)

The **Escape** key is often used to change (or 'escape') from one activity to another.

Function keys F1 , F2 , ...

Along the top of the keyboard is a row of **function** keys, labelled **F1** to **F12**. These are not normally used in SPSS for Windows though some of them can be used as shortcuts to menus or facilities - for example F1 opens the Help menu.

Number Lock (Num Lock)

Like **Caps Lock**, this is a toggle switch: one press brings a change of state, which is reversed when the key is pressed again. **Num Lock** is located above the numerical keys on the right of the keyboard. When the **Num Lock** light is on, the number pad functions are disabled and numbers are typed; when the light is off, the functions are operative. Of course, numbers can be entered from the keys above the top row of letters independently of the state of the **Num Lock** facility.

Return (Rtn, Enter or ↵)

On the PC keyboard, to the right of the letter keys, is a large key, which is marked with a crooked arrow ↵. Its main function is to **enter** (i.e. to transmit to the computer) the line that has just been typed by the user. It is therefore sometimes known as the **Enter** key. When one is typing material on the screen, however, the same key also returns the cursor to the start of the next line and so, in that context, the key is referred to as the **Return** key. In this book, we shall generally use the symbol ↵ to refer to this dual-purpose key.

Shift keys (⇧)

The two keys that are identically marked with wide, upward-pointing arrows are the **Shift** keys. Either key can be used. Their function was described at the beginning of this section.

Tabulation (Tab or |← →|)

On the left of the keyboard, above **Caps Lock**, is the **tabulation** key. As with an ordinary typewriter, pressing **Tab** moves the cursor directly to a predetermined position a set number of columns ahead. This is obviously invaluable to the typist who is producing tables of data. But **Tab** has other uses as well: for example, when in the Windows operating system (see below), the user can move from one application to another by using **Alt / Tab** .

1.3 GETTING STARTED

To the reader who has the exclusive use of a PC with Windows, there is little to say about the preliminaries: it is just a matter of turning on your machine and waiting for the first windows to appear. Many users, however, will have access to Windows only as users of a PC network, in which case there are various formalities which may have to be observed before Windows can be accessed.

1.3.1 Booting up the machine

The first step, assuming that the user's machine has not been switched on, is to do so and wait for the computer to **boot up**, that is, load the operating system and run through certain routine checks and diagnostic procedures. The term **boot** is short for **bootstrap**. Bootstrapping is an operation by which some preliminary computer operating instructions are loaded into main memory in order to bring in further material from an external storage device. Nowadays, bootstrapping is carried out automatically when a computer is switched on.

Sometimes, during the course of a computing session, the system may suddenly freeze, or **hang up**: that is, it will no longer respond to the user's instructions. When this happens, there is nothing for it but to **reboot**, that is, start the computer again. A complete rebooting, which involves all the checking routines, is known as a **hard reboot**. To carry out a hard reboot, however, the user is advised not to switch off the machine's power, but to press the **reset** button, which is often (though by no means always) located somewhere on the front of the PC.

For many purposes, a limited rebooting process, which omits many of the routine checks in a hard reboot, is sufficient. This is known as a **soft reboot**, and is achieved by pressing, simultaneously, the **Control**, **Alternate** and **Delete** keys, that is with **Ctrl-Alt-Delete**.

Even with a soft reboot, the user must accept the annoying fact that all the information in current memory that has not been saved to a file on disk will be lost. It is for this reason that you are advised to save frequently, so that if the machine hangs up, or the whole system fails, or 'crashes', only the processing that took place since the last save will be lost. (Note, however, that SPSS for Windows offers the option of frequent automatic saving.)

When the machine has been booted up, the user could be presented with any of several possible displays on the screen:

1) On many stand-alone computers the boot-up procedure starts **Windows** and the user works entirely within the Windows environment. This is the default for Windows 95.

2) When the user is on a **PC network**, it is usual for a menu to appear, offering a variety of choices, including access to Windows.

3) The user may first enter the DOS operating system, in which case the **DOS prompt C:\ >** will appear. This means that the user is in **Drive c** (the hard disk of the computer), in the **root directory**. To access Windows, type **win**.

1.3.2 Logging in and logging out

For security, and efficient resource management, access to a communal computing system may require a procedure by which the user, having already made arrangements to use the system beforehand, presents proof of identification, in the form of a **user number** and a **password**. This is known as **logging in**, and has the effect of making some of the computer's processing capacity and storage available to the user for the duration of the session. It is therefore essential, at the end of the session, to inform the system that these resources will no longer be needed, a procedure known as **logging out**. (It is bad practice simply to switch off, because part of the system's capacity may continue to be monopolised; moreover, other users may be able to access your files!)

SUMMARY

1) A computing system has 3 aspects:

   a) **input**;

   b) **central processing**;

   c) **output**.

   Information is input either from the **keyboard** or from storage in **files**. The output appears on the screen of a **visual display unit (VDU)** and is printed to obtain a **hard copy**.

2) Files are stored on **disks**, which are operated by **disk drives**. **Floppy disks** are portable; **hard disks** are not.

3) Since files are merely patterns of electromagnetic disturbance, they are fragile and must be **backed up** on other disks.

4) Although similar to that of a typewriter, the PC keyboard has a number of additional keys specific to computing, such as **Alt**, **Ctrl**, and the **number pad**.

5) An **operating system** creates a computing **environment**, within which the user accesses and applies task-oriented **programs** and **packages**.

6) An operating system is loaded by a process known as **booting**.

7) In the **Windows** operating system, commands are usually made by selecting items from graphic displays.

8) For reasons of security and efficient resource management, the user of a system will often be required to **log in** and **log out** of the system.

CHAPTER 2

WINDOWS OPERATIONS FOR SPSS

2.1 INTRODUCTION TO WINDOWS OPERATIONS

We can assume that the user with the exclusive use of a PC with **Windows** is already familiar with the system, at least to some extent. For the user of a network PC, however, Windows may be much less familiar, and it may be useful to outline those features that we have found particularly helpful when running SPSS.

We should also point out that there are already available several excellent, comprehensive texts on Windows (e.g. Microsoft, 1992). To use SPSS, however, only a few basic Windows operations will be needed..

There are several versions of Windows available, most commonly Windows 3.1, 3.11 (hereafter abbreviated to Windows 3) and the most recently released Windows 95. Much of what follows is common to all versions, but the reader should be aware that (especially with Windows 95) there are variations.

2.1.1 The Windows operating system

An operating system, such as Windows, sets the scene, or creates an **environment**, within which the user accesses or runs packages such as SPSS and word processors. The term **application** is often used to denote such items of software. For Windows the environment is essentially **graphical**, in which symbols appear as **icons**. Commands are given by selecting from arrays or lists of commands that appear on the screen. Selection is effected by controlling the position of an arrow (or other pointing symbol) on the screen.

Icons make their first appearance in a labelled rectangular area on the screen known as a **window**, which appears against a background known as the **desktop**. For example, Figure 1 shows the SPSS 6.1.3 and SPSS 7 icons. There are different kinds of windows, with different functions. Some contain arrays of icons; others invite the user either to adjust pre-set values or to enter further information. (The second type of window is known as a **dialog box**.)

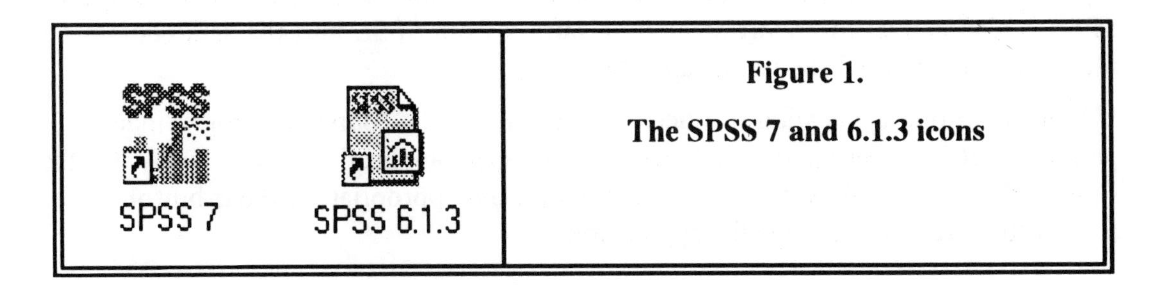

Figure 1.

The SPSS 7 and 6.1.3 icons

2.1.2 Controlling the screen pointer in Windows

In Windows, the position of the screen pointer can be controlled with a **mouse**. On the upper side of the traditional mouse are two buttons, left and right. When the arrow has been positioned at the correct point on the screen, clicking (or sometimes double-clicking) the left button of the mouse transmits the user's choice to the computer. **Double-clicking** means pressing the left button down twice in very quick succession; otherwise the desired effect will not be obtained. In **click-and-drag** operations, the left button is held down, while the mouse is moved. This technique is useful for moving windows and icons about on the screen. It can also be used to change the size of a window. The right button of the mouse is used only occasionally.

It will soon be noticed that the screen pointer assumes a variety of forms. Its first shape is that of a small hour-glass, which indicates that 'something is going on', and the user should do nothing until the shape changes. The hour-glass will appear at the point when **Windows** is being accessed and whenever processing is taking place thereafter. Since PCs vary enormously in their capacity to process information, the user of smaller machines will be more aware of the hour-glass, because processing takes longer. In any case, the user should always bear in mind that *processing takes time*.

The other common screen pointer shapes are: a cross; a girder or I-beam **I** ; a diagonal arrow ⇖ ; a horizontal double-arrow ⇔; a vertical double-arrow ⇕; a diagonal double-arrow ⤡. Each of these has its significance and is a useful cue, but we shall consider the meaning of each pointer shape as it arises.

In Windows, it is also possible to give commands by pressing keys. In fact, as the user becomes accustomed to Windows, key pressing often becomes the preferred mode of operation, since it is faster than manipulating the mouse.

2.1.3 Keeping more than one application open

One of the outstanding features of Windows is that the user can keep several applications open at the same time. This means that it is quite possible to be writing a report of an experiment in a word-processing application and, while doing so, (when SPSS is also active) to import computing output from SPSS into the same document file. This is an enormously useful capacity.

If more than one application has been opened, it will be found that for Windows 3, pressing **Alt/Tab** repeatedly will bring each open application successively to the screen. In the case of Windows 95, clicking on the appropriate taskbar button at the foot of the screen will change the application.

2.2 THE PROGRAM MANAGER WINDOW

In Windows 3, the first window to appear is the **Program Manager** window (Figure 2). (This caption appears in the coloured strip, or **title bar**, running across the top of the window. This bar is a feature of every window.)

Within the **Program Manager** Window, can be seen other smaller windows. The selection will vary depending on the applications and facilities that have been installed in the computer. The three most important windows shown in Figure 2 are **Main**, **Accessories**, and from the point of view of this book, **SPSS** (note that the SPSS icons within the SPSS window will vary depending on the version in use). The applications within **Main** effectively 'set the scene' for the running of packages such as SPSS. The layout of these windows can vary from one computer to another.

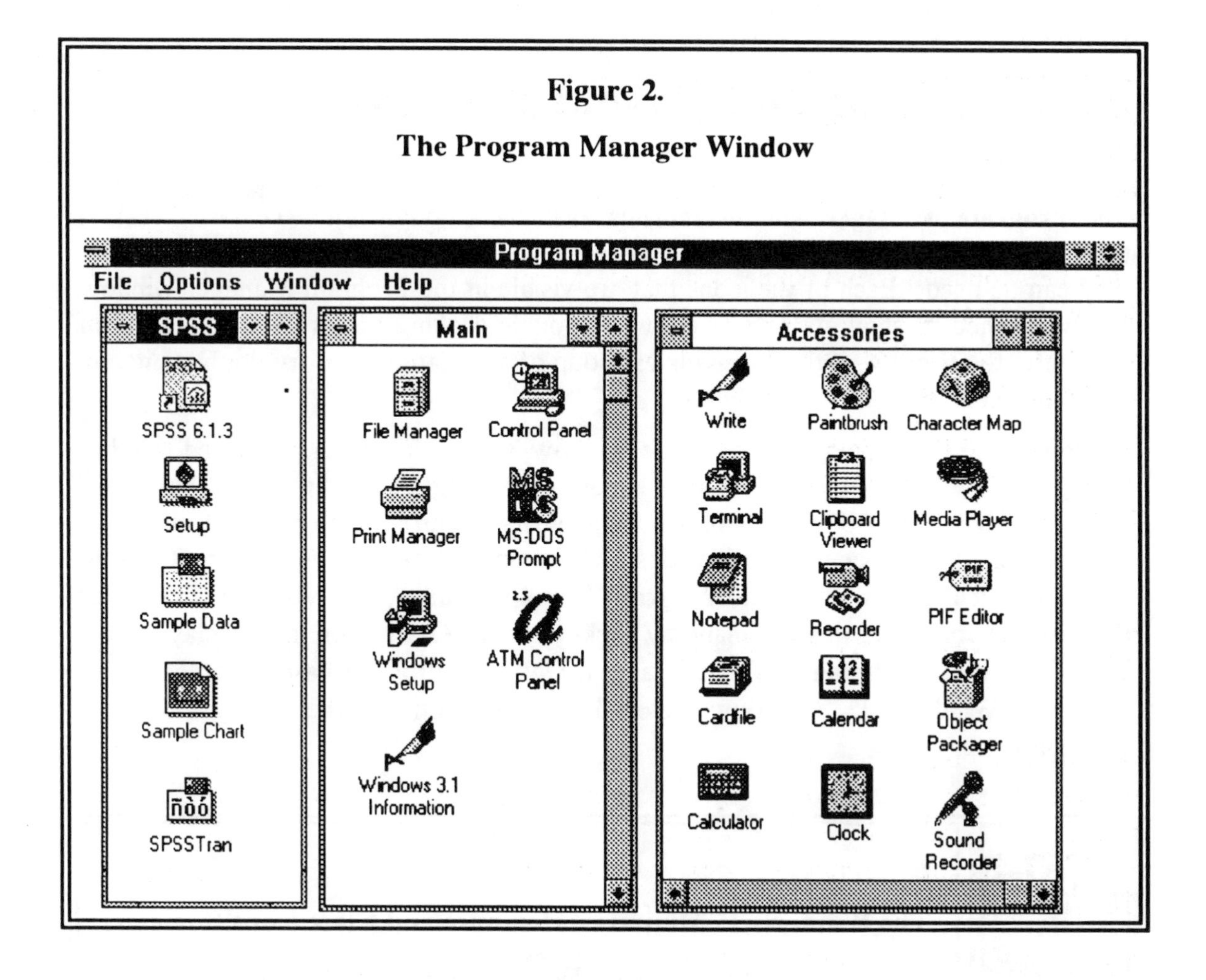

Figure 2.

The Program Manager Window

With **Windows 95** it is necessary to click the **Start** button in the desktop to open the menu shown in Figure 3. Pointing the cursor at **Programs** will produce a menu of programs.

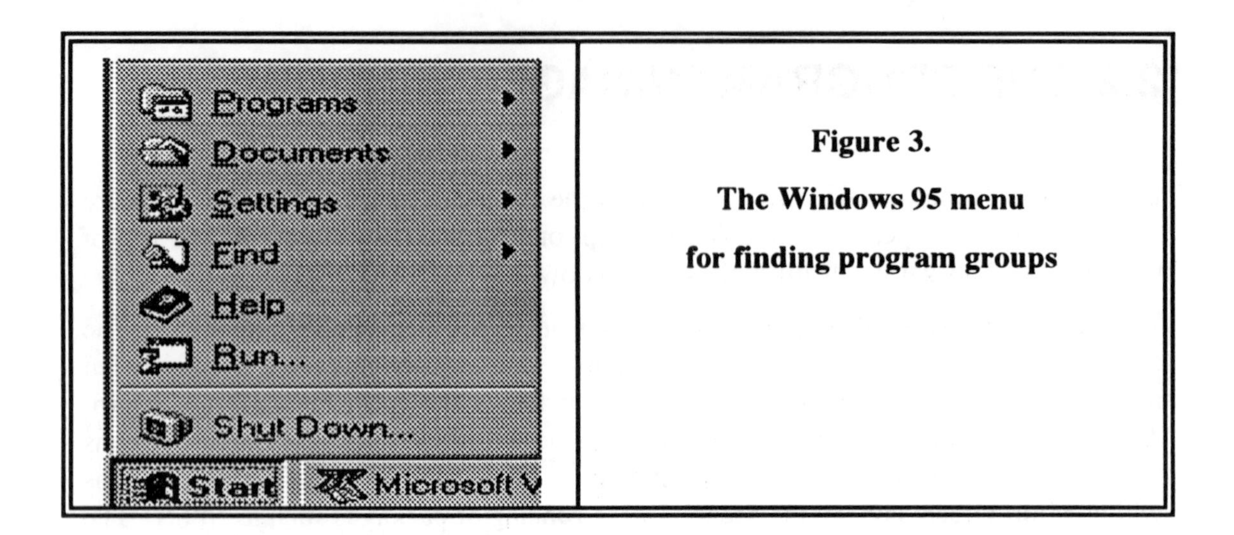

Figure 3.

The Windows 95 menu for finding program groups

2.2.1 Opening and closing a window

The **Program Manager** window remains available (though not necessarily visible) throughout a Windows 3 session. Other windows, however, must be opened before they can be used. Each of the icons that are visible in the Program Manager window can be opened to show its own window by double-clicking on its icon. To confirm this, enter the window of the **Accessories** group of applications and try double-clicking on **Clipboard Viewer**.

There is more than one way of closing a window. On the left of the coloured title bar in any window in Windows 3 is a small square containing a short horizontal bar. This is the **Control-menu** box. Double-clicking on its Control-menu box will close the window (or open a menu which includes a Close option) of any application. Clicking on the **Control-menu** box of the **Program Manager** quits Windows altogether, after the user has confirmed this command by clicking on the **OK** button in a display known as a **confirmation dialog**. (There is also a **Cancel** button, in case of a change of mind.) In Windows 95, a window is closed by clicking on × in the top right corner - see Figure 3.

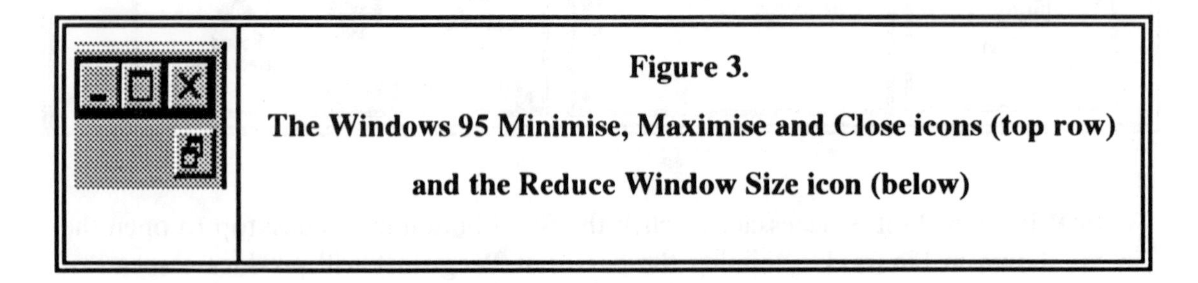

Figure 3.

The Windows 95 Minimise, Maximise and Close icons (top row) and the Reduce Window Size icon (below)

2.2.2 Controlling the size and position of a window

On the right hand side of the title bar are two small squares: the left (**Minimise**) contains a downward-pointing arrow; the right (**Maximise**) has an upward-pointing arrow. Clicking on **Minimise** reduces any window to an icon in the desktop. Try this with the **Program Manager** window. The effect is quite dramatic: the window is reduced to a tiny icon in the bottom left corner of the screen. Restore the window by double-clicking on the Program Manager icon. Clicking on **Maximise** expands the window to fill the entire screen, so that the desktop area previously outside the window now disappears. Restore the window to its original size by double-clicking on the **title bar** or by clicking on the outer of the two squares to the right of the title bar (see Figure 2). The equivalent icons for **Windows 95** windows are shown in Figure 3.

Finer control of the position and size of a window can be achieved by two **click-and-drag** operations (see Section 2.1.2). The **position** of the entire window can be adjusted by click-and-dragging on the window's title bar. The **height or width** of a window can be adjusted by click-and-dragging on a border. To change **both height and width**, click-and-drag on the lower right corner. The success of a **click-and-drag** window-shaping operation depends upon the shape of the screen pointer, which must assume the double-arrow shape (↔): horizontal for an adjustment of width; vertical for an adjustment of height; diagonal for an adjustment of both width and height.

2.2.3 Scrolling

Some lists of items are so long that they cannot all be seen at once through a window. On the borders of some windows, there are grey bars with arrows at either end: at vertical borders, the upper and lower arrows point up and down, respectively; those on the left and right sides of horizontal borders point left and right. These are known as **scroll bars**. By clicking on the arrows, the view through the window can be changed at will. The reader can experiment with scroll bars when studying the **File Manager** window, which is described in the next section.

2.2.4 The menu bar

In the **Program Manager** window (Figure 2), just underneath the title bar, is a white bar on which is written the words: **File**, **Options**, **Windows** and **Help**. The white bar is known as a **menu bar**, and the words it contains are the title captions of its menus. Notice that the first letter of each of these words is underlined: this is to indicate a keyboard shortcut to selecting the item because pressing **Alt** followed by the underlined letter will select the item.

When a menu's title caption is clicked on with the mouse, a **drop-down menu** appears as a list obscuring part of the window. (The drop-down menu can also be obtained by holding down **Alt** and typing the underlined letter in the menu's title: e.g. **Alt/f** obtains the **File** menu.) On the drop-down menu, each item on the list is a command which is run by clicking on its name in the menu or pressing the underlined letter. Among the items in the **File** menu, for example, is **Exit**. In the **Program Manager** window, clicking on **Exit** in the **File** menu quits Windows, as would pressing **Alt** followed by the underlined letter (here it is **x**). (Note: We shall not be including the underlining of menu and item letters in this book: mouse operations will be described instead.)

We shall denote a choice from a menu by indentation thus:

File

  Exit

2.3 THE FILE MANAGER WINDOW

Within the **Main** window, the icon representing the **File Manager** appears as a drawing of a filing cabinet. Double-click on this filing cabinet to obtain the **File Manager** window, part of which is shown in Figure 5. The specific directories and file names will, of course, vary; moreover, the manner in which these are displayed depends upon the options selected. The equivalent window in **Windows 95** is obtained by selecting **Start**, then **Programs**, and finally **Windows Explorer** (Figure 6).

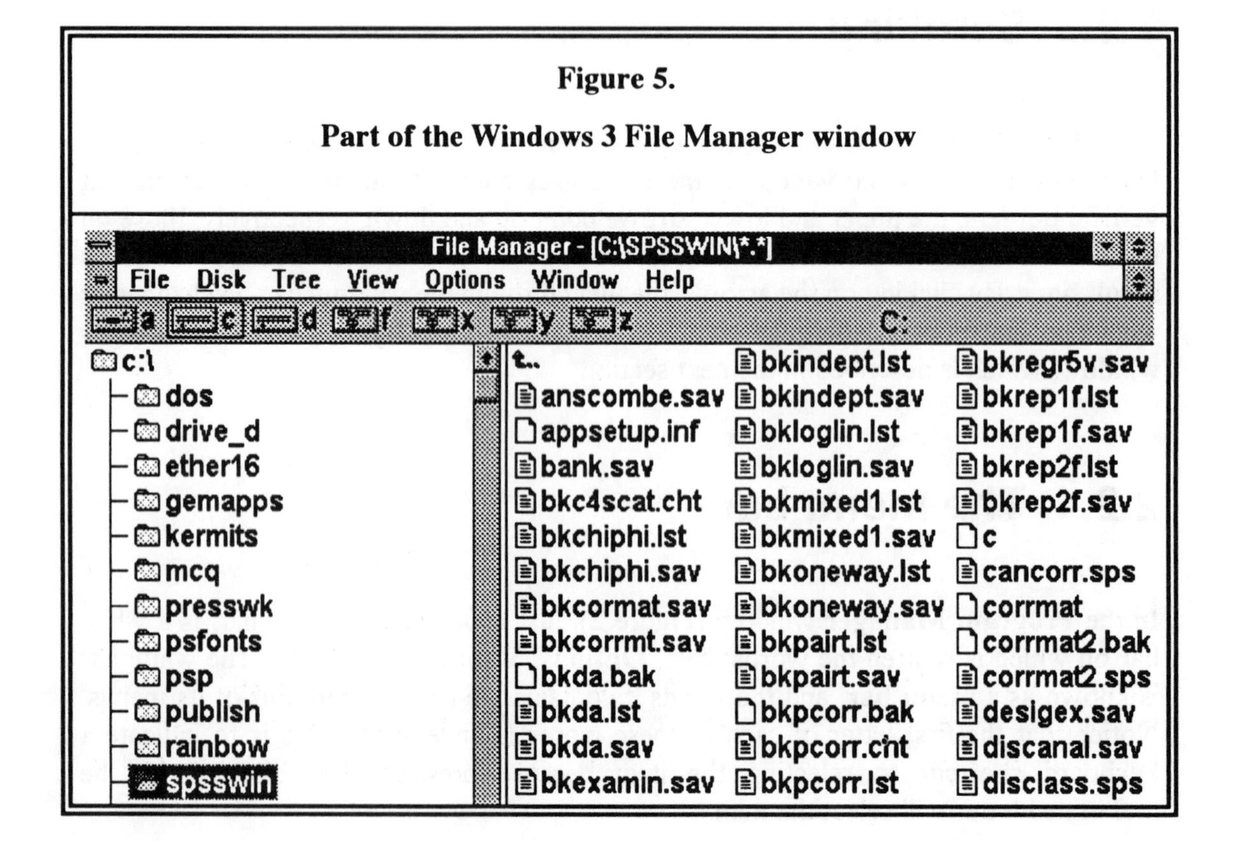

Figure 5.

Part of the Windows 3 File Manager window

The menu bar (Figure 5) has seven captions, of which only **File** and **Disk** will be discussed here. **Tree** and **View** provide options that control how the directories and files are tabulated and viewed.

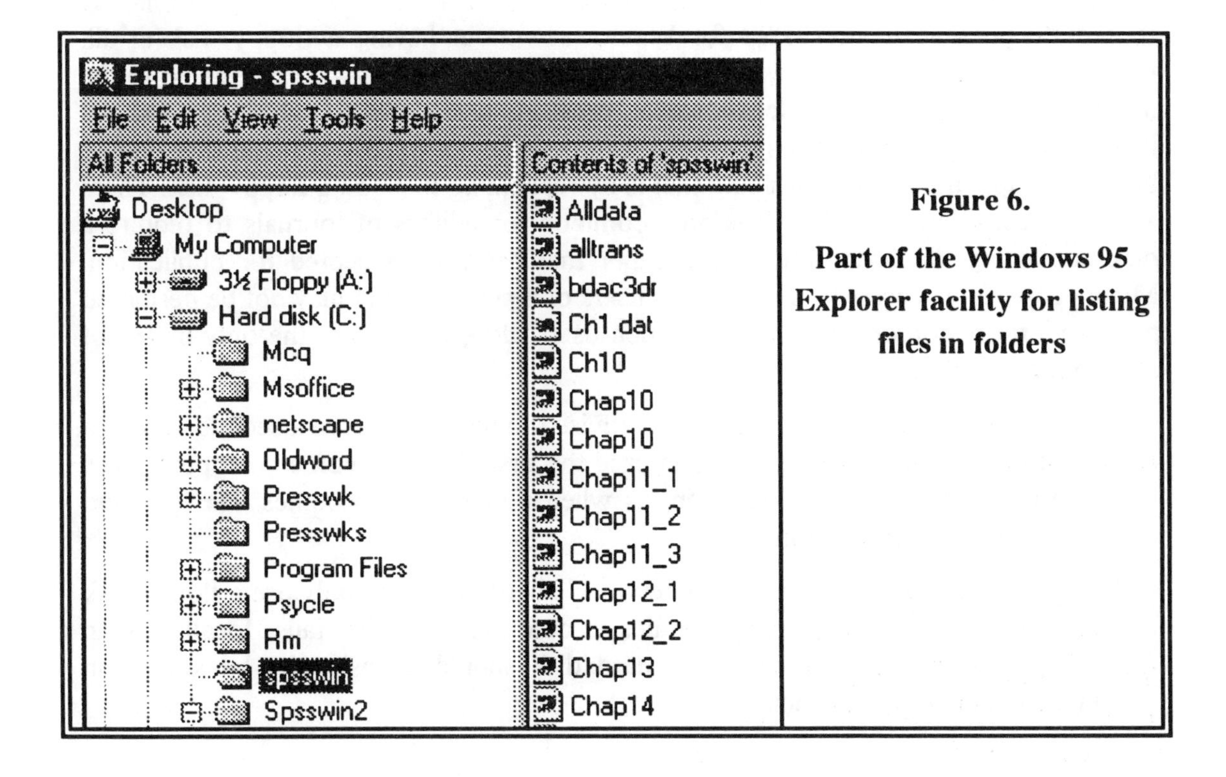

Figure 6.

Part of the Windows 95 Explorer facility for listing files in folders

2.3.1 Viewing the organisation of directories and files

Inside the title bar of the **File Manager** window (Figure 5), is the caption **C:\SPSSWIN*.*** . This path name locates the directory called SPSSWIN in drive **c** (i.e. the computer's hard disk). In the expression *.*, the left and right asterisks are, respectively, a **generic filename** and a **generic extension**: that is, the names of **all** the files in the directory, will be listed. (Because of its generic referent, the asterisk is known as a **wildcard character**.)

On the left of the window, is a list of directory icons, each icon depicting a schematic folder. One of these, **spsswin**, is highlighted and its icon is a picture of an opened folder. By clicking on the arrows above and below the central vertical scroll bar, the icons of other directories can be seen. The icons in the right half of the window may consist of several types of SPSS files in the directory called **spsswin**. Notice that if another directory, say **gemapps**, had been selected, the caption in the title bar would change to **C:\GEMAPPS*.*** , and a different collection of files would be visible through the right half of the window. By clicking on the arrows at the left and right ends of the horizontal scroll bar, the icons of other files within the directory can be seen.

2.4 FLOPPY DISKS

It is quite possible to use SPSS for Windows without having a floppy disk at all; moreover, if the user has the exclusive use of a PC, any new files can be saved to the machine's hard disk. In practice, however, most PC users need to use floppy disks at least occasionally. Since even a hard disk can become corrupted, valuable files should be backed up, and one way of doing that is by replicating them on a floppy disk. There are other considerations also. It is now common for editors of journals to require a disk containing the 'manuscript' of a paper that has been accepted for publication. Many people have access to a PC only as users of a network, and may not be permitted to store information on hard disk; for such users, floppy disks are the only means of storing important files.

- Users relying solely on floppy disks are advised to have in reserve a second disk as a back-up for storing important files in case the first should become corrupted; even this precaution can fail on occasion, as when a disk drive becomes damaged and destroys any disk inserted in it.
- Users with access to their own or a network's hard disk need only use a floppy disk as a back-up for storing important files in case the hard disk fails. Ideally, as an extra precaution, the contents of a hard disk should occasionally be stored on magnetic tape if that is available.

2.4.1 Inserting a floppy disk into the computer

When inserting a floppy disk into the slit of a disk drive, keep the label uppermost and insert the side with the metal piece first (Figure 7). A floppy disk has a **write-protect notch**. When you can see through the notch, the write-protect mechanism is in operation: fresh information cannot be stored on the disk, and any attempt to do so will result in an error message. Before inserting your first floppy disk, therefore, make sure that its plastic tab has been drawn across, closing the gap. This disables the write-protect mechanism.

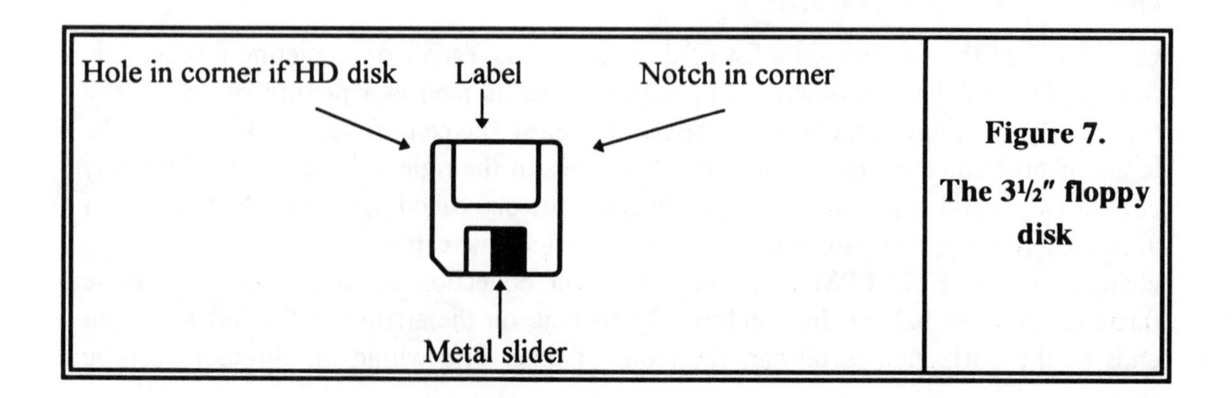

Figure 7.

The 3½" floppy disk

2.4.2 Formatting floppy disks

For a floppy disk to be usable by an operating system, it must be given a set of magnetic markings that the system can recognise. This process is known as **formatting**. On a floppy disk, information is stored in thin annuli known as **tracks**. Each track, in turn, is divided into a number of smaller storage units known as **sectors**. The tracks and sectors are numbered and the information they receive is determined by the formatting procedure.

It is only necessary for a floppy disk to be formatted once, either by the manufacturer or by the user. Thereafter, it can be used in session after session without further formatting - indeed further formatting would destroy any information already stored on the disk.

If formatting is necessary, check that a disk has already been inserted into the floppy disk drive. From the menu bar of the **File Manager** window, choose

Disk

Format Disk

This will bring to the screen the **Format Disk** dialog box (Figure 8).

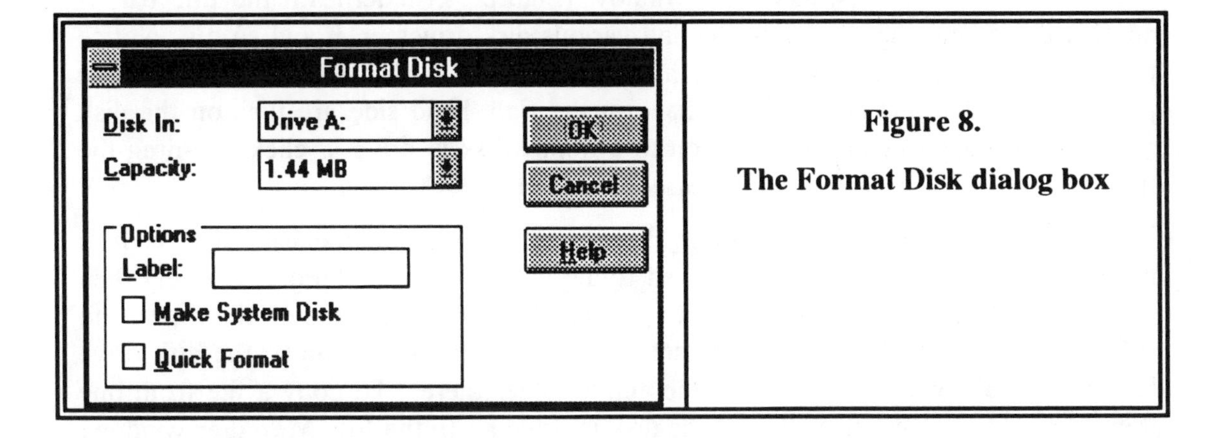

Figure 8.

The Format Disk dialog box

A **dialog box** is a special kind of window which requests information from the user, who must then type in values or change the settings indicated. Within the **Format Disk** dialog box are five labelled boxes, three of which are contained within a larger box, labelled **Options**. The small oblong boxes are known as **text boxes**. There are three text boxes in the dialog box, **Disk In**, **Capacity**, and **Label**. The two small square boxes (**Make System Disk** and **Quick Format**) are **check boxes**. If a check box is clicked on with the mouse, an X shows, indicating that the function is active. A second click will remove the X and uncheck the option. The grey rectangles labelled **OK**, **Cancel**, and **Help** are known as **command push-buttons**, because they tell the Windows File Manager to act immediately. Usually one command push-button will be highlighted by either appearing above its surround or having a dotted line around the command. Pressing the **Enter** key is a quicker alternative to clicking on the highlighted push-button. This is true for all Windows programs and applications, including SPSS.

Check that the **Disk In** box contains the label of the correct disk drive (usually **a**), and that the **Capacity** box shows the correct storage capacity (usually 1.44MB). If you are formatting a double-density disk, click on the scrolling arrow to the right of the **Capacity** box and select 720KB by clicking on that value when it appears. You will also be given the option of adding a label (your name, or that of the application). Click on the **OK** button to start the formatting procedure. Thereafter, all is plain sailing, with the system giving continuous information on the stage the formatting process has reached. When the formatting of the first floppy disk is complete, opt for **N** to terminate the process. If you want to format another disk, accept the offer to format another disk and repeat the process.

For users with **Windows 95**, insert the new disk in the disk drive, select **My Computer** from the Windows screen and click on the floppy disk icon. Then select **Format** from the **File** drop-down menu and follow the prompts thereafter, including selecting either 1.44MB or 720KB.

2.4.3 Copying files to and from a floppy disk

Copying files from a floppy disk to a hard disk or vice versa is a very simple operation in Windows. In the **File Manager** window (Figure 5), underneath the title bar, is another bar containing icons representing various disk drives: **a**, **b** and so on. Notice that in Figure 5 the icon for drive **c** has a box around it showing that it is the one presently selected and hence all the files on the right-hand side are files on the disk drive **c**. To copy one of these files on to a floppy disk in drive **a**, click-and-drag the file's icon to the drive icon **a**, and release the button.

To copy a file from a floppy disk in drive **a** to a folder on the hard disk **c**, it is necessary first to ensure that the desired folder is active on the hard disk **c** and then click on the disk drive icon **a** in order to get the filename icons listed on the right-hand side of the window. Then select the source file icon and drag it on to the disk drive icon **c**, where it will be copied into the active folder there. To copy a file from one floppy disk to another, place the source disk in drive **a**. In the **File Manager** window, click on the disk drive icon **a** to obtain the icons of the files on the disk. Click and drag the file's icon to the disk drive icon labelled **c**. This operation will duplicate the source file on the computer's hard disk, leaving the original on the source floppy disk. Now place the target floppy disk in drive **a**, click on the disk drive icon **c** to obtain the icons of the **c** disk files, and then click-and-drag the copy in **c** to the disk drive icon labelled **a**. This will transfer the file to the target disk.

An alternative method of copying a file is to select the file icon (e.g. **bank.sav**) of the file to be copied and then click on **Copy** within the **File** menu to open the **Copy** dialog box (Figure 9). The two small circles, one of which is marked, are known as **radio buttons**, and arise in situations where only one choice can be made from a list of items. In this case, we are given the choice between copying a file to a disk or placing it in a temporary store known as the **Clipboard**. Assuming that we want a permanent copy of the file, at a specified destination, the upper of the two buttons in Figure 9 is the one that should be marked. Enter the destination of the copied file in the **To** box and then click on **OK**.

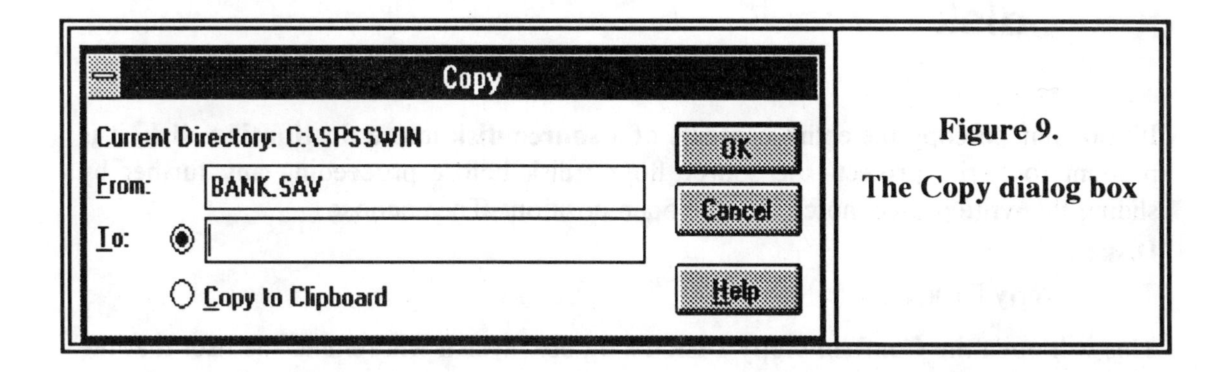

Figure 9.

The Copy dialog box

It should be noted that, when backing up an SPSS file, the foregoing procedures are unnecessary, because the user can save the file directly from SPSS to a floppy disk and repeat the procedure with a second disk.

For users with **Windows 95**, select **My Computer** from the Windows screen and click on the file to be copied. Then select **Send to** from the **File** drop-down menu and choose the appropriate floppy disk drive icon.

2.4.4 Deleting a file

Select the file icon of the file to be deleted (e.g. **bank.sav**) and then click on **Delete** in the **File** menu to open the **Delete** dialog box (Figure 10). Click on **OK** if the file name is correct: you will be asked to confirm the delete decision in a subsequent box.

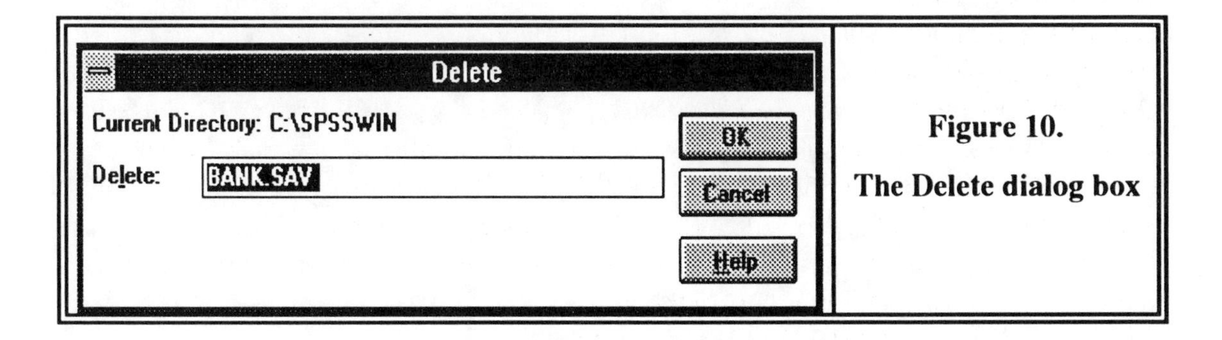

Figure 10.

The Delete dialog box

For users with Windows 95, select **My Computer** from the Windows screen and click on the file to be deleted. Then select **Delete** from the **File** drop-down menu. Clicking on the file and then pressing the **Delete** key has the same result.

2.4.5 Copying the contents of an entire floppy disk

If you want to copy the entire contents of a **source disk** into a **destination disk**, it is prudent to 'write protect' the source floppy disk before proceeding any further by sliding the write protect notch into the open position. Then choose

Disk

  Copy Disk

This will open the **Confirm Copy Disk** dialog box, which will remind the user that the copying process will erase all data previously stored on the **destination** disk. To proceed, click on the **Yes** box. Then comes an instruction to insert the **source disk** (the disk that is being copied). Do so and click on **OK**. The copying process will then proceed, its progress being shown in an information box on the screen. Presently, the user will be prompted to insert the **destination** disk. Do so and click on **OK**. When the process has been completed, the **File Manager** window will be restored.

For users with Windows 95, select **My Computer** from the Windows screen and click on the floppy disk icon. Then select **Copy Disk** from the **File** drop-down menu and follow the prompts thereafter.

SUMMARY

1) In Windows 3, the first window to appear is the **Program Manager**, which contains the window of the **Main** group of **Applications**. The equivalent Windows 95 window is obtained by clicking on **Start** and then selecting Programs. A window can be opened by double-clicking on its icon. A window can be closed by double-clicking on its control-menu box.

2) A window can be re-sized by the **click-and-drag** technique on a border or corner, **maximised** by pressing the maximise button and **minimised** to an icon by pressing the minimise button, restored by double-clicking on its icon, or moved by the click-and-drag technique on its title bar. Its size can be fine-tuned by the click-and-drag technique on either an edge (to widen or deepen it) or a corner (to do both). Often a complete list of items cannot be seen through a window, in which case scroll bars can be used to reposition the window.

3) If new floppy disks have not already been **formatted**, they must be formatted by entering the **File Manager**, and choosing

   Disk

   Format

   In the **Disk** menu is a command for copying an entire disk to a specified destination. Windows 95 users should use the formatting facility available in the **My Computer** option.

4) The **File** menu includes **Copy** for copying a file and **Delete** for deleting a file. A file can also be copied by dragging a file icon on to a disk drive icon. Windows 95 users should use the copying and deleting facility available in the **My Computer** option.

CHAPTER 3

DATA HANDLING IN SPSS

3.1 INTRODUCTION

Before any exploration of data or statistical analyses can take place, it is necessary to input the data to ***SPSS for Windows*** (hereafter referred to as SPSS) in a suitable form and to check that the data set has been correctly transcribed either by inspecting it on the screen or by printing it out. Any corrections or modifications can then be made by invoking one of the editing procedures. It may also be desirable to select (or exclude) cases and to invoke the **Weight Cases** procedure if the data represent frequencies rather than scores. In this chapter, the operations of inputting, editing, saving, listing, printing, selecting and case-weighting will be fully explained and demonstrated with examples.

3.2 SOME RESEARCH TERMS

3.2.1 Variables

A **variable** is a characteristic, or property, of a person, an object or a situation, which comprises a set of different values or categories. **Quantitative variables**, such as height, weight or extraversion, are possessed in **degree** and can be measured; **qualitative** variables, such as sex, blood group or nationality, are possessed in **kind**.

3.2.2 Hypothesis

A **hypothesis** is a provisional supposition about nature, which is stated in such a way that it can be tested empirically, that is, by gathering data. Often, a hypothesis states that there is a causal relationship between two variables, that is, the value of one variable at least partially determines that of another.

3.2.3 Experimental and correlational research

In **correlational research** (a strategy often forced on the psychological investigator), variables are measured as they occur in the individuals studied. As a consequence, it is often difficult to make an unequivocal decision about the research hypothesis, because the effects of the supposedly causal variables are entangled, or **confounded**, with the effects of other variables, such as the personal characteristics of the subjects studied.

Most importantly, the difficulty with correlational research can be summed up in the aphorism:

Correlation does not imply causation

The correlation of two variables may indeed reflect the fact that one variable influences the other; but the pattern is equally compatible with the view that both the correlated variables are themselves caused by a third variable which has not been studied.

In **experimental research**, as opposed to correlational research, one variable, which is hypothesised to exert a causal influence upon another, is manipulated directly by the experimenter, the manipulated variable being known as the **independent variable (IV)**, the variable it supposedly influences being known as the **dependent variable (DV)**. (Should a mnemonic be necessary, one might think of the values of the DV as 'depending' upon - i.e. partly determined by - those of the IV.) The IV is decided upon and controlled *before the experiment is carried out*; the DV is *measured during the course of the investigation.* While this usage of the term independent variable is common, there are several well-known authors (e.g. Tabachnick & Fidell, 1996; Howell, 1997) who use the term to refer to *any* supposedly causal variable, whether it is manipulated directly by the experimenter or not. Those authors use the term *independent variable* in the context of correlational, as well as experimental, research. At times, for convenience, we shall also follow this practice.

3.2.4 The principle of control

The great advantage of the experimental strategy is that, since there is an independent variable, the experimenter is in a stronger position to draw causal inferences from the data, provided that there has been adequate **control** of the effects of potential confounding, or **extraneous variables**. In correlational research, on the other hand, the absence of an independent variable makes it impossible to draw causal inferences unequivocally.

3.2.5 Factors

In experimental design, a **factor** is a set of related conditions or categories. The conditions or categories making up a factor are known as **levels**, even though, as in the qualitative factor of gender, there is no sense in which one category can be said to be 'higher' or 'lower' than the other. Some factors are independent variables: that is, the experimenter manipulates them to ascertain their effects upon selected dependent variables. They are not inherent subject characteristics. Other factors, however, such as gender, or age, are **subject variables**, and are usually included in the experimental design for purposes of control. For most purposes, such as statistical analysis, subject variables are treated as if they were true independent variables.

It should be noted that the term **factor** has more than one meaning in psychological data analysis. In this section, it has been presented as a term in experimental design. Experimental factors are decided upon at the planning stage of the research: they do not emerge from the data yielded by the investigation. Later, however, in the context of correlational research, the statistical technique known as **factor analysis** (Chapter 15) will be introduced. This technique is applicable when a battery of tests is given to a (large) sample of subjects, the purpose being to identify the comparatively few underlying variables that the researcher suspects may underlie the observed correlations among the tests in the battery. In this second usage, a **factor** is a classificatory variable derived from the data gathered in the process of an investigation.

In summary, the terms **factor** and **level** are the equivalents, in the context of experimental design, of the more general terms **variable** and **value**, respectively. A **factor** is a special kind of variable, created by the design of an experiment. In the context of experimental design, a factor is either a true independent variable or a grouping variable such as gender, which we 'manipulate' *statistically*, rather than experimentally, by sampling so many men and so many women.

3.2.6 Between subjects and within subjects factors

Some factors are **between subjects**: that is, the subject is tested under only one condition, or level, of the factor. (Subject variables such as Gender must always be between subjects factors.) Other factors are **within subjects**, that is, the subject is tested under all the different conditions (levels) making up the factor. A design with a within subjects factor is also said to have **repeated measures** on the factor.

In order to ascertain the effectiveness of a drug, an investigator tests the performance on a vigilance task of two groups of subjects:

(1) a group who have ingested a dosage of the drug;

(2) a comparison, or **control**, group, who have received a placebo.

In the terminology of experimental design, this experiment has **one treatment factor (Drug)**, comprising two conditions or **levels**: Drug Present and Drug Absent. Since different samples of subjects perform under the different conditions, this is a **between subjects experiment**. Should the investigator wish to study the effectiveness of more than one drug, the performance of two or more groups of subjects could be compared with that of the controls. In that case, the experiment would still have one treatment factor, but with three or more levels.

A second investigator wishes to test the hypothesis that words presented in the right visual hemifield are recognised more quickly than those presented in the left hemifield. Fifty subjects are each presented with 40 words in the left and right hemifields and their median response times are recorded. In this experiment (as in the drug experiment), there is **one treatment factor** (Hemifield of Presentation) comprising two conditions: Left Field; Right Field. But this time, *the same subjects perform under both conditions*. This experiment is said to be of **within subjects** design, or to have **repeated measures on the hemifield factor.** In the general case of a one-factor, within subjects experiment, the factor would comprise three or more treatment conditions, or levels, and each subject would perform under all conditions.

For example, to test the hypothesis that the accuracy with which a subject shoots at a target depends upon the shape of the target's perimeter, each subject might be tested with circular, square and triangular targets, in which case the treatment factor (Shape of Target) would have three levels.

In Table 1, the designs of the between subjects and within subjects one-factor experiments are shown schematically.

Table 1.

Between subjects and within subjects experiments with one treatment factor

(a) The one-factor between subjects experiment

	Factor: Drug			
Levels	Control	Drug A	Drug B	Drug C
Subjects	Group 1	Group 2	Group 3	Group 4

(b) The one-factor within-subjects experiment

	Factor: Shape of Target			
Levels	Circle	Square	Triangle	Diamond
Subjects	The same group of subjects perform with all four shapes			

3.2.7 Factorial designs: Between subjects, within subjects and mixed designs

It is common for experiments to have two or more factors. For example, our drugs researcher might wish to investigate, in addition to the effects of different drugs upon fresh subjects, the effects of the drugs upon those who have voluntarily gone without sleep for twenty-four hours. Accordingly, an experiment is planned, the design of which is shown in Table 2.

Table 2.

A two-factor factorial between subjects experiment.

	Drug	
State	Drug A	Drug B
Fresh	Group 1	Group 2
Tired	Group 3	Group 4

Notice that a different sample of subjects performs at each of the four combinations of the two treatment factors, Subject's State (Fresh, Tired) and Drug (A, B). Since each subject is tested only once, this type of experiment is said to be of **between subjects factorial** design. It is also described as having **two factors with no repeated measures**.

Table 3.

A two-factor factorial within subjects experiment.

Factor				
Shape:	Triangle		Square	
Colour:	Blue	Green	Blue	Green
Subjects	The same subjects perform under all four combinations of shape and colour.			

Table 3 shows a **within subjects** experiment, in which there are two factors:

(1) Shape of Target (Triangle, Square);

(2) Colour of Target (Blue, Green).

Alternatively, the experiment can be said to have **repeated measures on both factors.**

Suppose that, in addition to the effects of target colour, the experimenter wishes to test the hypothesis that men and women may not produce their best performances with targets of the same colour. Table 4 shows the experimental design.

It will be noticed that in this experiment, there are two factors:

(1) Sex (Male, Female);

(2) Colour of Target (Red, Blue).

Moreover, Sex is a between subjects factor, whereas Colour of Target is within subjects. Factorial experiments in which some (but not all) factors are within subjects are known as **mixed** (or **split-plot**) factorial experiments.

Table 4.

A two-factor mixed factorial experiment with one between subjects factor (sex) and one within subjects factor (colour of target).

	Colour of Target	
Sex	**Red**	**Blue**
Male	Each is tested with red and blue targets.	
Female	Each is tested with red and blue targets.	

3.3 INPUTTING DATA: AN EXAMPLE

In this section, the results of a simple experiment are recast in a form suitable for entry as a data set into SPSS.

3.3.1 A between subjects experiment

In an experiment on the relative efficacy of two mnemonic methods for the recall of verbal material, each individual in a pool of 30 participants is randomly assigned to one of three equal-sized groups:

(1) a **control** group, which receives no training;

(2) a group trained to use the **Galton's Walk** method **(Mnemonic A)**;

(3) a group trained to use the **Peg** method **(Mnemonic B)**.

Each participant is presented with verbal material and asked (at a later stage) to reproduce it in free written recall. The dependent variable is the number of words recalled.

The results of the experiment are shown in Table 5.

Table 5.

The numbers of words recalled by subjects with different mnemonic training histories

Control Group	3	5	3	2	4	6	9	3	8	10
Mnemonic A	10	8	15	9	11	16	17	17	7	10
Mnemonic B	20	15	14	15	17	10	8	11	18	19

3.3.2 Laying out the data in a form suitable for entry into SPSS

Data for SPSS is entered into a spreadsheet format called the **Data Editor** window (Figure 1).

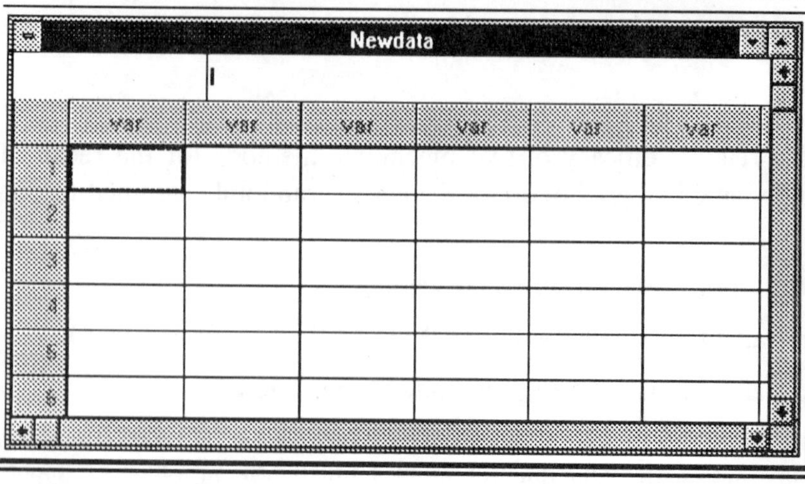

Figure 1.
The Data Editor window

Notice that the rows are already numbered and that the columns are labelled *var*. At this stage they are shaded grey because they have not yet been activated with data or variable names.

Thus:

- Each row represents a subject, or **case**.
- Each column represents a **variable**.

Each cell, rather like a point on graph, has a vertical and a horizontal co-ordinate: here the *horizontal co-ordinate* represents a particular subject or case and the *vertical co-ordinate* represents a particular variable. Within generous limits there can be any number of subjects and any number of variables. It is not generally necessary to identify each subject with a name or number (each row in the Data Editor is already numbered) but if a data set is large or there is a possibility that the rows may be re-ordered using the **Sort Cases** command (obviously the Data Editor row numbers do not move during such a process), then subject identification is recommended. However, it is strongly recommended that a name is specified for each variable because, by default, SPSS will label each variable with the name *var00001*, *var00002* and so on when data are entered if variable names are not supplied.

Data from an experiment or survey may need to be rearranged in order to fit into this spreadsheet type of format. On the basis of what has just been described, the data shown in Table 5, where each row represents the scores of ten subjects are unacceptable for entering into SPSS in that form. The data have to be re-arranged into a format where each row represents the scores of just one subject. But there remains a problem: how will SPSS know whether a row (a subject) belongs to the Control group, the Mnemonic A group or the Mnemonic B group?

Before entering the Data Editor window, it is strongly recommended that the user makes a list of the names and types of variables. In this experimental design, there is one factor, Learning Method, with three levels: Control, Mnemonic A, and Mnemonic B. There is also one dependent variable, Number of Words Recalled. Note that, in contrast with a factor such as Gender, the factor Learning Method is a true independent variable, since subjects are assigned at random to its three component conditions. Since different subjects are used for each learning method, the experimental design is of the **between subjects** type.

The next stage is to decide how these variables will be entered in the Data Editor window. The actual variable names cannot be as long as 'Learning Method' or 'Number of Words Recalled', because variable names (which will be discussed in Section 3.4.3.2) cannot exceed 8 characters and there must be no gaps. We shall therefore abbreviate the variable names to *group* and *score*. The requirement that each row in the Data Editor window contain information on only one subject is met by entering all the scores in Table 5 into one single column of the Data Editor.

- This single column, containing the number of words recalled by each subject, is the DV.

Each learning method is identified with a code: for example, the code numbers *1*, *2* and *3* could be assigned to the Control, Mnemonic A, and Mnemonic B conditions, respectively. These values are entirely arbitrary: any three numbers will do, as long as they are different, because the numbers are to function as **labels**, rather than expressing the degree to which some property is possessed. The entire set of code numbers indicating the experimental conditions under which scores were obtained is an example of what is known as a **grouping variable**. Alternatively, letters such as C, A, B could be used, but for this illustration it is simpler to use digits.

- The condition under which each subject (the IV) was tested is entered in another single column of the Data Editor as a series of codes.

In summary, each column in the Data Editor window will contain the values of one (and only one) variable: in the present case, the first column will contain the independent (grouping) variable, that is, the code numbers (*1*, *2* or *3*) identifying the condition under which each subject in each row performed; the second column contains the scores that all the subjects achieved in the experiment.

In Table 6, the results in Table 5 have been recast, so that each row now contains two data per subject:

(1) A code number showing the learning method *group* (the **IV**) to which that person was assigned.

(2) The *score* (the **DV**) that person achieved under the coded condition.

Moreover, each row now contains data on <u>only one subject</u>.

Table 6.

The data of Table 5, recast in a form suitable for entry into SPSS

(Note that the shaded items have been included here for explanation only: they are not actually entered into SPSS. Only the unshaded variable names and values are entered in the Data Editor window.)

	Variable Names		
	group	score	
Subject 1	1	3	Group 1: The controls
Subject 2	1	5	
...	...	...	
Subject 9	1	8	
Subject 10	1	10	
Subject 11	2	10	Group 2: Mnemonic A
Subject 12	2	8	
...	...	...	
Subject 19	2	7	
Subject 20	2	10	
Subject 21	3	20	Group 3: Mnemonic B
Subject 22	3	15	
...	...	...	
Subject 29	3	18	
Subject 30	3	19	

3.4 ENTERING DATA

Now that the data from the experiment has been re-organised into a format suitable for entry into the Data Editor window, we are ready to proceed to enter the data.

3.4.1 Obtaining the Data Editor window

In Chapter 2, we saw that when Windows 3 is accessed, the first window to appear is the **Program Manager**, which itself contains several other open windows. Among these is usually a window labelled **SPSS**. This is the window of the **SPSS program group** (though in some networks the SPSS icon may be in another window such as **Applications**). Double-click on the SPSS icon to obtain three overlapping windows:

(1) the **SPSS application window** (captioned **SPSS for Windows**);

(2) the **Output window** (captioned **!output1**);

(3) the **Data Editor window** (captioned **Newdata**).

As the **Data Editor** window was forming on the screen, the reader may have noticed the appearance of the hour-glass, which always appears when 'something is happening', and also various messages in the bar that runs horizontally across the base of the SPSS Application window. The final message to appear there is: 'SPSS Processor is ready'. This bar is known as the **status bar**. Like the hour-glass, the status bar apprises the user of the stage of operations: for example, if a large data set is being read from a file, progress is continually monitored, case by case, in the status bar. This **case counter** is one of several useful types of message that appear in different parts of the status bar: there are also messages about the weighting of cases (**weight status**), the selection of specified portions of the data set (**filter status**), and whether the data set has been split into several separate groups for analysis (**split file status**).

Notice that in both the **Data Editor** and the **SPSS Application** windows, the title bars are coloured on the screen; whereas that in the **Output** window is grey. This indicates that, of the three windows, only the first two (in order of mention) are presently **active**, that is, the items therein can be accessed directly by clicking within the appropriate areas.

Initially, every column in the **Data Editor** window (Figure 1 in Section 3.3.3) has the heading *var*, and all the cells are empty.

3.4.2 How many decimal places?

Since we are about to enter numbers into the **Data Editor** window, we need to consider the form (i.e. how many decimal places - if any) in which those values will be displayed. A convenient procedure is to specify a standard, or **default**, format for all values, which can then be over-ridden (if necessary) for specified variables only.

In the menu bar of the **SPSS application** window are the headings of nine drop-down menus (Figure 2).

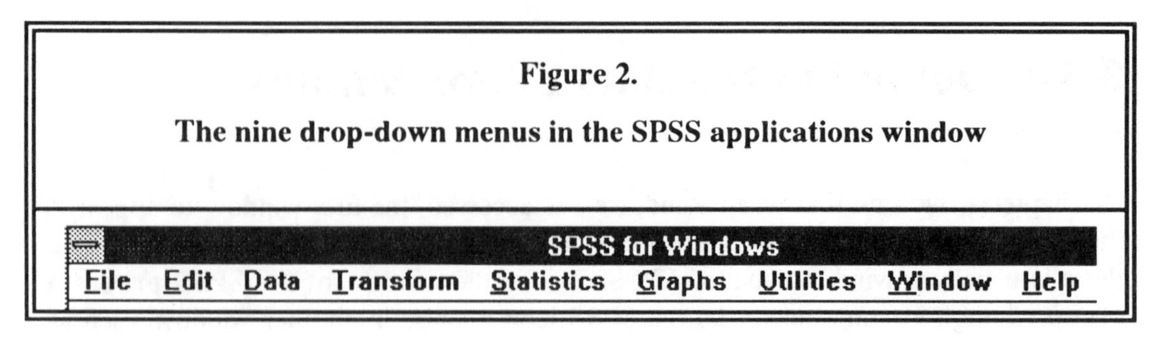

Figure 2.

The nine drop-down menus in the SPSS applications window

Choose
Edit

Preferences

to obtain the **Preferences** dialog box (Figure 3).

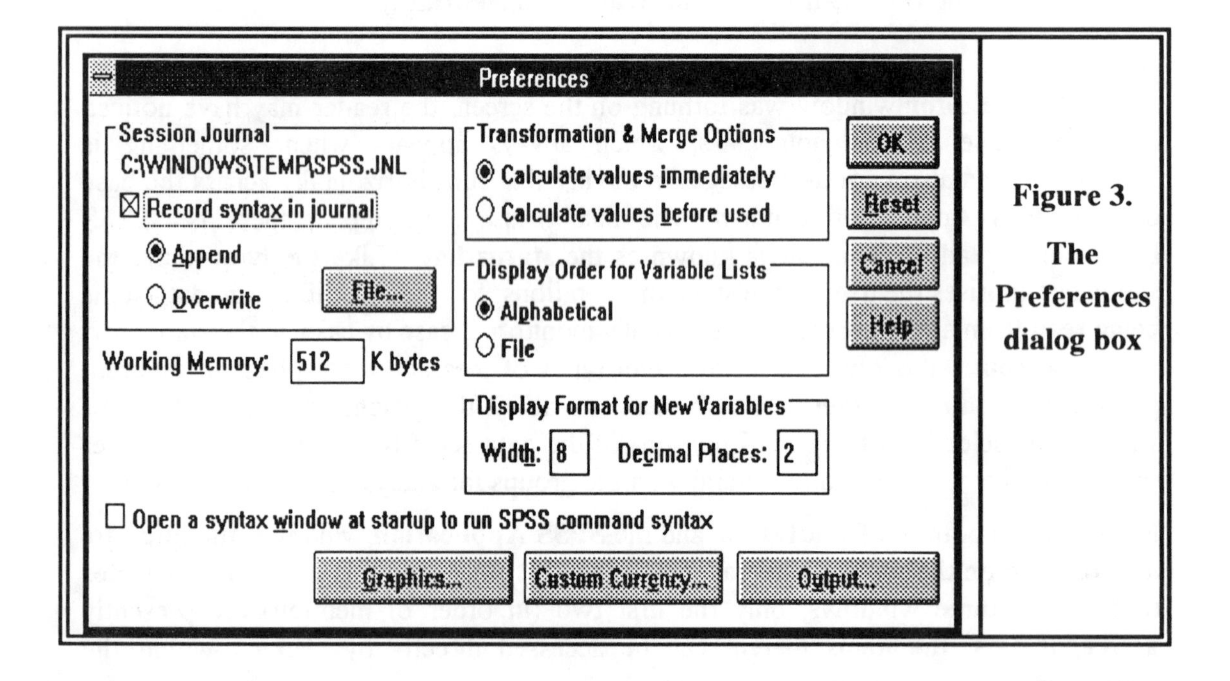

Figure 3.

The Preferences dialog box

Within the **Display Format for New Variables** box are two text boxes, labelled **Width** and **Decimal Places**, in each of which a number is already entered. If those numbers are *8* and *2*, respectively, a total of eight spaces will be allocated to each value and all values will be displayed to two places of decimals, even if they are integers (i.e. *3* will appear as *3.00*). All the data in Table 5, however, are integers, so there is no need for values to be written as decimals at all. Click on the **Decimal Places** box, press the backshift key ← to erase the number and type in a zero. The effect of this change will be to show all values as integers, and the data display will be much easier to read. Leave the **Preferences** dialog box by clicking on **OK**. Note that the default preferences for your system may be different from those shown: Windows is a very flexible system which can be set up in many different ways.

Incidentally, the user might take the opportunity to change the **Display Order for Variable Lists** to **File** instead of **Alphabetical**: this has the effect of listing variable names within dialog boxes in the same order as they are displayed in the Data Editor, rather than in alphabetical order.

3.4.3 Variable names and value labels

Having recast the results in Table 5 into the form shown in Table 6, we are now almost ready to begin entering the data into SPSS. Before doing that, however, we must first assign sensible names to our variables and (for the grouping variable) explanatory labels to the values. In Table 6, the first column contains the code numbers of the grouping variable, and the second contains the scores of the subjects tested under the conditions codified in the first column. We shall name the first and second columns *group* and *score*, respectively.

3.4.3.1 A notation convention

In this book, we shall use *italics* to indicate those variable names and values which are to be typed into the Data Editor grid. Note that whether we type in lower or uppercase, the Editor will record (at the head of the appropriate column) a name in lower case only: for example, if we type *Field*, the name will be recorded as *field*. This is not true, however, of variable name labels and values (see below), which will appear in the SPSS output as they have been typed. We shall use a **bold** typeface for the names of menus, the names of dialog boxes and the items therein. Emboldening will also be used for emphasis and for technical terms.

3.4.3.2 Rules for assigning variable names

The choice of names for variables is governed by a set of six rules: A variable name...

(1) must not exceed **eight characters**. (A **character** is a letter, a digit or a symbol.)

(2) must **begin with a letter**.

(3) must **not end with a full stop**.

(4) **can** contain letters, digits or any of the characters @, #, _, or $.

(5) must **not** contain any of the following:

- (i) a blank;
- (ii) special characters, such as !, ?, and *, other than those listed in (4).

(6) must **not be** one of the keywords (such as AND, NOT, EQ, BY and ALL) that SPSS uses as special computing terms.

The names we have chosen, *group* and *score,* clearly meet the requirements of all the above rules. Note, however, that while the name *group1* would also have been satisfactory, *group 1* would not, because it contains a space, violating rule 5. The name *1group* would violate rule 2 since it does not start with a letter. Watch out for length too (rule 1): *red_cube* is satisfactory; but *red_cubes* is not, because the total number of characters (including the underline symbol) exceeds the permitted limit of 8.

3.4.3.3 Assigning the chosen variable names

To assign the variable name *group* to the first column in the Data Editor window, proceed as follows:

Double-click on the grey area at the top of the first column. This will obtain the **Define Variable** dialog box (Figure 4).

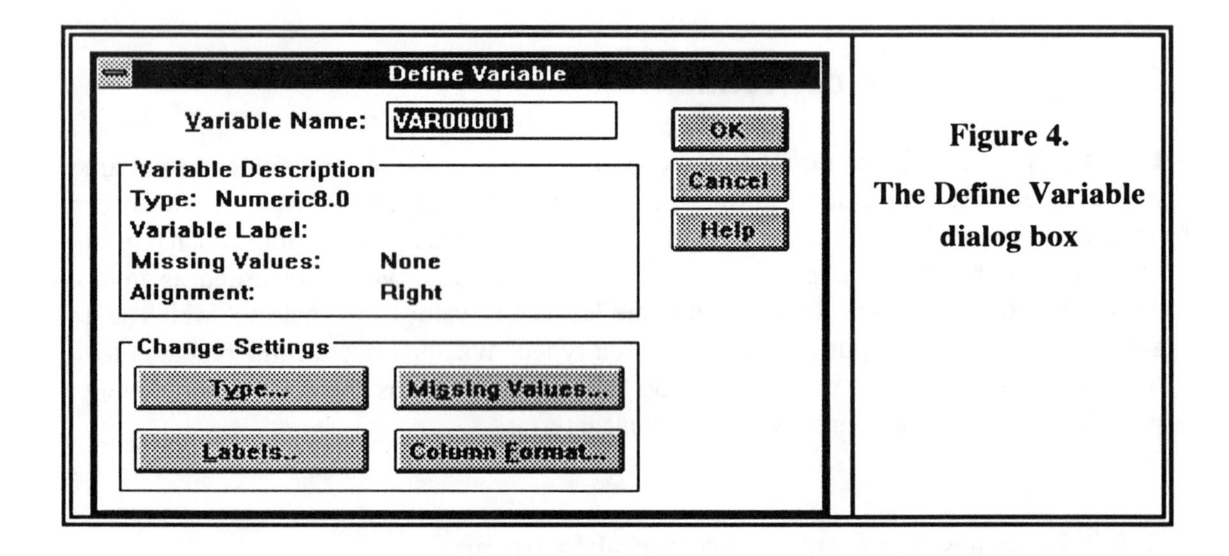

Figure 4.

The Define Variable dialog box

The Variable Name text box contains a default variable name, *var00001.* The **Variable Description** box contains the information that the **Type** (of variable) is **Numeric8.0**. These are the default specifications that were set in **Preferences** (see Section 3.4.2). Notice that the **Change Settings** box contains four **subdialog command buttons**: **Type**, **Labels**, **Missing Values** and **Column Format**. These permit the user to make specifications that apply only to one particular variable. For example, although the variable type has been set at **Numeric8.0**, clicking on **Type** will bring to the screen the **Define Variable Type** dialog box (Figure 5).

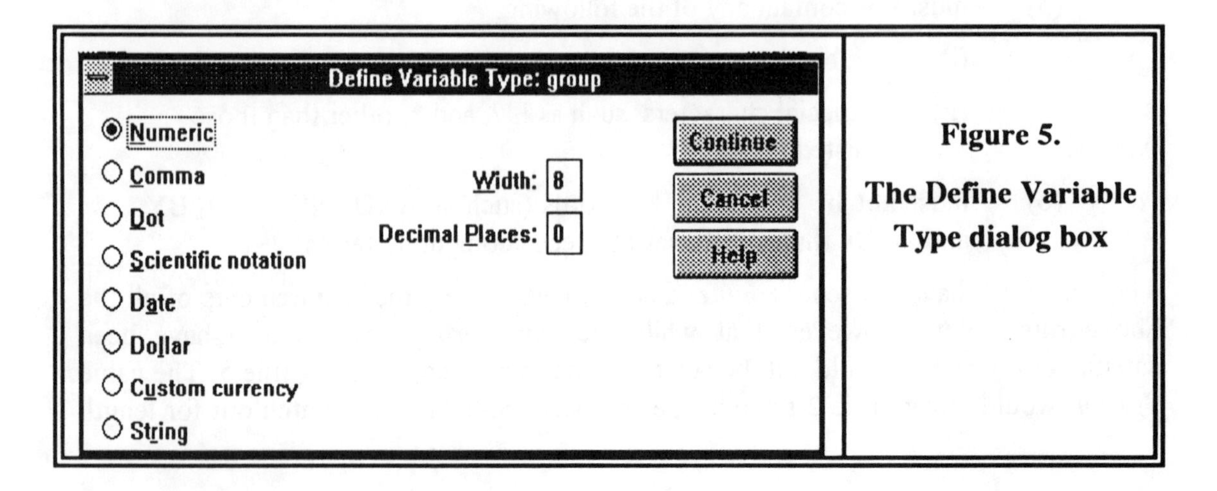

Figure 5.

The Define Variable Type dialog box

Within the **Define Variable** dialog box is the **Variable Name** text box: type *group* into it. There is no need to remove the default variable name (*var00001*) first: that will be overwritten when the chosen name is typed in. The chosen name, *group,* although reminding the reader that this is a grouping variable, conveys no further information. A longer, more meaningful, label is required. To assign one, click on the **Labels** subdialog button to obtain the **Define Labels** dialog box (Figure 6).

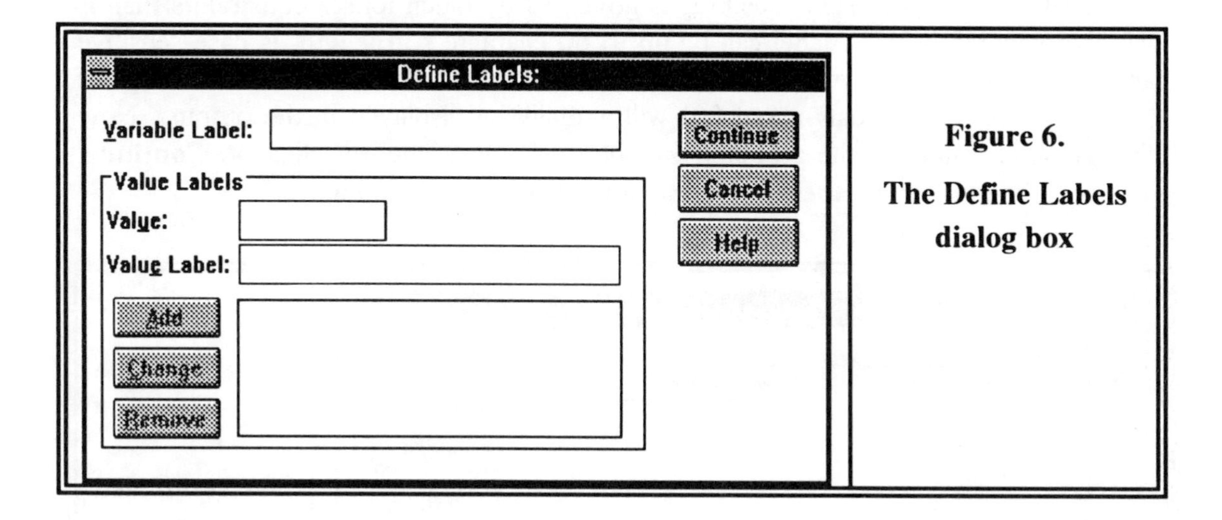

Figure 6.

The Define Labels dialog box

The **Variable Label** text box gives the user the opportunity to supply a fuller label for the grouping variable. This will make the statistical output easier to interpret. Type in an informative name such as *Mnemonic Training History.*

The rules governing the naming of variables (Section 3.4.3.2) do not apply to the assignment of labels in the **Define Labels** dialog box. Here, the name can be anything up to 120 characters in length and (as in *Mnemonic Training History)* can include spaces. Expanded variable names often clarify the output when these fuller names appear in tables and diagrams. Moreover, unlike the naming of variables, assigned variable labels are case sensitive and displayed exactly as they are entered. It should be borne in mind, however, that should a name with the maximum of 120 characters be chosen, fewer characters (usually the first 40) will actually be displayed in the output though the precise number varies in different procedures.

3.4.3.4 Assigning value labels

With a grouping variable comprising a set of arbitrary codes such as the treatments used in an experiment, it is useful but not essential to assign **value labels** showing what these codes represent especially if numbers have been used.

With the **Define Labels** dialog box (Figure 6) on the screen, type the lowest code number *1* into the **Value** text box. In the **Value Label** text box, type *Control.* This will embolden the **Add** button below. When **Add** is clicked, the following will appear in the lowest box:

1 = “Control”.

In a similar manner, proceed to label the values *2* and *3,* so that in the lowest box can be seen:

1 = "Control"

2 = "Mnemonic A"

3 = "Mnemonic B"

Value labelling, like variable labelling, is governed by much looser constraints than is variable naming. A value label can be up to 60 characters in length, is case sensitive and can contain spaces. As with variable labels, however, fewer than the maximum of 60 characters (usually only about 20) will actually be displayed in the output. Now that all three values of the grouping variable have been labelled, click on **Continue**. The completed **Define Labels** dialog box for *group* is shown in Figure 7.

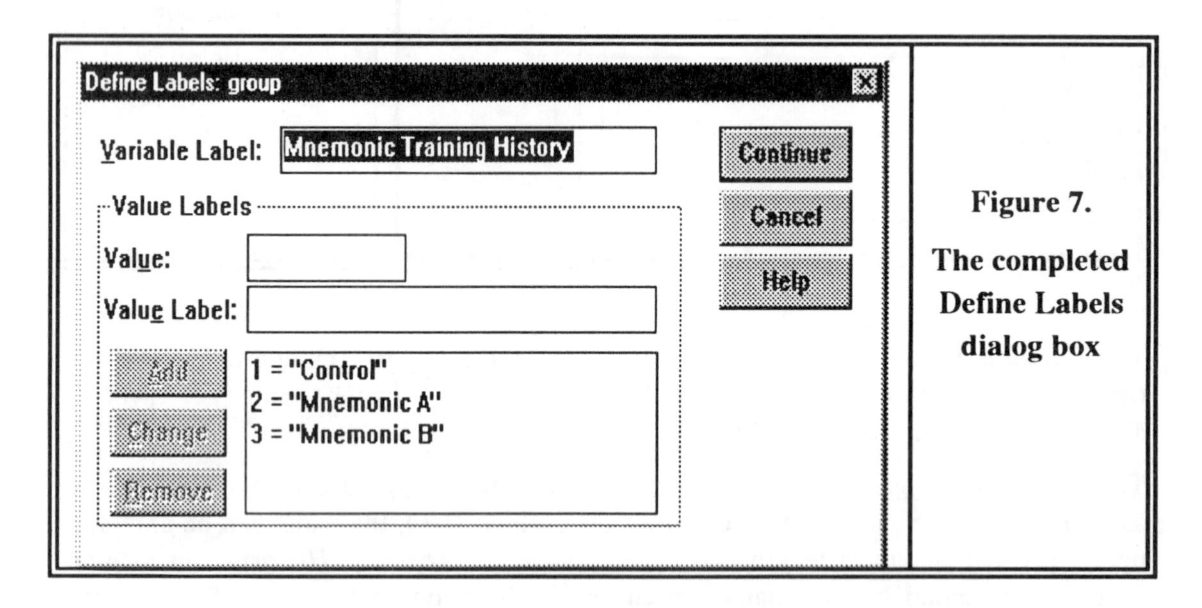

Figure 7.

The completed Define Labels dialog box

We are now back in the **Define Variable** dialog box again (Figure 4). This time, however, it will be found that the **Variable Description** box contains a fuller label for the grouping variable. Return to the **Data Editor** window by clicking on **OK**. Notice that after a pause (during which the hour glass symbol appears on the screen), the first column is now headed *group*.

Double click on *var* at the top of the second column and name the variable *score*. As *score* is a quantitative variable, it does not have value labels but an expanded variable label can be added if desired. Click on **OK** to return to the **Data Editor** window. This completes the naming of the two variables required for the data in Table 5. The next few subsections describe the manner in which data are entered into SPSS.

3.4.4 Using the keyboard to enter data

In the **Data Editor** window (Figure 1), just underneath the title bar, is a white bar. This is the **cell editor**. Beneath can be seen a black rectangle, the **cell highlight**, formed by the thickened borders of one of the cells. (When the **Data Editor window** is first accessed, the highlight will be located at the top cell of the leftmost column.)

In the cell editor, on the left, is an entry showing the current location of the cell highlight: for example, the entry **2:group** locates the highlight at the cell in the *second* row of the column headed *group*. A value typed in from the keyboard will appear in the cell editor. If a cursor key (or ↵) is pressed, this value or its associated label as defined in the **Define Labels:** dialog box is transferred to the highlighted cell. Whether the value or its label appears is determined by the state of the toggle item **Value Labels** in the **Utilities** drop-down menu: if it is ticked, then the label will appear; if not, the value will appear.

The subsequent location of the highlight depends upon which key is pressed: if the ↑ or ↓ cursor key is pressed, the new location is a cell above or below the original position; if the ← or → cursor key is pressed, the highlight moves to the left or the right, respectively. An alternative way of moving down is to use ↵. The position of the cell highlight can also be controlled by using the mouse. Clicking on any cell will highlight it and its row and column co-ordinates will appear in the cell editor.

3.4.5 Entering the data of Table 6

Having already named the variables, the data are very simply typed in. It is easier to enter the data by columns. Thus in the first column labelled *group*, type in ten ones, ten twos and ten threes to identify the subjects in the three treatment groups. (In Section 3.5.2, a quicker way of entering repeated numbers will be described.) The values in the second column *score* of Table 6 are entered as described in Section 3.4.4 since each cell contains a different value.

The completed Data Editor window is shown in Figure 8.

This method of data entry is easily extended to deal with **more than one grouping variable** by adding extra variables (columns). This will be illustrated in Section 3.12.2 where two grouping variables are needed.

A different data entry procedure is required for entering **within subjects (repeated measures)** data: this will be discussed in Section 3.6.

	group	score
1	1	3
2	1	5
3	1	3
4	1	2
5	1	4
6	1	6
7	1	9
8	1	3
9	1	8
10	1	10
11	2	10
12	2	8
13	2	15
14	2	9
15	2	11

(continued in next column)

16	2	16
17	2	17
18	2	15
19	2	7
20	2	10
21	3	20
22	3	15
23	3	14
24	3	15
25	3	17
26	3	10
27	3	8
28	3	11
29	3	18
30	3	19

Figure 8.

The completed Data Editor window for the 30 subjects taking part in the learning experiment

3.5 EDITING DATA

The **Data Editor** offers a range of functions, some of which are extremely useful, not only for amending data that are already in the Data Editor window, but also for inputting data values that are to be repeated many times.

3.5.1 Changing individual values

Enter a few numbers in the **Data Editor** window. Any of these can be changed at will by targeting the cell concerned with the black rectangle, typing a new value and pressing a cursor key or ↵.

3.5.2 More complex editing: Blocking, copying and pasting

Initially, only one cell in the Data Editor window is highlighted. It is possible, however, to highlight a whole block of cells. This **blocking** operation is achieved very simply, either by a click-and-drag with the mouse or by proceeding as follows:

Press and hold **Shift** and press the ↓ cursor a few (say four) times. It will be seen that five cells are now highlighted: the original cell and four new ones below, whose entries now appear in **inverse video** (that is, in white against a black background).

The blocking operation can be used to copy, say, the values in one column into another column or to lower down in the same column (see below). Highlight a column of values that you wish to copy. Now, choose

Edit

  Copy

Next, highlight the cells of the target column and choose

Edit

  Paste

The values in the source column will now appear in the target column.

As an example, the repeated values 1, 2, 3 used for identifying the learning method group in Section 3.4.3.4 could have been entered using this copy-and-paste method. To enter the first (unbracketed) column of values of Table 5 into the window, place the value *1* in the first (topmost) cell of the first column *group*. Choose

Edit

  Copy

Using the **Shift** and downward cursor keys, highlight the first 10 cells in the first column.

It will be found that on choosing

Edit

  Paste

the value *1* will appear in each of the highlighted cells. Target the 11th cell in the first column and enter the value *2* in that cell. Proceed as above to enter the value *2* in all of the cells from 11 to 20, inclusive. In similar fashion, enter the value *3* in each of the cells from 21 to 30, inclusive.

3.5.3 Deletion of values

To delete the values in a cell (or block), highlight the area concerned and press **Shift/ Delete**. To delete a whole row of values, click on the grey box containing the row number (see Figure 1). This will highlight every cell in the row. Pressing **Delete** will remove the whole row from the Data Editor window. (Press firmly and look for the hour-glass screen pointer: this means that the **Delete** procedure has been successfully activated.) Similarly, clicking the grey box containing the name of a column will highlight all the cells in the column, and pressing **Delete** will remove the entire column of values from the Data Editor window.

3.5.4 Inserting additional variables and cases, and changing the order of variables

Additional variables (i.e. new named columns) and additional cases (i.e. new rows) can always be added on at the right and foot of the existing data respectively, but it is sometimes convenient to be able to insert a new variable beside an existing variable within a large data set or to insert a new case (e.g. an additional male) at the end of a block of cases rather than at the foot of the list. Likewise it is sometimes useful to change the positions of variables so that certain variables are adjacent to one another.

All these operations are easily achieved by highlighting the variable in the Data Editor window to the right of the position desired for the new variable or by highlighting the case above which the desired new case is to be inserted, choosing the **Data** drop-down menu and then selecting the appropriate item (Figure 9). A blank column or a blank row will then be created. If a variable is to be moved to this new column, highlight the existing variable, select **Cut** form the **Edit** drop-down menu, highlight the new column, and finally select **Paste** from the **Edit** drop-down menu. The variable will then be pasted into its new position.

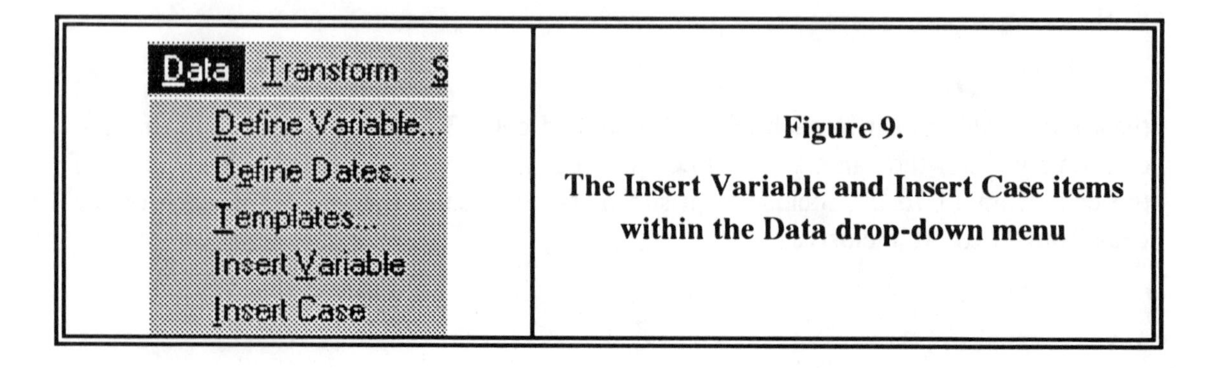

Figure 9.

The Insert Variable and Insert Case items within the Data drop-down menu

3.6 INPUTTING DATA FROM A WITHIN SUBJECTS EXPERIMENT

Suppose ten subjects participate in an experiment designed to investigate whether recognition of patterns is affected by the shapes of their perimeters. Perhaps, for instance, it is easier to recognise a pattern with a square perimeter than one with a circular perimeter. Each subject is tested on pattern recognition with three perimeter shapes: a triangle, a circle and a square. In this experiment, there is one treatment factor, Shape of Perimeter, comprising three levels, or conditions: (1) Triangle; (2) Circle; and (3) Square. The dependent variable is Recognition Time.

Notice that, in contrast to the mnemonics experiment, each subject is tested under all the three conditions making up the treatment factor. The factor Shape of Perimeter, therefore, has **repeated measures**: it is a **within subjects factor**.

Table 7 shows how the data are entered in the SPSS Data Editor.

Table 7.

Recognition times for 3 shapes viewed by the same sample of subjects.

(Only the unshaded items are entered in the Data Editor window)

	Shape		
Subject	triangle	circle	square
1	220	300	260
2	250	290	300
3	260	280	290
4	230	340	190
5	190	300	250
6	220	270	240
7	250	320	270
8	280	290	260
9	270	340	250
10	240	300	350

In Table 7, notice the heading Shape, which is the treatment factor in this experiment. But Shape is not entered in the Data Editor window: only the conditions *triangle*, *circle*, *square* are entered as variable names.

We have seen earlier that the Data Editor can accept only two kinds of variables:

(1) **grouping variables**, which identify (by codes) the condition under which each subject has been tested;

(2) **dependent variables**, comprising measurements.

At the moment, therefore, the Data Editor has no knowledge of the experimenter's interest in making comparisons among the three different shape columns. As far as the Data Editor is concerned, the data comprise **three dependent variables**. Later, we shall see that some statistical programs can be informed that the three columns in the Data Editor are to be treated, not as separate dependent variables, but as comprising a single (repeated measures) treatment factor.

After defining the variable names as *triangle*, *circle*, *square* and entering the recognition times, the Data Editor window appears as in Figure 10.

	triangle	circle	square
1	220	300	260
2	250	290	300
3	260	280	290
4	230	340	190
5	190	300	250
6	220	270	240
7	250	320	270
8	280	290	260
9	270	340	250
10	240	300	350

Figure 10.

The layout in the Data Editor window for a within subjects (repeated measures) design

Data from an experiment with **both between subjects variables and within subjects factors** is entered in the **Data Editor** window as a combination of the procedures illustrated in this Section and previously in Section 3.3. For example, if the subjects for the recognition of patterns experiment had been coded for sex, then all that would be required is an extra column for the variable *sex* with codes such as *M* for Males and *F* for Females.

3.7 ENTERING STRING VARIABLES

A **string** is a sequence of characters (letters, symbols, blanks, digits) which is treated as a label by the system. A **string variable** is a qualitative variable whose categories are entered into the window as strings, rather than numbers. Thus a string can be a simple letter M, a word such as French, or a person's name such as Abraham Lincoln.

A **short string variable** has string values of up to eight characters in length; a **long string variable** has values exceeding eight characters in length. The distinction is important, because some SPSS procedures only work with short string variables or truncate long string variables to the first eight characters.

Suppose we want to record the names of all the subjects taking part in the learning experiment and that the longest name does not exceed 20 characters in length. In the **Data Editor** window (Figure 1), double-click on the grey area at the top of the third column to obtain the **Define Variable** dialog box (Figure 4). In the **Variable Name** text box, type the name of the string variable *name*. Notice, however, that in the **Variable Description** box is the entry **Type: Numeric8.0**. In fact, until it receives information to the contrary, SPSS for Windows always assumes that variables will be of the numeric type.

To specify a string variable, click on **Type**, to obtain the **Define Variable Type** dialog box (Figure 5). In the box is a list of eight variable types, each with a radio button. SPSS initially marks the **Numeric** button. Click on the **String** button at the foot of the list. The **Decimal Places** text box immediately disappears, leaving only the **Width** box, with the value *8* that was set in **Preferences**. Delete *8* in the **Width** box and type in *20*. Click on **Continue** and then on **OK.** The variable *name* will now appear at the head of the third column, which is now much wider than before. The names of the subjects can now be typed into each row of this column.

3.8 MISSING VALUES

When the user enters a number into a previously empty Data Editor window, a default variable name (such as *var00001*) will appear at the head of the column concerned. Enter, say, five such numbers into the first column of the Data Editor window. Now enter a single value into the first cell of the second column. You will see that a period (a dot) appears in each of the four cells beneath. In SPSS, there are no empty cells within the data file, which is assumed to be rectangular. If no value has been entered, the system supplies the **system-missing** value, which is indicated in the Data Editor window by a full stop. SPSS will exclude system-missing values from its calculations of means, standard deviations and other statistics.

It may be, however, that for some purposes the user wishes SPSS to treat certain responses actually present in the data set as missing. For example, suppose that, in a survey of political opinion, five categories are used (A, B, C, D & E), but category E was recorded when the person refused to answer and D was a category that indicated a failure to understand the question. The user wants SPSS to treat responses in both categories as missing, but to retain information about the relative frequencies of such responses in categories D and E in the output listings. In SPSS terminology, the user wants certain responses to be treated as **user-missing** values.

To define user-missing values, open the **Define Variable** dialog box and click on **Missing Values**. This will obtain the **Define Missing Values** dialog box (Figure 11).

Initially, the **No missing values** radio button is marked. The three text boxes underneath give the user the opportunity to specify up to three **Discrete Missing Values**, referred to in SPSS as *missing (1)*, *missing (2)*, and *missing (3)*. These may either be numerical, as with a grouping variable, or short string variables, but must match the original variable type. The other options in the dialog box are for quantitative variables: the user may define a missing value as one falling within a specified range, or one that falls either within a specified range or within a specified category.

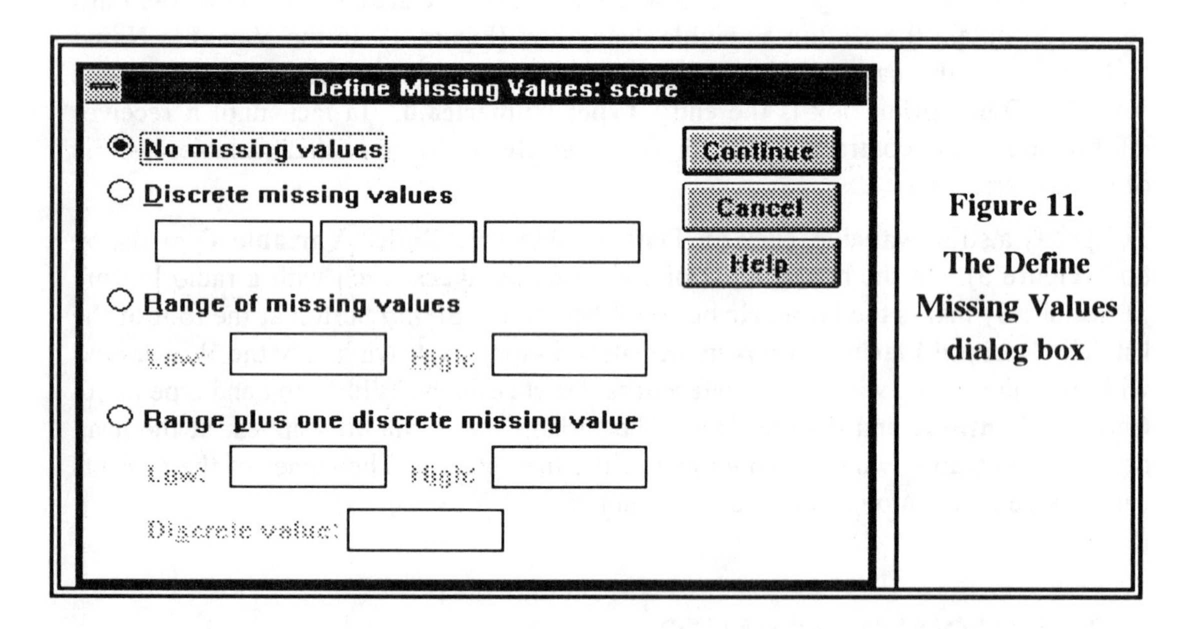

Figure 11.
The Define Missing Values dialog box

In analysing a set of exam results, for instance, the user might wish SPSS to treat as missing:

(1) any marks between, say, 0 and 20;

(2) cases where the candidate walked out without giving any written response. (A walk-out could be coded as an arbitrary, but salient, number, such as *-9*: the negative sign helps it to stand out and cannot be a valid exam mark.)

This coding can be achieved by clicking on the **Range plus one discrete missing value** button, entering the values *0* and *20* into the **Low** and **High** boxes, respectively, and *-9* into the **Discrete value** box. Click on **Continue** to return to the **Define Variable** dialog box.

3.9 SAVING AND RETRIEVING THE DATA SET

3.9.1 Saving the data

Having gone to considerable trouble to enter the data into the Data Editor window, the user will wish to save them in a form that can be called up instantly at the next session, rather than having to type in all the values again. To save the data to a file, proceed as follows.

In the **SPSS application** window, choose
File

Save As

This obtains the **Save Data As** dialog box (Figure 12).

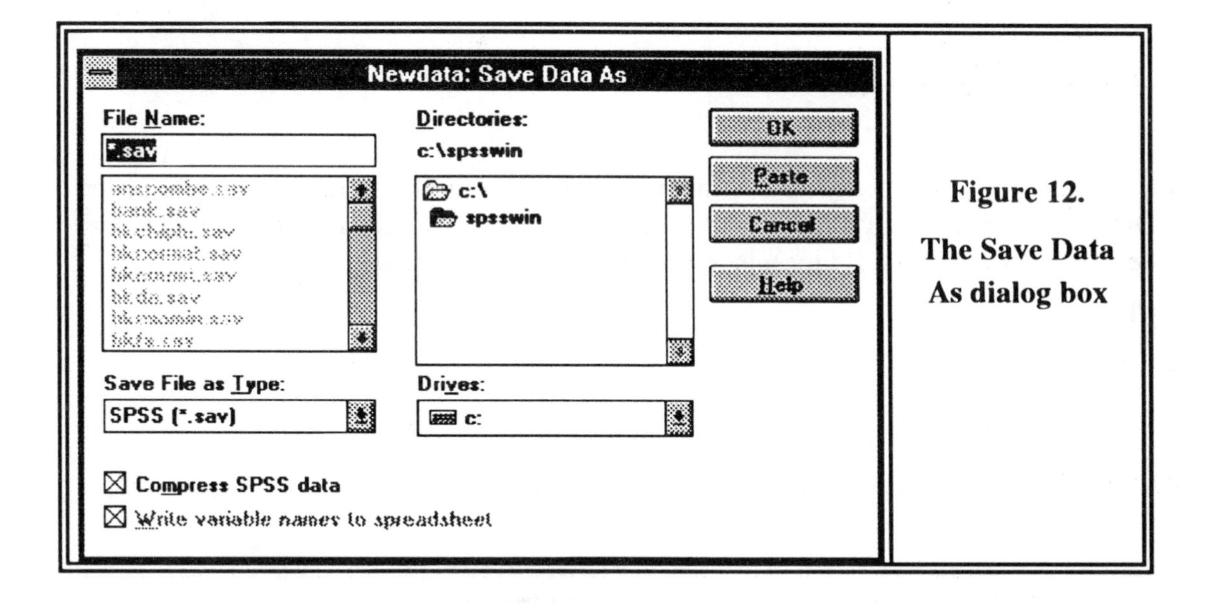

Figure 12.

The Save Data As dialog box

In the **File Name** text box, is * with the extension **.sav**, reminding the user that SPSS data files are normally saved with the extension **.sav**. Notice also that, in the **Save File as Type** text box, is already entered **SPSS(*.sav)**. It is convenient to use this extension because whenever **Open** or **Save** dialog boxes are opened, SPSS will list files with this extension. The user can type into the **File Name:** box any name with the extension **.sav** and it will be saved as a file of the type displayed in the **Save File as Type** box. (Note, however, that the file name assigned must conform to the rules for naming variables (Section 3.4.3.2).) In the present example, a suitable file name would be **firstset.sav**. The faint names in the box beneath the **File Name:** box are the names of data files already saved.

Notice that under the caption **Directories:** is the entry **c:\spsswin**. We have seen that a directory can be thought of as a folder containing documents (files). The entry **c:\spsswin** means that, unless instructed otherwise, SPSS will save the data to the file

firstset.sav, located on the PC's hard disk (drive **c**) in the directory **spsswin**. The path name for the file will be **c:\spsswin\firstset.sav**. The saving is effected by pressing **OK**. In some network configurations, this may be disallowed because the **spsswin** directory is 'read only'.

Generally it is better to avoid placing files in program directories. If files are to be saved to the same hard disk as the program directory, then create another directory for this purpose before starting SPSS, such as **data**, by choosing in the **Windows File Manager**

File

  Create Directory

The path name would be **c:\data\firstset.sav**.

It is often better to save to a floppy disk, especially when using a computer in a network. In that case, the entry in the **Drives** box (Figure 12, bottom right) must be changed to **a**, by scrolling the arrow in the grey area to the right, and selecting **a**. Clicking on **OK** will now save the file **firstset.sav** to the disk in drive **a**.

3.9.2 Reading in data

Suppose that, prior to ending a Windows session, the user has saved the data in the Data Editor window to a file named **firstset.sav** on floppy disk **a**. Later, the data can be restored to the Data Editor window by proceeding as follows:

Choose

File

  Open

    Data

This will produce the **Open Data File** dialog box (Figure 13).

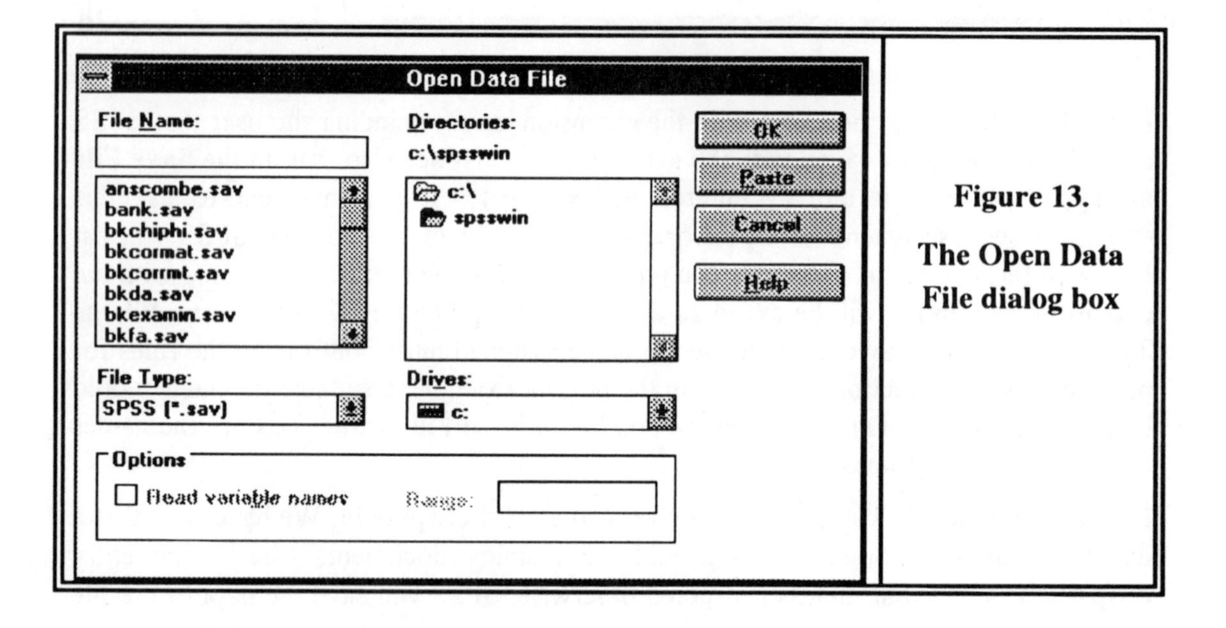

Figure 13.

The Open Data File dialog box

In appearance, this box is very similar to the **Save Data As** box. There are the same **File Name**, **File Type** and **Drives** boxes, and the directory is specified as **c:\spsswin.**

If the data set has been saved to the file **a:\firstset.sav**, drive **a** (not drive **c**, as shown in Figure 13) must be specified by clicking on the arrow to the right of the **Drives** text box and selecting drive **a**. The **File Type** specification should already be correct **SPSS(*.sav)**, so all the files in drive **a** with a **.sav** extension should then be listed in the file box. Select the required file by clicking on its name in the list: the filename will then appear in the **File Name:** box.

Click on **OK** to restore the **Data Editor** window (Figure 1), which will now contain the data from the nominated file in its cells. While data are being read into the Data Editor window from a file, the hour-glass will appear and messages will appear in the Status Bar at various stages in the operation. The message '**SPSS Processor is ready**' signals the end of the procedure.

3.9.3 Importing and exporting data

It is possible to import data such as SPSS/PC+ data files, Microsoft Excel spreadsheet files, and ASCII tab-delimited (i.e. values are separated by tabulation symbols) or fixed format (i.e. variables are recorded in the same column locations for each case) files into SPSS and to export an existing SPSS data file in a format compatible with another application (e.g. Excel spreadsheet, ASCII tab-delimited or fixed format). For example, to import an Excel file, choose **Open** and then click ▼ on the right of the **Files of type** box to open the list of file types (Figure 14), click on the Excel (*.xls) line and a list of Excel files in the current path will be displayed. Click on the required file to transfer it to the **File Name:** box or type the name of the file in the **File Name:** box and select the appropriate location of the file in the **Look in** box.

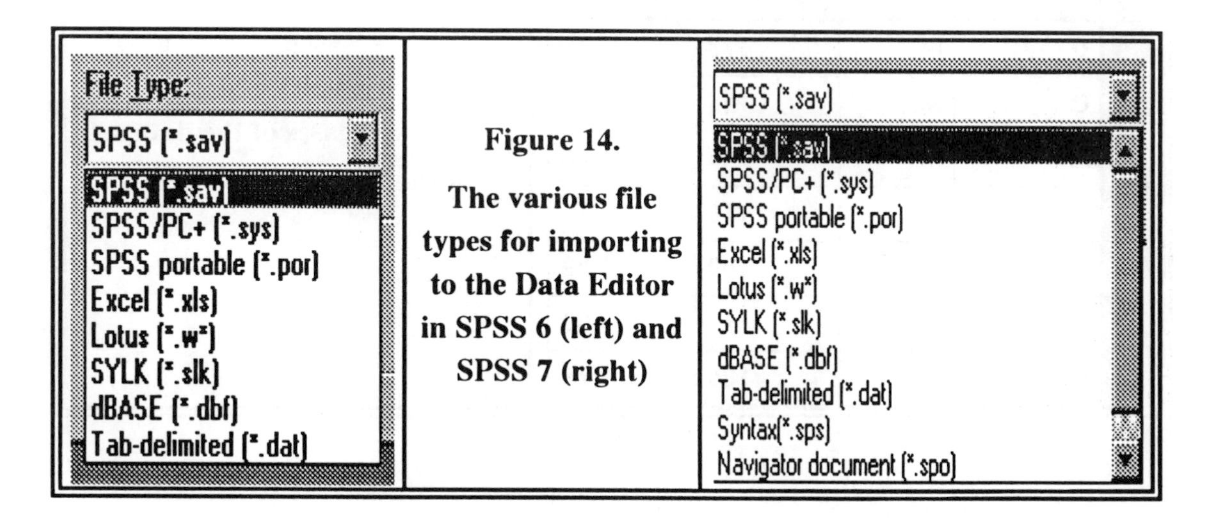

Figure 14. The various file types for importing to the Data Editor in SPSS 6 (left) and SPSS 7 (right)

In the case of ASCII material, choose instead of **Open**

Read ASCII data ...

and follow the prompts. If the original file does not have fixed format or tab delimiters, it is possible to edit out excess spaces and insert tab delimiters within a word-processing package in order to make it suitable for importing to SPSS.

Similarly an existing SPSS data file can be saved in a wide range of formats for exporting to other applications.

Full details of importing and exporting files are available in the **Help** facility.

3.10 LISTING DATA

3.10.1 Listing cases

It is sometimes convenient to be able to list the data for a particular variable (or perhaps a few variables) rather than having to scan a particular column (or columns) in the **Data Editor** window. For example, the user might wish to see two variables side-by-side which in the **Data Editor** window are several columns apart.

Let us assume that a data set (Table 8) consisting of two quantitative variables Weight and Height, and two qualitative variables Gender and Blood, has already been set up in the Data Editor window (see the first seven of thirty-two cases in Figure 15).

	bloodtyp	gender	height	weight
1	O	M	178	75
2	O	M	196	100
3	A	M	145	60
4	O	M	170	71
5	B	M	180	80
6	O	M	175	69
7	AB	M	185	78

Figure 15.
The first 7 cases of the data set in the Data Editor window

Choose:

Statistics

Summarize

List Cases (SPSS 6) or **Case Summaries (SPSS 7)**

and then complete the **SPSS 6 List Cases** dialog box (Figure 16) or the **SPSS 7 Summarize Cases** dialog box (not reproduced) to indicate which variables are to be listed.

Table 8.

Blood group, sex, height & weight of 32 subjects

Blood	Sex	Height	Weight	Blood	Sex	Height	Weight
O	M	178	75	O	M	183	70
O	M	196	100	B	M	182	85
A	M	145	60	A	M	170	72
O	M	170	71	O	M	160	77
B	M	180	80	O	M	170	95
O	M	175	69	AB	M	172	68
AB	M	185	78	B	M	190	120
A	M	190	90	O	M	180	75
O	F	163	60	O	F	162	62
O	F	142	51	B	F	182	80
A	F	150	55	O	F	165	67
O	F	165	64	A	F	171	50
A	F	160	53	O	F	146	55
O	F	175	50	AB	F	151	48
O	F	182	72	O	F	164	59
B	F	169	65	B	F	176	71

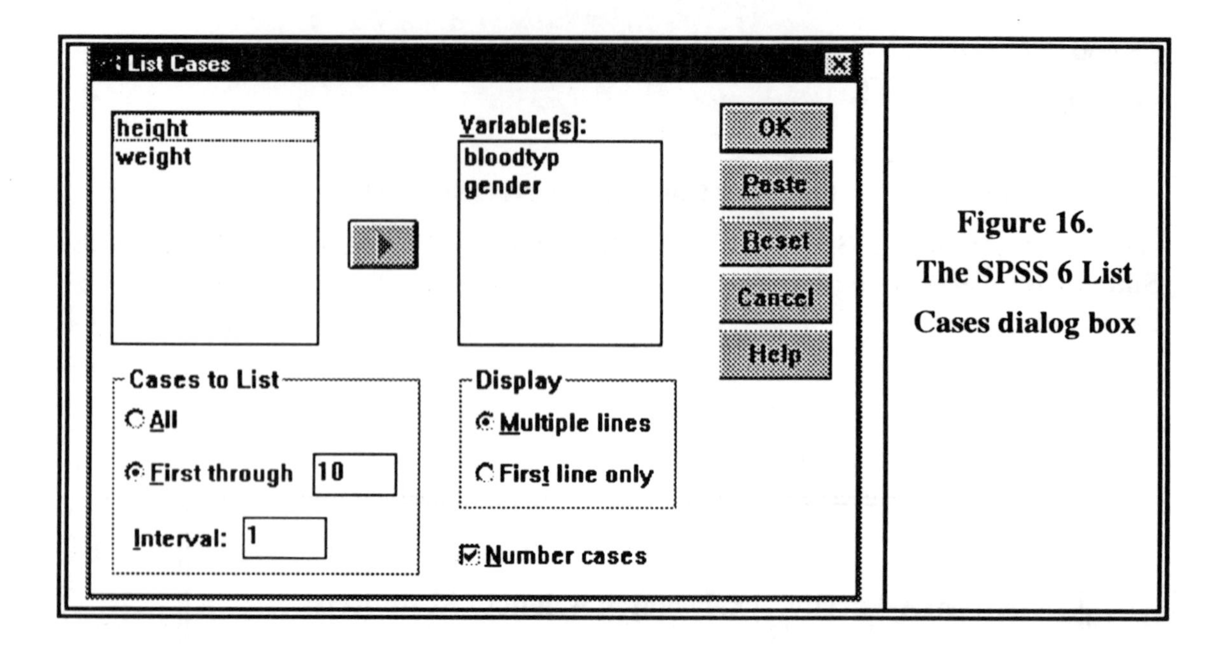

Figure 16. The SPSS 6 List Cases dialog box

Select the variables of interest (for example, *gender* and *bloodtyp*) by clicking on the variable name and then on ▶ to enter it into the **Variable(s)** box. It is also useful to click on the **Number cases** box in order to have the data listed with case numbers. For illustrative purposes, only the first ten cases will be listed; this is achieved by specifying *10* in the **Cases to List** box. Finally click on **OK**.

The output is shown in Output Listing 1. Notice that SPSS 6 lists data values whereas SPSS 7 lists value labels.

	BLOODTYP	GENDER
1	O	M
2	O	M
3	A	M
4	O	M
5	B	M
6	O	M
7	AB	M
8	A	M
9	O	M
10	B	M

Output Listing 1.

Output from SPSS 6 List Cases (left) and SPSS 7 Case Summaries (right)

Case Summaries[a]

		BLOODTYP	GENDER
1		Group O	Male
2		Group O	Male
3		Group A	Male
4		Group O	Male
5		Group B	Male
6		Group O	Male
7		Group AB	Male
8		Group A	Male
9		Group O	Male
10		Group B	Male
Total	N	10	10

a. Limited to first 10 cases.

3.10.2 Displaying data file information

It is useful to be able to see details of variables such as their names, types, values and value labels (if any) in a data file, particularly if it is a large one and one has perhaps forgotten how many values were defined for several variables. Note that this cannot be done for a file currently in the **Data Editor window**.

Choose
File
　　Display Data Info...

and then select the appropriate file name from the **Display Data Info** dialog box.

Output Listing 2 (identical for SPSS 6 and 7) shows the information for the data file, part of which is shown in Figure 15.

Output Listing 2. Display Data Information for a saved data file

```
                          -- SYSFILE INFO --

File c:\spsswin\chap4.sav
   Label:     SPSS
   Created:   18 Feb 97 12:37:48 - 4 variables and 32 cases
File Type:  SPSS Data File
N of Cases: 32
Total # of Defined Variable Elements: 4
Data Are Not Weighted
Data Are Compressed
File Contains Case Data


Variable Information:

Name                                                         Position

GENDER     * No label *                                          1
           Format: A1
           Value    Label
               F    Female
               M    Male

WEIGHT     Weight in Kilograms                                   2
           Format: F8

HEIGHT     Height in Centimetres                                 3
           Format: F8

BLOODTYP   * No label *                                          4
           Format: A2
           Value    Label
              A     Group A
              AB    Group AB
              B     Group B
              O     Group O
```

The listing shows the following:

- There were 32 cases.
- None of the variables was weighted (weighting is explained in Section 3.12.2).
- The variable GENDER has two defined string levels M and F together with their value names with a format of just one character in width (A1).
- WEIGHT and HEIGHT are numeric variables with a format of 8 non-decimal digits (F8).
- BLOODTYP has four defined string values together with their value names with a format of two characters (A2).

3.11 PRINTING IN SPSS

It is always reassuring to have in one's possession a hard copy of important computer output. For example, after a series of complicated editing operations, the user may wish to print out the contents of the Data Editor window to have a permanent record of the finalised data set. It may be necessary to check that a suitable printer is connected to the computer (or to the network) by inspecting the information within the **Printer Setup** item in the **File** drop-down menu where an option for changing the orientation of the printing from Portrait to Landscape may be invoked if the data set is very wide. Local advice may be required.

When the **Print** item in the **File** drop-down menu is selected, the **Print** dialog box will appear. Bear in mind that only the contents of the **active** window will be printed: thus if the data set is to be printed out, the **Data Editor** window must be active (a window is activated by clicking anywhere on it or by selecting the appropriate window name from the list of windows at the foot of the **Windows** drop-down menu). Similarly, if it is the output listing that is to be printed, the **Output** window must be active. Charts and graphs are in the **Chart Carousel** window.

3.11.1 Printing out the entire data set

To print out the entire contents of the Data Editor window, ensure that it is active as described above and choose

File

  Print...

This obtains the **Print** dialog box, which has the caption **a:\firstset.sav** in its title bar (see Figure 17).

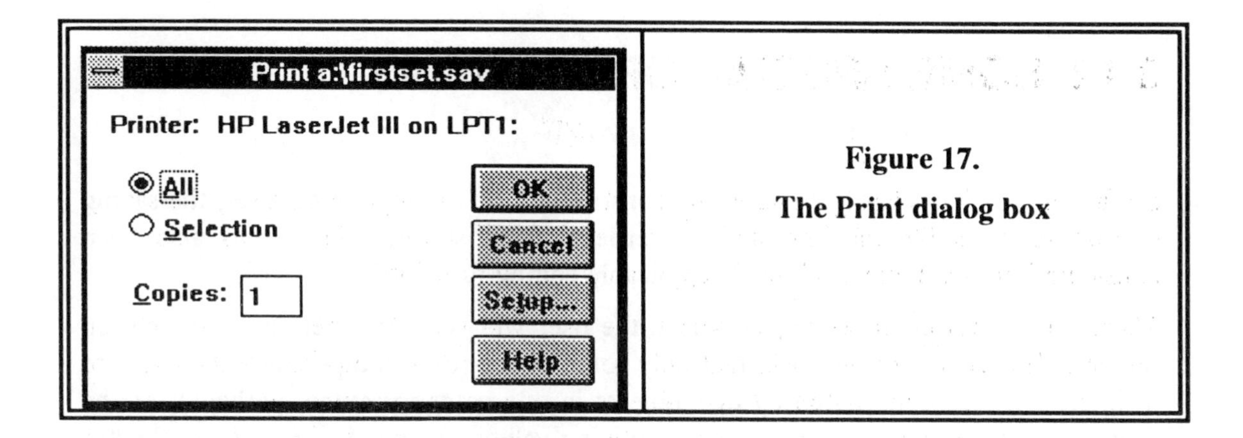

Figure 17.
The Print dialog box

If the **All** button is marked, the entire data set will be printed out. (If the **Selection** button is marked, only a selected part of the data set will be printed out - see below.) The user can also amend the entry in the **Copies** text box to obtain multiple hard copies.

Click on **OK** to start the printing (which may take some time).

3.11.2 Printing out a selection from the data set

To print out only selected parts of the data set, use the click-and-drag method to define the target sections by blackening them. This requires a little practice: it will be found that when the mouse arrow touches the lower border of the window, the latter will scroll down to extend the blackened area to the desired extent. If it touches the right border, it will scroll rightwards across the Data Editor window.

When the **Print** dialog box (Figure 17) appears, the marker will now be on **Selection**. Click on **OK** to obtain a hard copy of the selected areas.

3.11.3 Printing other items

To print items such as listings of tables and results, graphs, scatterplots, and diagrams, ensure that the correct window is active before following the procedures that have just been described.

3.12 SOME SPECIAL OPERATIONS

So far, the emphasis has been upon the construction of a complete data set, the saving of that set to a file on disk, and its retrieval from storage. There has also been consideration of a number of widely applicable editing functions.

There are occasions, however, on which the user will want to operate selectively on the data. It may be, for instance, that only some of the rows comprising a data set are of interest (those contributed by the subjects in one category alone, perhaps); or the user may wish to exclude subjects with outlying values on specified variables. In this section, some of these more specialised manoeuvres will be described.

Transformations and recoding of data will be discussed in Chapter 4.

3.12.1 Case selection

Let us assume that we have the data of our learning methods example in the Data Editor window: there are two variables, *group* and *score*.

Suppose, for example, that we want to analyse only the data from the two mnemonic groups (i.e. exclude the control group) of the experiment presented in Section 3.3.

Choose

Data

Select Cases

This will produce the **Select Cases** dialog box (see Figure 18).

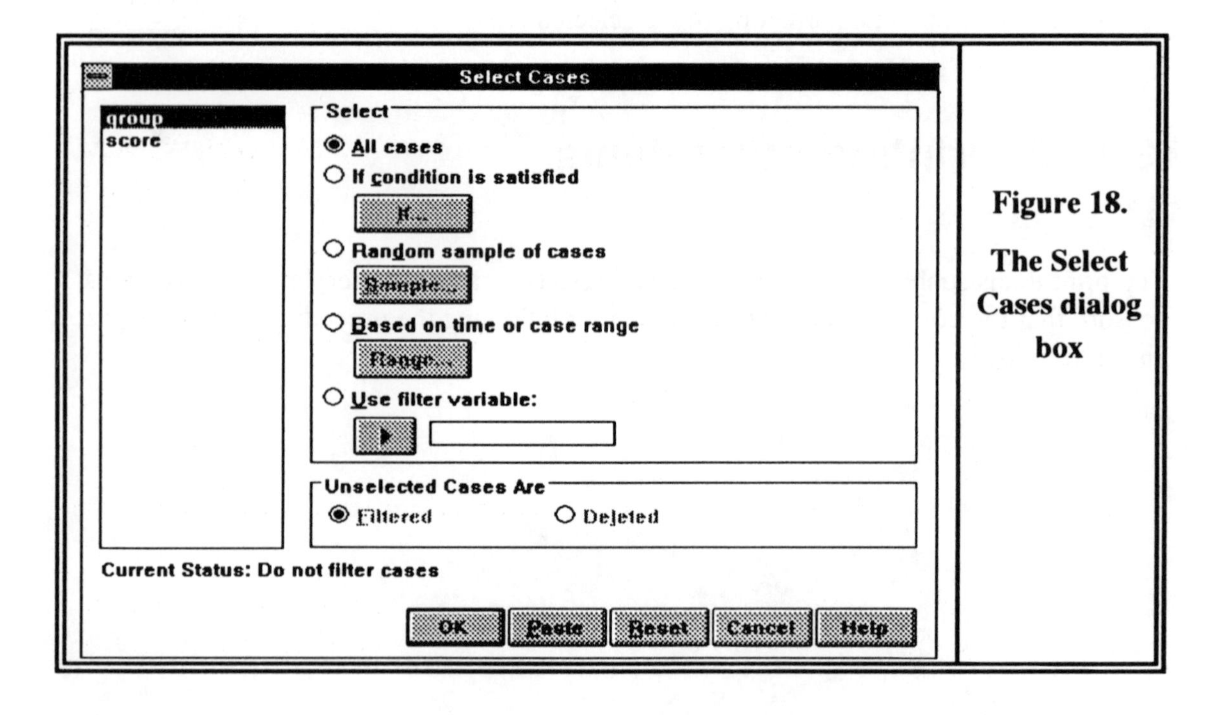

Figure 18. The Select Cases dialog box

On the left in Figure 18 is a list of the variables in the data set: *group* and *score*. We want to include a case in the data if the row contains the values *2* or *3* for the variable *group*. To do this, we must make what is known as a **conditional** instruction (of the form **Select cases if ...**), which will only be carried out if the condition is met. Notice that in Figure 18, the **All cases** radio button is marked, a default setting telling SPSS that there is to be no selection. Use the mouse to mark the button labelled **If condition is satisfied**. Clicking on **If...** will select the **Select Cases If** dialog box (Figure 19).

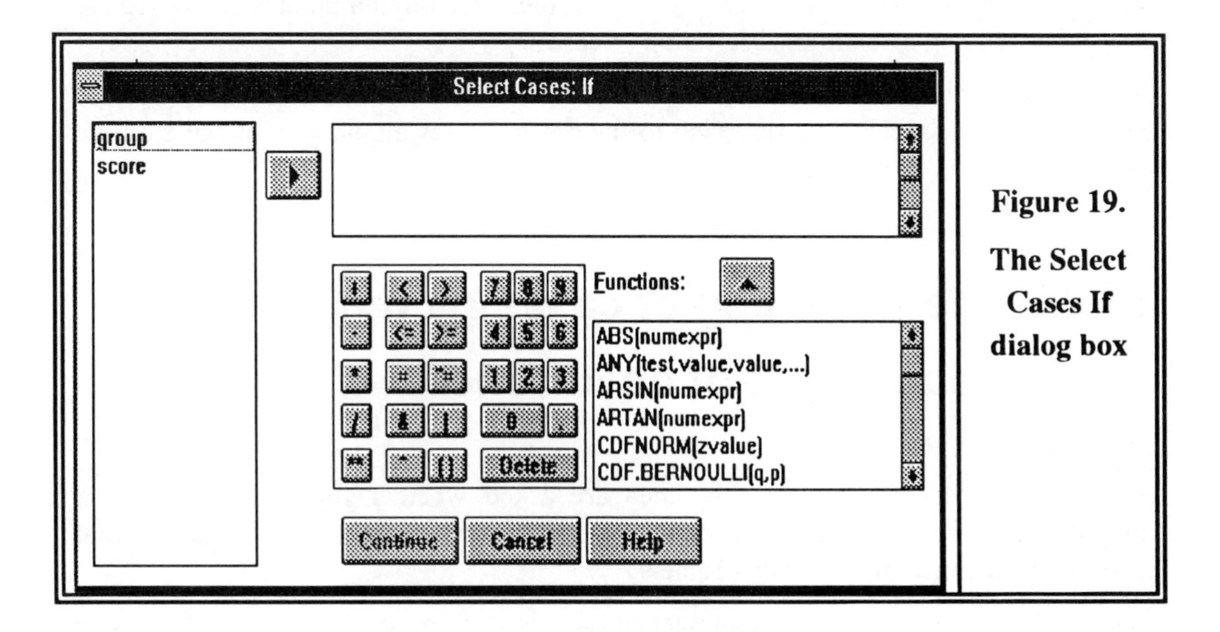

Figure 19.

The Select Cases If dialog box

On the left in Figure 19 is the same list of the variables. Highlight *group* and click on ► to transfer it to the upper box on the right. The conditional expression can be typed directly into this box or it can be assembled by clicking on buttons in the lower box. Click on = to transfer it to the box above, and then on *2* in order to select the cases in group 2. Click on | (this is the logical operator OR and is located beside the logical operator AND, which is represented by the symbol &). Highlight the variable name *group* within the variable name box and click on ► to transfer it again to the conditional expression box. Finally select = and *3* to complete the expression shown in Figure 20 which means 'select cases if group = 2 OR group = 3'. Note that the expression must be in the form shown: SPSS will not understand *group = 2 | 3* and will report it as an error.

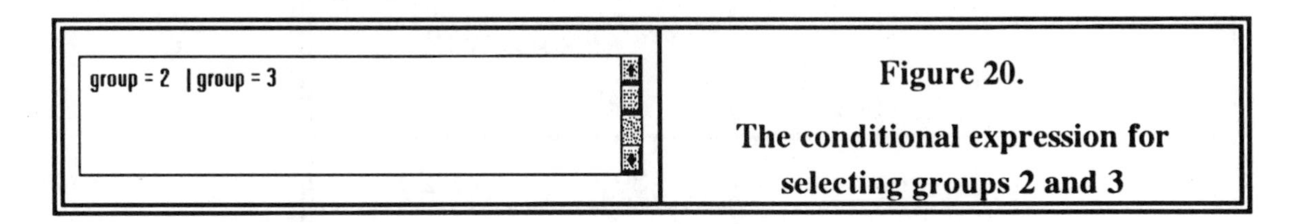

Figure 20.

The conditional expression for selecting groups 2 and 3

When the conditional expression has been completed, click on **Continue** and then on **OK** to return to the **Data Editor** window, where it will be noticed that a new column labelled **filter_$**, and containing *1*s and *0*s, has appeared. The *1*s and *0*s represent the selected and unselected cases, respectively. The row numbers of the unselected cases have also been marked with an oblique bar. This is a useful indicator of **case selection status.** The status bar (if enabled at the foot of the Data Editor window) will also indicate **Filter On**.

The reader will have noted that the selection could equally have been made with the expression **group ~= 1** (the symbol ~= means *not equal to* and can either be selected from the keypad in the dialog box - it is the key to the left of 1 in Figure 19 - or typed from the keyboard using ~ and then =). In fact there are often a number of alternative ways of specifying a conditional selection of cases.

Any further analyses of the data set will exclude the cases within group 1. The case selection can be cancelled by returning to the **Select Cases** dialog box, clicking on **All cases**, and then on **OK**.

3.12.2 The weighting of cases by their frequencies of occurrence

Suppose that fifty women and fifty men are asked whether they disapprove of a popular, but violent, television programme. Their responses can be summarised in what is known as a **contingency table** (Table 9).

The purpose of constructing a contingency table is to bring out whatever relationship there may be between two qualitative or nominal variables. In the present example, the qualitative variables are Sex of Respondent and Answer to Question. The former comprises the categories Male and Female; the latter's categories are Yes and No. It is clear from Table 9 that there is indeed a relationship between the two variables: a markedly higher proportion of the female respondents disapproved of the programme.

Table 9.

A contingency table

	Disapprove?	
Sex	**Yes**	**No**
Female	30	20
Male	10	40

As with the data in Table 5, a contingency table must be recast to make it suitable for entry into SPSS. Earlier, it was said that SPSS expects a data set in the form of a matrix whose rows are subjects and whose columns are variables. Clearly, the arrangement of the data in Table 9 does not conform to this requirement: the two columns represent values of the same variable; and a row represents the responses of several subjects.

In part, the solution is to carry the variables in columns of codes, as we did with the data from the mnemonics experiment (see Table 6). This meets the requirement that each column in the Data Editor window relates to a single variable. In the present case, however, it remains to be made clear that each cell entry represents the response not of one person but of several. This is achieved by entering the cell frequencies into the third column in the **Data Editor** window. In Table 10, the categories of the *sex* variable have been assigned the codes *M* and *F* for *female* and *male*, respectively; and the response categories *Yes* and *No* have been coded as *Y* and *N*, respectively. SPSS can then be instructed to weight the category combinations by multiplying them by the corresponding frequencies in the third variable *freq* using the **Weight Cases** option with the **Data** drop-down menu.

Table 10.

A recasting of the data in Table 9, to make the data suitable for entry into SPSS

sex	disapp	freq
M	Y	30
M	N	20
F	Y	10
F	N	40

Name the variables taking care to change the **Type** for *sex* and for *disapp* to **String** as described in Section 3.4.3.3, and assign labels as described in Section 3.4.3.4. Enter the data in Table 10 into the **Data Editor** window.

It is now necessary to inform SPSS that each row of entries under *sex* and *disapp* is to be weighted by the corresponding entry in *freq*.

Choose

Data

Weight Cases

to open the **Weight Cases** dialog box (Figure 21).

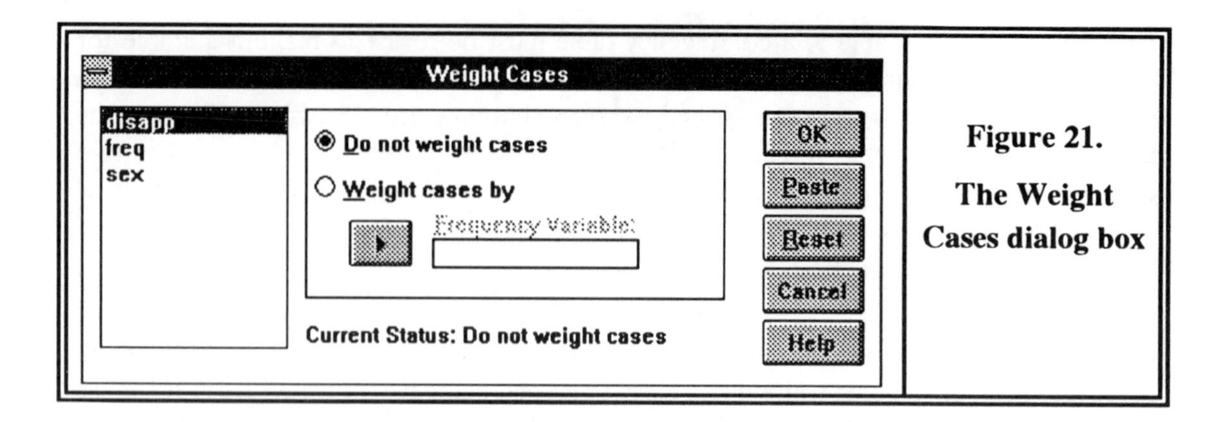

Figure 21.

The Weight Cases dialog box

On the left is a list of the variables in the data set: *sex, disapp, freq.* We want to weight each row (case) by the corresponding frequency in the third column. Click on the **Weight cases by** button. Next, highlight the variable *freq.* This will embolden the arrow button which, when clicked, will transfer the name *freq* to the **Frequency Variable** text box. Click on **OK** to run the procedure. The weighting of cases is an essential preliminary to the analysis of nominal data in the form of contingency tables, as described in Chapter 11.

3.12.3 Splitting files

It is sometimes convenient to split a file by the levels of a grouping variable (or by combinations of more than one grouping variable) so that any subsequent exploratory data analysis or statistical analysis is conducted automatically on each level (or combinations of levels) separately. For example, the blood group data in Table 8 could be split by the levels of *bloodtyp* as shown in the completed **Split File** dialog box (Figure 22). **Split File** is an option within the **Data** drop-down menu.

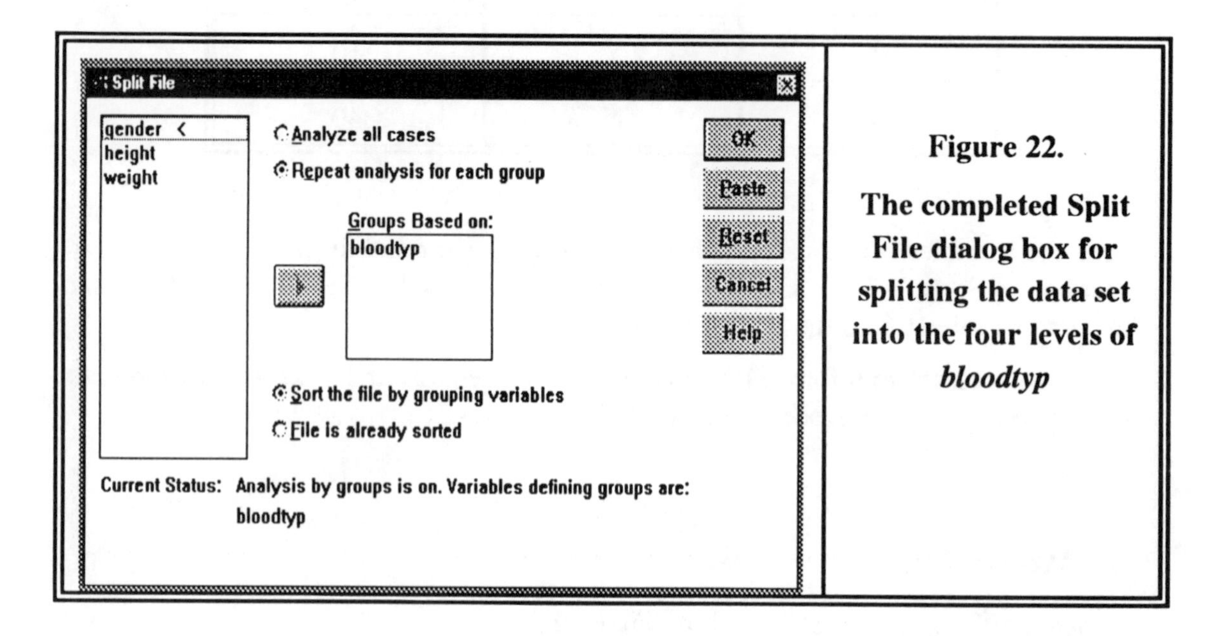

Figure 22.

The completed Split File dialog box for splitting the data set into the four levels of *bloodtyp*

SUMMARY

1) **Quantitative variables** are possessed in **degree**; **qualitative variables** are possessed in **kind**.

2) Variables manipulated by the experimenter consisting of two or more treatment conditions are **independent variables (IVs)**; variables observed or measured during the experiment to assess the effect(s) of the IV(s) are **dependent variables (DVs)**. In the context of experimental design, a **factor** is a set of related conditions or categories, the latter being known as **levels**. Factors may be either **between subjects** or **within subjects**.

3) A **hypothesis** is often a provisional supposition that a specified **independent variable** has a causal effect upon a specified **dependent variable**.

4) SPSS expects to receive a data set in which **each row represents one** (and **only one) subject**, or case, and whose **columns represent the variables** on which the subjects have been measured. Experimental results may require to be recast into a suitable format for entering into the Data Editor window.

5) The format in which values will appear in the **Data Editor** window can be predetermined by choosing

   Edit

   Preferences

6) The **naming of variables** is achieved by double-clicking on the head of the column. With a grouping variable, assign **value labels** by clicking on the **Labels** subdialog button in the **Define Variable** dialog box. The choice of a **variable name** is governed by strict rules, as in Section 3.4.3.2.

7) There are several editing facilities available including **blocking, copying** and **pasting** which are useful for inserting blocks of numbers in a column such as the groups of a grouping variable.

(continued)

8) The procedure for entering data from a **within subjects** (repeated measures) design differs from that for a **between subjects** (independent samples) design because there is no grouping variable for the within subject design. Instead the levels for each within subjects variable have to be entered in separate columns.

9) When entering **string (non-numeric) values**, make sure that the **Variable Type** has been set to **String**. This is achieved by pressing the **Type** subdialog button in the **Define Variable** dialog box and marking the **String** radio button in the **Define Variable Type** dialog box.

10) On the assumption that the data set is rectangular, SPSS assigns a **system-missing value** to any cell in which no entry has been made. This assignment is indicated by a point in each of the cells concerned. The user, however, may wish to designate certain values that are actually in the data set as missing by assigning **user-missing values**.

11) To **save a data set** that has been entered into the Data Editor window, ensure that this is the active window by clicking anywhere within it or selecting it from the list of windows at the foot of the Windows pull-down menu. Then choose

    File

    Save As

    and type in a suitable file name with the extension **.sav** after selecting the appropriate disk drive.

12) To **retrieve a data set** from a file, choose

    File

    Open

    Data

    and highlight the required file name after selecting the appropriate disk drive.

13) Data from SPSS/PC+ and from other applications can be **imported** into SPSS for Windows. Likewise an SPSS for Windows data file can be **exported** to other applications.

(continued)

14) Data can be **listed** on the screen by choosing

Statistics

Summarize

List Cases (or Case Summaries in SPSS 7)

and then specifying the variable desired to be listed.

Details of a stored data file (but not one currently in the Data Editor window) can be listed by choosing

File

Display Data Info...

and then selecting the appropriate file name.

15) Items or selected sections of items can be **printed** from any window by ensuring that it is active. (Click anywhere within it or select it from the list of windows at the foot of the Windows drop-down menu.) Then choose

File

Print

A selected part of a window can be printed by highlighting the selection.

16) To **select cases**, choose

Data

Select Cases

and prepare a suitable conditional expression within the **Select Cases: If** dialog box.

17) When a variable contains counts, or frequencies, it is necessary to indicate that fact to SPSS by invoking the **weight cases** procedure. Choose

Data

Weight Cases

and identify the variable that contains the frequencies or counts.

18) Files can be split by levels (or combinations of levels) of a grouping variable (or variables) using the **Split File** option within the **Data** drop-down menu.

CHAPTER 4

EXPLORING AND GRAPHING DATA

4.1 INTRODUCTION

The SPSS package has been designed to carry out a wide range of statistical tests with ease and rapidity. Before the user can proceed with any data analysis, however, certain preparatory steps must first be taken.

First of all, it is essential to check whether the data have been correctly entered into the computer: a chain is no stronger than its weakest link and it is of paramount importance to ensure that all subsequent inferences rest upon a firm factual foundation. Having checked that the data have been correctly entered using the procedures described in Chapter 3, one might be tempted to proceed immediately to command SPSS to perform various formal statistical tests. The user is strongly warned against this.

The process of data analysis should be thought of as taking place in two phases:

(1) **exploration and description** of the data;

(2) **confirmatory statistical analysis**.

This chapter is primarily concerned with the first phase: exploration and description of the data.

4.1.1 Exploratory data analysis (EDA)

Hartwig & Dearing (1979) provide a readable account of a set of more recent statistical measures known collectively as **exploratory data analysis (EDA)**. These useful methods have now found their way into all good modern computing packages.

The availability of powerful computing packages such as SPSS has made it a simple matter to subject a data set to all manner of statistical analyses and tests of significance. To proceed immediately to such formal analysis, however, is a decidedly risky practice.

There are two main reasons for taking such a cautious approach. Firstly, the user who proceeds immediately to carry out various tests may miss the most illuminating features of the data. Secondly, the performance of a statistical test always presupposes that certain assumptions about the data are correct. Should these assumptions be false, the results of statistical tests may be misleading.

The researcher who explores a data set thoroughly may discover therein things of profound scientific import. There is always the possibility, however, that these patterns are chance occurrences and that, were the research to be repeated with fresh subjects, they might not reappear. The purpose of a statistical test is to **confirm** the characteristics of a data set, in the sense that the researcher wants to be able to say, with a high degree of confidence, that a characteristic of the data has not arisen through chance and is **robust** to replication of the study.

The researcher works with several kinds of data:

(a) **interval data** (measurements on an independent scale with units);

(b) **ordinal data** (ranks or assignments to ordered categories);

(c) **nominal data**, which are merely statements of qualitative category membership.

Of the three kinds of data, types (a) and (b) relate to **quantitative** variables; whereas (c) refers to **qualitative** variables. The term *categorial* is sometimes used to include qualitative data and quantitative data in the form of assignments to ordered categories. This term thus straddles the distinction between types (b) and (c).

Suppose we have a set of measurements, say the heights in inches of a group of women. There are usually three things we want to know about such a data set:

(1) the general **level**, or **average value**, of their heights;

(2) the **dispersion** of height, i.e. the degree to which the individual scores tend to **vary** around or **deviate** from the average, as opposed to clustering closely around it;

(3) the **distribution shape**, i.e. the relative frequencies with which heights are to be found within various regions of the total range of the variable.

In this book, we must assume that you already have some knowledge of the statistics that measure the level and dispersion of a set of scores. The most well-known measures of level are the **mean**, the **median** and the **mode**; and dispersion is measured by the **standard deviation** and **quantile range** statistics. We also assume that you understand some terms relating to the distribution of the data set, such as **skewness**, **bimodality** and so on. Should you be a little rusty on such matters, we strongly recommend that you read the relevant chapters of a good text on the topic, such as Gravetter & Wallnau (1996), chapters 1 to 4, Howell (1997), chapters 1 and 2, or Anderson (1989), chapters 1 to 3.

While there can be no question that the availability of a package with the versatility and power of SPSS is of great assistance to the researcher, there are, nevertheless, a number of cautions and caveats that should be borne in mind.

4.1.2 The influence of outliers and asymmetrical distributions

There are other, equally important, reasons for a thorough preliminary examination of the data set. Statistics such as the mean and standard deviation are intended to express, in a single number, some characteristic of the data set as a whole: the former is intended to express the **average**, that is, the general level, typical value, or **central tendency**, of a set of scores; the latter is a measure of their **spread**, or **dispersion**. There are circumstances, however, in which the mean and standard deviation are very poor measures of central tendency and dispersion, respectively, as when the distribution of scores is markedly skewed, or when extreme values, or **outliers**, exert undue **leverage** upon the values of these statistics.

4.1.3 Formal tests, statistical models and their assumptions

There is yet another potential problem. The ease of access to formal tests of significance that a modern computing package confers upon the user belies the risk involved in applying such tests before the properties of a data set (even one that has been entered without transcription error) have been fully investigated. The making of a formal statistical test of significance always presupposes the applicability of a statistical **model**, that is, an interpretation (usually in the form of an equation) of the data set as having been generated in a certain manner. The model underlying the one-sample t-test, for example, assumes that the data are from a normal population. To some extent, statistical tests have been shown to be robust to moderate violations of the assumptions of the models upon which they are predicated. But there are limits to this robustness, and there are circumstances in which a result, declared by an incautious user to be significant beyond, say, the 0.05 level, may actually have been much more probable under the null hypothesis than the given tail probability would indicate. There is no way of avoiding this pitfall other than by thoroughly exploring the data first to ascertain their suitability for specified formal tests.

4.2 FINDING MENUS

Before considering the various exploratory statistical measures available on SPSS, it might be useful to remind the reader how to find the various menus, how to complete the dialog boxes, and how to amend information in dialog boxes.

In the menu bar of the **SPSS Application** window are 9 drop-down menus (Figure 1):

Figure 1.

The nine drop-down menus

SPSS for Windows

File Edit Data Transform Statistics Graphs Utilities Window Help

Some items in the **Data Menu (Define Variable, Select Cases, Weight Cases)** have already been considered in Chapter 3. For this chapter, the relevant menus are **Statistics, Graphs**, and **Transform**. Within the **Statistics** menu, the relevant items are **Summarize** and **Compare Means**. The **Summarize** menu (Figure 2) includes **Frequencies, Descriptives, Explore**, and **Crosstabs**; the **Compare Means** menu includes **Means**.

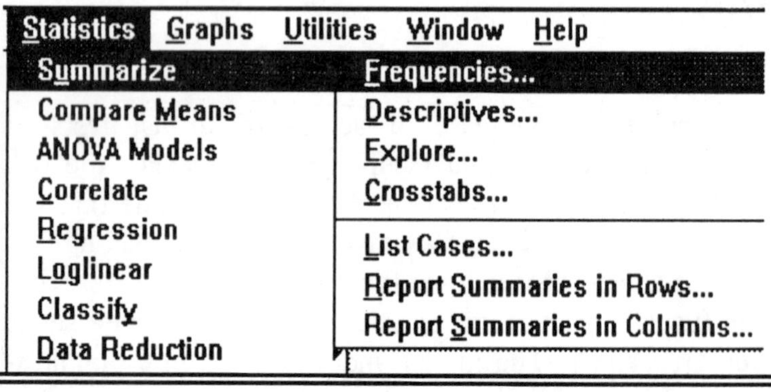

Statistics Graphs Utilities Window Help

Summarize | Frequencies...
Compare Means | Descriptives...
ANOVA Models | Explore...
Correlate | Crosstabs...
Regression | List Cases...
Loglinear | Report Summaries in Rows...
Classify | Report Summaries in Columns...
Data Reduction

Figure 2.

The Summarize menu

Within the **Graphs** menu (Figure 3) are various types of graph such as **Bar, Line, Pie, Boxplot, Error Bar, Scatter** (for a scatterplot) and **Histogram**. Since, however, some of these graphs are available in other procedures in the **Summarize** menu, we shall consider them later. Finally, within the **Transform** menu (Figure 4) are **Compute** and **Recode**. The meanings of these items will be explained later.

Figure 3.

The Graphs drop-down menu

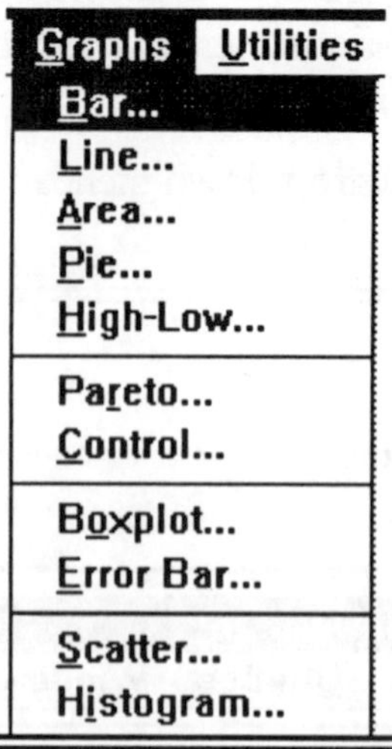

Graphs Utilities

Bar...
Line...
Area...
Pie...
High-Low...
Pareto...
Control...
Boxplot...
Error Bar...
Scatter...
Histogram...

Figure 4.

The Transform drop-down menu

Transform Statistics Graph

Compute...
Random Number Seed...
Count...
Recode
Rank Cases...
Automatic Recode...
Create Time Series...
Replace Missing Values...

4.3 DESCRIBING DATA

Before illustrating the use of various menu items, it is necessary to have a suitable data set such as the one already used in Chapter 3 (Table 8) consisting of two quantitative variables *weight* and *height*, and two qualitative variables *gender* and *bloodtyp*. Let us assume the data have already been set up in the **Data Editor** window (only the first seven of the thirty-two cases are shown in Figure 5).

	bloodtyp	gender	height	weight
1	O	M	178	75
2	O	M	196	100
3	A	M	145	60
4	O	M	170	71
5	B	M	180	80
6	O	M	175	69
7	AB	M	185	78

Figure 5.

The first 7 cases of the data set in the Data Editor window

4.3.1 Describing categorial data

The **summarize** item within the **statistics** drop-down menu contains procedures for describing qualitative and categorial data, namely **Frequencies** and **Crosstabs**. Items from the **Graphs** drop-down menu can also be used; but these will not be described in this section, since some of them are also available within **Frequencies**.

Frequencies gives frequency distributions for all types of data (nominal, ordinal, and interval). There are options for additional statistics, and for plots such as barcharts and histograms (see also **Explore** below for other ways of displaying barcharts and histograms).

Crosstabs generates contingency tables, which list cell frequencies for categorial data classified on at least two variables. The tables also show row and column frequencies and percentages. Various statistics computed from contingency tables, such as **chi-square**, the **phi coefficient**, the **contingency coefficient**, **lambda**, **Kendall's tau-b** and **tau-c**, **Pearson's correlation coefficient r**, and **gamma**, are available in the **Options** box in Crosstabs.

4.3.1.1 Frequencies

The following example demonstrates the use of the descriptive statistics procedures for the two qualitative variables *gender* and *bloodtyp*.

Click on

Statistics

Summarize

Frequencies

to open the **Frequencies** dialog box (Figure 6).

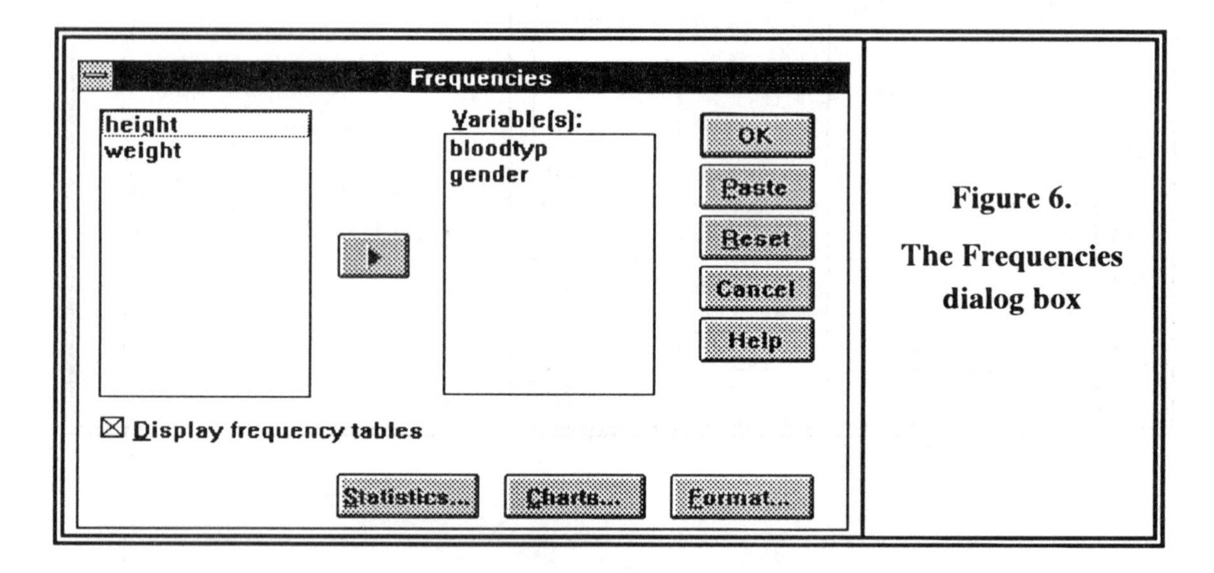

Figure 6.

The Frequencies dialog box

Highlight the variables *bloodtyp* and *gender* and then click on ▶ to transfer them to the **Variable(s)** box. Click on **Charts** to obtain the **Frequencies: Charts** dialog box (Figure 7) and then on the **Bar Chart(s)** button. There is also the choice of frequencies or percentages for the y axis in the **Axis Label Display** box. Click on **Continue** and then on **OK** in the **Frequencies** dialog box. The output consists of a table and bar chart for each variable.

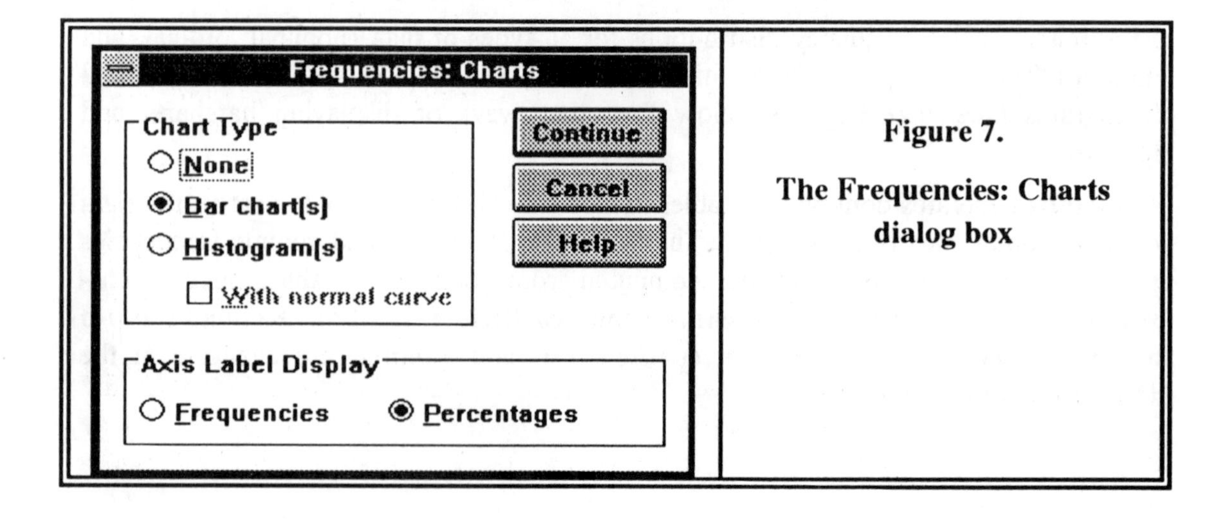

Figure 7.

The Frequencies: Charts dialog box

Note about SPSS 6 and SPSS 7 outputs

Since the SPSS 6 and SPSS 7 outputs differ considerably in their layout, both versions will be included in most of the examples in this Chapter.

- SPSS 6 lists and tables appear in the **Output window**, whereas charts and graphs appear in the **Chart Carousel window**, where further editing can be carried out.
- All SPSS 7 output (lists, tables, charts and graphs) appears in a single window called the **SPSS Output Navigator**, which consists of two panes.

The left-hand pane of the **Output Navigator** lists the items of output in a hierarchical iconic manner showing whether the item is visible (open-book icon) or invisible (closed-book icon). By double-clicking on the icon, the item can be made visible or invisible in the right-hand pane, where all output is presented in full. The output can also be arranged in a different order simply by moving the appropriate icons around in the left-hand pane. Much the best way of learning how to move around the **Output Navigator** is to choose

Help

Tutorial

and double-click to open the tutorial menu. Then select

Examining results

Using the output navigator

and follow the prompts through the illustrated tutorial.

The first example of SPSS 7 output includes the left-hand pane; but thereafter only the principal table, chart or graph in the right-hand pane will be reproduced.

A feature of the SPSS 7 output is the ease with which it can be edited to improve the layout of materials in tables or to remove items which the user may not wish to reproduce in a document. After double-clicking anywhere within a boxed item, the item will be surrounded by a hatched box indicating that it is in editing mode. If the cursor is then moved on to a vertical line, a double arrow appears and it is then possible to slide the line sideways by holding down the left-hand mouse button and moving the line left or right. Items can be deleted by highlighting them and pressing the Delete key. Several of the SPSS 7 tables reproduced in this and later chapters have been edited in this manner.

The output tables are listed in Output Listing 1 (SPSS 6 and 7) and the bar chart for *bloodtyp* is shown in Figure 8 (the bar chart for *gender* is not reproduced). Note that the bar chart can also be requested directly from the **Bar** option within the **Graphs** drop-down menu.

Output Listing 1 (SPSS 6).

Frequency listings for *bloodtyp* and *gender*

BLOODTYP

Value Label	Value	Frequency	Percent	Valid Percent	Cum Percent
Group A	A	6	18.8	18.8	18.8
Group AB	AB	3	9.4	9.4	28.1
Group B	B	6	18.8	18.8	46.9
Group O	O	17	53.1	53.1	100.0
	Total	32	100.0	100.0	

GENDER

Value Label	Value	Frequency	Percent	Valid Percent	Cum Percent
Female	F	16	50.0	50.0	50.0
Male	M	16	50.0	50.0	100.0
	Total	32	100.0	100.0	

Output Listing 1 (SPSS 7).

Frequency listing for *bloodtyp* (*gender* is not reproduced here)

Left-hand pane

(This shows the items and order of output. Notice all items have an open-book icon except Notes which has a closed-book icon showing that it is invisible)

File Edit View Insert Statistics G

- SPSS Output
  - Frequencies
    - Title
    - Notes
    - Statistics
    - BLOODTYP
    - Bar chart of bloodtyp
    - GENDER
    - Bar chart of gender

One of the right-hand pane tables:

The *bloodtyp* frequencies

BLOODTYP

		Frequency	Percent	Valid Percent	Cumulative Percent
Valid	Group A	6	18.8	18.8	18.8
	Group AB	3	9.4	9.4	28.1
	Group B	6	18.8	18.8	46.9
	Group O	17	53.1	53.1	100.0
	Total	32	100.0	100.0	
Total		32	100.0		

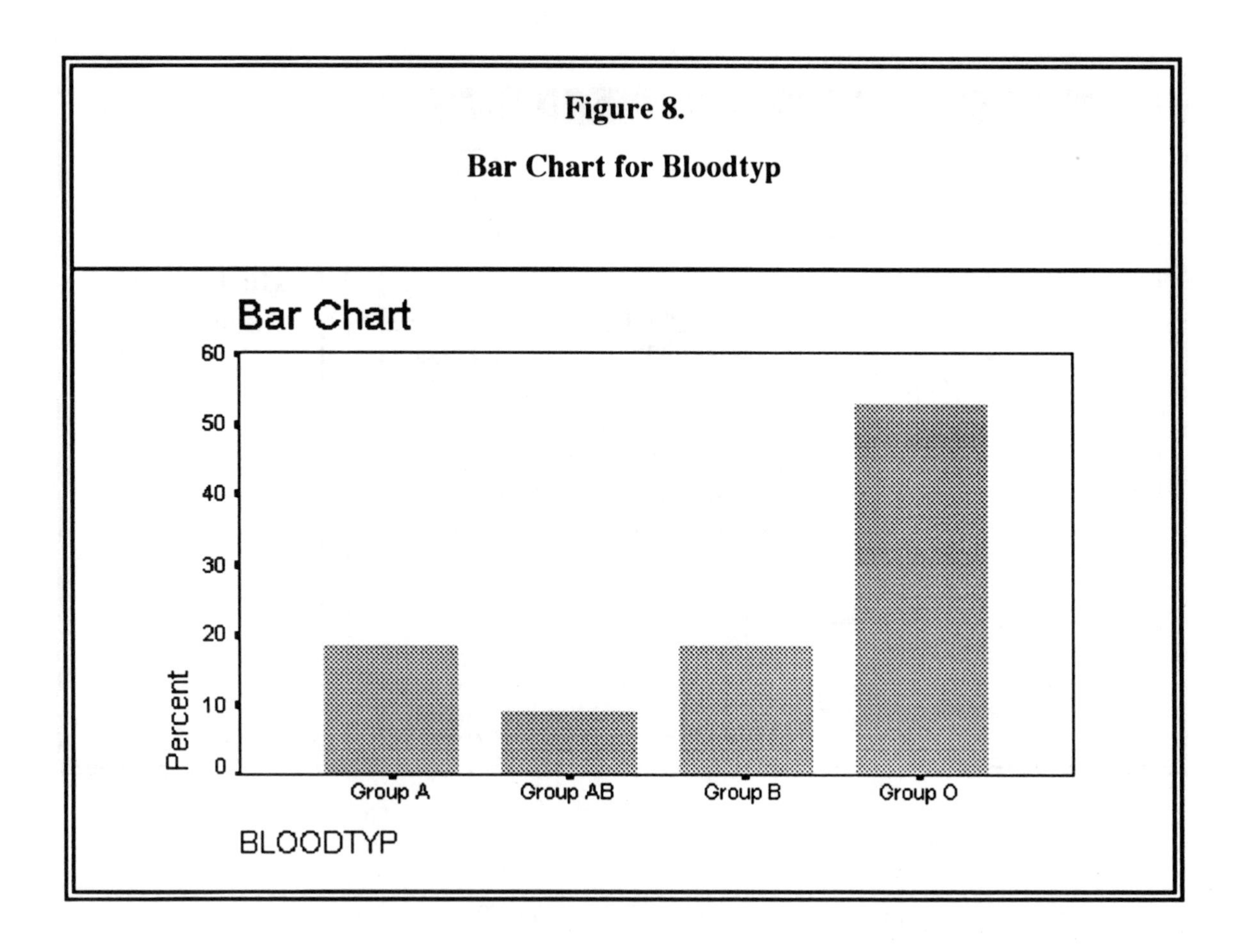

Figure 8.

Bar Chart for Bloodtyp

4.3.1.2 Crosstabs

Crosstabs generates contingency tables from nominal or ordinal categorial data. Here we illustrate the procedure with *bloodtyp* and *gender.*

Choose
Statistics

  Summarize

    Crosstabs

to open the **Crosstabs** dialog box (Figure 9).

Enter one of the variables into the **Row(s)** box by clicking on its name and then on ▶. Enter the other variable into the **Column(s)** box. Click on **OK**.

In the case of SPSS 7, it is necessary to click on the **Cells...** box within the **Crosstabs** dialog box and then click on the **Total** box within **Percentages** to get row and column percentages listed in the output.

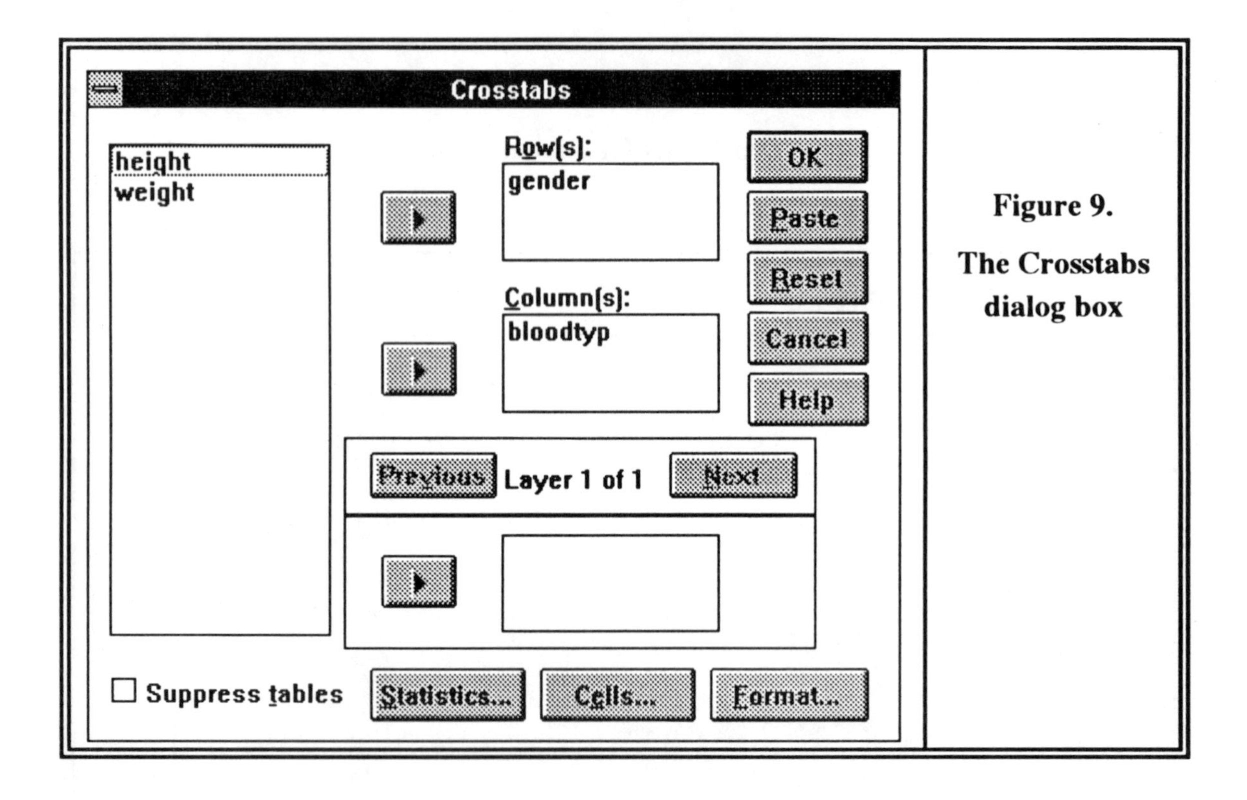

Figure 9.

The Crosstabs dialog box

The output is shown in Output Listing 2 (SPSS 6 and 7).

Output Listing 2 (SPSS 6).

Contingency table from Crosstabs

GENDER by BLOODTYP

GENDER	Count	BLOODTYP Group A A	Group AB AB	Group B B	Group O O	Row Total
Female	F	3	1	3	9	16 50.0
Male	M	3	2	3	8	16 50.0
	Column Total	6 18.8	3 9.4	6 18.8	17 53.1	32 100.0

Output Listing 2 (SPSS 7).

Contingency table from Crosstabs

GENDER * BLOODTYP Crosstabulation

			BLOODTYP				
			Group A	Group AB	Group B	Group O	Total
GENDER	Female	Count	3	1	3	9	16
		% of Total	9.4%	3.1%	9.4%	28.1%	50.0%
	Male	Count	3	2	3	8	16
		% of Total	9.4%	6.3%	9.4%	25.0%	50.0%
Total		Count	6	3	6	17	32
		% of Total	18.8%	9.4%	18.8%	53.1%	100.0%

It is important to be clear that **Crosstabs** is only applicable to contingency tables as described in Section 3.12.2 of Chapter 3: it should be requested only for **categorial data** (i.e. nominal data or those that are assignments to ordered categories). Crosstabs should not be requested for interval data or ranks.

4.3.2 Describing interval data

Descriptives and **Explore** within the **Summarize** drop-down menu, and **Means** within the **Compare Means** drop-down menu, are the principal procedures for describing and exploring interval data, the last two procedures also allowing quantitative variables to be classified by categories of a qualitative variable (e.g. *gender*). **Descriptives** provides a quick way of obtaining a range of common descriptive statistics, both of central tendency and of dispersion. **Means** calculates the means and standard deviations of sub-populations (as defined by values of a grouping or coding variable). There is also the option of a one-way analysis of variance. Note especially that **Means** cannot be used for variables that have not been grouped by another variable; **Descriptives** must be used instead. **Explore** contains a large variety of graphs and diagrams (also available directly from the **Graphs** drop-down menu) as well as a variety of statistics.

Frequencies within the **Summarize** drop-down menu, though primarily suited for nominal and ordinal data, can be used for computing specified percentile values, measures of central tendency and dispersion, and drawing histograms (with or without a superimposed normal curve) of interval data. However in order to prevent a possibly very large range of scores being listed along with their frequencies in the output, it is essential to turn off the frequency table by clicking off the **Display frequency tables** box (see Figure 6).

4.3.2.1 Frequencies

The first example iillustrates the use of **Frequencies** to draw a histogram, compute some descriptive statistics, and to display some percentile values with the variable *height*. Enter the variable name *height* into the **Variable(s)** box within the **Frequencies** dialog box (Figure 6) and click on **Charts** to open the **Frequencies: Charts** dialog box (Figure 7). Click on the **Histogram** button and turn on the **With normal curve** box within the **Chart Type** box and then on **Continue**. Click on the **Statistics** button to open the **Frequencies: Statistics** dialog box (Figure 10).

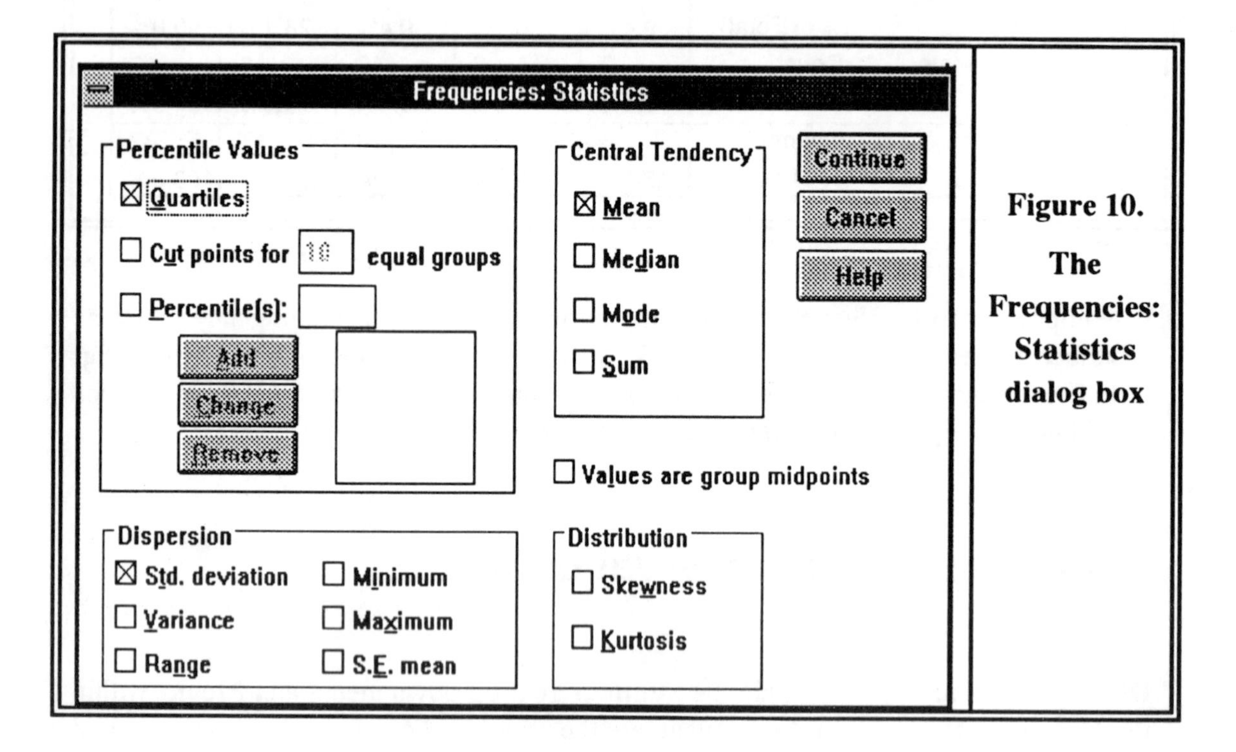

Figure 10. The Frequencies: Statistics dialog box

Within the **Central Tendency** box, click on the **Mean** check box; within the **Dispersion** box, click on the **Std. deviation** check box. Within the **Percentile Values** box, click on the **Quartiles** check box: this will print the 25th, 50th and 75th percentile values. Other percentiles can be specified if desired by clicking on the **Percentile(s)** box and filling in whatever values are wanted (e.g. 90, 95). Click on **Continue** and then on **OK** to run the procedure. A histogram can also be requested by selecting **Histogram** from the **Graphs** drop-down menu instead of using **Frequencies**. Ensure that the **Display frequency tables** box is turned off.

The statistical output is shown in Output Listing 3 (SPSS 6 and 7) and the histogram in Figure 11 (SPSS 6 and 7 versions are similar).

Output Listing 3 (SPSS 6).

The mean, standard deviation, and quartiles for height

```
HEIGHT     Height in Centimetres

Mean            170.281        Std dev       13.679

Percentile      Value          Percentile    Value         Percentile    Value

  25.00         162.250          50.00       170.500         75.00       181.500

Valid cases        32          Missing cases       0
```

Output Listing 3 (SPSS 7).

The mean, standard deviation, and quartiles for height

Statistics

	N		Mean	Std. Deviation	Percentiles		
	Valid	Missing			25.00	50.00	75.00
Height in Centimetres	32	0	170.28	13.68	162.25	170.50	181.50

Figure 11.

Histogram as requested from Frequencies

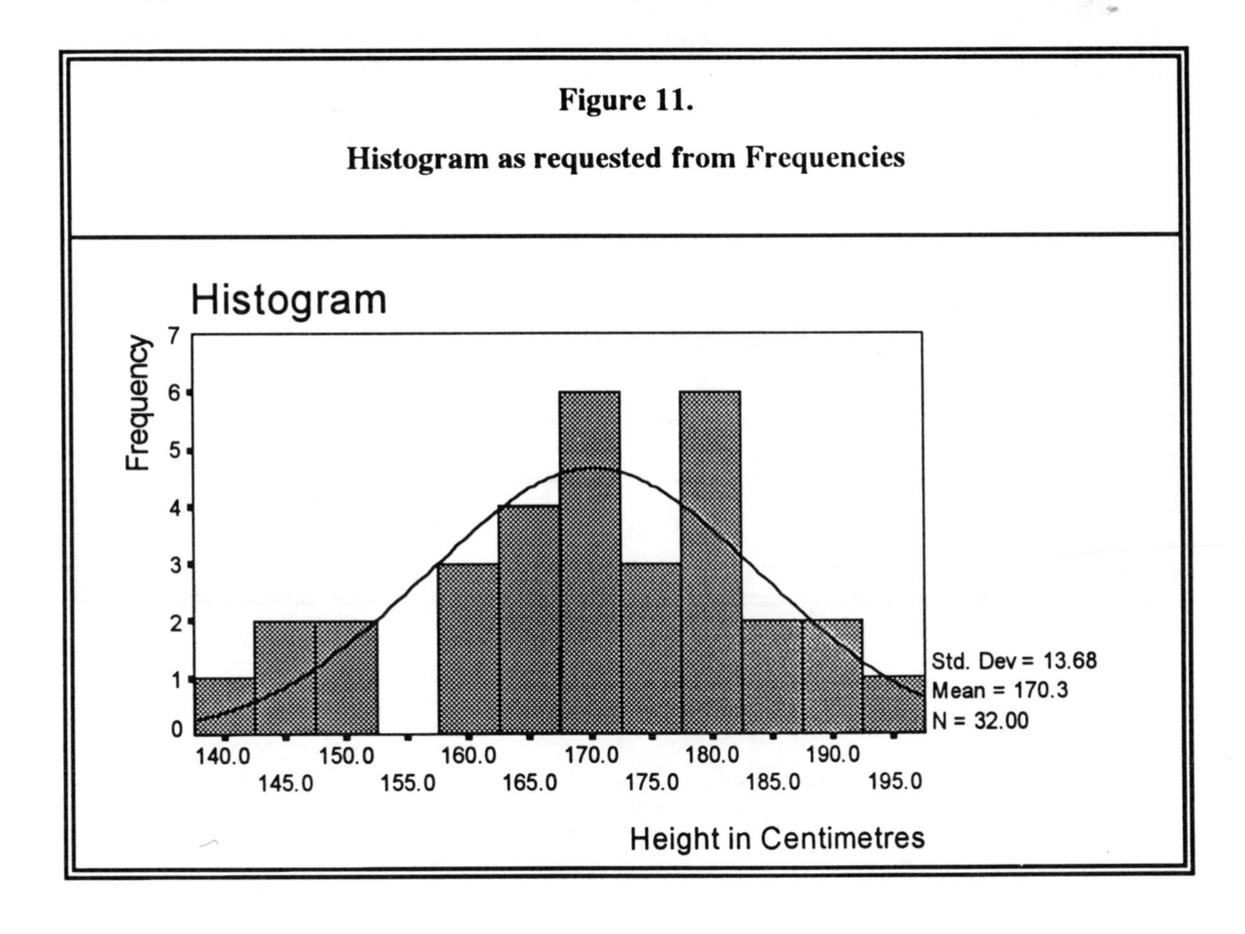

4.3.2.2 Descriptives

Descriptives provides a quick way of generating several well-known statistics such as the mean, standard deviation, variance, maximum and minimum values, range and sum. Choose

Statistics

  Summarize

    Descriptives

and open the **Descriptives** dialog box. Transfer the variables names *height* and *weight* into the **Variable(s)** box and then click on **Options** to open the **Descriptives: Options** dialog box (part of which is shown in Figure 12).

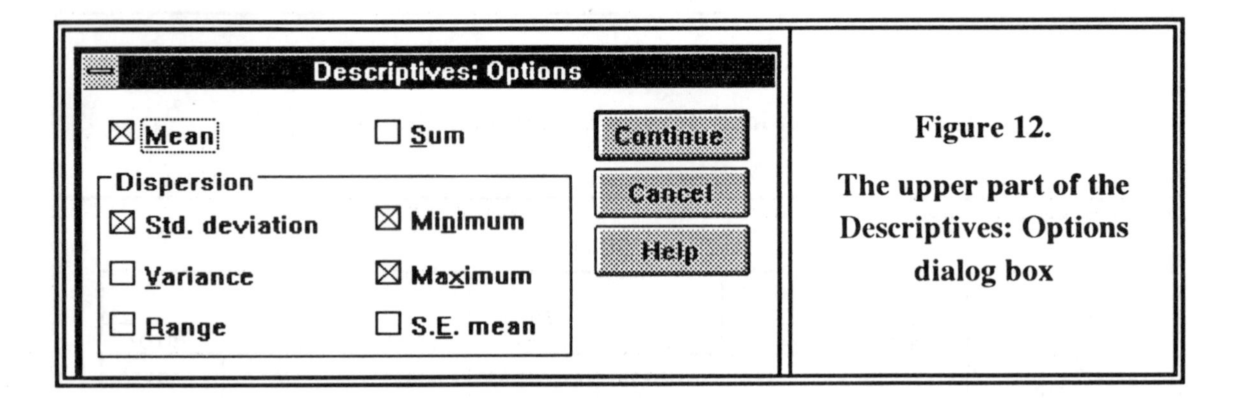

Figure 12.

The upper part of the Descriptives: Options dialog box

Select the statistics of interest by clicking on the check boxes (here we have selected just a few of them). Click on **Continue** and then on **OK**. The output is shown in Output Listing 4 (SPSS 6 and 7).

Output Listing 4 (SPSS 6).

The descriptive statistics for weight and height

Variable	Mean	Std Dev	Minimum	Maximum	Valid N	Label
WEIGHT	70.22	15.93	48	120	32	Weight in Kilograms
HEIGHT	170.28	13.68	142	196	32	Height in Centimetre

Output Listing 4 (SPSS 7).

The descriptive statistics for weight and height

Descriptive Statistics

	N	Minimum	Maximum	Mean	Std. Deviation
Height in Centimetres	32	142	196	170.28	13.68
Weight in Kilograms	32	48	120	70.22	15.93
Valid N (listwise)	32				

4.3.2.3 Means

When statistics such as the mean and standard deviation are required for one variable that has been grouped by categories of another (e.g. *height* grouped by *gender*), the appropriate procedure is **Means**. Choose

Statistics

Compare Means

Means

to open the **Means** dialog box.

Click on *height* and on ▶ to transfer the name *height* into the **Dependent List** box. Click on *gender* and on ▶ to transfer the name *gender* into the **Independent List** box. The completed dialog box is shown in Figure 13. Click on **OK** to run the procedure.

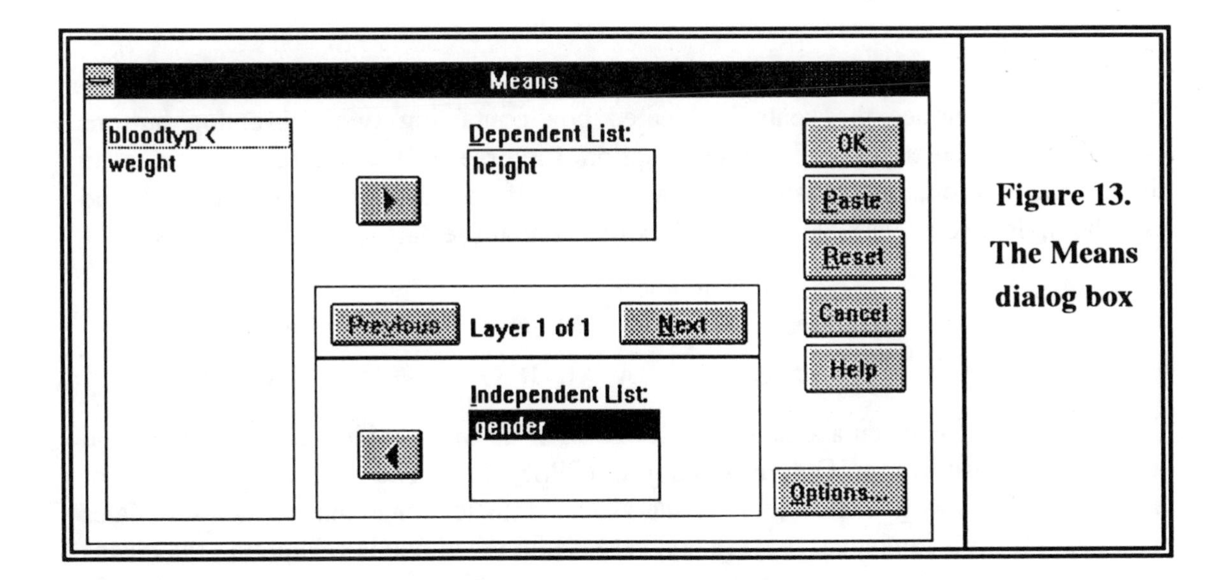

Figure 13.

The Means dialog box

The output is listed in Output Listing 5 (SPSS 6 and 7).

Output Listing 5 (SPSS 6).

The mean height for each level of gender requested with Means

```
Summaries of       HEIGHT      Height in Centimetres
By levels of       GENDER

Variable        Value  Label                     Mean      Std Dev     Cases

For Entire Population                        170.2813     13.6789        32

GENDER          F      Female                163.9375     12.0635        16
GENDER          M      Male                  176.6250     12.4626        16
```

Report

Height in Centimetres

Female	Mean	163.94
	N	16
	Std. Deviation	12.06
Male	Mean	176.63
	N	16
	Std. Deviation	12.46
Total	Mean	170.28
	N	32
	Std. Deviation	13.68

Output Listing 5 (SPSS 7).

The mean height for each level of gender requested with Means

In Figure 13, notice the centrally located box containing two sub-dialog buttons **Previous** and **Next,** as well as the caption **Layer 1 of 1.** Here a **layer** is an independent (grouping) variable, such as *gender*. If you click on **Next**, you can add another independent variable such as *bloodtyp*, so that the data are classified thus:

1st Layer	***Gender***	**Male**	**Female**
2nd Layer	***Bloodtype***	**A AB B O**	**A AB B O**

SPSS will give the mean and standard deviation of all the combinations of gender and bloodtype as shown in Output Listing 6 (SPSS 6). The SPSS 7 output (not reproduced) is a long vertical table listing all the statistics for Females, then for Males and then for both combined. Layering is very useful when one is calculating the means and standard deviations for data from a factorial analysis of variance (see Chapters 8-10).

Output Listing 6 (SPSS 6).

The use of layering to compute means and standard deviations

```
Summaries of        HEIGHT      Height in Centimetres
By levels of        GENDER
                    BLOODTYP

Variable          Value   Label                    Mean     Std Dev    Cases

For Entire Population                           170.2813    13.6789       32

GENDER              F       Female              163.9375    12.0635       16
  BLOODTYP          A       Group A             160.3333    10.5040        3
  BLOODTYP          AB      Group AB            151.0000       .           1
  BLOODTYP          B       Group B             175.6667     6.5064        3
  BLOODTYP          O       Group O             162.6667    12.4700        9

GENDER              M       Male                176.6250    12.4626       16
  BLOODTYP          A       Group A             168.3333    22.5462        3
  BLOODTYP          AB      Group AB            178.5000     9.1924        2
  BLOODTYP          B       Group B             184.0000     5.2915        3
  BLOODTYP          O       Group O             176.5000    10.6637        8
```

4.3.2.4 Explore

The **Explore** procedure offers many of the facilities already illustrated with the other procedures and allows quantitative variables (such as *height*) to be subdivided by the categories of a qualitative variable, such as *gender*: for example, if a data set comprises the heights of 50 men and 50 women collected into a column headed *height* and (in another column) sex is carried by the grouping variable *gender*, **Explore** can be commanded to produce statistical summaries, graphs and displays either for the 100 height measurements considered as a single group, or the heights of males or females (or both) considered separately.

A useful first step in the analysis of data is to obtain a picture of the data set as a whole, that is, to construct a **graph** of the data. The **Explore** routine offers three kinds of graphs:

(1) histograms;

(2) stem-and-leaf displays;

(3) boxplots.

Readers unfamiliar with these can find clear descriptions in Howell (1997) of histograms (and bar graphs) on pp17-20, of stem-and-leaf displays on pp21-23, and of boxplots on pp54-57.

The basis of all three types of graphs is a table called a **frequency distribution**, which sets out either (in the case of qualitative or nominal data) the categories comprising a qualitative variable and gives the frequency of observations in each category or (with interval data) divides the total range of values into arbitrary **class intervals** and gives the frequency of measurements that fell within each interval, that is, had values within the upper and lower **bounds** of the interval concerned. With data on height recorded in centimetres, for example, the total range could be divided into the class intervals (140-149, 150-159, 160-169, and so on), and the frequency distribution would give the **frequencies** of heights within each of these ranges.

A **bar graph** (SPSS calls it a 'bar chart': see Figure 8) is suitable for qualitative (nominal) data, such as the numbers of people in a sample belonging to the various blood groups. In a bar graph, the bars are separated to clarify the fact that the horizontal axis contains no scale of measurement; in fact, the order of the bars in Figure 8 is arbitrary, since the Group B bar could as well have followed the Group A bar. A **histogram**, on the other hand, is appropriate for interval data such as a set of height measurements: the class intervals are stepped out on the horizontal axis; and on each interval, a bar is erected, whose height represents the number of people whose heights fell within that interval. *In a histogram, the bars touch one another - there are no spaces.*

Choose
Statistics
Summarize
Explore

to open the **Explore** dialog box (the completed version is shown in Figure 14).

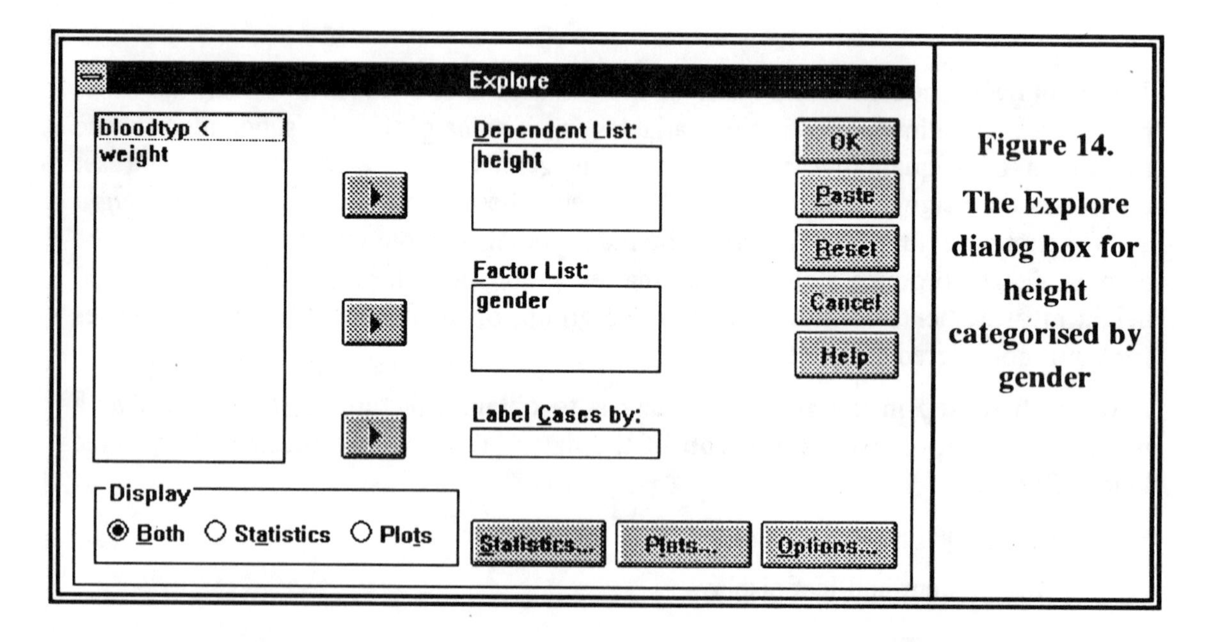

Figure 14. The Explore dialog box for height categorised by gender

To see how height varies with gender, click on the variable name *height* and on ▶ to transfer it to the **Dependent List** box, and then click on *gender* and on ▶ to transfer it to the **Factor List** box.

Click on **Plots** to open the **Explore: Plots** dialog box (part of which is shown in Figure 15) and select the **Stem-and-leaf** check box in the **Descriptive** box. The default setting for the **boxplots** is a side-by-side plot for each level of the factor (i.e. Female and Male). Click on **Continue** and then on **OK** to run the procedure.

If we had wished to plot boxplots of height and weight side-by-side at each level of gender (not very sensible since height and weight measurements are totally different in range of values), it would have been necessary to enter both *height* and *weight* in the **Dependent List** box and to mark the **Dependents together** radio button within the **Boxplots** box.

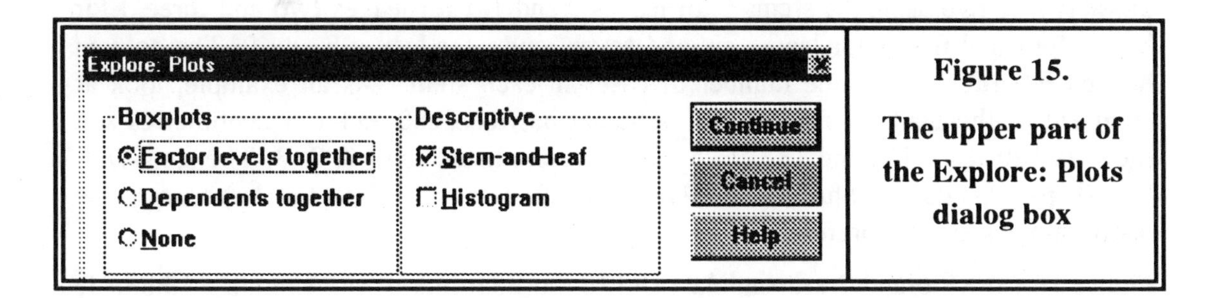

Figure 15.

The upper part of the Explore: Plots dialog box

The descriptive statistics and the stem-and-leaf display for *heights* on Males (one of the levels of *gender*) is shown in Output Listing 7 (the SPSS 6 and 7 versions are similar); the output for Females is not reproduced here.

Output Listing 7 (SPSS 6).

Descriptive statistics, and stem-and-leaf display for height categorised by gender (only Males shown here)

```
    HEIGHT     Height in Centimetres
By  GENDER     M          Male

Valid cases:          16.0   Missing cases:         .0   Percent missing:        .0

Mean        176.6250  Std Err      3.1157  Min       145.0000  Skewness     -.9470
Median      179.0000  Variance   155.3167  Max       196.0000  S E Skew      .5643
5% Trim     177.3056  Std Dev     12.4626  Range      51.0000  Kurtosis     1.6419
95% CI for Mean (169.9841, 183.2659)       IQR        14.5000  S E Kurt     1.0908

Frequency     Stem &  Leaf

    1.00 Extremes     (145)
    1.00        16 *  0
     .00        16 .
    4.00        17 *  0002
    2.00        17 .  58
    4.00        18 *  0023
    1.00        18 .  5
    2.00        19 *  00
    1.00        19 .  6

Stem width:         10
Each leaf:        1 case(s)
```

Look at the example of a **stem-and-leaf display** given in the lower half of Output Listing 7. The central column of numbers (16, 16, 17, 17, ..., 19) is the **stem** of the display representing the leading digit or digits (here they are the hundreds and tens of centimetres); the numbers in the column headed **Leaf** are the final digits (here the units of centimetres). Each stem denotes the lower bound of the class interval: for example, the first number, 16, represents the lower bound of the class interval from 160 upwards. If there is a large number of leaves for a single stem, SPSS may split the stem into two using an asterisk * for the leaves 0-4 and a dot for the leaves 5-9, or possibly into five using the stems * for leaves 0 and 1, t for leaves two and three, f for leaves four and five, s for leaves six and seven, and . for leaves 8 and 9. The column headed **Frequency** lists the number of cases in each stem. As an example, look at stem 18 *: there are four cases with a height between 180 and 184 centimetres and they are 180, 180, 182 and 183 since the leaves are listed as 0, 0, 2, 3. The stem-and-leaf display is very useful for displaying small data sets, but for large sets, the histogram is generally preferred.

Figure 16 (SPSS 6 and 7 are simiular) shows the **boxplots** of the heights of the male and female subjects considered separately, but plotted side-by-side, for comparison. In a boxplot, the box itself represents that portion of the distribution falling between the 25th and 75th percentiles. (The xth percentile is the value below which x% of the distribution lies: so 50% of the heights lie between the 25th and 75th percentiles.) The horizontal line across the interior of the box represents the median. If the median line is eccentrically placed within the box, a skewed distribution is indicated. The vertical lines outside the box, which are known as **whiskers**, connect the largest and smallest values that are not categorised as outliers or extreme values.

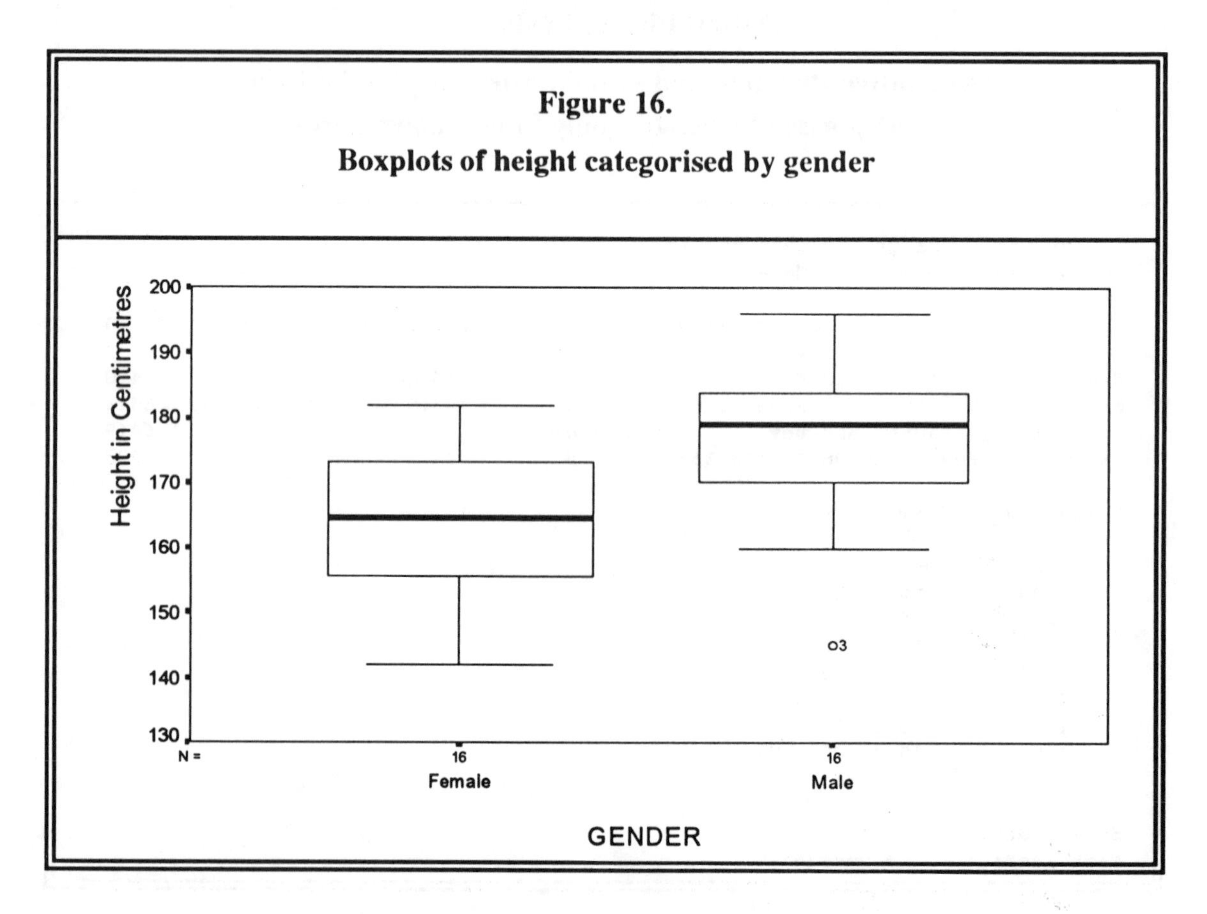

Figure 16.

Boxplots of height categorised by gender

A boxplot **outlier (o)** is defined as a value more than 1.5 box-lengths away from the box, and an **extreme value** (*) as more than 3 box-lengths away from the box. The number(s) alongside O and * are the case number(s).

Skewness is indicated by an eccentric location of the median within the box. Notice that the distribution of heights for females is much more symmetric than that for males. The $\mathbf{o}^3$ under the Male boxplot indicates the existence of an outlier and that it is the value for case 3. This value (145cm) is much lower than the average height for males and its presence is also noted in the stem-and-leaf display in Output Listing 7.

Boxplots are especially useful for identifying outliers and extreme values in data sets, and can be requested directly by choosing the **Boxplot** item within the **Graphs** drop-down menu.

4.3.3 Other graphical procedures

A wide range of graphs and charts is available for exploring and representing data. Some of these have already been discussed; here further details are given. Before moving on to actual examples, some general information about requesting graphs and plots will be presented.

4.3.3.1 Requesting graphs and charts

The dialog boxes for specifying graphs and charts are accessed from the **Graphs** drop-down menu or from options within various procedures - for example, the **Frequencies** dialog box (Figure 6) contains an option **Charts**, as shown in Figure 7.

It is worth spending a few moments considering the variable names and labels that may be plotted in charts or graphs in case the user might want to change some of them within the data file before going ahead with the graph or chart. If the data file has missing data, remember to specify whether missing data should be plotted (for example, in bar charts); missing data can be excluded by turning off the **Display groups defined by missing values** box in the **Options** dialog box.

If extensive editing is not anticipated, it is quicker to add a title (if desired) at this stage rather than at the editing stage (though for boxplots this can only be done at the editing stage) by clicking on the **Titles** box and typing in the desired title.

It should be noted that not all boxes in a dialog box need necessarily be used. For example, **Label Cases by** boxes may be left unfilled when that option is not required. The critical test of whether enough information has been specified in a dialog box is whether the **OK** box is operative or not.

4.3.3.2 Seeing the graph or chart on screen

After a graph or chart has been completed by SPSS 6, it will either appear directly on the screen or a **Carousel** icon will appear, in which case it is necessary to click on the icon to open the **Chart Carousel** window. In SPSS 7, the graph or chart will appear in the **Output Navigator**.

4.3.3.3 Editing a graph or chart

After a graph or chart has appeared on the screen, the following options are available:

1. Accept the image as it is and save it, print it or copy it for pasting into a document.
2. Reject the image. (In SPSS 6, this is done by clicking on the **Discard** box; in SPSS 7, click on the appropriate item in the left-hand pane of the Output Navigator and then press the **Delete** key).
3. Edit the image. (For details, see below).

It is tempting to save all relevant charts but the reader should be aware that charts take up a lot of computer space. If storage space is limited, save only the most important charts: it is easy to recreate charts from saved data files on later occasions if necessary.

Editing of the image allows a wide range of alterations and additions to be made to the graph or chart; but it is a slow process. For example, axis legends can be changed, titles and subtitles can be added or altered, colours can be changed or eliminated, shadings can be added or altered instead of colours, spacing of bars can be revised, and so on. To edit an image, click on the **Edit** box in SPSS 6 or double-click on the actual image in SPSS 7 to make available a new set of drop-down menus (the **Chart Editor** menu bar) and the **Chart Window** toolbar of icons representing most of the items in the **Attributes** drop-down menu.

The **Chart** drop-down menu allows titles, subtitles and legends to be added or changed, axis annotations to be changed, inner and outer frames to be added or deleted, and so on.

The **Attributes** drop-down menu allows the following to be modified (the icons in the toolbar are also shown):

- fill patterns  and colours of bars  .
- styles of markers  , lines  and bars  .
- text fonts and sizes  .
- axis position

Some of the menu items can also be accessed by double clicking on a feature of the graph or chart (for example, clicking on an axis legend will bring the **Legend** dialog box on to the screen). It will also be necessary to select the value or item to be changed on the graph or chart by single-clicking it when using items from the **Attributes** menu.

If a series of similar graphs or charts are going to be requested, the reader should consider saving the edited first chart and then specifying the file when using the **Chart Template** option for the second and subsequent charts.

In summary, it is possible to customise a graph or a chart to a considerable extent and to maximise clarity for reproduction by a monochrome printer by replacing colours with patterns.

4.3.3.4 Clustered bar charts

Several types of bar charts can be drawn. The example shown in Figure 17 is derived from SPSS's data bank file called *bank.sav* showing the mean current salary (in dollars) for males and females in various employment categories. Note that there are no females working as security officers, or in technical work.

Figure 17.

Clustered bar chart

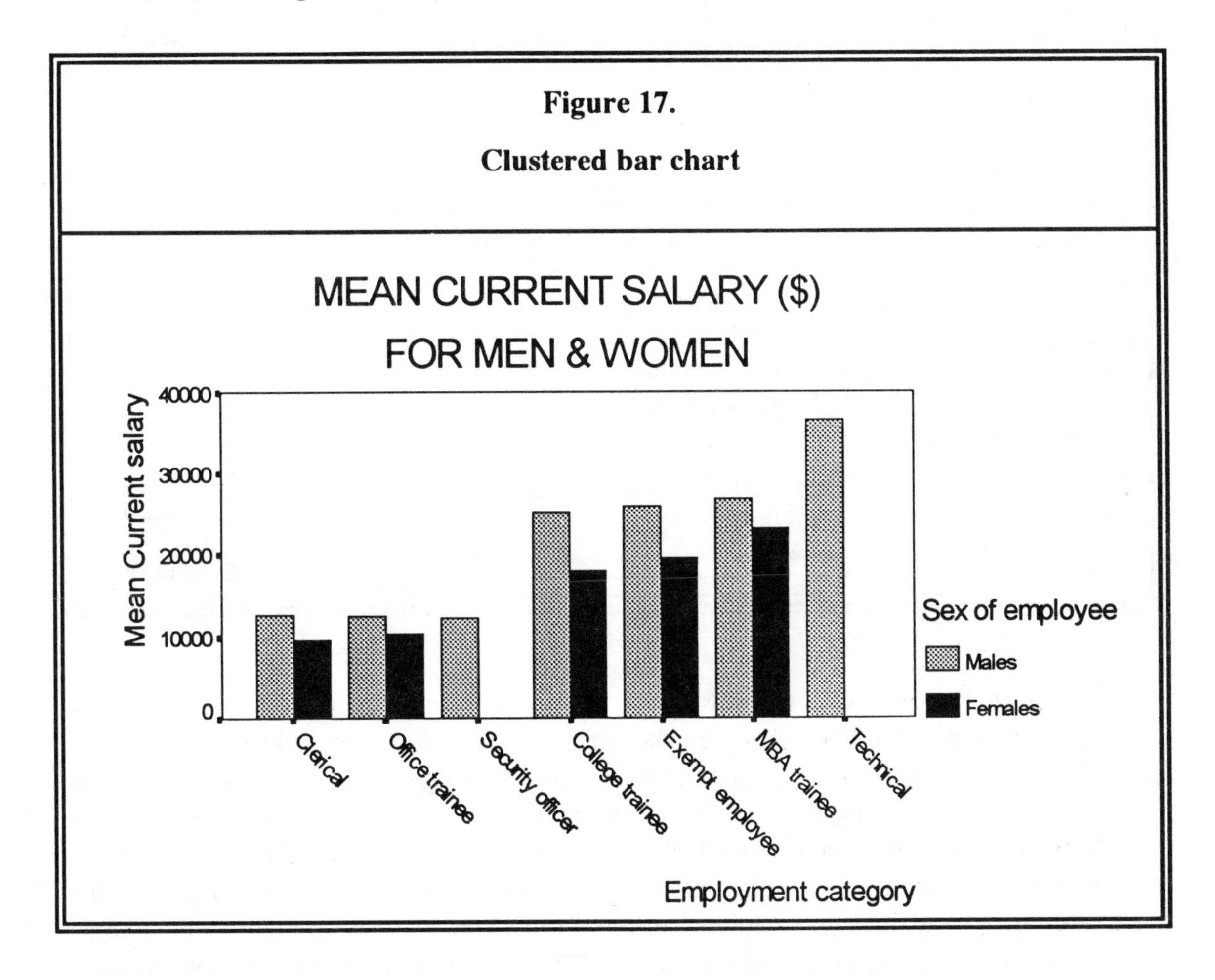

Access the **Data Editor** window and open the file *bank.sav*. Then a clustered bar chart can be specified by choosing

Graphs

Bar.

Select the **Clustered** option from the dialog box and click on the **Define** box to open the **Define Clustered Bar: Summaries for Groups of Cases** dialog box. Click on the **Other summary function** button and transfer the variable name *salnow* into the **Variable** box (the default statistic **MEAN** is supplied but other statistics can be obtained by clicking on the **Change Summary** box). Transfer the variable name *jobcat* for the categories along the x-axis into the **Category Axis** box, and transfer the variable name *sex* for the clusters into the **Define Clusters by** box. The completed dialog box is shown in Figure 18.

Figure 18.

The completed dialog box for the clustered bar chart in Figure 17

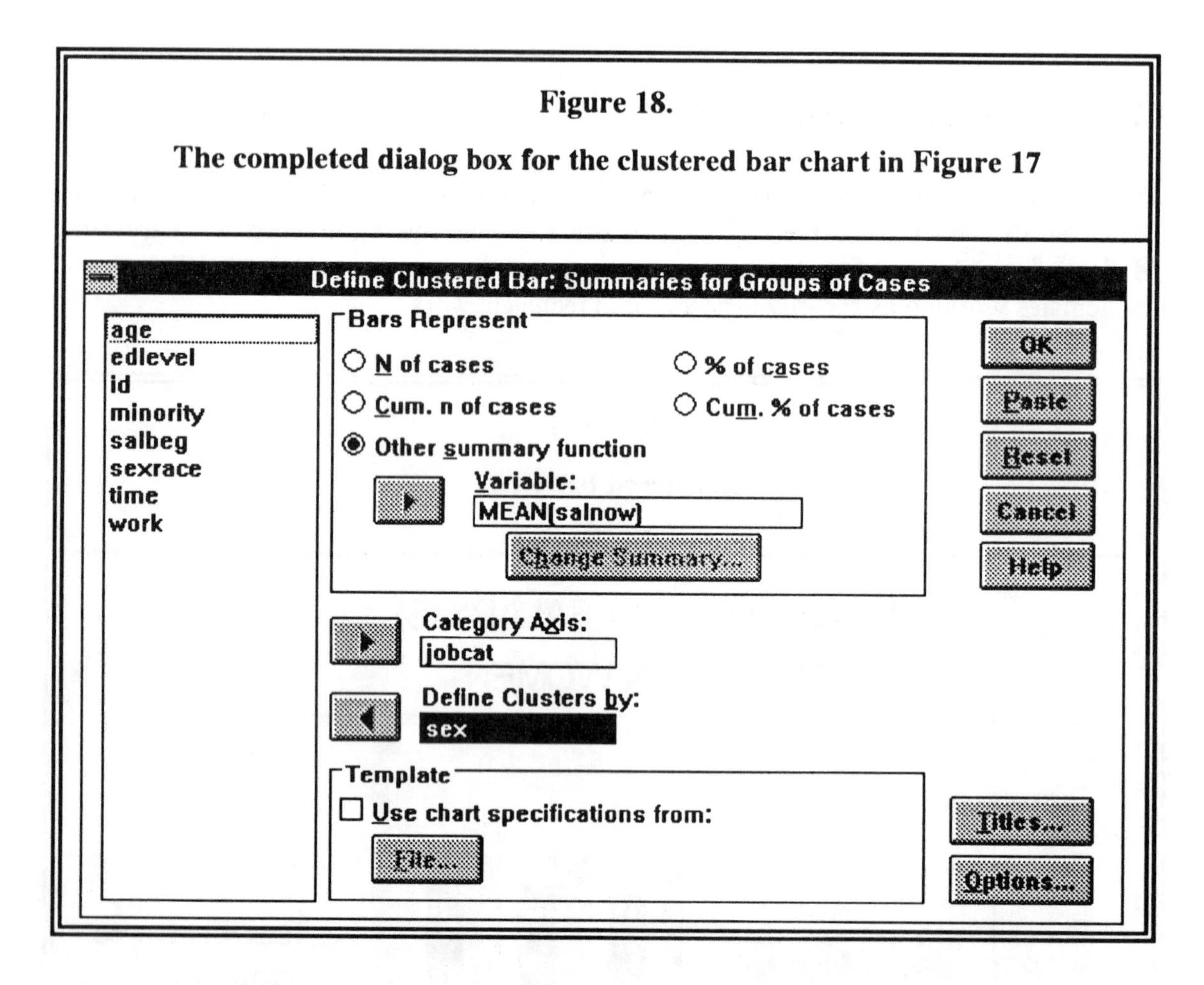

A bar chart can be edited to improve reproduction clarity by replacing the default colour shadings of the boxes by grey and black. This is done by clicking on the **Edit** box in SPSS 6 (or double-clicking anywhere on the image in SPSS 7) to reveal the editing icon bar, selecting the *male* boxes for editing by clicking on one of them (all the *male* boxes should then have a small black square marker at each of their corners), and then clicking on the icon of a crayon to open the **Colors** dialog box. By changing the **Fill** colour to grey, and then clicking on the **Apply** box, the ticked boxes will change to grey. After completing this alteration, click anywhere in the Chart window to turn off the box highlighting. The same procedure can be applied to the *female* boxes except that black was selected for the fill.

The abscissa and ordinate legends in Figure 17 were moved to the **right** and to the **top** respectively, the job category legends changed to **diagonal**, and a title added using other editing facilities.

Remember that it is always necessary to select the aspect of the figure to be edited by clicking on it *before* any of the editing options will work. Failure to do so will result in the **Apply** box of an editing dialog box remaining inoperative, or it may apply unintentionally to a previously selected aspect of the figure.

Several modifications are available for changing the pattern of bars in the chart as shown in the **Bar Spacing** dialog box in Figure 19, which is obtained by choosing

Chart

  Bar Spacing

The percentages can then be altered as desired.

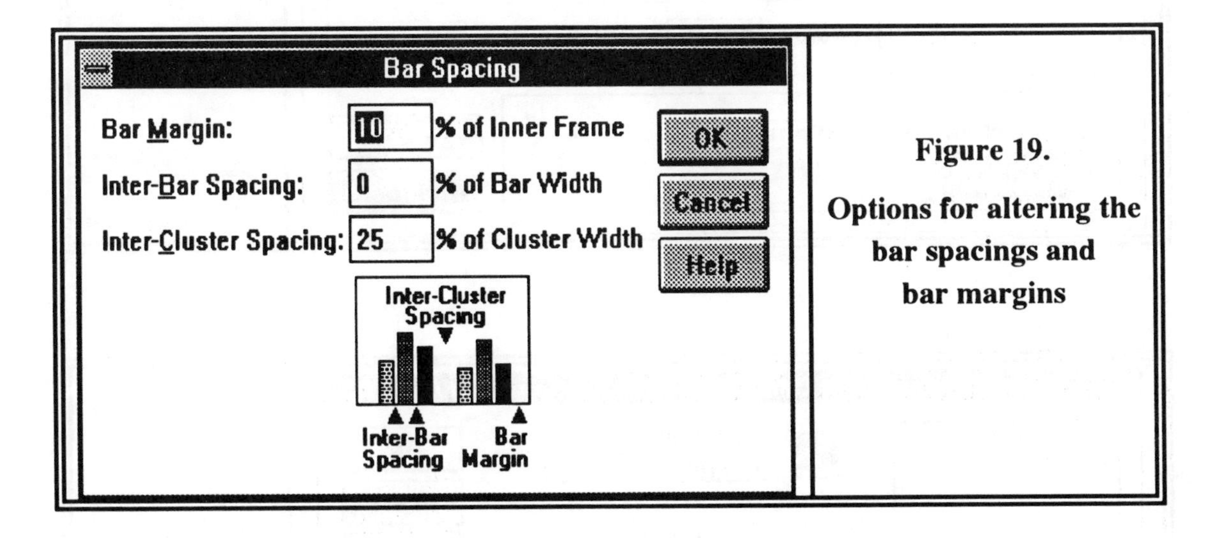

Figure 19.

Options for altering the bar spacings and bar margins

4.3.3.5 Bar chart with error bars

The height data represented as boxplots in Figure 16 can be plotted in a chart showing the means together with error bars representing multiples of standard deviations or standard errors (SPSS calls this a bar chart with error bars).

After checking that the appropriate data are in the Data Editor window, a bar chart with error bars can be specified by choosing

Graphs

  Error Bar

and then completing the **Define Simple Error Bar: Summaries for Groups of Cases** dialog box (Figure 20) by transferring the variable name *height* to the **Variable** box and *gender* to the **Category Axis** box. Within the **Bars Represent** box, click on the arrow to the right of **Confidence interval for mean** to reveal **Standard Deviation** and then specify how many **SDs** are desired: the default value is 2, but this can be changed to 1 as shown in the completed dialog box (Figure 21). The title MEAN HEIGHTS & SDs was added by clicking on the **Titles** box and typing in the title.

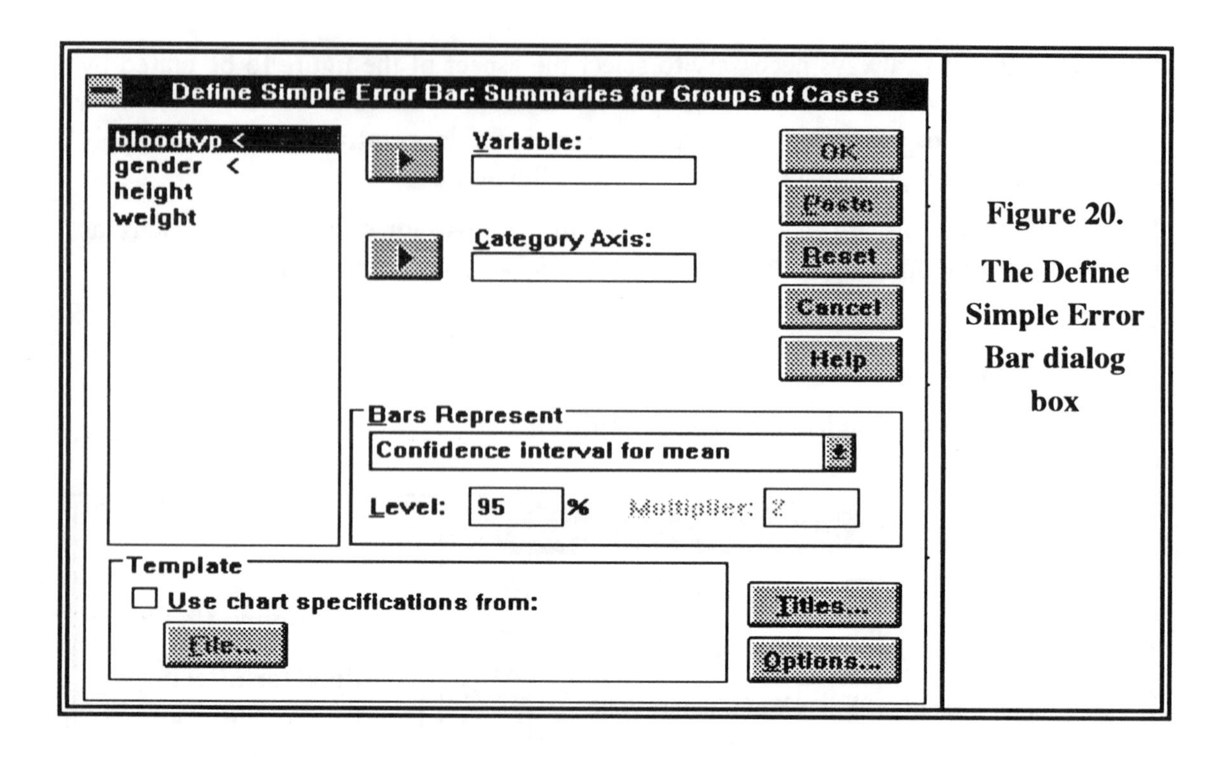

Figure 20. The Define Simple Error Bar dialog box

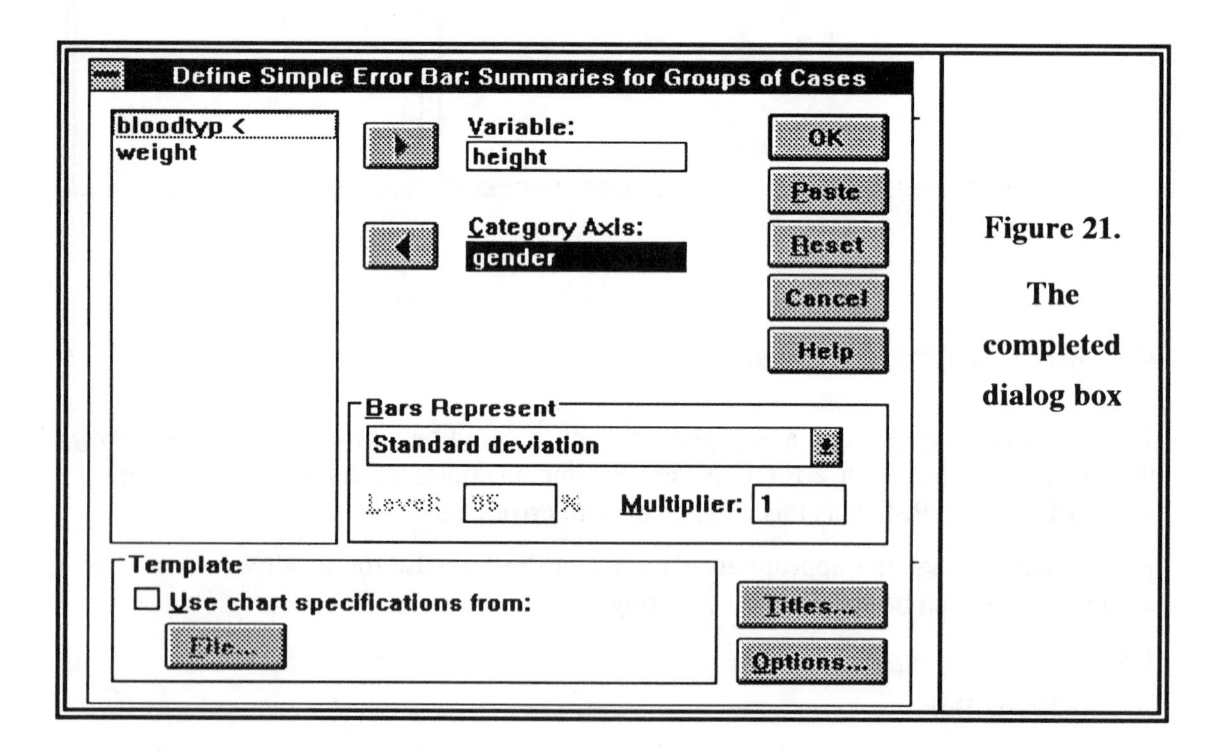

Figure 21. The completed dialog box

The result is shown in Figure 22. The means (edited as described below with an extra large solid circle to highlight them) are shown with ± 1 SD error bars.

The representation of the means was changed to a much larger black solid circle in the following manner. To do this, click on the **Edit** box to reveal the editing icon bar, and then move the cursor arrowhead on to the small circles representing the means and click once.

Next, choose

Attributes

Marker

to open the **Markers** palette. (Alternatively, select the marker icon in the toolbar). Within the **Style** box, select the solid circle symbol instead of the open square by clicking on it, and within the **Size** box, select the radio-button labelled **Large** instead of **Tiny**. To effect these changes, click the **Apply** box and finally close the palette by clicking on the **Close** box.

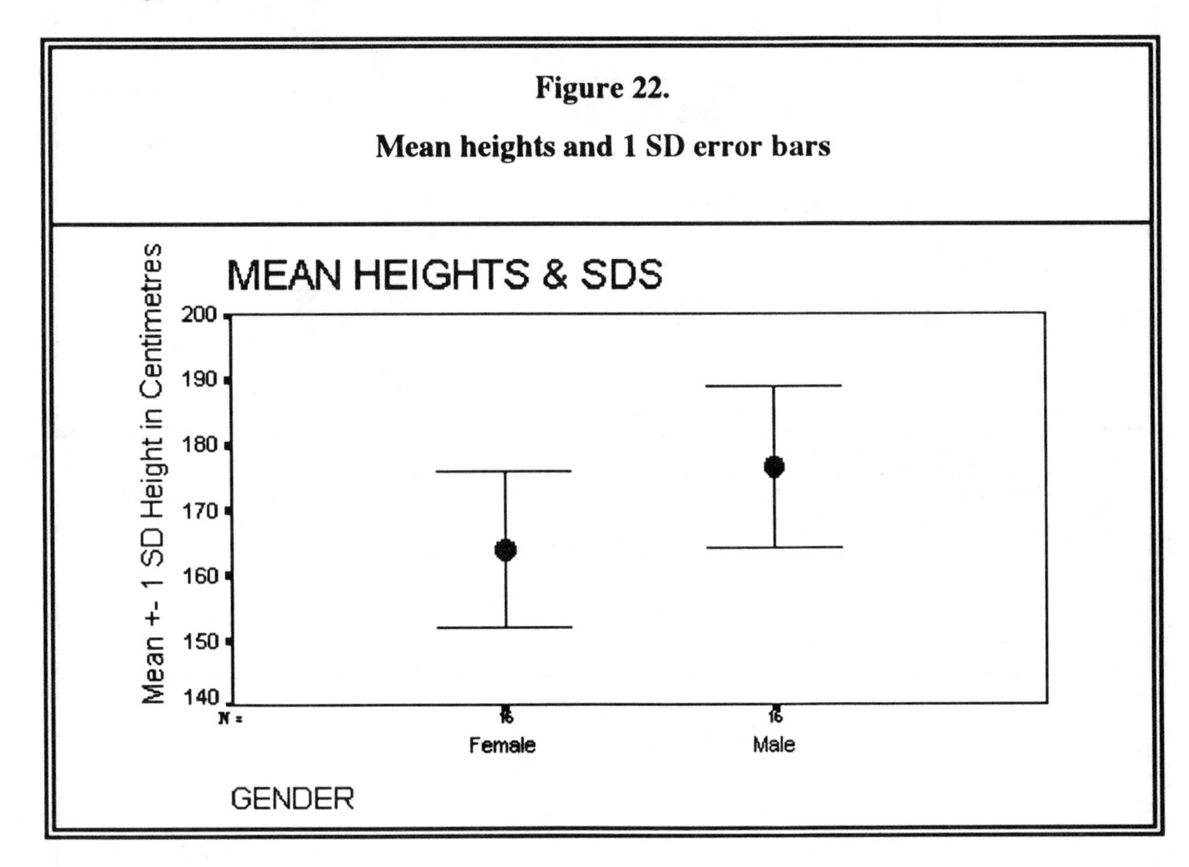

Figure 22.

Mean heights and 1 SD error bars

4.3.3.6 Pie Chart

The pie-chart provides a picturesque display of the frequency distribution of a qualitative variable.

To draw a pie chart of the categories within *bloodtyp*, choose

Graphs

Pie

to open the first of the **Pie Charts** dialog boxes (not reproduced here).

Click on **Define** to open the **Define Pie: Summaries for Groups of Cases** dialog box (the completed version is shown in Figure 23). Click on *bloodtyp* and on ▶ to paste the name into the **Define Slices by** box. Click on **% of cases** so that the slices represent percentages rather than the values of N. Finally, it is desirable to have a title:

click on **Titles** and type the desired title into the box (e.g. BLOOD GROUPS), click **Continue** and then **OK** to draw the pie-chart, which is reproduced in Figure 24.

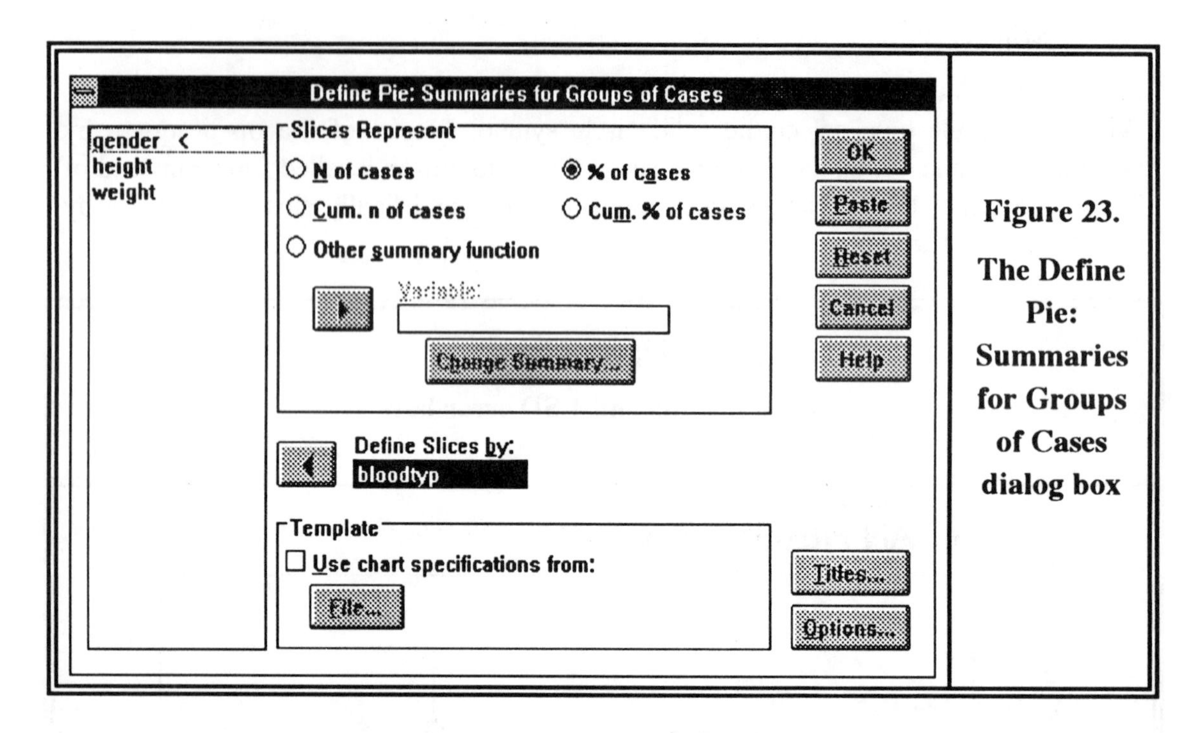

Figure 23.
The Define Pie: Summaries for Groups of Cases dialog box

Figure 24.
Pie Chart of blood groups

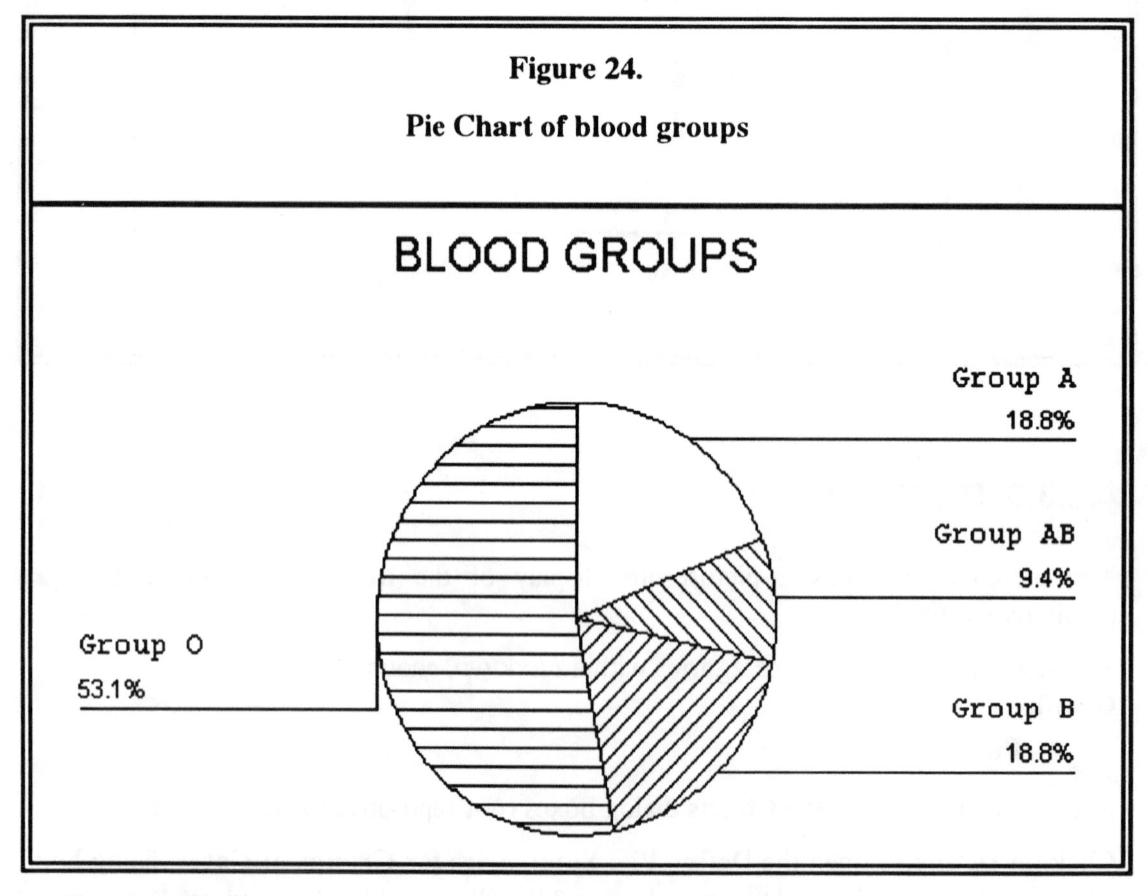

4.3.3.7 Scatterplot

The scatterplot depicts the bivariate distribution of two quantitative variables and should always be examined before calculating a correlation coefficient (Chapter 11) or conducting a regression analysis (Chapter 12).

To obtain the scatterplot of *height* against *weight*, choose

Graphs

Scatter

to open the **Scatterplot** dialog box (not reproduced here).

Click on **Define** to open the **Simple Scatterplot** dialog box (the completed version is shown in Figure 25).

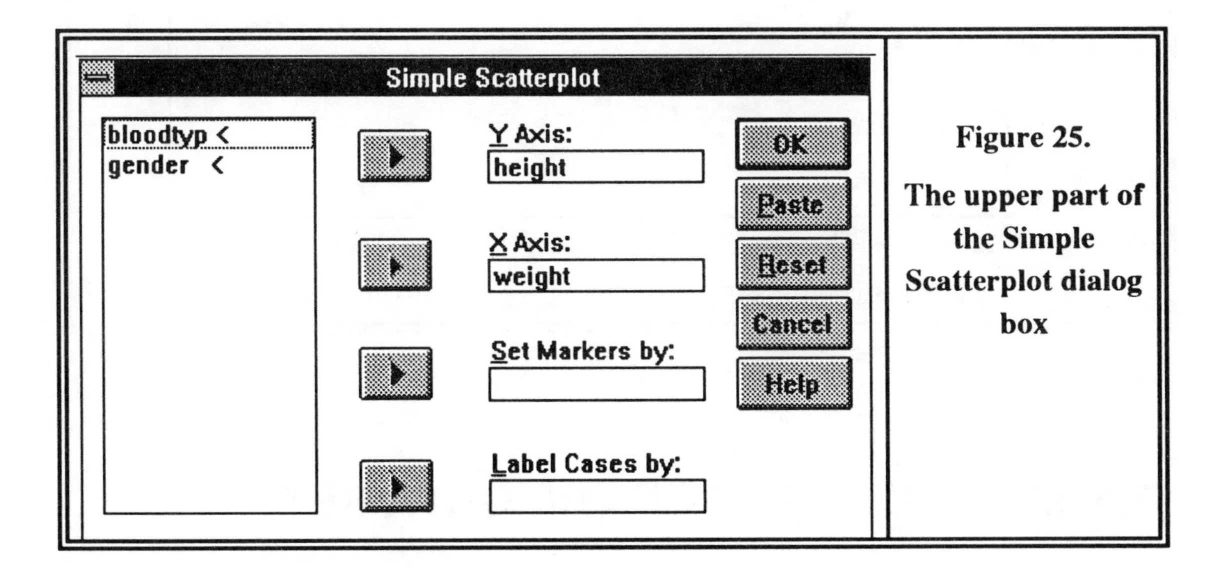

Figure 25.

The upper part of the Simple Scatterplot dialog box

Enter *height* into the **Y Axis** box and *weight* into the **X Axis** box by clicking on each variable name and then on the corresponding ▸ button. Click on **OK** to execute the plot, which is shown in Figure 26.

Further examples of scatterplots (e.g. plotting bivariate data subdivided by a grouping variable such as sex; adding regression lines to the plots) will be presented in Chapters 11 and 12.

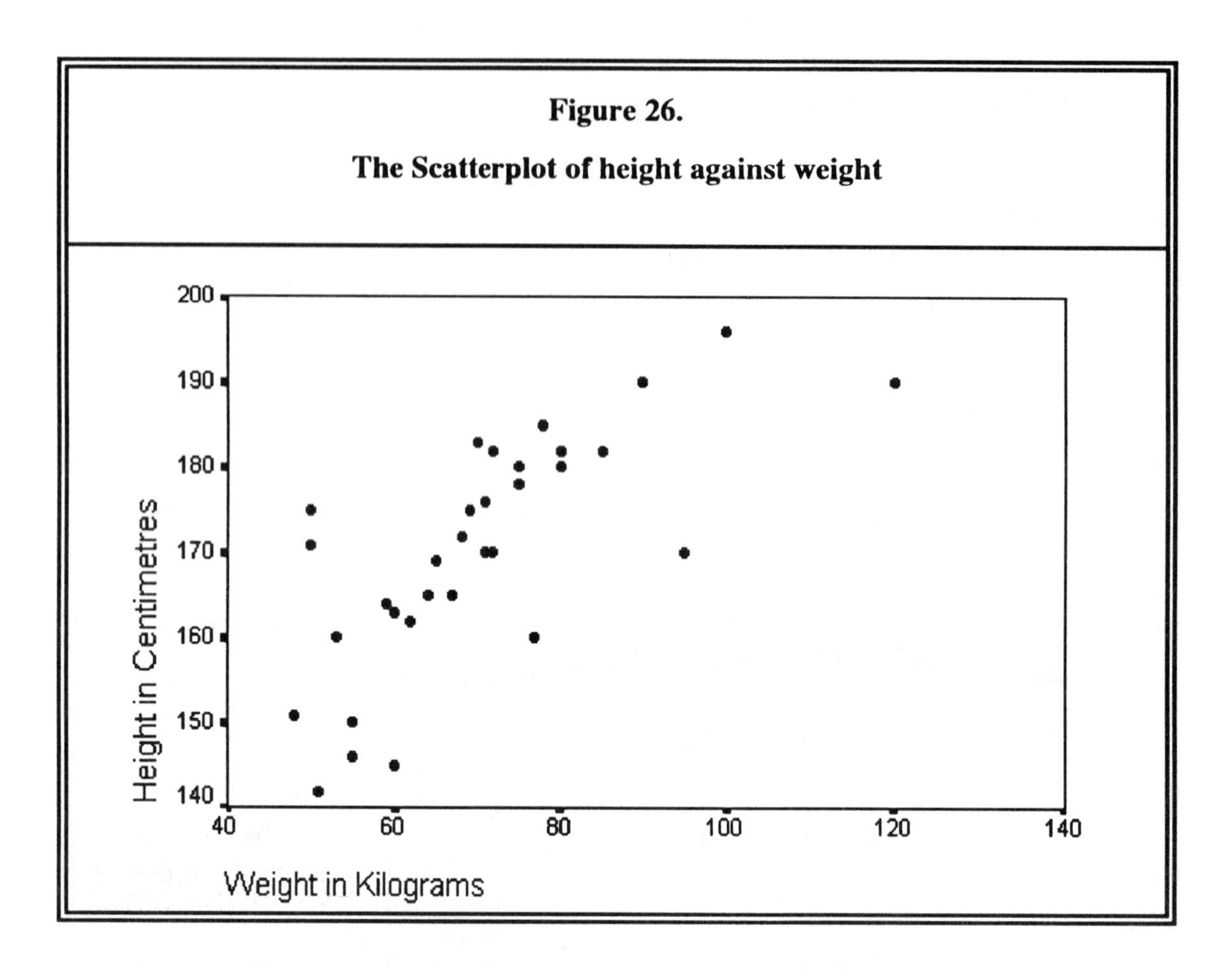

Figure 26.

The Scatterplot of height against weight

4.4 MANIPULATION OF THE DATA SET

4.4.1 Reducing and transforming data

After a data set has been entered into SPSS, it may be necessary to modify it in certain ways. For example, an exploratory data analysis may have revealed that atypical scores, or **outliers**, have exerted undue influence, or **leverage**, upon the values of statistics such as the mean and standard deviation (for a discussion of outliers, see Hartwig & Dearing, 1979). One approach to this problem is to remove the outliers and repeat the analysis with the remaining scores, on the grounds that it is better to have statistics that describe 95% of the data well than 100% of it badly. Cases can be dropped from the analysis by using **Select Cases** (Chapter 3).

Sometimes it is necessary to **transform** the values of a variable in order to satisfy the distribution requirements for the use of a particular statistic. Transformations such as the square root or the logarithm, are easily made with **Compute**.

Finally, it is sometimes convenient to combine or alter the categories that make up a variable. This is achieved with the **Recode** procedure, which can construct a new variable with the new category assignments.

4.4.2 The COMPUTE procedure

The **Compute** procedure is used to transform the values (say their square roots, or logarithms) of a variable. The transformed values can either replace the existing values in a variable (not recommended) or form a new variable (recommended). For example, suppose the user wants the square roots of values in a variable *score*, then the recommended procedure is to create a new variable *sqrtval*, whose values are the square roots of those in *score*.

Click on
Transform
  Compute

to open the **Compute Variable** dialog box (Figure 27).

Figure 27.

The upper part of the Compute Variable dialog box

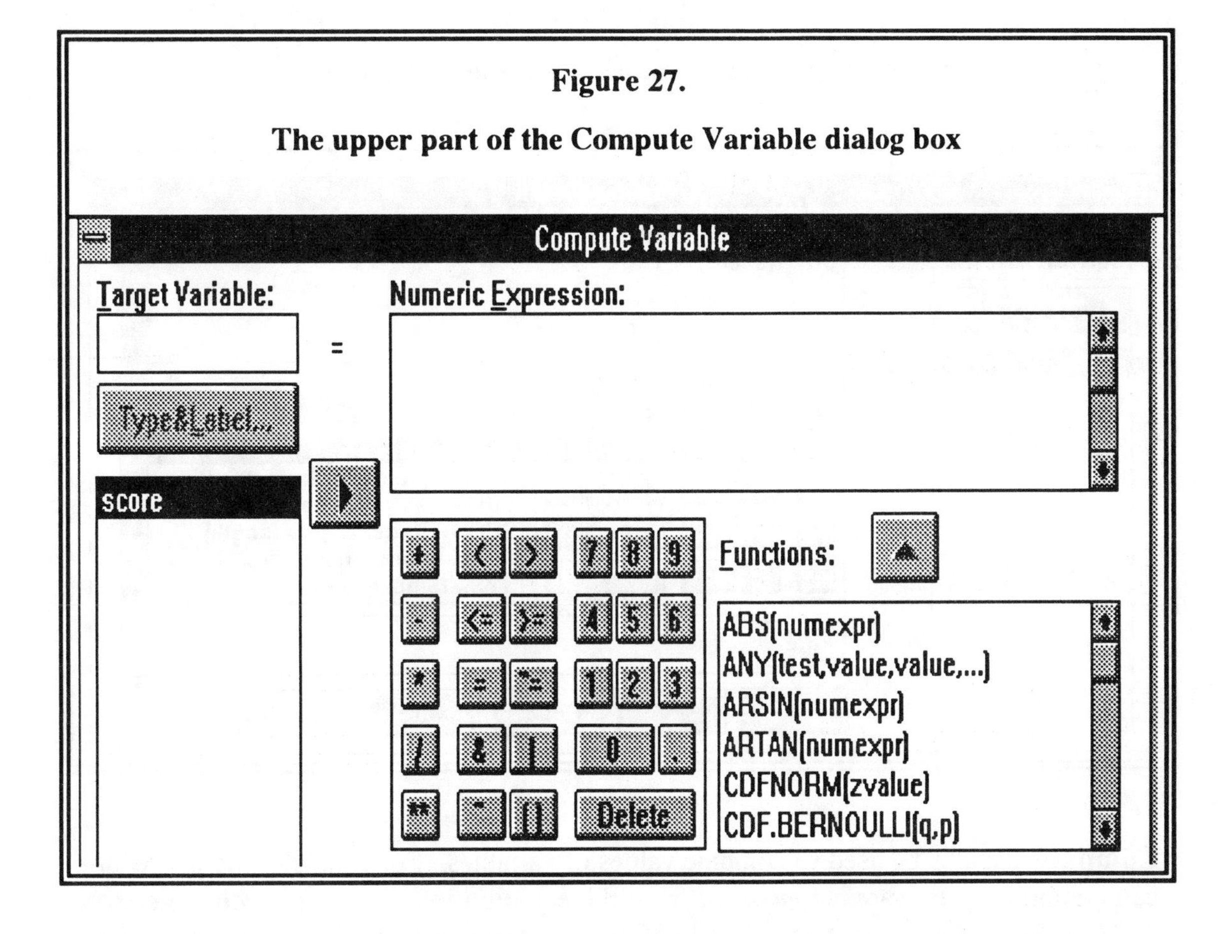

Assuming there is a variable *score* already in the **Data Editor** window, the box will appear as shown, with the existing variable names printed in the lower left-hand box, a blank space for the name of the target variable in the upper left-hand box, and a menu of operators and functions in the middle. Type in the name of the target variable *sqrtval*, and click on the arrow on the right of the **Functions** box to scroll down through the functions to **SQRT[numexpr]**. Click on this and then ▲ to paste it into the **Numeric Expression** box where it will appear as **SQRT[?]**. Click on *score* and ▶

to make this variable the argument of the square root function (i.e. replacing ?). The expression **SQRT[score]** will now appear in the **Numeric Expression** box. The final pattern of the dialog box is shown in Figure 28.

The most commonly used transformation functions are:

LG10	logarithm to the base 10
SQRT	square root
LN	natural logarithm
ABS	absolute value

Click on **OK** to run the procedure. A new column *sqrtval*, containing the square roots of the values of *score*, will appear in the **Data Editor** window. (It may be necessary to change **Variable Type** to show decimals - see Chapter 3.)

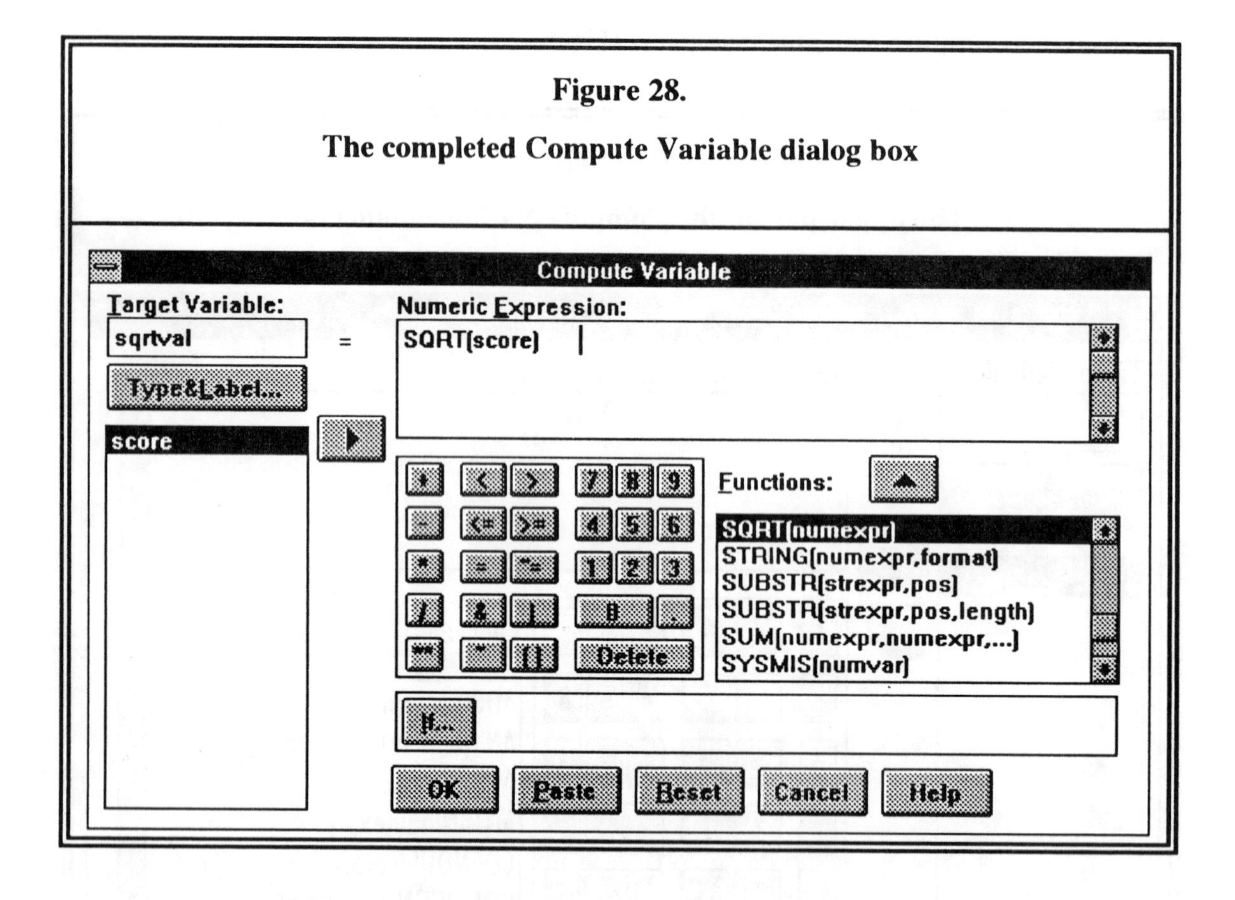

Figure 28.

The completed Compute Variable dialog box

Compute can also be used to combine values of variables. For example, the procedure can compute a new variable *meanval* from the equation *meanval = (french + german + spanish)/3*, which sums the three scores and divides by three; if any value is missing, a system-missing result is recorded. Alternatively, the function *mean* can be used (e.g. *meanval = mean (french, german, spanish)*). *Mean* computes the mean of the valid values; the result is recorded as missing only if all three scores are absent.

Finally, conditional computations can be commanded by clicking on the **If** button in the **Compute Variable** dialog box and then clicking on **Include if case satisfies the condition**. A conditional statement, such as the one in Figure 29, can then be compiled within the box.

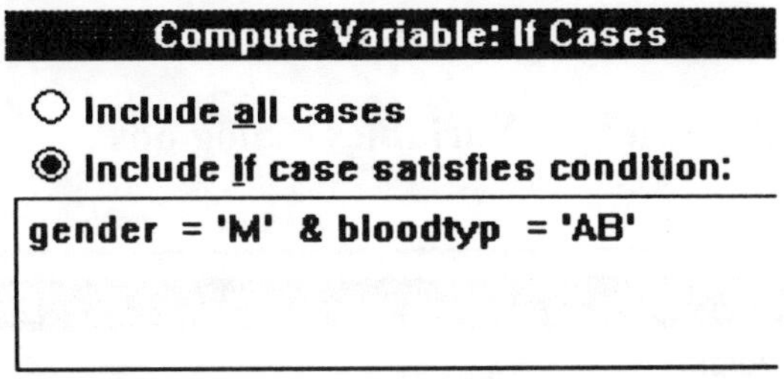

Compute Variable: If Cases ○ Include all cases ◉ Include If case satisfies condition: gender = 'M' & bloodtyp = 'AB'	**Figure 29.** **A conditional statement in the Compute Variable: If Cases dialog box.**

Click on **Continue** to return to the **Compute Variable** dialog box where, for example, the **Target Variable** might be nominated as *group* and the **Numeric Expression** as *1*. This would then have the effect of categorising all males with bloodgroup AB into value *1* of the variable *group*. Other values for *group* could be assigned by specifying other combinations of *gender* and *bloodtyp*.

4.4.3 The RECODE procedure

We have seen that the **Compute** procedure operates upon one or more of the variables in the data set, so that there will be as many values in the transformed variable as there were in the original variable. Sometimes, however, the user, rather than wanting a transformation that will convert all the values of one or more variables systematically, may want to alter only some of the values. Having defined a variable such as social class (*socclass*) as comprising five categories, for example, the researcher may subsequently wish to combine two or more of the original categories into a single category. Suppose that categories *3*, *4* and *5* are now to be given the single value of *3*. This can be achieved by using the **Recode** procedure.

Choose
Transform
    Recode

and click on **Into Different Variables** to open the **Recode into Different Variables** dialog box (the completed version is shown in Figure 30).

Just as in the case of **Compute**, it is possible to change the values to the recoded values within the same variable; but we recommend storing the recoded values in a new variable, perhaps *newsclas*. The procedure for recoding categories *4* and *5* into the single category *3* (while keeping the existing values *1*, *2* and *3* as they are) is as follows:

Click on *socclass* and on ▶ to paste the name into the **Numeric Variable -> Output Variable** box. Type the name of the output variable (*newsclas*) into the **Name** box and click **Change** to insert the name into the **Numeric Variable -> Output Variable** box, which will now appear as shown in Figure 30.

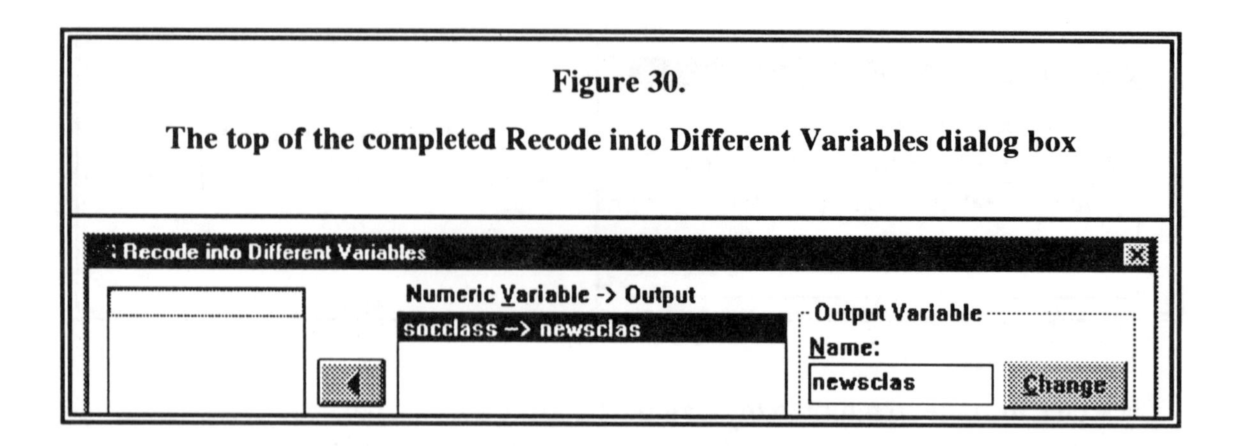

Figure 30.

The top of the completed Recode into Different Variables dialog box

Click on the **Old and New Values** box to open the next dialog box **Recode into Different Variables: Old and New Values** dialog box (the completed version is shown in Figure 31).

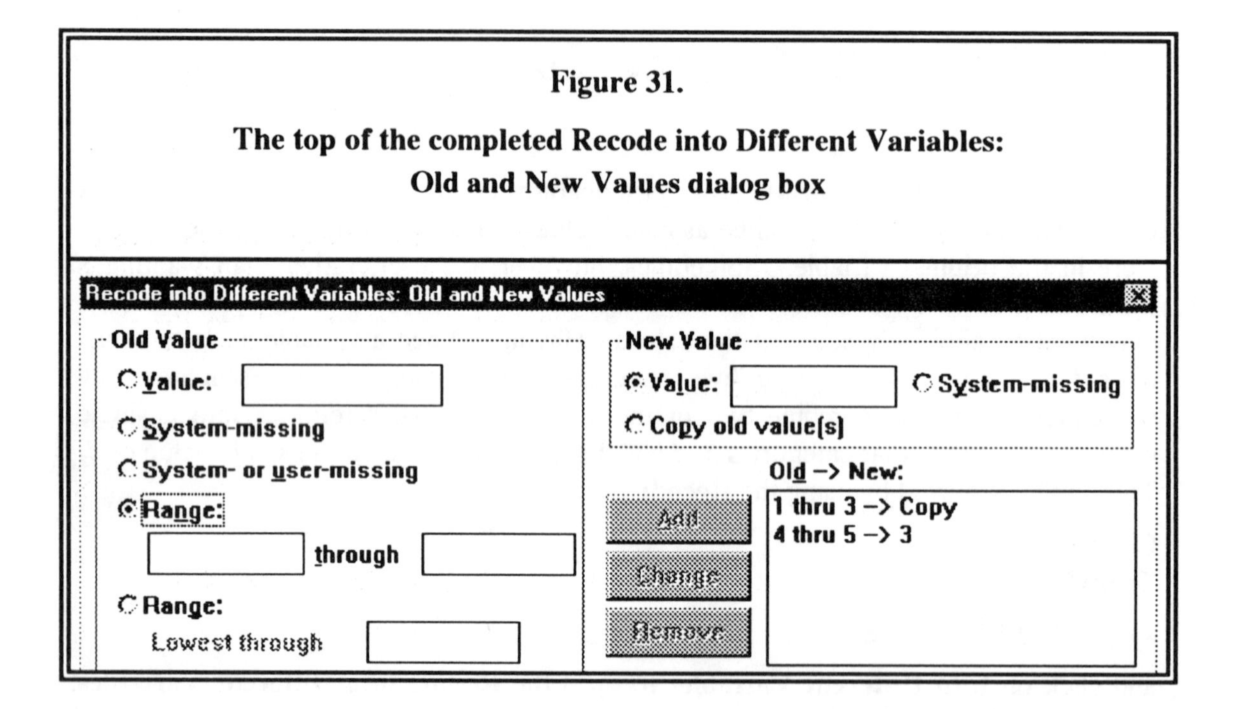

Figure 31.

The top of the completed Recode into Different Variables: Old and New Values dialog box

Click on **Continue** and then on **OK** to run the procedure. A new column, headed *newsclas* and containing the recoded values, will appear in the **Data Editor** window.

The **Recode** procedure can also be used to recode ordinal or interval data into coded categories. For example, a set of examination marks in the variable *score* (all falling within the range from 0 to 100) can be recoded into two categories *Pass* and *Fail* in a new variable *passfail* by entering the information shown in the dialog box in Figure 32.

The first range of scores *Lowest thru 39* is prepared by clicking on the fifth radio button and entering the value *39* in the box. Then click on the check box **Output variables are strings**. Type *Fail* into the **New Value** box and click on **Add**. The second range of scores *40 thru Highest* is prepared in a similar manner after clicking on the sixth radio button, entering the value *40* in the box, and then *Pass* in the **New Value** box.

Figure 32.

Recoding values into two categories Pass and Fail

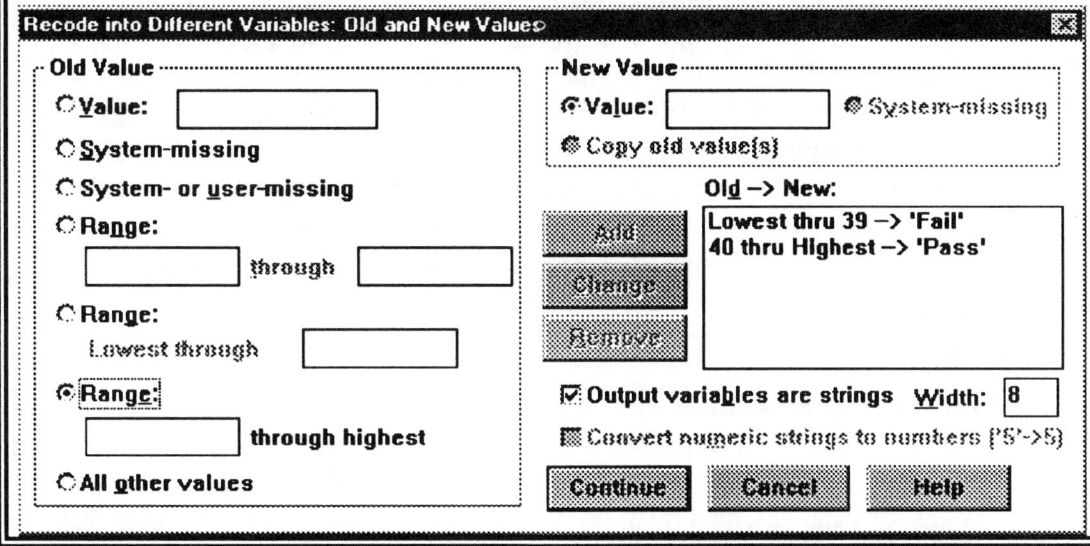

Recode into Different Variables: Old and New Values

Old Value

Value:

System-missing

System- or user-missing

Range:

through

Range:

Lowest through

Range:

through highest

All other values

New Value

Value:

System-missing

Copy old value(s)

Old –> New:

Lowest thru 39 –> 'Fail'

40 thru Highest –> 'Pass'

Add

Change

Remove

Output variables are strings Width: 8

Convert numeric strings to numbers ('5'->5)

Continue Cancel Help

Notice that the word **thru** includes the specified value either before or after the word. Thus this procedure will categorise all exam marks less than 40 as *Fail* and all those of 40 and above as *Pass*. A section of the **Data Editor** window showing the new variable *passfail*, together with its categories of Pass or Fail, is shown in Figure 33.

	score	passfail
1	34	Fail
2	45	Pass
3	76	Pass
4	87	Pass
5	34	Fail

Figure 33.

Part of the new variable *passfail* created by Recode

If a variable has non-integer values (e.g. height in metres), great care has to be taken in recoding the values into ranges such as tall, medium and short. For example, if short is to be defined as less than 1.6 metres, medium as 1.6 to 1.8 metres, and tall as more than 1.8 metres, then the ranges should be set within the **Recode** dialog box as follows:

Lowest thru 1.5999 –> 'Short'
1.6 thru 1.8 –> 'Medium'
1.8001 thru Highest –> 'Tall'

SUMMARY

1) Before carrying out formal statistical tests, a set of data should always be explored to check for possible transcription errors, to ascertain whether there are outliers, and to examine distribution shape. The drop-down menus **Transform**, **Statistics** and **Graphs** contain several procedures for listing and exploring data. Once a menu item has been selected, a dialog box appears on the screen containing the list of variables that are contained in the **Data Editor** window. The user can then select the appropriate variables and various options (often by opening additional, optional, sub-dialog boxes before returning to the original dialog box).

2) The procedures **Frequencies** and **Crosstabs** are suitable for exploring *categorial data*. **Frequencies** lists frequency distributions, and draws plots such as bar charts and histograms. **Crosstabs** generates contingency tables for data classified by at least two categorial variables. The plots can also be requested from the **Graphs** drop-down menu.

3) The procedures **Frequencies, Descriptives, Means** and **Explore** are suitable for exploring *interval data*, the last two being especially useful if it is desired to subdivide a quantitative variable by levels of a qualitative variable. **Explore** contains a range of descriptive statistics, graphs and plots. The graphs and plots can also be requested from the **Graphs** drop-down menu.

4) When graphs and charts are selected from the **Graphs** drop-down menu, additional options and editing facilities become available. Clustered bar charts and bar charts with error bars can be requested. There are also Pie-charts for depicting the distributions of qualitative variables and scatterplots for showing bivariate distributions.

5) The **Compute** procedure can be used to modify variables by transforming them or combining them. The **Recode** procedure changes the categories of a variable.

CHAPTER 5

CHOOSING A STATISTICAL TEST

5.1 INTRODUCTION

5.1.1 The need for formal statistical tests

Chapter 4 was concerned with the first stage of data analysis, the description and exploration of the data set. In the present chapter, we turn to the second stage, namely, the making of formal statistical tests. Neither stage can be omitted: to rush into formal testing without first examining the data is foolhardy; but to rest one's case purely on the characteristics of one's own data is to ignore the possibility that a fresh sample of data, even one gathered in exactly the same way, might not show those characteristics. We shall need to confirm that the patterns we have observed in our data were not merely chance occurrences and are 'robust', in the sense that they would be replicated were the research project to be repeated.

While this is not a statistics textbook, it was felt that in view of the great variety of statistical tests offered to the user by SPSS, there should be at least some guidance here on how to make a reasonable choice from among such a daunting array of possibilities.

5.1.2 Considerations in choosing a formal statistical test

It may be helpful to suggest that choosing a statistical test depends upon three general considerations:

(1) the **research question**;

(2) the **nature of the data**;

(3) the plan, or **design**, of the research.

5.2 THE RESEARCH QUESTION

Consider the following two situations:

a) Suppose that, in order to determine whether it is easier to shoot at a square target than at a circular one, you ask a group of subjects to shoot, say fifty times, at square and circular targets. Each person will have a score in the range from 0 to 50, inclusive. You want to know whether the accuracy rate is typically higher in one group than in the other. Translating your question into statistical terms, you want to know whether the *average* hit rate is higher for one target than for the other: your research question is one of **comparing averages**. In terms of formal statistical testing, you want a statistical test that will tell you whether the difference, *in your own data set*, between people's hit rates when shooting at square and circular targets is sufficiently great for you to be able to claim that if someone else were to repeat your experiment, they would find a similar difference.

b) Now suppose that you want to know whether there is a tendency for tall and short fathers to have tall and short (first) sons, respectively. In statistical terms, you are asking whether there is an **association** between the measured variables of Father's Height and First Son's Height.

The answers to questions of comparison (situation a) and association (situation b) are provided by quite different statistical tests. There are, of course, many other questions you might ask about a set of data. For example, you might be interested in the spread of scores obtained under one condition in comparison with another. Or you might be interested the sequencing of a subject's choices. Such questions, however, often arise in the context of research that has basically been designed to compare averages, or establish the presence of an association.

5.2.1 The nature of the data

The choice of a specific test depends on other considerations apart from the research question that motivated the enquiry. Another crucial consideration when choosing a statistical test is the nature of the data set.

In Chapter 4 (Section 4.1.1), three kinds of data were described:

(1) **interval** data, which are measurements on an independent scale with units;

(2) **ordinal** data, consisting of ranks, of assignments to ordered categories, or of sequencing information;.

(3) **nominal** or **categorial** data, which are records of qualitative category membership.

Strictly, only the first category contains 'measurements', in the familiar sense of the term; although the first and second categories both refer to quantitative variables. While *all* data are numerical, in the sense that even the categories making up a qualitative variable may be assigned arbitrary code numbers, a nominal datum is merely a *label*, not an expression of the degree to which the attribute is possessed.

Different statistics are appropriate for descriptions of the three types of data; and the corresponding formal tests are also different.

Another important aspect of a data set is the number of measured variables. If a data set comprises measurements on only **one** variable (e.g. reaction time), the data are **univariate data**. If, on the other hand, subjects are measured on **two** variables (e.g. height and weight), the data are **bivariate**. If there are **three or more** variables, the data are **multivariate**.

5.2.2 The plan or design of the research

5.2.2.1 The number of samples

A crucial consideration in the choice of a statistical test is the number of samples in the data set. The exercise of observing and noting the sex of people passing through a theatre door would yield one sample of nominal data. If, on the other hand, we were to note which of three theatre doors people pass through over a period of time, the operation would also yield one sample of nominal data; but since there are now three categories in the variable we are studying, the choice of a statistical test would be different in the second case.

If the skilled performance (measured on a scale from 0 to 100) of a group of people who have ingested a drug A is compared with that of a control (placebo) group, we shall obtain two samples of scores; but if, on the same skilled task, we test a third group, who have ingested drug B, there will be three samples. Again, the choice of formal statistical tests will be different in the two cases.

5.2.2.2 Independent versus related samples

If we select, say, 100 subjects for an experiment and randomly assign half of them to an experimental condition and the rest to a control condition, we have a situation where the assignment of an individual to a particular group has no effect on the group to which another subject is assigned, or vice versa. This experiment will yield two **independent samples** of scores. With independent samples of data, there is no basis for pairing the scores in one sample with those in the other.

Now suppose that each of fifty people shoots fifty times at a triangular target and fifty times at a square target of the same area. This experiment will also yield two samples of scores. This time, however, every score in either sample can be paired with the score in the other sample that the same subject produced. This experiment will yield two **related samples** of scores.

The scores in two related samples are likely to be substantially correlated; whereas that is unlikely to be the case with scores in independent samples. Accordingly, different statistical tests are appropriate for use with independent and related samples of data.

5.2.2.3 Between subjects and within subjects factors

In Chapter 3, some basic terms in research design were introduced. A pivotal concept is that of a **factor**, a related set of conditions, treatments or categories known as **levels**. Another key notion, from the point of view of selecting a statistical test, is the distinction between **within subjects** (or **repeated measures**) **factors** and **between subjects** factors.

If an experimental design has only between subjects factors, the experiment will yield independent samples of scores. If, on the other hand, there are within subjects factors, that is, if there are repeated measures on some factors, the experiment will yield related samples of scores.

5.3 TWO OR MORE SAMPLES

Suppose we have a set of data comprising two or more samples from a one-factor experiment. In the simplest case, there are two samples; but in principle, there can be any number of samples, provided each sample was obtained under one of a single set of related conditions or categories, that is, from an experiment (or study) with a *single treatment factor*.

Table 1 outlines a scheme for classifying situations and research questions in the manner described in the Introduction to this chapter. In each cell of the table, a statistical test is specified.

To enter the table, one must consider:

(1) whether the samples of data are related or independent (i.e. whether the design is between subjects or within subjects);

(2) how many samples of data there are;

(3) the type of data (interval, ordinal or nominal) that will be used in the test.

Table 1.
Choosing a test for comparing averages of two or more samples of scores from experiments with one treatment factor.

Type of data	Experimental Design: Between subjects (independent samples)	Experimental Design: Within subjects (related samples)
	TWO SAMPLES	**TWO SAMPLES**
Interval	Independent samples t-test	Paired samples t-test
Ordinal	Wilcoxon-Mann-Whitney test	Wilcoxon signed ranks test, Sign test
Nominal	Chi-square	McNemar
	THREE OR MORE SAMPLES	**THREE OR MORE SAMPLES**
Interval	One-way ANOVA	Repeated measures ANOVA
Ordinal	Kruskal-Wallis k-sample	Friedman
Nominal	Chi-square	Cochran's Q (dichotomous nominal data only)

5.3.1 Choosing tests for comparing averages between (or among) samples of interval data

To explore Table 1, we shall begin by assuming that we have a set of interval data, that is, independent measures on a scale with units.

Suppose we have two samples of data. Table 1 suggests that an **independent samples t-test** may be the appropriate test for comparing the means of the two samples. The decision about whether the design is between subjects (producing independent samples) or within subjects (producing related samples) is absolutely crucial for a correct choice of test. Consideration of the theory behind the independent and related t-tests is beyond the scope of this book: the reader is referred to statistical texts such as Howell (1997) or Winer, Brown & Michels (1991). In the present book, the computerisation of a t-test is described in Chapter 6.

As another example, suppose we have three or more samples of scores, as when people's performance under two or more experimental conditions is compared with their performance under a control condition for comparison. To test the null hypothesis of a constant level of performance in the population at all levels, the **one-way analysis of variance (ANOVA)** can be used as described in Chapters 7 and 8. Note that 'one-way' means 'one-factor'.

5.3.2 Reducing interval data: Parametric and nonparametric tests

The safe use of the independent t-test presupposes that the samples have been drawn from populations with the same variance. It may be, however, that the variance estimates of the samples are highly disparate: in fact, it is not uncommon for one sample to have a variance many times that of the other. This can have consequences for formal testing; and the dangers are greater when the samples sizes are also very disparate. With small data sets, there is the additional consideration that the t statistic is very vulnerable to the leverage exerted by atypical scores or **outliers**, which tend to inflate the standard error.

5.3.2.1 Parametric and nonparametric (distribution-free) statistics

The t-test is an example of a **parametric test**, that is, it is assumed that the data are samples from a population with a specified (normal) distribution. Other tests, known as **nonparametric tests**, do not make specific assumptions about the population distributions. For that reason, they are often referred to as **distribution-free tests**. When strong contra-indications against the use of parametric tests are present, one possible solution (though one not without its drawbacks) is to use a nonparametric test instead of the t-test.

While some authors (e.g. Siegel & Castellan, 1988) strongly recommend the use of nonparametric tests, others (e.g. Howell, 1997) emphasise the robustness of the parametric t-tests to violations of their assumptions and the loss of power incurred by the use of equivalent nonparametric tests. We suggest that, provided the data show no obvious contra-indications such as the presence of outliers or marked disparity of variances (especially if this is coupled with greatly disparate sample sizes), a t-test can safely be used; otherwise a nonparametric equivalent should be considered. If, however, the data comprise measurements at the ordinal level in the first place, as in sets of ranks or ratings, a nonparametric or distribution-free test is the only option.

5.3.2.2 Comparing levels of samples of ordinal data

Nonparametric tests can be used with samples of interval data by converting the original data into another, derived data set which preserves only some of the information present in the original. For example, suppose two samples of children have taken part in a between subjects experiment: one sample have performed a task under an experimental condition; the other have performed the same task under a control condition. Such an experiment will result in two independent samples of scores. The **Wilcoxon-Mann-Whitney statistic W** is obtained by ranking all the scores in order, noting which group each score came from. The value of W is calculated by counting the numbers of scores in, say, the experimental group that have ranks higher than each of the scores in the control group. The Wilcoxon-Mann-Whitney test, therefore, uses only the sequential or ordinal information present in the original data set. Of course, all the procedures just described are carried out automatically by SPSS (see Chapter 6).

Nonparametric tests are also available for comparing the averages of the related samples of data resulting from a within subjects experiment. If, say, thirty subjects identify material presented to the left and right visual hemifields, the experiment will result in a set of paired data. In the **Wilcoxon signed ranks test**, a single column of difference scores is obtained, the differences are ranked in order of their absolute size, and the test is made with the statistic T+, which is the sum of the ranks of the positive differences.

Another test available for paired data is the **sign test**, which uses only the nominal information present in the original paired samples of interval data. As in the Wilcoxon signed ranks test, the values in each column of data are subtracted from the corresponding data in the other column; but *only the sign* of each difference is noted. The result is a sequence of pluses and minuses. The null hypothesis implies equal numbers of pluses and minuses, and the binomial test is used to ascertain whether the number of pluses (or, equivalently, the number of minuses) is such as to constitute evidence against the null hypothesis.

So far, we have been considering the use of nonparametric alternatives to t-tests. For data sets comprising more than two sets of interval data, however, there are also equivalent nonparametric tests. The **Kruskal-Wallis k-sample test** is equivalent to the one-way ANOVA (which is appropriate for independent samples of interval data). The **Friedman test** is a nonparametric equivalent of the one-factor within subjects ANOVA.

5.3.3 Using nonparametric tests with inherently ordinal data

Consider, however, an experiment in which subjects rank ten objects in order of preference. This would generate ten related samples of data, each sample comprising the ranks given by the subjects to one particular object. Here we have a set of inherently ordinal data, not independent measurements on a scale with units. In this case, the use of a nonparametric test is required by the nature of the data: a parametric ANOVA is not an option here.

5.3.4 Comparing levels of samples of dichotomous nominal data

With nominal data, the question of comparing *averages* does not really arise, because all we have are the frequencies of people in each category. Nevertheless, it is often of interest to know whether there is a robust tendency for people to produce a response more often in some conditions than in others.

5.3.4.1 Independent samples of dichotomous nominal data

Suppose that twenty-four subjects are divided into three groups: two experimental groups (Group A and Group B) and a Control group, eight subjects being randomly assigned to each group. Each subject is tested with a criterion problem, a 1 being recorded if they pass, and a 0 if they fail. Table 2 shows the results of the experiment.

Table 2.

A set of nominal data from a one-factor between subjects experiment

	Control		Group A		Group B
Subject	*Score*	*Subject*	*Score*	*Subject*	*Score*
1.	0	9.	0	17.	1
2.	0	10.	1	18.	1
3.	0	11.	0	19.	1
4.	0	12.	0	20.	1
5.	1	13.	0	21.	1
6.	0	14.	0	22.	1
7.	0	15.	0	23.	1
8.	0	16.	1	24.	1

With such a nominal data set, a **chi-square test** can be used to test the null hypothesis that, in the population, there is no tendency for the problem to be solved more often in some conditions than in others. This is described in Chapter 11.

5.3.4.2 Three or more sets of correlated dichotomous nominal data: Cochran's Q test

A nominal data set resembling the data in Table 2 would also result from a within subjects experiment, that is, if each person had been tested under all three conditions. In that case, however, the data set would comprise three *related samples* of nominal data.

Table 1 shows that an appropriate test of the null hypothesis of no difference in performance among the three conditions is the **Cochran's Q test**, which is described in Chapter 9.

5.3.4.3 Two correlated samples of dichotomous nominal data: McNemar test

Suppose that ten people are asked whether they are for or against a proposal before and after hearing a debate on the issue. On both occasions of testing, each person's response is coded either as 0 (against) or 1 (for). Table 3 shows the results.

Table 3.

A set of correlated nominal data from a one-factor within subjects experiment

Subject	Before	After	*Subject*	Before	After
1.	0	1	6.	0	1
2.	0	1	7.	0	1
3.	0	0	8.	0	1
4.	1	0	9.	0	1
5.	0	1	10.	0	1

Here an appropriate test of the null hypothesis that hearing the debate has no effect upon people's opinions on the issue is tested with **McNemar's change test** described in Chapter 6.

5.4 ONE-SAMPLE TESTS

Much psychological research involves the drawing of two or more samples of data. This is by no means always true, however: sometimes the researcher draws a *single* sample of observations in order to study just one population.

5.4.1 One-sample tests with nominal data

A question about a single population is often one of **goodness-of-fit**: has the sample been drawn from a population with certain specified characteristics? For example, suppose a researcher wants to know whether 5-year-old children of a certain age, when leaving a room, show a preference for one of two doors, A and B. One hundred 5-year-olds are observed leaving the room and their choices are noted. Here the population comprises the choices (A or B) of 5-year-olds in general. Of the hundred children in our study, 60 leave by door A and 40 by door B. The null hypothesis states that the probability of choosing A (or B) is 0.5 : more formally, it states that we have sampled 100 times from a Bernoulli population with $p = 0.5$. Does this theoretical distribution fit our data?

Table 4 is a scheme for choosing appropriate one-sample tests in various situations. Selection of a test from the table is on the basis of (1) the type of data, and (2) whether there are more than two categories or values.

Table 4.

Scheme for choosing a one-sample test

Type of data	Number of categories or values		
	Two	More than two	
Nominal	Binomial test	Chi-square test	
Ordinal		Randomness Runs test	Distribution Kolmogorov-Smirnov test
Interval		Mean t-test	Distribution Kolmogorov-Smirnov test

According to Table 4, with a sample of nominal data such as the children's choices in the present example, the **binomial test** is appropriate. Should the children have had more than two doors to choose from, a **chi-square** test could have been used to test the null hypothesis of no preferences among the three or more alternatives.

5.4.2 Using sequential information: Tests of randomness

Many of the most well-known statistical tests assume that the scores in the data set are a random sample from the population. There are circumstances, however, in which this fundamental assumption can be questioned. Suppose we learn that a child, when given a choice between two apparently identical objects on each of ten trials, chose the left on five trials and the right on the remainder. On the basis of this information alone, it would seem reasonable to suppose that the child has been choosing at random. But if we know that the sequence of choices was L, L, L, L. L, R, R, R, R, R, the supposition of randomness seems less tenable. To test the assumption of randomness in such sequences of events, the **runs test** can be used. Notice that the use of the runs test requires that we have the necessary **ordinal** information (see Table 4).

5.4.3 Testing for goodness-of-fit with ordinal and interval data: Kolmogorov-Smirnov test

The histogram of a sample of scores may suggest that it has been drawn from a normal population (or one which is nearly so). The **Kolmogorov-Smirnov** test can be used to test the assumption of normality of distribution. This test compares the centiles of the observed distribution of the data with the corresponding centiles of the normal distribution. The test statistic is the largest discrepancy between the observed and theoretical centiles. The Kolmogorov-Smirnov test is not confined to testing for normality: as long as the theoretical centiles can be specified, the test is also applicable to Poisson distributions, rectangular distributions, chi-square distributions, and so on.

5.4.4 Has the sample been drawn from a population with a specified mean value?

With interval data, as when we ask whether the performance, on a standardised test, of a group of schoolchildren is typical of those in their age group, a **one-sample t-test** can be used to test the null hypothesis that the population mean has the putative 'population' value (i.e. the mean performance of the test's standardisation sample). See Table 4.

Note that the t-test that is used with two samples of correlated interval data is really a one-sample t-test. Essentially, a single column of differences is created by consistently subtracting the scores in one column from the corresponding scores in the other. If the null hypothesis is true, there is no difference, in the population, between people's average performance under the two conditions. In terms of the columns of differences (rather than the original scores), the mean difference, in the population, is zero. Here, rather than thinking of having correlated samples from two populations (or a single sample from a bivariate population) we have reinterpreted the situation as one in which a single sample (of differences) has been drawn from a population (of differences). Now, we need only carry out a one-sample t-test to test the null hypothesis of a population mean (μ) of zero (see Howell, 1997, pp. 175 - 188).

5.5 THE ANALYSIS OF DATA FROM FACTORIAL EXPERIMENTS

There may be two, three or more factors in an experimental design. Experiments with more than one factor are known as **factorial** experiments. In Chapter 3 (Section 3.2), three different types of factorial experiments were described:

(1) between subjects;

(2) within subjects;

(3) mixed.

The basis of this classification is whether the experiment has factors with repeated measures, and if so, whether *all* factors have repeated measures (within subjects designs), *some* (but not all) factors have repeated measures (mixed designs), or *none* has repeated measures (between subjects designs). Beware of an alternative use of the term *mixed* (usually in the term *mixed model*) in some textbooks such as Howell (1997, p422) which refers to the mixed model as the combination of *fixed* and *random effects* factors, a fixed effects factor being one with fixed selected levels whereas a random effects factor is one with randomly selected levels. Random effects factors are rare in psychological experiments.

Corresponding to the three different types of factorial experiment described, between subject, within subjects and mixed, are three different analysis of variance models, the between subjects, within subjects and mixed models, respectively. A separate chapter will be devoted to the use of SPSS to analyse data from each of these three different types of experiments - see Chapters 8, 9 and 10.

5.6 MEASURING STATISTICAL ASSOCIATION BETWEEN TWO VARIABLES

Consider the following research question: do tall fathers tend to have tall sons? Select 200 fathers who have sons and measure the height of each father and that of his eldest (or only) son. Your question is whether there is a statistical association between the two variables Father's Height and Son's Height: are these two variables **correlated**?

Table 5 shows some of the correlation coefficients and other measures of strength of association that are available for the different kinds of psychological data. As before, the choice of a measure depends upon consideration of the type of data one has.

Table 5.

Measures of association between two variables

Type of data	Statistic
Interval	Pearson correlation (r)
Ordinal	Spearman's rho, Kendall's tau-a, tau-b, tau-c
Nominal	Phi; Cramér's V

5.6.1 Measuring association with interval data: Pearson correlation

If we have the heights of 200 fathers, paired with those of their 200 eldest sons, we have a set of interval data. According to Table 5, we should consider the use of a correlation coefficient to measure the strength of association between the variables of father's height and son's height.

It may be well, however, even at this point, to warn the reader of the dangers lurking in the incautious use of the correlation coefficient. Some of the difficulties are discussed in Chapter 11. For the moment it should suffice to say that, taken by itself, the value of a correlation coefficient, whether calculated by SPSS or by any other means, may give quite a wrong impression about the real nature of the association (if any) between two variables. It is always necessary to examine the scatterplot of the two variables in a correlation. Fortunately, it is very easy to command SPSS to produce a scatterplot (see Chapter 11).

5.6.2 Measuring association with ordinal data: Spearman rank correlation and Kendall's tau statistics

If two judges rank ten paintings on order of their quality, we shall have a set of ordinal data in the form of ranks. Most statistical packages now offer two alternative measures of association for such data:

(1) Spearman's rank correlation;

(2) one of Kendall's tau statistics.

The manner in which one enters bivariate data in the form of ranks into the SPSS Data Editor window and obtains a rank correlation or a Kendall statistic are considered in detail in Chapter 11.

5.6.3 Measuring association in nominal data: Contingency tables

Suppose that Fred has claimed telepathic powers. Accordingly, in an experiment designed to test this claim, an experimenter tosses a coin 100 times, and Fred, seated behind a screen, states, on each occasion, whether the coin turned up heads or tails. Table 6 presents the results of the experiment.

Table 6.
A contingency table.

	Experimenter's toss	
Subject's Guess	Head (H)	Tail (T)
H	45	9
T	8	38

The presence of an association can be confirmed by using a **chi-square test** (see Chapter 11). Since the value of the chi-square statistic depends partly upon the sample size, it is unsuitable as a measure of the strength of association between two qualitative variables. Table 5 specifies two statistics, **Cramér's V** and the **phi coefficient**, which measure such association.

5.6.4 The point-biserial correlation

Table 5 is by no means comprehensive; in fact, many other measures of association are in use. One of the most important of these is the **point-biserial correlation**.

Suppose that in an experiment on skilled performance, the scores of 20 subjects under a special experimental condition are compared with the scores of 20 controls. The results of such an experiment can be entered into the SPSS Data Editor window in the manner described in Chapter 3: all the scores are entered into a single column of the grid, and the group membership of each subject is carried by another column containing code numbers, such as 0 for the control group and 1 for the experimental group. Such a variable is known as a **grouping variable**.

The Data Editor thus contains two columns of numbers:

(1) the scores;

(2) values of the grouping variable.

The Pearson correlation between the two columns of numbers, where one variable has been measured and the other is merely a grouping variable, is known as the **point-biserial correlation**.

It will be found that if a point-biserial correlation proves to be significant, then so also will be the pooled t-test of the difference between the means of the two groups, and *vice versa*. This is because the point-biserial correlation and the t-statistic are both completely determined by the difference between the group means and the spread of the scores within the groups. It will be found that the values used to label the groups are entirely arbitrary: *any* numbers will do, as long as they are different. This fact, though interesting, may not seem to be particularly useful. Nevertheless, the point-biserial correlation is a useful conceptual bridge between the making of comparisons and the measurement of association.

5.7 REGRESSION

5.7.1 Simple regression

If there exists an association between two variables, this can be exploited to estimate the values of one variable from knowledge of those of the other. For example, if there is an association between the heights of fathers and their sons (which there certainly is), can we make use of this association to estimate the height of a son whose father is, say, five feet ten inches in height? This is a problem in **simple regression**, which is described in Chapter 12.

5.7.2 Estimating one variable from knowledge of two or more other variables: Multiple regression

It may be that a young man's height is associated not only with that of his father but also the father's financial circumstances. In **multiple regression** (Chapter 12), knowledge of a person's scores on two or more variables (the **regressors**) is used to estimate that person's score on a target variable (the dependent variable, or **criterion**). We can expect that if height and father's income are indeed correlated, multiple regression will produce a more accurate prediction of a young man's height than will a simple regression upon either of the two regressors considered on its own.

5.8 MULTIVARIATE STATISTICS

In all the experimental examples so far considered, there was just one dependent variable. In factorial ANOVA, for example, there may be several *independent* variables (i.e. factors); but there is only one *dependent* variable. The ANOVA, therefore, is a **univariate** statistical method. There is, however, available a set of methods designed for situations in which there are two or more dependent variables. These methods are known as **multivariate statistics**.

5.8.1 Multivariate analysis of variance (MANOVA)

Suppose that in a one-way experiment on memory, the performance of two groups of subjects, each group trained in a different mnemonic technique, is compared with that of a control sample. Suppose also that performance is measured in two ways:

(1) number of items recalled;

(2) number of errors in recall.

In **multivariate analysis of variance (MANOVA),** these dependent variables are combined into a single variable in such a way that the mean scores of the different groups on this new variable are spread out, or dispersed, to the greatest possible extent. The differences among the group means on the single new dependent variable are then tested by methods similar in rationale to univariate analysis of variance. Although we shall not consider MANOVA in any detail in this book, references will be made to the technique from time to time, in the hope that the foregoing simplified characterisations of ANOVA and MANOVA may serve as useful co-ordinates in the exploration of what may be unfamiliar territory.

5.8.2 Discriminant analysis

In an experimental study where cases have been classified into two or more groups with two or more dependent variables, the dependent variables can be combined to produce a new dependent variable for maximising the correct classification of the cases into the groups. This new combination variable can then become a **regressor** for predicting group membership of other non-classified cases. Thus **discriminant analysis (DA)** is the obverse of MANOVA: the same composite variable is computed with a view to predicting group membership. In fact, in many ways, discriminant analysis is mathematically equivalent to MANOVA. Discriminant analysis is the subject of Chapter 14.

5.8.3 Factor analysis

In all the situations so far described, the variables, whether measured during the course of the study, or manipulated by the experimenter, have been *overt*, in the sense of being directly observable. Suppose, however, that people are tested on a number of psychological tests, and the correlations among them are calculated. Among the correlations, certain patterns may emerge suggesting that subgroups of the original set of variables are manifestations of underlying, or **latent**, psychological variables. **Factor analysis** (see Chapter 15) is a set of methods designed to identify the latent psychological variables thought to underlie the correlations among a set of tests.

5.8.4 Complex contingency tables

In the past two decades, there have been dramatic developments in the analysis of nominal data in the form of multiway contingency tables. In particular, the application of **loglinear models** of the cell frequencies in such tables has made it possible to tease out the relationships among the attributes in the classification in a way that was not possible before. Loglinear analysis is the subject of Chapter 13.

5.9 DATA ANALYSIS WITH SPSS

The analysis of a set of data takes place in two phases:

(1) **data entry and exploration** at a general level;

(2) **formal statistical analysis**.

5.9.1 Phase 1 - Data Entry and Exploration

The scheme below shows the steps taken in entering data into SPSS, their subsequent exploration, inspection, transcription corrections, data transformations, case selections and so on.

Prepare data file in Data Editor window

Within the **Statistics** drop-down menu, explore data with procedures from the **Summarize** submenu such as **Frequencies, Descriptives, Explore, Crosstabs**

Inspect listings on the screen, check for outliers, study the distributions

If necessary, deselect outliers or transform distributions with procedures from the **Data** or **Transform** drop-down menus

5.9.2 Phase 2 - Statistical Analysis

After the data have been entered, corrected, and explored as described in Phase 1, the user is then ready to engage in further statistical analysis of the data. Table 7 tabulates the SPSS statistical procedures which will be discussed in subsequent chapters of this book. The names in bold type are items within the **Statistics** drop-down menu; the names in italics are sub-items from the main items.

Table 7.
SPSS statistical procedures (bold type) within the Statistics drop-down menu and their sub-items (italics)

Significance of differences in level between or among variables	Degree of relationship among variables	Prediction of group membership	Finding latent variables
Compare Means:	**Summarize:**	**Classify:**	**Data reduction:**
Various T-Tests	*Crosstabs*	*Discriminant*	*Factor*
One-way ANOVA	**Correlate:** *Bivariate*		
ANOVA Models:	**Regression:** *Linear*		
Simple Factorial	**Loglinear**		
Repeated measures	**Nonparametric Tests**		
Nonparametric Tests			

After running a statistical analysis and inspecting the output, the user can run it slightly differently by returning to the original dialog box(es) and changing the variables or selecting different options. The analysis may lead to the identification of more outliers and the need to repeat the analysis with a reduced data set. Further refinements may be added: additional statistics can be commanded; tables of residuals can be requested; and plots of the results obtained. Once an analysis has been carried out to the user's satisfaction, the various outputs (listings, charts, graphs) may be stored and/or printed.

5.10 GETTING HELP

In a book of this sort, which is primarily concerned with the use of a computing package, it is not possible to offer more than a few signposts to the reader wishing to select and use a statistical test correctly. In the following sections we offer two suggestions.

5.10.1 Useful textbooks

Of the many textbooks that offer advice on the selection of statistical tests, we have found Howell (1997) to be among the most consistently helpful. Like several other authors (Siegel & Castellan, 1988; Tabachnick & Fidell, 1996), Howell offers a decision tree to help the reader make the correct selection. The trees offered by different authors vary considerably in appearance, a fact reflecting the different approaches advocated by their authors (Siegel was an advocate of nonparametric statistics; Howell emphasises parametric univariate ANOVA methods; Tabachnick & Fidell are more concerned with multivariate statistics). From the point of view of the modern experimental psychologist, Howell's decision tree is perhaps the most helpful.

While such decision trees are very helpful in the early stages of study, one inevitably meets situations to which none of the proposed schemes really applies convincingly. Some situations, in fact, require the construction of a special statistical model, rather than the application of any standard test.

5.10.2 Getting help in SPSS

SPSS offers a very useful Help facility. By entering the **Help** drop-down menu and selecting the Search option, one can, by typing in key phrases, obtain useful information about how to find and run procedures.

For example, for a one-sample t-test, the user is directed to the dialog box for a **related-samples t-test** and is given clear instructions there on how to modify the data set for the one-sample test.

SUMMARY

1) To select an appropriate statistical test, several aspects of the research situation must be kept in mind:-
   (a) the research question;
   (b) the nature of the data;
   (c) the plan or design of the research.

2) In experiments with two or more samples, there is a range of tests available depending on whether the data are of the interval, ordinal or nominal type. Apart from the more well-known t-tests and analysis of variance (ANOVA) for interval data, there are several nonparametric tests for ordinal and nominal data. Nonparametric tests make fewer underlying assumptions about the population distributions than equivalent parametric tests, but are usually less powerful.

3) In experiments with just one sample, there is also a range of nonparametric tests and the one-sample t-test.

4) Between subjects, within subjects, and mixed (or split-plot) ANOVA designs are available for multi-factorial experiments.

5) Various correlation methods and cross-tabulations statistics are available for measuring the statistical association between variables. Simple and multiple regression can be used to estimate values of one variable from knowledge of one or more other variables (regressors).

6) In the case of experiments with more than one dependent variable, various multivariate methods such as MANOVA (analogous to ANOVA), discriminant analysis (for determining the best combination of variables to predict group membership), factor analysis (for determining combinations of variables that might act as latent variables accounting for the correlations among all the variables), and loglinear analysis (for analysing multi-variable contingency tables) are available.

7) A scheme for analysing data with SPSS is presented along with a table showing the SPSS menu names of the principal statistical tests and procedures. There is also information about useful textbooks and how to get help within SPSS.

CHAPTER 6

COMPARING THE AVERAGES OF TWO SAMPLES

6.1 INTRODUCTION

Suppose that an experiment has been carried out, in which the performance of two groups of people has been measured under two conditions, an experimental condition and a control. For example, the task could be the memorisation of the content of a written passage, and the purpose of the experiment might be to compare the recall performance of a group of subjects who have been given special training in a mnemonic technique with that of an untrained control group. We may find that the mean performance of the experimental (trained) group is higher than that of the untrained (control) group. If this experiment were to be repeated, however, the averages for the two groups would almost certainly take different values. In statistical terms, this is because the scores actually obtained from each group are merely a **sample** from an infinite pool, or **population**, of possible values. Can we be confident that if the experiment were to be repeated, we would get the same result? To answer this question we need to carry out a formal statistical test.

Possibly the best known statistical test for comparing the average levels of two samples of interval data is the **t-test**, which is designed to test the difference between two **means** for **significance**. Our hypothesis is that the mnemonic technique enhances recall. This is the **experimental hypothesis**. In traditional significance testing, however, it is not the experimental hypothesis that is directly tested but its **negation**, which is known as the **null hypothesis** (H_0). In this example, H_0 states that, in the population, there is no difference between performance under the mnemonic and control conditions. If H_0 fails the test, we shall conclude that our experimental hypothesis, which in statistical terms is known as the **alternative hypothesis**, is correct.

The performance of a statistical test requires a knowledge of the **sampling distribution** of the test statistic. The **p-value** of a statistic such as ***t*** or ***F*** (or some other test statistic) is the probability, assuming that H_0 is true, of obtaining a value **at least as extreme as the one actually obtained**. Should the p-value be small, this is taken as evidence against H_0 , because a value that extreme is unlikely (though possible) under H_0 . Traditionally, H_0 is rejected if the p-value is no more than 0.05; but in many areas, an even lower p-value, say 0.01, is now the conventional criterion for rejection. When the p-value of a statistic is at least as small as the conventional value, the value of the statistic is said to be **significant**.

Should the p-value be larger than the conventional small value, H_0 is **accepted**. This does not mean that it is actually true: it means only that the evidence is insufficient to justify rejection.

To sum up:

1) if the p-value is greater than 0.05, $\mathbf{H_0}$ is accepted and the result is **not significant**;

2) if the p-value is less than 0.05 but greater than 0.01, $\mathbf{H_0}$ is rejected and the result is **significant beyond the 5 per cent level**;

3) if the p-value is smaller than 0.01, H_0 is rejected and the result is **significant beyond the 1 per cent level**.

In this book, we assume that you are familiar with the t-test, at least to some extent. If you are not, we strongly recommend that you read the relevant sections of a good statistical text: e.g. Gravetter & Wallnau (1996; chapters 9-11) give a lucid account. With independent samples, the t statistic is calculated by dividing the difference between the sample means by an estimate of the standard deviation of the distribution of differences, known as the **standard error of the difference**. Should the sample variances have similar values, it is common practice to work with a pooled estimate of the supposedly constant population variance; but if they do not, the pooled estimate is not used and a **separate variance** test is made. The null hypothesis is rejected if the obtained value of t lies in either tail of the sampling distribution. The precise value of t needed for significance depends upon the **degrees of freedom** of the distribution, which in turn depends upon the sizes of the samples in the experiment; but an absolute value of t greater than or equal to 2 is usually significant, unless the samples are very small indeed. Very small samples should be avoided in any case, because the test would have insufficient power to reject H_0 . (The **power** of a statistical test is the probability that H_0 will be rejected given that it is false.)

Table 1 shows the SPSS menus and sub-menus (in upper case letters) for the various two-sample situations.

Table 1.

SPSS menus and submenus (upper case words) within the Statistics drop-down menu for various two-sample situations

Data derived from populations assumed to have normal distributions and equal variances		No specific assumptions about the population distributions	
Independent samples	Paired samples	Independent samples	Related samples
COMPARE MEANS	COMPARE MEANS	NON-PARAMETRIC TESTS	NON-PARAMETRIC TESTS
↓	↓	↓	↓
INDEPENDENT SAMPLES T-TEST	PAIRED SAMPLES T-TEST	2 INDEPENDENT SAMPLES	2 RELATED SAMPLES

↓ indicates that the item below is part of the submenu of the item above

The left half of Table 1 deals with parametric tests (i.e. those making assumptions about population distributions), the right half with nonparametric tests (i.e. those making no assumptions about population distributions). Each half is subdivided according to whether the samples are independent or related (SPSS refers to related samples as **paired samples** in the case of the t-test, but as **related samples** for nonparametric tests).

6.2 PARAMETRIC METHODS: THE t-TESTS

6.2.1 Assumptions underlying the use of the t-test

The model underlying a t-test assumes that the data have been derived from normal distributions with equal variance. Computer simulations have shown that even with moderate violations of these assumptions, one may still safely proceed with a t-test, provided the samples are not too small, do not contain outliers (atypical scores), and are of equal (or nearly equal) size. Should a preliminary exploration of the data (as recommended in Chapter 4) indicate that the assumptions of a t-test model have been seriously violated, an alternative test should be chosen from the portfolio of **nonparametric** tests in the **Nonparametric Tests** menu. Nonparametric tests do not carry specific assumptions about population distributions and variance.

6.2.2 Paired and independent samples

In an experiment on lateralisation of cortical functioning, a subject looks at a central spot on a computer screen and is told to press a key on recognition of a word which may appear on either side of the spot. As a check on whether the word has been truly recognised, the subject is also asked to type the word just identified. The experimental hypothesis is that words presented in the right visual field will be more quickly recognised than those in the left visual field, because the former are processed by the left cerebral hemisphere, which is thought to be more proficient with verbal information. For each subject, the median response time to forty words in each of the right and left visual fields is recorded, as indicated in Table 2:

Table 2.

Paired data: Median word recognition times in milliseconds for words in the left and right visual fields

Subject	Left Field	Right Field
s1	323	304
s2	512	493
s3	502	491
s4	385	365
s5	453	426
s6	343	320
s7	543	523
s8	440	442
s9	682	580
s10	590	564

This experiment is of **repeated measures**, or **within subjects**, design, because the performance of the same subjects has been measured under both conditions (word in right field, word in left field). Now suppose that **different** subjects had been tested with words in the right and left visual fields. The data table might appear as in Table 3.

This variant of the experiment has **no repeated measures**, or is of **between subjects** design: each subject is tested under only one condition. Notice that there is no basis on which the subjects in the two conditions can meaningfully be paired; indeed, with no repeated measures, the samples can be of different sizes. It is recommended, however, that samples should always be the same size wherever possible.

With suitable paired data, the **paired samples t-test** can be used to test the difference between the means of the two sets of scores for significance. With suitable independent data, the **independent samples t-test** is used. These tests are available in the **Compare Means** section of the **Statistics** menu. Note that the data are entered differently in the two cases, as explained below.

Table 3.

Independent samples: Median word recognition times in milliseconds for words in the left and right visual fields

Subject	Left Field	Subject	Right Field
s1	500	s11	392
s2	513	s12	445
s3	300	s13	271
s4	561	s14	523
s5	483	s15	421
s6	502	s16	489
s7	539	s17	501
s8	467	s18	388
s9	420	s19	411
s10	480	s20	467

6.2.3 The paired samples t-test

Prepare the data file from the data in Table 2 as follows:

Using the techniques described in Chapter 3 (Section 3.5), define the variables *leftfld* and *rightfld* (fuller names, such as *Left Visual Field* and *Right Visual Field* can be assigned by using the **Define Labels** procedure). Type the data into the two columns and save the data set to a file. The t-test is selected by choosing

Statistics (see Figure 1)

Compare Means

Paired-Samples T Test ...

to open the **Paired-Samples T Test** dialog box (the completed version is shown in Figure 2).

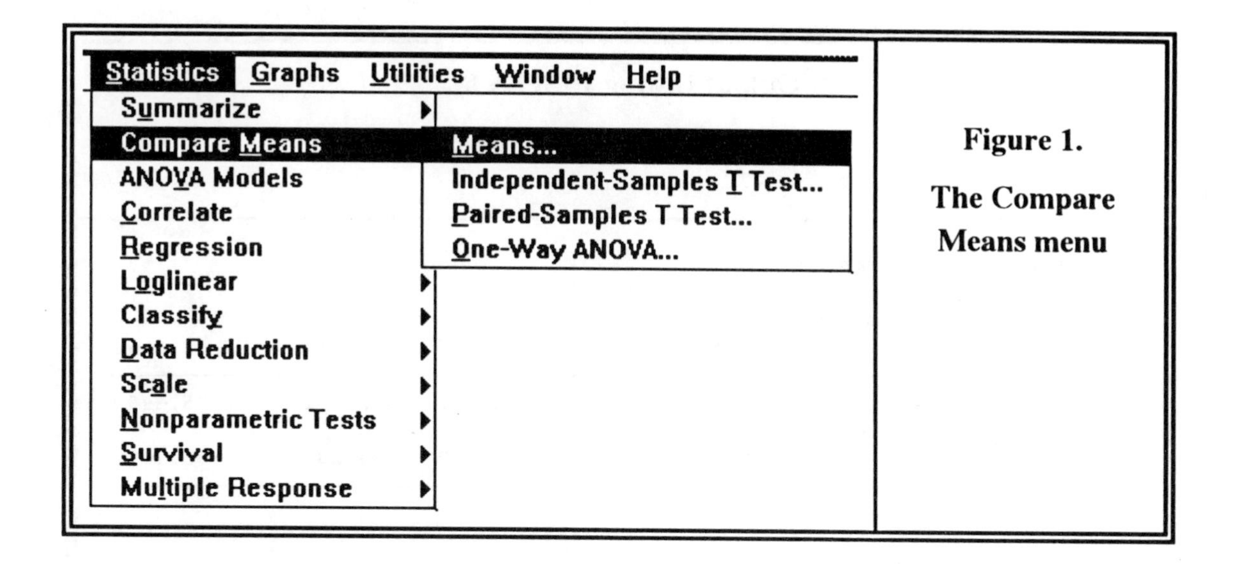

Figure 1.

The Compare Means menu

Highlight the two variable names in the left-hand box (by clicking on them with the mouse), and then click on the ▶ box to transfer the names into the **Paired Variables** box. Click on **OK** to run the t-test.

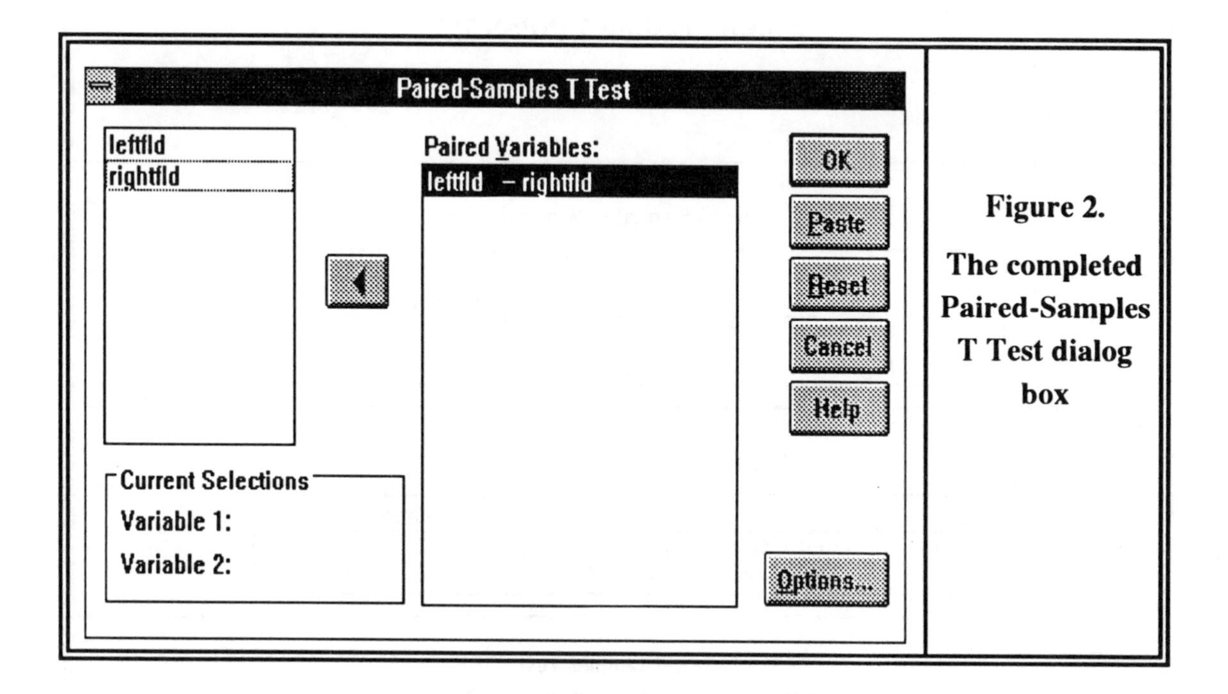

Figure 2.

The completed Paired-Samples T Test dialog box

The output is shown in Output Listing 1 (SPSS 6 and 7). The listing begins with some statistics for each of the two variables considered separately, followed by statistics of the distribution of differences between the paired scores (Paired Differences).

Output Listing 1 (SPSS 6).

t-test output for paired samples

```
t-tests for Paired Samples

                  Number of           2-tail
Variable            pairs      Corr   Sig          Mean          SD    SE of Mean

LEFTFLD    Left Visual Field                    477.3000     112.091       35.446
                     10        .975    .000
RIGHTFLD    Right Visual Field                  450.8000      97.085       30.701


          Paired Differences
   Mean              SD     SE of Mean  |        t-value         df      2-tail Sig

26.5000        27.814           8.796   |         3.01            9          .015
95% CI (6.603, 46.397)                  |
```

Output Listing 1 (SPSS 7).

t-test output for paired samples

Paired Samples Statistics

		Mean	N	Std. Deviation	Std. Error Mean
Pair 1	Left Visual Field	477.30	10	112.09	35.45
	Right Visual Field	450.80	10	97.09	30.70

Paired Samples Correlations

		N	Correlation	Sig.
Pair 1	Left Visual Field & Right Visual Field	10	.975	.000

Paired Samples Test

		Paired Differences					t	df	Sig. (2-tailed)
		Mean	Std. Deviation	Std. Error Mean	95% Confidence Interval of the Difference Lower	Upper			
Pair 1	Left Visual Field - Right Visual Field	26.50	27.81	8.80	6.60	46.40	3.013	9	.015

The correlation coefficient for the two variables (0.975), the t-value (3.01) with its associated degrees of freedom (9), and the 2-tail p-value (0.015) are also given. The final item in the Output Listing 1 reads as follows:

95% CI (6.598, 46.402)

In words this is: 'The ninety-five per cent confidence interval is from 6.598 to 46.402'. The same values are listed in the Output Listing 1 under the heading: **95% Confidence Interval of the Difference**. In statistical inference there are two kinds of estimates:

(1) **point estimates**, which are single values (the sample mean and variance are point estimates of the corresponding population parameters);

(2) **interval estimates**, which are intervals within which the true values are stated, with specified levels of confidence, to lie.

The **ninety-five percent confidence interval (95% CI)** is an interval calculated from the data in such a way that it should include the true value of the parameter (in this case the mean difference in the population) in 95% of samples. This is what is meant by the term '95% confidence': the stated confidence interval does **not** mean: 'The probability that the true mean lies between 6.598 and 46.402 is 0.95'. Since this interval does not include the H_0 value of 0, the result is clearly significant. The listing shows that the null hypothesis can also be rejected on the basis of the t-test, since the t-test tail probability (labelled **Sig**) .015 (or 1.5%) is less than .05 (or 5%). Thus the difference between the means is significant.

To check for anomalies in the data, it is recommended that a scatterplot of the data points be constructed. Use the **Scatter** item within the **Graphs** pull-down menu (previously described in Section 4.3.3.7) to obtain the scatterplot (Figure 3) with *leftfld* in the **Y Axis** box and *rightfld* in the **X Axis** box.

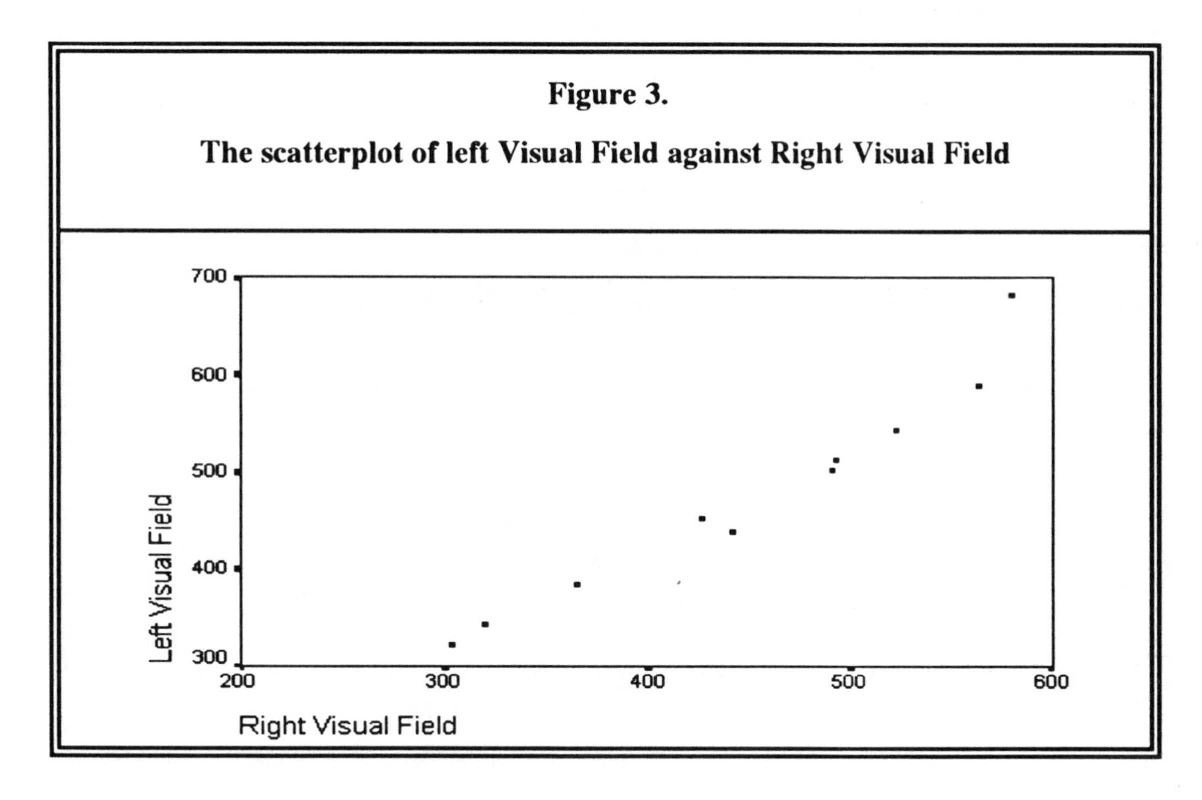

Figure 3.

The scatterplot of left Visual Field against Right Visual Field

No outlier appears in the scatterplot. It should be noted that the presence of an outlying pair of scores, even one showing a difference in the same direction as the others, can have the effect of increasing the denominator of the **t** statistic more than the numerator and so reduce the value of **t** to insignificance. This effect is illustrated in one of the Exercises. The vulnerability of the standard deviation to the leverage exerted by outliers derives from the fact that the elements of the variance are the **squares** of deviations from the mean, and large deviations thus continue to have a disproportionate influence, even after the square root operation by which the standard deviation is derived from the variance has been carried out.

When outliers are present, the user can either consider removing them or choose a nonparametric method such as the **Sign test** or the **Wilcoxon matched pairs test**. The former is completely immune to the influence of outliers; the latter is much more resistant than the t-test. Should there be no contra-indications against the use of the t-test however, the parametric t-test is preferable to a nonparametric test because the latter would incur the penalty of a loss of power.

6.2.4 The independent samples t-test

In this analysis, each score is identified by a code number indicating the condition under which the score was obtained. The code numbers are carried in a grouping variable. Using the techniques described in Chapter 3 (Section 3.5), define the grouping (independent) variable as *field* and the dependent variable as *rectime*. Fuller names (e.g. *Visual Field* and *Word Recognition Time*) and value labels (e.g. *Left Field* and *Right Field*) can be assigned by using the **Define Labels** procedure. Type in the data and save to a file. The t-test is selected by choosing

Statistics

Compare Means

Independent-Samples T Test ...

to open the **Independent-Samples T Test** dialog box (Figure 4).

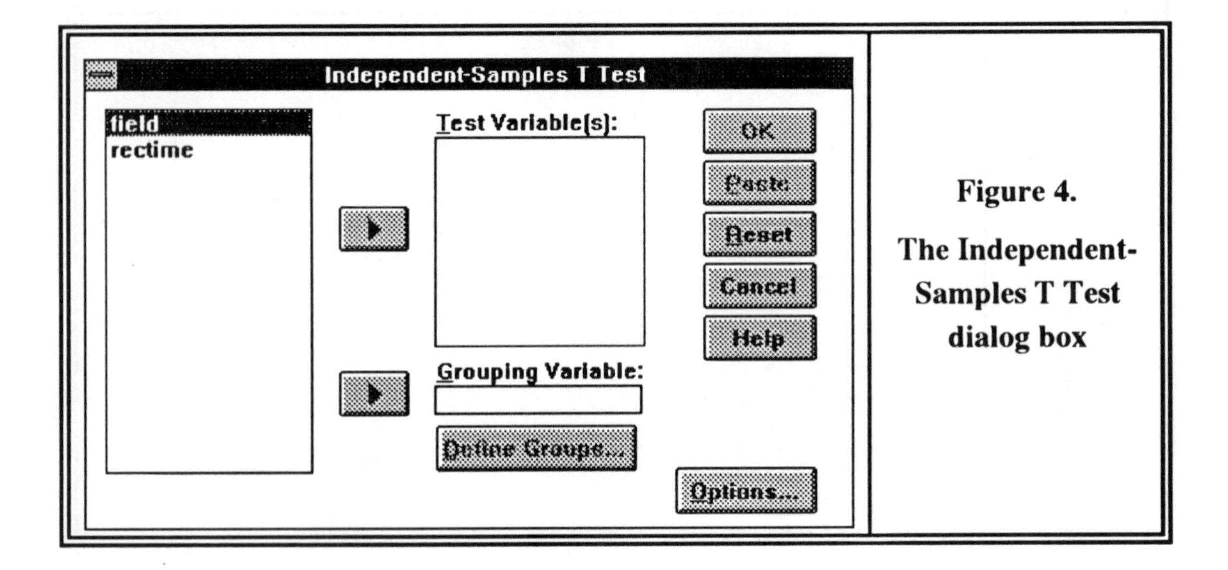

Figure 4.

The Independent-Samples T Test dialog box

Highlight the variable *rectime* in the left-hand box. Transfer *rectime* to the **Test Variable(s)** box by clicking on ▶. Similarly, highlight the grouping variable *field* and transfer it to the **Grouping Variable**. At this point the **Grouping Variable** box will appear with **? ?** as shown in Figure 5.

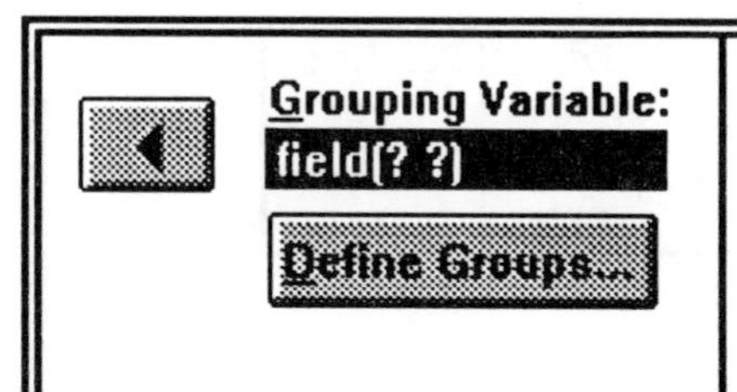

Figure 5.

The Grouping Variable part of the Independent-Samples t-test dialog box before defining the groups

It remains to define the values of the groups by clicking on **Define Groups** (Figure 4), typing the value *1* into the **Group 1** box and the value *2* into the **Group 2** box, and clicking on **Continue**. The values 1, 2 will then appear in brackets after *field* in the Grouping Variable box. Click on **OK** to run the t-test, the output for which is shown in Output Listing 2 (SPSS 6 and 7).

Output Listing 2 (SPSS 6).

t-test output for Independent Samples

```
t-tests for Independent Samples of FIELD     Visual Field

                                 Number
 Variable                       of Cases       Mean            SD   SE of Mean
 -----------------------------------------------------------------------------
 RECTIME  Word Recognition Time

 Left Field                         10      476.5000       73.083       23.111
 Right Field                        10      430.8000       72.793       23.019
 -----------------------------------------------------------------------------

         Mean Difference = 45.7000
         Levene's Test for Equality of Variances: F= .068    P= .797

      t-test for Equality of Means                                   95%
 Variances    t-value       df     2-Tail Sig   SE of Diff     CI for Diff
 ---------------------------------------------------------------------------------
 Equal           1.40       18          .178        32.619   (-22.830, 114.230)
 Unequal         1.40    18.00          .178        32.619   (-22.830, 114.230)
 ---------------------------------------------------------------------------------
```

Output Listing 2 (SPSS 7).

t-test output for Independent Samples

Group Statistics

	Visual Field	N	Mean	Std. Deviation	Std. Error Mean
Word Recognition Time	Left Field	10	476.50	73.08	23.11
	Right Field	10	430.80	72.79	23.02

Independent Samples Test

		Levene's Test for Equality of Variances		t-test for Equality of Means						
									95% Confidence Interval of the Mean	
		F	Sig.	t	df	Sig. (2-tailed)	Mean Difference	Std. Error Difference	Lower	Upper
Word Recognition Time	Equal variances assumed	.068	.797	1.401	18	.178	45.70	32.62	-22.83	114.23
	Equal variances not assumed			1.401	18.0	.178	45.70	32.62	-22.83	114.23

The output starts with statistics of the two groups, followed by the value of the difference between means (Mean Difference). Since one of the assumptions for a valid t-test is homogeneity of variance, the **Levene Test** for homogeneity of variance is included. Provided the F value is **not significant** ($p > 0.05$), the variances can be assumed to be homogeneous and the **Equal Variances** line of values for the t-test can be used. If $p < 0.05$, then the homogeneity of variance assumption has been violated and the t-test based on separate variance estimates (**Unequal Variances** or **Equal variances not assumed**) should be used.

In this example, the Levene Test is not significant, so the t value calculated with the pooled variance estimate (Equal Variances) is appropriate. With a **2-Tail Sig** (i.e. p-value) of 0.178 (i.e. 17.8%), the difference between means is not significant. This is confirmed by the **95% Confidence Interval** for the difference between means (-22.83 to 114.23) which includes the H_0 mean difference of 0. Had this interval been entirely positive, the result would have been significant.

6.3 NONPARAMETRIC METHODS

When there are serious violations of the assumptions of the t-test, nonparametric tests can be used instead. They should not be used as a matter of course, however, because should the data meet the requirements of the t-test, the comparable nonparametric test may lack the **power** to reject the null hypothesis, should that be false. It is best, therefore, to consider the parametric test first, resorting to the nonparametric alternative only if the data seriously violate the requirements.

SPSS has a wide selection of nonparametric tests in the **Nonparametric Tests** submenu of **Statistics**. The **Sign** and **Wilcoxon** tests are nonparametric counterparts of the paired samples t-test; the **Mann-Whitney** test is an alternative to the independent samples t-test.

Most nonparametric methods use measures, such as the median, that are resistant to outliers and skewness. In the tests described here, H_0 states that, in the population, the two **medians** are equal.

6.3.1 Related samples: Wilcoxon, Sign and McNemar tests

Choose

Statistics

Nonparametric Tests

2 Related Samples ...

to obtain the **Two-Related-Samples** dialog box (Figure 6).

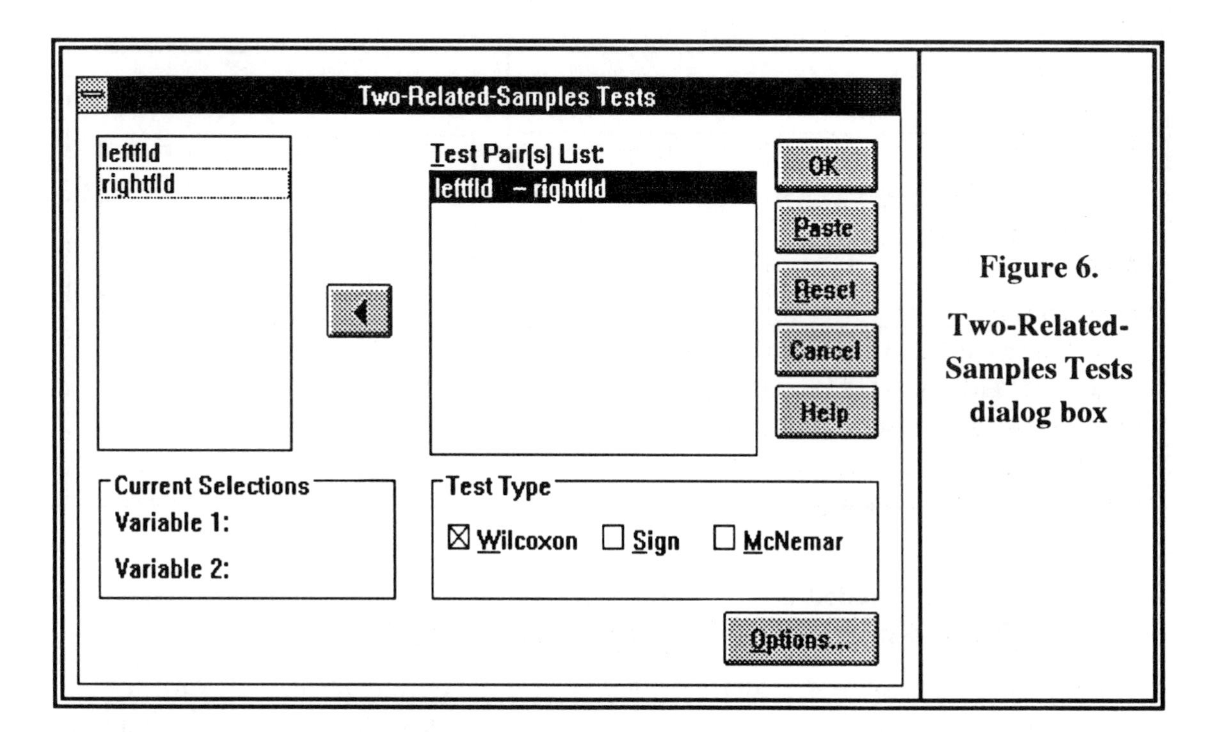

Figure 6. Two-Related-Samples Tests dialog box

Highlight the variable names and transfer them to the **Test Pair(s) List** box. Click on **OK** to run the test. The results are shown in Output Listing 3 (SPSS 6 and 7).

Output Listing 3 (SPSS 6).

The output for the Wilcoxon test

```
Wilcoxon Matched-Pairs Signed-Ranks Test

     LEFTFLD   Left Visual Field
with RIGHTFLD  Right Visual Field

     Mean Rank     Sum of Ranks  Cases

      6.00             54.00      9   - Ranks  (RIGHTFLD LT LEFTFLD)
      1.00              1.00      1   + Ranks  (RIGHTFLD GT LEFTFLD)
                                  0   0 Ties   (RIGHTFLD EQ LEFTFLD)
                                 --
                                 10     Total

      Z =    -2.7046             2-Tailed P =  .0068
```

Output Listing 3 (SPSS 7).

The output for the Wilcoxon test

Ranks

		N	Mean Rank	Sum of Ranks
Right Visual Field - Left Visual Field	Negative Ranks	9[a]	6.00	54.00
	Positive Ranks	1[b]	1.00	1.00
	Ties	0[c]		
	Total	10		

a. Right Visual Field < Left Visual Field

b. Right Visual Field > Left Visual Field

c. Left Visual Field = Right Visual Field

Test Statistics[a]

	Right Visual Field - Left Visual Field
Z	-2.705[b]
Asymp. Sig. (2-tailed)	.007

a. Wilcoxon Signed Ranks Test

b. Based on positive ranks.

The p-value for Z (**2-tailed p** or **Asymp. Sig.**) is less than 0.05, confirming the t-test result that there is a significant difference between the visual fields.

Although the Wilcoxon test assumes neither normality nor homogeneity of variance, it does assume that the two samples are from populations with the same distribution shape. It is also vulnerable to the influences of outliers - though not to nearly the same extent as the t-test. The **Sign test**, which is even more robust than the Wilcoxon, can be requested by clicking on its check box. The **McNemar test** is applicable to paired data relating to dichotomous qualitative variables.

6.3.2 Independent Samples: Mann-Whitney test

Choose
Statistics
Nonparametric Tests
2 Independent Samples ...

to obtain the **Two-Independent-Samples** dialog box (Figure 7).

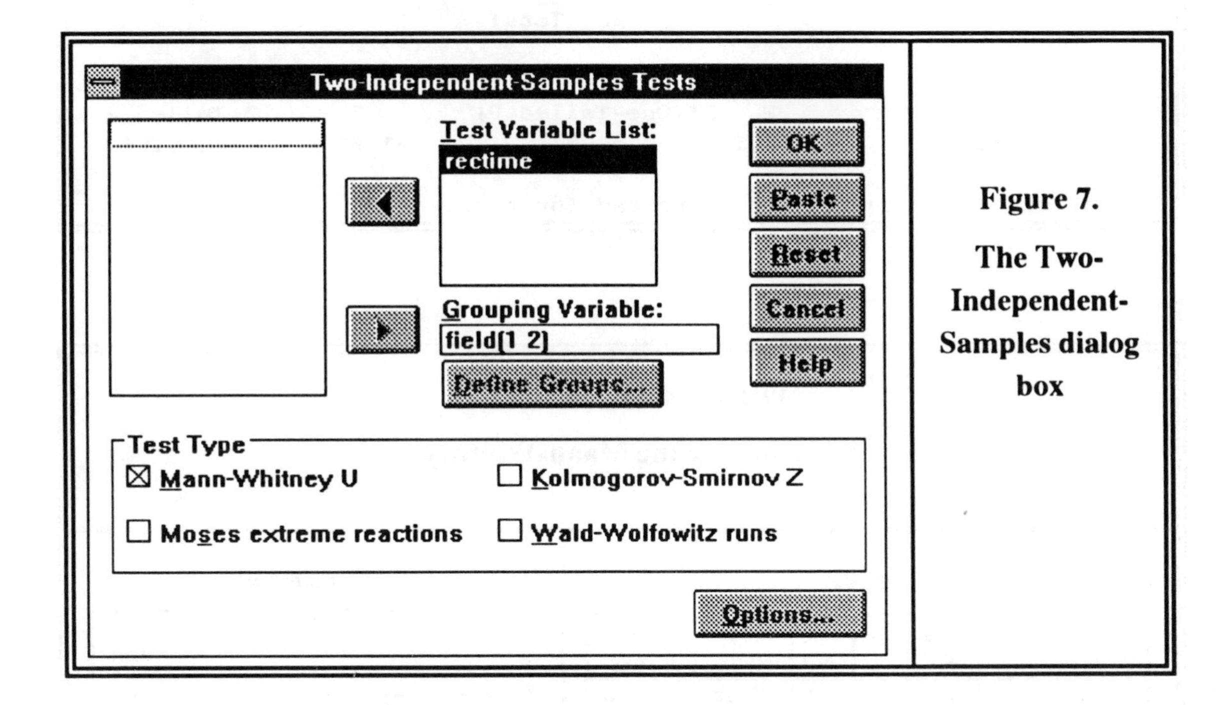

Figure 7. The Two-Independent-Samples dialog box

Highlight the test variable name *rectime* and transfer it to the **Test Variable List** box. Highlight the grouping variable name *field* and transfer it to the **Grouping Variable** box; click on **Define Groups** and add the group numbers *1* and *2* in the usual way. Click on **Continue** and then on **OK** to run the test. The results are shown in Output Listing 4 (SPSS 6 and 7).

Output Listing 4 (SPSS 6).

The output for the Mann-Whitney test

```
Mann-Whitney U - Wilcoxon Rank Sum W Test

     RECTIME    Word Recognition Time
  by FIELD      Visual Field

     Mean Rank      Sum of Ranks  Cases
         12.65             126.5     10  FIELD     =     1    Left Field
          8.35             83.50     10  FIELD     =     2    Right Field
                                     --
                                     20  Total

                                   Exact**
           U                W   2*(One-Tailed P)       Z         2-Tailed P
          28.5            83.5        .1051        -1.6259            .1040

**This exact p-value is not corrected for ties.
```

Output Listing 4 (SPSS 7).

The output for the Mann-Whitney test

Ranks

	Visual Field	N	Mean Rank	Sum of Ranks
Word Recognition Time	Left Field	10	12.65	126.50
	Right Field	10	8.35	83.50
	Total	20		

Test Statistics[a]

	Word Recognition Time
Mann-Whitney U	28.500
Wilcoxon W	83.500
Z	-1.626
Asymp. Sig. (2-tailed)	.104
Exact Sig. [2*(1-tailed Sig.)]	.105[b]

a. Grouping Variable: Visual Field

b. Not corrected for ties.

The p-value for Z (**2-tailed p** or **Asymp. Sig.**) is greater than 0.05, confirming the t-test result that there is a no significant difference between the visual fields.

SUMMARY

1) The **t-test** can be used to test for a significant difference between the means of two samples of interval data, provided the data are normally-distributed, and the samples have similar variances.

2) For independent samples, use

   Statistics

   Compare Means

   Independent-Samples T Test ...

   The group to which each subject belongs is identified by a coding variable.

3) For paired samples, use

   Statistics

   Compare Means

   Paired-Samples T Test ...

   A scatterplot is recommended. Use

   Graphs

   Scatter

   Simple

   and define the variables for each axis.

4) If the assumptions for the t-test are violated, a **nonparametric** test can be used. Nonparametric tests do not assume normality and homogeneity of variance; though they may require that the two distributions have the same shape. These tests are available in

   Statistics

   Nonparametric Tests

   2 Independent Samples ... or **2 Related Samples ...**

CHAPTER 7

THE ONE-FACTOR BETWEEN SUBJECTS EXPERIMENT

7.1 INTRODUCTION

Suppose that an experiment has been carried out to compare the performance of two groups of subjects: an **experimental** group and a **control** group. Provided the data have certain characteristics (i.e. the samples have approximately normal distributions and comparable variances), an independent samples t-test can be used to test the null hypothesis (H_0) of equality of the two population means. If the test shows significance, we reject H_0: we conclude that there is a difference between the two population means, which is equivalent to the conclusion that the experimental manipulation does have an effect.

The same null hypothesis, however, can also be tested by using one of the set of techniques known as **analysis of variance (ANOVA** for short). Despite its name, the ANOVA, like the t-test, is concerned with the testing of hypotheses about **means**. In fact, if the ANOVA and the (pooled variance) t-test are applied to the data from a simple, two-group experiment, the tests will give the same result: if the t-test shows the difference between the means to be significant, then so will the ANOVA and vice versa.

The ANOVA, however, is more versatile than the t-test. Suppose that in an investigation of the effects of mnemonic strategies upon recall, three groups of subjects were tested:

(a) a group trained in Mnemonic Method A;

(b) a group trained in Mnemonic Method B;.

(c) a Control group, who had merely been asked to memorise the material as well as possible.

This type of experiment, in which each subject performs under only one of the conditions making up a single independent variable, is said to have **one treatment factor** with **no repeated measures**. It is also known as the **completely randomised experiment**. From such an experiment, we would obtain three samples of scores, one for each of the three groups. The 'one-way' ANOVA can test the null hypothesis that all three population means are equal, i.e. neither mnemonic technique improves recall (in comparison with the control group). Note that, unlike ANOVA, the t-test cannot be used to evaluate a hypothesis about three or more population means: it can substitute for ANOVA only if there are two groups in the experiment.

Why couldn't a series of t-tests be used to make comparisons among the three group means? Couldn't we simply use three t-tests to compare the Control group with the Mnemonic A and Mnemonic B groups, and Mnemonic A with Mnemonic B? The problem with that approach is that when multiple comparisons are made among a set of treatment means, the probability of at least one test showing significance **even when the null hypothesis is true** is higher than the conventional significance level (i.e. critical p-value) of 0.05 or 0.01; in fact, if there is a large array of treatment group means, the probability of at least one test showing significance is close to 1 (certainty)! This point is explained in greater detail in Gravetter & Wallnau (1996; p402).

A lucid account of the rationale of the one-factor between subjects (one-way) ANOVA is given in Gravetter & Wallnau (1996), Chapter 13. Basically, the ANOVA works like this. A group mean is taken to be an estimate of people's typical level of performance under that particular condition. But individual performance can vary widely and at times deviates markedly from the group mean. Think of this **within group** variability as background noise, or **error**. It may be, however, that mnemonic groups A and B achieved much higher average levels of performance than did the control group: in other words, there is high variability **between (i.e. among) groups**. The **ANOVA F statistic** is calculated by dividing an estimate of the variability **between groups** by the variability **within groups**:

$$F = \frac{\text{variance between}}{\text{variance within}}$$

If there are large differences among the treatment means, the numerator of F (and therefore F itself) will be inflated and the null hypothesis is likely to be rejected; but if there is no effect, the numerator and denominator of F should have similar values, giving an F close to unity. A high value of F, therefore, is evidence against the null hypothesis of equality of all three population means.

There remains a problem, however. If H_0 states that all the means are equal, the alternative hypothesis is that they are not. If the ANOVA F test gives significance, we know there is a difference **somewhere** among the means, but that does not justify us in saying that any **particular** comparison is significant. The ANOVA F test, in fact, is an **omnibus test**, and further analysis is necessary to localise whatever differences there may be among the individual treatment means.

The question of exactly how one should proceed to further analysis after making the omnibus F test in ANOVA is not a simple one, and an adequate treatment of it earns an extensive chapter in many statistical texts (e.g. Kirk, 1982, Chapter 3; Howell, 1997, Chapter 12). It is important to distinguish between those comparisons that were **planned** before the data were actually gathered, and those that are made as part of the inevitable process of unplanned **data-snooping** that takes place after the results have been obtained. Planned comparisons are often known as **a priori** comparisons. Unplanned comparisons should be termed **a posteriori** comparisons, but unfortunately the misnomer **post hoc** is more often used.

SPSS offers the user both planned comparisons and an assortment of unplanned data-snooping tests, such as **Tukey's Honestly Significant Difference (HSD) test**, **Scheffé's test**, and so on. If these are unfamiliar to you, we urge you to read the relevant chapters in the books we have cited.

7.2 THE ONE-FACTOR BETWEEN SUBJECTS (ONE-WAY) ANOVA

7.2.1 The mnemonics experiment revisited

In Chapter 3 (Section 3.3.1), an experiment was described in which the performance of two groups of subjects, each trained in a different mnemonic technique (Mnemonic A or Mnemonic B), was compared with that of a group of untrained controls. The results are shown in Table 1, which is a reproduction of Table 2 in Chapter 3.

Table 1.
The numbers of words recalled by subjects with different mnemonic training histories

Control Group	3	5	3	2	4	6	9	3	8	10
Mnemonic A	10	8	15	9	11	16	17	17	7	10
Mnemonic B	20	15	14	15	17	10	8	11	18	19

In Chapter 3, Section 3.3.3 describes how this set of results is recast into a form suitable for entry into SPSS. The SPSS data set (shown in Table 3, Chapter 3) comprises two columns: the first, headed *group*, contains the code numbers *1*, *2* and *3*, identifying the Control, Mnemonic A and Mnemonic B, groups respectively. The second column, headed *score*, contains each subject's score, which was achieved under the condition coded by the *group* variable on the same line.

The **Data Editor** was used to assign to the independent (grouping) variable the more informative variable label *Mnemonic Training History*, and to assign the value labels *Control*, *Mnemonic A* and *Mnemonic B* to the values *1*, *2* and *3*, respectively.

We shall assume that the data set was saved and can therefore be recalled immediately to the **Data Editor** by using the procedure in Section 3.9.2.

7.2.2 Procedure for the one-way ANOVA

The following instructions assume that the data set shown in Table 3, Chapter 3, has been restored to the **Data Editor**.

The one-way analysis of variance is selected by choosing (Figure 1)
Statistics

Compare Means

One-Way ANOVA

to open the **One-Way ANOVA** dialog box.

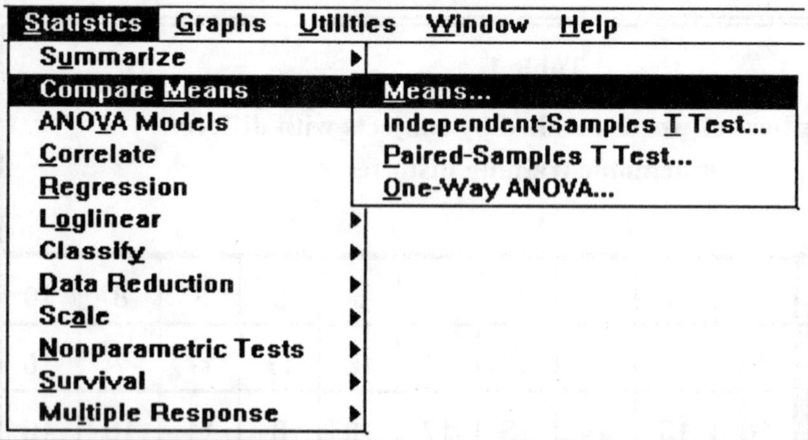

Statistics Graphs Utilities Window Help
Summarize ▶
Compare Means ▶ Means...
ANOVA Models ▶ Independent-Samples T Test...
Correlate ▶ Paired-Samples T Test...
Regression ▶ One-Way ANOVA...
Loglinear ▶
Classify ▶
Data Reduction ▶
Scale ▶
Nonparametric Tests ▶
Survival ▶
Multiple Response ▶

Figure 1.

The Compare Means menu

Click on *group* and then on ▶ to transfer it to the **Factor** box. Click on the **Define Range** box and type *1* into **Minimum** box and *3* into the **Maximum** box. Click on **Continue**. Return to the variable names, click on *score* and then on ▶ to transfer it to the **Dependent List** box.

Unplanned multiple pairwise comparisons among the means can be obtained by clicking **Post Hoc** and then clicking on the check box opposite **Tukey's honestly significant difference**. If descriptive statistics are desired, they can be obtained by clicking on **Options** and then on the check box opposite **Descriptive**. The completed dialog box is shown in Figure 2. Click on **Continue**, and then on **OK** to run the ANOVA.

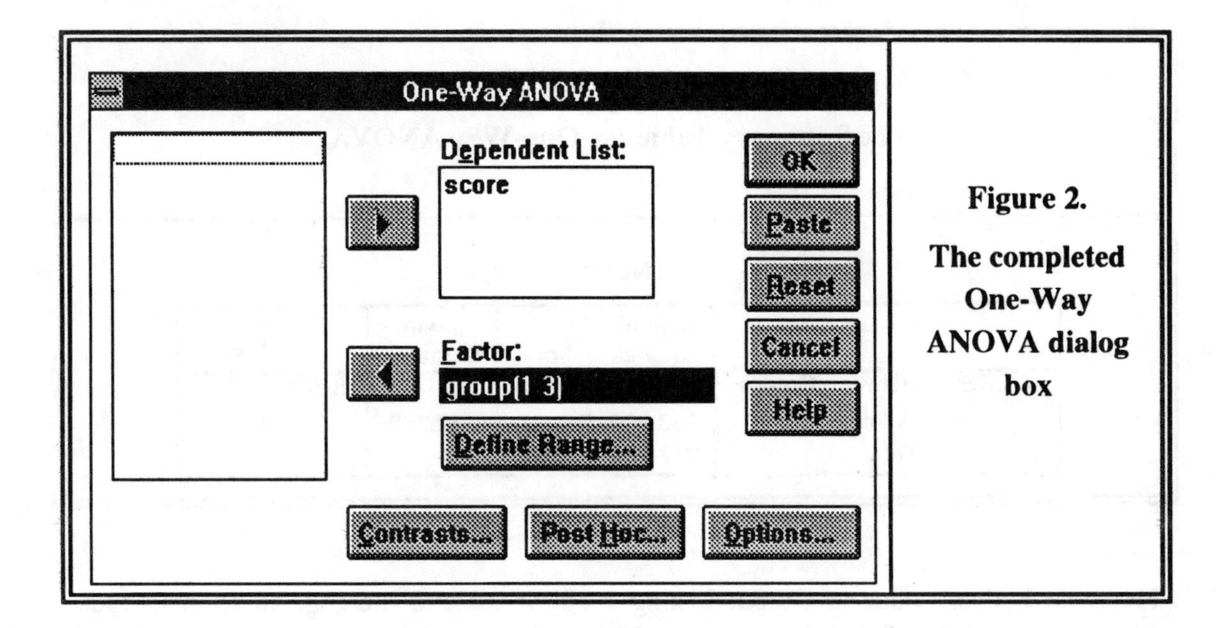

Figure 2.

The completed One-Way ANOVA dialog box

7.2.3 Output listing for the one-way ANOVA

7.2.3.1 The ANOVA summary table

Output Listing 1 (SPSS 6 and 7) shows the summary table for the one-way ANOVA..

Output Listing 1 (SPSS 6).

The Summary Table for One-Way ANOVA

```
     Variable  SCORE
  By Variable  GROUP       Mnemonic Training History

                                  Analysis of Variance

                                  Sum of          Mean           F        F
       Source            D.F.    Squares        Squares       Ratio    Prob.

Between Groups             2     463.4000       231.7000    18.7415    .0000
Within Groups             27     333.8000        12.3630
Total                     29     797.2000
```

Output Listing 1 (SPSS 7).

The Summary Table for One-Way ANOVA

ANOVA

		Sum of Squares	df	Mean Square	F	Sig.
SCORE	Between Groups	463.400	2	231.700	18.741	.000
	Within Groups	333.800	27	12.363		
	Total	797.200	29			

Note the **F Prob** value in Output Listing 1 (SPSS 6) and the **Sig.** value in Output Listing 1 (SPSS 7). This is the p-value of F, i.e. the probability under H_0 of a value at least as extreme as the one obtained. If the p-value is less than 0.05, F is statistically significant. The smaller the p-value, the stronger the evidence against the null hypothesis. In this example, H_0 can be rejected, since the p-value is very small indeed. (It is shown as *.0000* in the listing, which means that it is less than *0.00005*).

7.2.3.2 Descriptive statistics for a one-way ANOVA

Output Listing 2 (SPSS 6 and 7) continues with the descriptive statistics, which include standard deviations, standard errors, 95% confidence intervals (confidence intervals are explained in Chapter 6, Section 6.2.3) and extreme values.

Output Listing 2 (SPSS 6).

Descriptive statistics for One-Way ANOVA

```
                                 Standard   Standard
Group     Count         Mean    Deviation      Error    95 Pct Conf Int for Mean

Grp 1        10       5.3000       2.8304      .8950      3.2753  TO    7.3247
Grp 2        10      11.8000       3.6148     1.1431      9.2141  TO   14.3859
Grp 3        10      14.7000       4.0014     1.2654     11.8376  TO   17.5624

Total        30      10.6000       5.2431      .9572      8.6422  TO   12.5578


GROUP         MINIMUM      MAXIMUM

Grp 1          2.0000      10.0000
Grp 2          7.0000      17.0000
Grp 3          8.0000      20.0000

TOTAL          2.0000      20.0000
```

Output Listing 2 (SPSS 7).

Descriptive statistics for One-Way ANOVA

Descriptives

			N	Mean	Std. Deviation	Std. Error	95% Confidence Interval for Mean Lower Bound	95% Confidence Interval for Mean Upper Bound	Minimum	Maximum
SCORE	Mnemonic Training History	Control	10	5.30	2.83	.90	3.28	7.32	2	10
		Mnemonic A	10	11.80	3.61	1.14	9.21	14.39	7	17
		Mnemonic B	10	14.70	4.00	1.27	11.84	17.56	8	20
		Total	30	10.60	5.24	.96	8.64	12.56	2	20

7.2.3.3 Unplanned multiple comparisons with Tukey's HSD test

The results of **Tukey's HSD test** are tabulated in Output Listing 3 (SPSS 6 and 7), the presentation differing slightly between them.

Output Listing 3 (SPSS 6).

The Tukey-HSD test output

```
      Variable  SCORE
   By Variable  GROUP       Mnemonic Training History

Multiple Range Tests:  Tukey-HSD test with significance level .050

The difference between two means is significant if
  MEAN(J)-MEAN(I)  >= 2.4863 * RANGE * SQRT(1/N(I) + 1/N(J))
  with the following value(s) for RANGE: 3.50

    (*) Indicates significant differences which are shown in the lower triangle

                          G G G
                          r r r
                          p p p

                          1 2 3
     Mean       GROUP

     5.3000     Grp 1
    11.8000     Grp 2     *
    14.7000     Grp 3     *
```

For SPSS 6, the listing specifies the formula used for calculating the critical differences between means in which **RANGE** is the critical value ($q_{critical}$) of the **Studentized Range Statistic** (to be explained later) and then indicates which pairs of groups differ at the 5% level. (This is the *per family* error rate, i.e. the probability under the hypothesis of equality of all the population means, that at least one comparison in the set will show significance.) The means are ordered and displayed from smallest to largest in the first column, and the asterisks in the lower part of the matrix indicate which pairs of groups differ significantly at the 5% level. Notice that groups 2 and 3 each differ from group 1, but they do not differ from each other.

Output Listing 3 (SPSS 7).

The Tukey HSD test output

Multiple Comparisons

Dependent Variable: SCORE
Tukey HSD

(I) Mnemonic Training History	(J) Mnemonic Training History	Mean Difference (I-J)	Std. Error	Sig.	95% Confidence Interval	
					Lower Bound	Upper Bound
Control	Mnemonic A	-6.50*	1.572	.001	-10.40	-2.60
	Mnemonic B	-9.40*	1.572	.000	-13.30	-5.50
Mnemonic A	Control	6.50*	1.572	.001	2.60	10.40
	Mnemonic B	-2.90	1.572	.175	-6.80	1.00
Mnemonic B	Control	9.40*	1.572	.000	5.50	13.30
	Mnemonic A	2.90	1.572	.175	-1.00	6.80

*. The mean difference is significant at the .05 level.

Output Listing 3 (SPSS 7) does not show the formula for calculating the critical differences in means nor does it list the group means - their values are available in Output Listing 2 (SPSS 7); instead it lists each pair of means and indicates with an asterisk whether the means are significantly different at the 5% level. In the column labelled **Sig.**, is the p-value based on the Studentized Range Statistic (see below).

Finally, in Output Listing 4 (SPSS 6 and 7), the groups are divided into homogeneous subsets, thus showing which means do *not* differ from one another (i.e. the members within each subset). In SPSS 7, the listing excludes any subset with just one member. In this case, therefore, it shows only one subset containing the means for Mnemonic A and Mnemonic B (Groups 1 and 2).

Output Listing 4 (SPSS 6).

The homogeneous subsets from Tukey's HSD test

```
Homogeneous Subsets (highest and lowest means are not significantly different)

Subset 1

Group         Grp 1

Mean          5.3000

Subset 2

Group         Grp 2           Grp 3

Mean          11.8000         14.7000
```

Output Listing 4 (SPSS 7).

The homogeneous subsets from Tukey's HSD test

SCORE

Tukey HSD[a]

		Subset for alpha = .05
Mnemonic Training History	N	1
Control	10	
Mnemonic A	10	11.80
Mnemonic B	10	14.70
Sig.		.175

Means for groups in homogeneous subsets are displayed.

a. Uses Harmonic Mean Sample Size = 10.000

The rationale of Tukey's HSD is this: if the treatment means are arranged in order of magnitude, and the smallest is subtracted from the largest, the probability of obtaining a large difference increases with the size of the array of means. **The Studentized Range Statistic (*q*)** expresses the difference between a pair of means in any array as so-many standard errors of the mean, the latter being estimated with

$$\sqrt{\frac{MS_{error}}{n}}$$

where n is the number of subjects in each treatment condition and MS_{error} is the ANOVA error mean square in SPSS 7 Output Listing 1, the quantity **Mean Square** for the row labelled **Within Groups**.

The **Tukey HSD** test requires that, to achieve significance, any pairwise difference must exceed a critical value which depends partly upon a critical value of q ($q_{critical}$), the latter being fixed by the values of two parameters:

(1) the number of means in the array;

(2) the degrees of freedom of MS_{error} . [If there are k treatment means and n subjects in each treatment group, the degrees of freedom of the error term is k(n - 1).]

The 95th percentile of q is obtained by looking up a table of critical values of the **Studentized Range Statistic** (see Howell, 1997; pp680-681). To obtain the critical value, enter the table with the values of the two parameters (here the number of means = *3* and the df for the **Within Groups** (error) source of variance = *27*). For these values, $q_{critical}$ from the table is 3.50.

The critical difference (**CD**) is given by the formula

$$CD = q_{critical}\sqrt{\frac{MS_{error}}{n}}$$

where $q_{critical}$ is the 95th percentile of the distribution of the Studentized Range Statistic. Hence in this example,

$$CD = 3.50\sqrt{\frac{12.363}{10}} = 3.89$$

which is the same value as that from the formula given in SPSS 6 Output Listing 3.

Note that in **Tukey's HSD** test, the critical value for the significance of any of the pairwise comparisons is determined partly by the size of the *entire array* of means. There are other tests, such as the **Newman-Keuls**, which adjust the critical value according to whether the two means are close together or far apart in the left-to-right order of magnitude: in the Newman-Keuls test, the critical value for q is less for a pair of means that are close together in the ordering than for, say, the greatest and smallest means, which are at opposite ends of the ordered array. **Tukey's HSD** test, therefore, is more conservative than the **Newman-Keuls** test: that is, it gives fewer significant differences.

7.3 NONPARAMETRIC TESTS FOR ONE-FACTOR BETWEEN SUBJECTS EXPERIMENTS

Should the data be unsuitable for ANOVA (as when there is marked heterogeneity of variance, or the data are highly skewed), one should consider using **nonparametric** tests, which assume neither homogeneity of variance nor a normal distribution. With inherently ordinal data, the parametric ANOVA cannot be used in any case (see Chapter 5).

7.3.1 The Kruskal-Wallis test

In the **K Independent Samples ...** item of the **Nonparametric Tests** menu (Figure 3) is the **Kruskal-Wallis one-way ANOVA.**

Choose

Statistics

Nonparametric Tests

K Independent Samples

to open the **Tests for Several Independent Samples** dialog box (Figure 4).

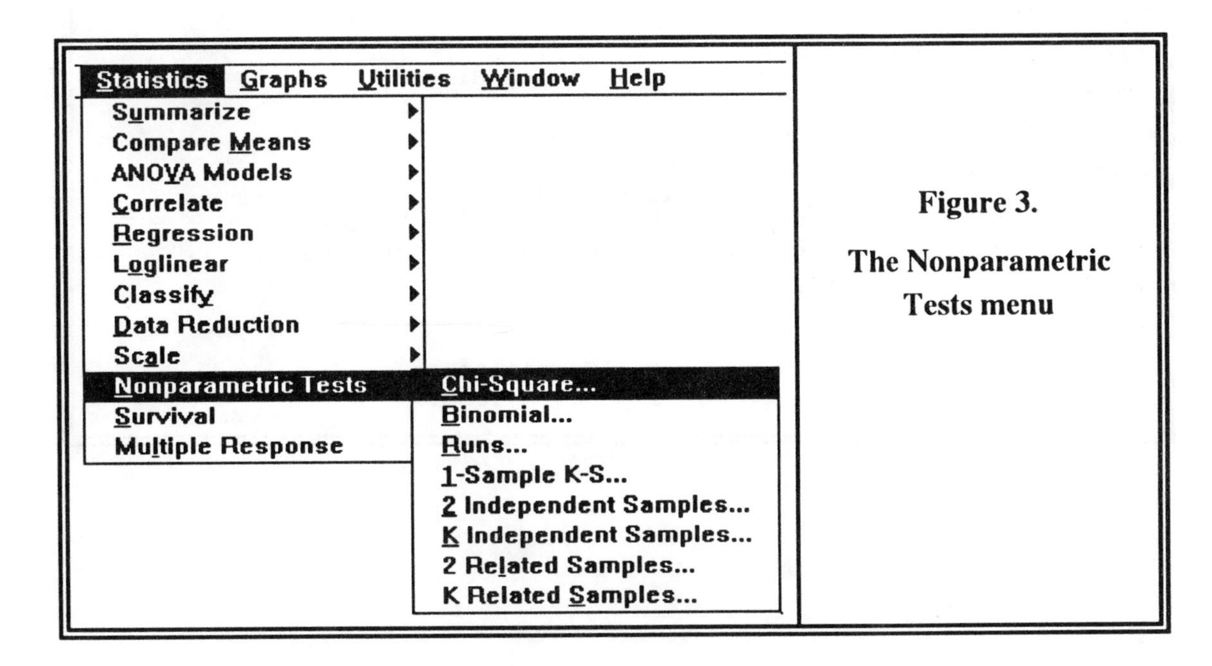

Figure 3.

The Nonparametric Tests menu

Complete the dialog box as for one-way ANOVA and click on **OK**.

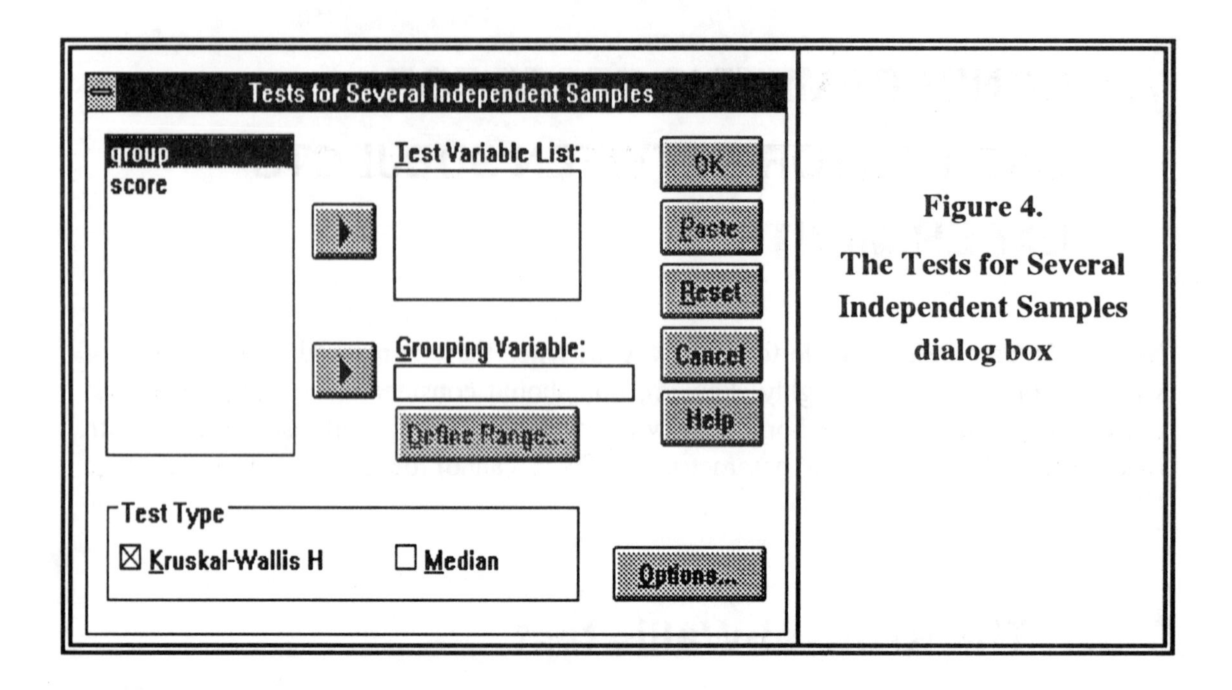

Figure 4.

The Tests for Several Independent Samples dialog box

The result of the test is shown as a value of the **Chi-Square statistic** together with its p-value in Output Listing 5 (SPSS 6 and 7).

Output Listing 5 (SPSS 6).

The Kruskal-Wallis 1-Way ANOVA output

```
Kruskal-Wallis 1-Way Anova

     SCORE
  by GROUP      Mnemonic Training History

     Mean Rank    Cases

          6.60       10    GROUP = 1    Control
         17.65       10    GROUP = 2    Mnemonic A
         22.25       10    GROUP = 3    Mnemonic B
                     --
                     30    Total

  Chi-Square         D.F.   Significance
    16.8121            2          .0002
```

Output Listing 5 (SPSS 7).

The Kruskal-Wallis 1-Way ANOVA output

Ranks

	Mnemonic Training History	N	Mean Rank
SCORE	Control	10	6.60
	Mnemonic A	10	17.65
	Mnemonic B	10	22.25
	Total	30	

Test Statistics[a,b]

	SCORE
Chi-Square	16.812
df	2
Asymp. Sig.	.000

a. Kruskal Wallis Test

b. Grouping Variable: Mnemonic Training History

The p-value (**Significance** or **Asymp. Sig.**) is much smaller than 0.01, confirming the parametric test that performance is not at the same level in all three groups.

7.3.2 Dichotomous data: Chi-square test

When data are in the binary (dichotomous) form shown in Table 2 in Chapter 5, the **chi-square test** can be used to test the null hypothesis that, in the population, there is no tendency for the problem to be solved more often in some conditions than in others. The procedure is described in Chapter 11.

SUMMARY

1) The one-way analysis of variance (ANOVA) is used for analysing data from a one-factor between subjects experiment. The test assumes that the data are normally distributed and that there is **homogeneity of variance**. Should these assumptions be violated (the homogeneity assumption is especially important), other methods are available, such as the **Kruskal-Wallis** test.

2) The procedure for **one-way ANOVA** is

   Statistics

   Compare Means

   One-Way ANOVA

3) Options include unplanned multiple pairwise comparisons, such as **Tukey's honestly significant difference (HSD)** test, and descriptive statistics.

4) For the **Kruskal-Wallis one-way ANOVA**, select

   Statistics

   Nonparametric Tests

   K Independent Samples

5) Dichotomous data can be analysed with the **chi-square test**.

CHAPTER 8

FACTORIAL EXPERIMENTS - BETWEEN SUBJECTS

8.1 INTRODUCTION

Chapter 7 was concerned with the type of experiment in which there is a single independent variable, or factor. The experimental design is shown in Table 1. In order to see whether training in the use of a mnemonic method improved recall, three groups of subjects were tested:

(1) a **Control** group, untrained in the use of any mnemonic;

(2) another group trained in the use of **Mnemonic A**;

(3) a third group trained in **Mnemonic B**.

Since the three conditions all relate to the type of mnemonic training the subjects receive, they can all be regarded as values or **levels** of a single treatment factor, Mnemonic Training History (or more briefly, Mnemonic Method).

Table 1.

Design of the Mnemonics experiment

	Mnemonic Method		
	Control	Mnemonic A	Mnemonic B
Subjects	Group 1	Group 2	Group 3

An important feature of the mnemonics experiment is that each subject performed under only one condition: that is, there were **no repeated measures**. As a result, the experiment yielded three independent samples of scores. The one-factor experiment with no repeated measures on its single factor is also known as the **completely randomised** experiment.

Now suppose that the experimenter, having divided the subjects into the three groups, splits each group into two subgroups. Both subgroups perform under the same mnemonic condition; but one subgroup is tested first thing in the morning and the other last thing at night. If there are equal numbers of subjects in all subgroups, half the subjects in the entire experiment perform while fresh and the other half while tired. This version of the experiment now has **two factors**:

(1) **Mnemonic method**, whose levels are **Control, Mnemonic A and Mnemonic B**;

(2) **Alertness**, whose levels are **Fresh** and **Tired**.

Notice that in this design, each level of either factor is to be found in combination with every level of the other factor: the two factors are said to **cross**. The design can be represented as a table in which each row or column represents a particular level of one of the treatment factors, and a **cell** of the table represents one particular treatment **combination** (Table 2). The cell on the bottom right represents the combination Tired, Mnemonic B. The participants in Group 6 were tested under that treatment combination.

Table 2.

Design from a completely randomised, two-factor experiment

	Mnemonic Method		
Alertness	Control	Mnemonic A	Mnemonic B
Fresh	Group 1	Group 2	Group 3
Tired	Group 4	Group 5	Group 6

Experiments with two or more crossed treatment factors are called **factorial** experiments. The experiment just described is a **two-factor** factorial experiment. Note also that each subject is tested under only one treatment combination: for example, a subject, having been trained in Mnemonic A and tested first thing in the morning, is not tested again in the evening. In other words, **neither factor in the experiment has repeated measures**. Factorial experiments with no repeated measures on any of their treatment factors are also termed **completely randomised factorial** experiments. Since the levels of a factor can be said to vary **between subjects**, factors with no repeated measures are called **between subjects** factors. A factorial experiment in which all factors are between subjects (i.e. have no repeated measures) is known as a **between subjects experiment**.

Table 3 shows the mean scores of the subjects tested under the six treatment combinations. The row and column means, which are known as **marginal means**, are the mean scores at each level of either factor considered separately, ignoring the other factor in the classification.

In a two-factor experiment, there are two kinds of possible treatment effects:

(1) **main effects**;

(2) an **interaction**.

If the performance level is not the same at all levels of either treatment factor (ignoring the other factor in the classification), that factor is said to have a **main effect**. For example, should the scores of those subjects tested first thing in the morning be higher than those tested at night, there would be a main effect of the Alertness factor. Looking at the marginal row means, it is clear that this is indeed the case: the Fresh subjects performed better. Turning now to the marginal column means, it is clear that performance under either mnemonic training condition was superior than under the control condition: there is a main effect of the Mnemonic Method factor.

Table 3.

Summary of the results of a two-factor experiment

Alertness	Mnemonic Method			Means
	Control	Mnemonic A	Mnemonic B	
Fresh	15	15	15	15
Tired	5	14	14	11
Means	10	14.5	14.5	13

So far, it has been seen that by looking at the marginal means alone, possible main effects can be discerned. Turning now to the cell means, however, it is clear that the data show another striking feature. If we look at the Fresh subjects only, the performance means show a flat profile: the use of a mnemonic technique failed to produce any improvement with Fresh subjects. It was quite different with the Tired subjects: without the mnemonic training, their performance was markedly lower than that of the Fresh subjects; whereas, when trained, they performed nearly as well. The performance means of the Tired subjects thus show a very uneven profile, which does not parallel that of the Fresh subjects. The effect of one treatment factor (such as Mnemonic Method) at one particular level of another factor (say Fresh subjects) is known as a **simple main effect** of that factor. In general, if we have two factors, A with levels a_1, a_2, . . ., a_a and B with levels b_1, b_2, ...,b_b, there will be two sets of simple mains effects:

(1) A at b_1, A at b_2, ..., A at b_b;

(2) B at a_1, B at a_2, ..., B at a_a,

where the upper case letters are factor labels and the lower case are the levels comprising the factors.

The factor Mnemonic Method has different simple main effects at different levels of the Alertness factor: it works strongly with Tired subjects; but it does not work at all with Fresh subjects. When one treatment factor does not have the same simple main effects at all levels of another, the two factors are said to **interact**. The analysis of variance of data from a factorial experiment offers tests for the presence not only of main effects of each factor considered separately but also of interactions between (or among) the factors.

The interaction we have just described can be pictured graphically, as plots of the cell means against mnemonic method for each of Fresh and Tired groups (see Figure 1). There is thus a **Fresh** subjects profile, which is horizontal, and a **Tired** subjects profile below it, with a different shape. The possible presence of an interaction is always indicated by profile heterogeneity across the levels of one of the factors.

Algebraically, main effects and interactions are defined as independent: it is quite possible to obtain main effects without any interaction between the factors; and it is also possible to have an interaction without any main effects.

Figure 1.

A pattern of cell means suggestive of an interaction

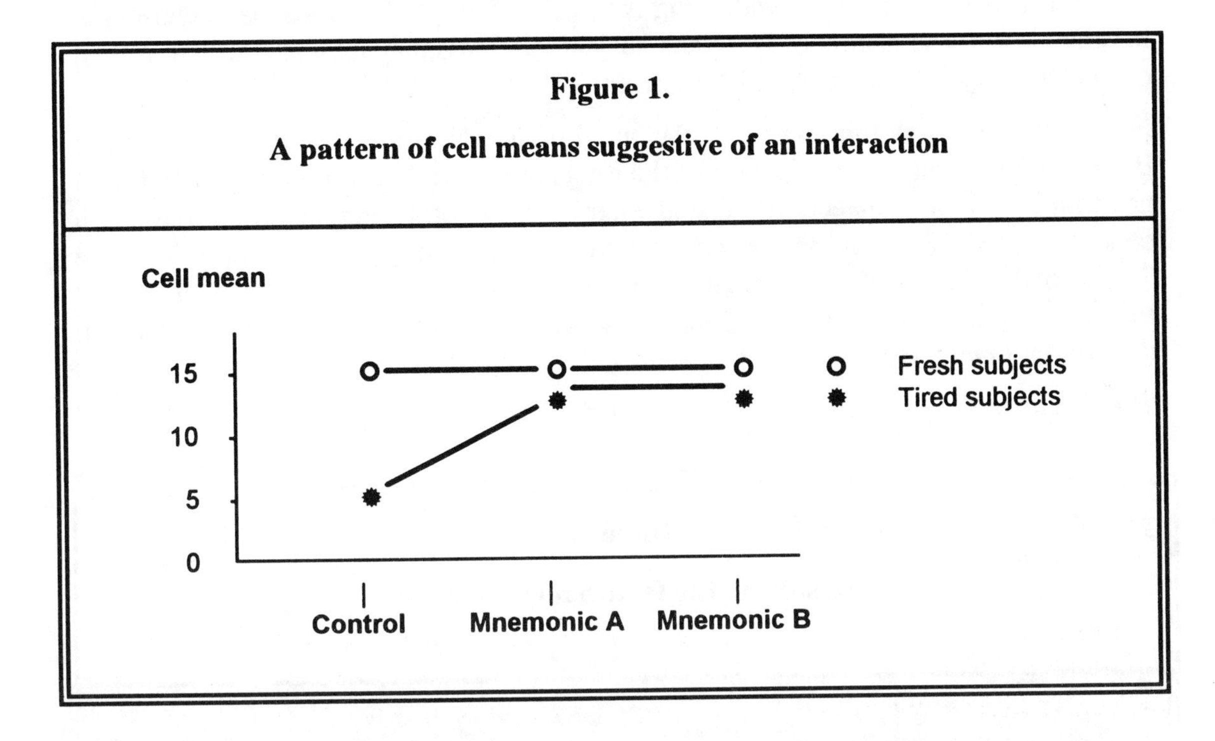

The manner in which the ANOVA tests for the presence of main effects and an interaction is lucidly described in Gravetter & Wallnau (1996, Chapter 15). If you are unfamiliar with such ANOVA terms as **sum of squares, mean square** and **degrees of freedom**, we urge you to read their chapter.

8.2 FACTORIAL ANOVA

In recent years, developments in computer graphics have given an enormous fillip to the study of **human-machine interaction**. In **driving simulation**, for example, the participant sits in a car whose controls are linked to computer-generated images of an imaginary road to create a realistic driving experience. It is thus possible to test a person's performance in heavy traffic, icy conditions, or in emergencies requiring evasive action. A researcher plans to investigate the effects upon driving performance of two new anti-hay fever drugs, A and B. It is suspected that at least one of the drugs may have different effects upon fresh and tired subjects.

The researcher decides to carry out a two-factor experiment, in which the factors are:

(1) **Drug**, with levels **Placebo**, **A**, and **B**;

(2) **Alertness**, with levels **Fresh** and **Tired**.

There is already some reason to believe that both drugs may increase the level of arousal in tired subjects, in which case their driving should improve after ingestion of either drug. With fresh subjects, however, the effects of the drugs may be rather different: it is suspected that, with Drug A at least, their performance may deteriorate. In other words, the factors of Drug and subject Alertness may interact, so that at least one of the drugs may be dangerous to drivers.

In the experiment, all subjects take a flavoured drink which contains either (in the A or B conditions) a small dosage of one of the drugs or (in the Control, Placebo condition) no drug. Half the subjects are tested after reading for twenty minutes (the Fresh condition); the other half are tested after cycling vigorously for the same time (the Tired condition). A different sample of ten subjects is tested under each of the six treatment combinations (Fresh, Control); (Fresh, A); (Fresh, B); (Tired, Control); (Tired, A); (Tired, B).

The results of the experiment are shown in Table 4.

Table 4.

Results of the factorial experiment

	Drug		
Alertness	**Placebo**	**A**	**B**
Fresh	24 25 13 22 16 23 18 19 24 26	18 8 9 14 16 15 6 9 8 17	27 14 19 29 27 23 19 17 20 25
Tired	13 12 14 16 17 13 4 3 2 6	21 24 22 23 20 13 11 17 13 16	21 11 14 22 19 9 14 11 21 18

8.2.1 Preparing the data for the factorial ANOVA

It will be necessary to use *two* **coding (grouping) variables** to indicate the treatment combination under which each score was achieved. If the coding variables are *alert* and *drug*, and performance in the driving simulator is named *drivperf*, the data file will consist of three columns, the first two for the coding variables, with the dependent variable in the third.

Define the three variables as described in Chapter 3, Section 3.5. Use the **Define Labels** dialog box to assign more meaningful names to the three variables: *Alertness*, *Drug Treatment*, and *Driving Performance* will be suitable. The **Value Labels** dialog box can be used to provide keys to the code numbers that make up the grouping variables *alert* and *drug*: in the *alert* column, the values *1* and *2* can be assigned the value labels *Fresh* and *Tired*, respectively; in the *drug* column, the values *1*, *2*, and *3* can be assigned the value labels *Placebo*, *Drug A*, and *Drug B*, respectively.

Use the cell editor to enter the data into the **Data Editor** window (Figure 2). The three values in row 1 indicate that subject 1 achieved a score of *24* while still fresh and without ingesting any drug; row 12 indicates that subject 12 achieved a score of *8* while still fresh, but having ingested a dose of Drug A. Save the file in the usual manner.

	alert	drug	drivperf
1	1	1	24
2	1	1	25
3	1	1	13
4	1	1	22
5	1	1	16
6	1	1	23
7	1	1	18
8	1	1	19
9	1	1	24
10	1	1	26
11	1	2	18
12	1	2	8

Figure 2.

Section of the Data Editor window showing some of the data from Table 4

(Each row represents one subject's score and the conditions under which it was achieved.)

8.2.2 Exploring the data: Obtaining cell means and standard deviations

Before conducting the ANOVA, it is important to explore the data by computing the cell means and standard deviations to check for any wayward distributions. This information is also useful for interpreting any significant interactions which may appear in the ANOVA summary table.

To obtain the mean performance levels under each of the six treatment combinations, choose
Statistics
 Compare Means
  Means

to open the **Means** dialog box (see Figure 14, Chapter 4). In the box on the left are the variables *alert*, *drug* and *drivperf*. Highlight *drivperf* and click on ▶ to transfer it to the **Dependent List** box. Highlight *alert* and click on ▶ to transfer it to the **Independent List** box.

Notice that the box above the **Independent List** box contains the caption **Layer 1 of 1**. So far, SPSS knows only of one layer of classification, created by classifying the dependent variable *drivperf* by the coding variable *alert*. Click the **Next** subdialog button and enter the next layer according to the grouping variable *drug*. The central caption will now read **Layer 2 of 2**, indicating that SPSS now knows of the two layers of classification. Click on **OK** to run the **Means** procedure, the output for which is shown in Output Listing 1 (SPSS 6 and 7).

Output Listing 1 (SPSS 6).

The means and standard deviations for each cell and for levels of Alert

```
                 - - Description of Subpopulations - -

Summaries of      DRIVPERF    Driving Performance
By levels of      ALERT       Alertness
                  DRUG        Drug Treatment


Variable          Value  Label                 Mean     Std Dev     Cases

For Entire Population                       16.5000      6.3846        60

ALERT                 1  Fresh              18.3333      6.3481        30
  DRUG                1  Placebo            21.0000      4.2947        10
  DRUG                2  Drug A             12.0000      4.4222        10
  DRUG                3  Drug B             22.0000      4.9441        10

ALERT                 2  Tired              14.6667      5.9731        30
  DRUG                1  Placebo            10.0000      5.6569        10
  DRUG                2  Drug A             18.0000      4.6428        10
  DRUG                3  Drug B             16.0000      4.7842        10

  Total Cases =  60
```

Unfortunately Output Listing 1 (SPSS 6) does not show the means for the levels of *drug* (i.e. for *Placebo, Drug A, Drug B*). To get those means, it is necessary to reset the dialog box and re-run it with *drivperf* as before in the **Dependent List** box but with just *drug* in the **Independent List** box.

The layout of the table in SPSS 7 is different, as shown in Output Listing 1 (SPSS 7). Here the means for the levels of *drug* are shown in the section of the table labelled **Total**.

Report

Driving Performance

Fresh	Placebo	Mean	21.00
		N	10
		Std. Deviation	4.29
	Drug A	Mean	12.00
		N	10
		Std. Deviation	4.42
	Drug B	Mean	22.00
		N	10
		Std. Deviation	4.94
	Total	Mean	18.33
		N	30
		Std. Deviation	6.35
Tired	Placebo	Mean	10.00
		N	10
		Std. Deviation	5.66
	Drug A	Mean	18.00
		N	10
		Std. Deviation	4.64
	Drug B	Mean	16.00
		N	10
		Std. Deviation	4.78
	Total	Mean	14.67
		N	30
		Std. Deviation	5.97
Total	Placebo	Mean	15.50
		N	20
		Std. Deviation	7.47
	Drug A	Mean	15.00
		N	20
		Std. Deviation	5.38
	Drug B	Mean	19.00
		N	20
		Std. Deviation	5.65
	Total	Mean	16.50
		N	60
		Std. Deviation	6.38

Output Listing 1 (SPSS 7).

The means and standard deviations for each cell and for levels of Alert

8.2.3 Choosing a factorial ANOVA

For SPSS 6, the factorial analysis of variance is executed by choosing (Figure 3)
Statistics
    ANOVA models
        Simple Factorial

to open the **Simple Factorial ANOVA** dialog box (the completed version is shown in Figure 5)

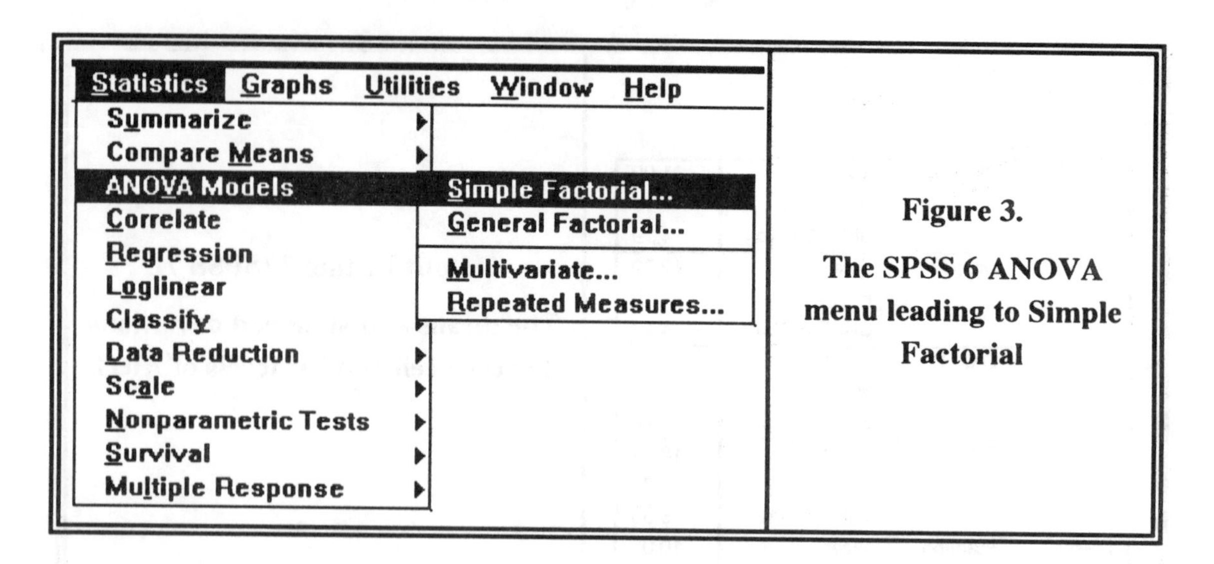

Figure 3.

The SPSS 6 ANOVA menu leading to Simple Factorial

For SPSS 7, the factorial analysis of variance is executed by choosing (Figure 4)

Statistics

General Linear Model

Simple Factorial

The Simple Factorial ANOVA dialog box is similar to that for SPSS 6 (Figure 5).

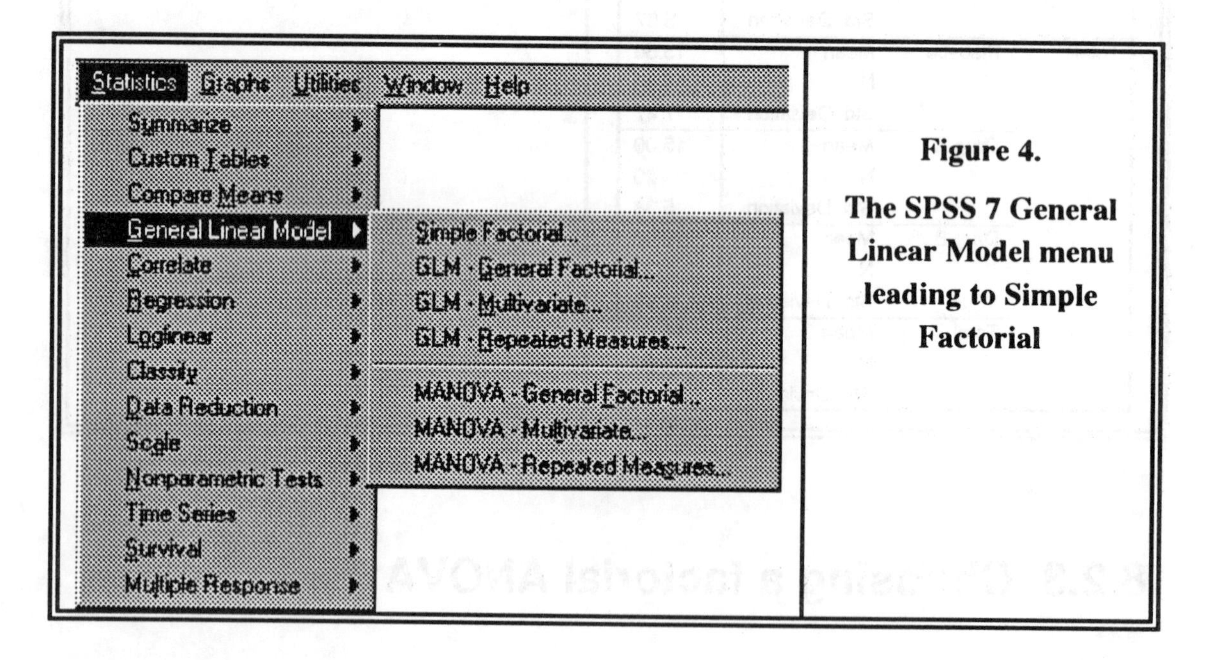

Figure 4.

The SPSS 7 General Linear Model menu leading to Simple Factorial

Complete the box in the same manner as for the Independent Samples T Test (see Chapter 6) by clicking the grouping variables into the **Factors** box and adding the minimum and maximum values of their levels using the **Define Range** box. The dependent variable is *drivperf*.

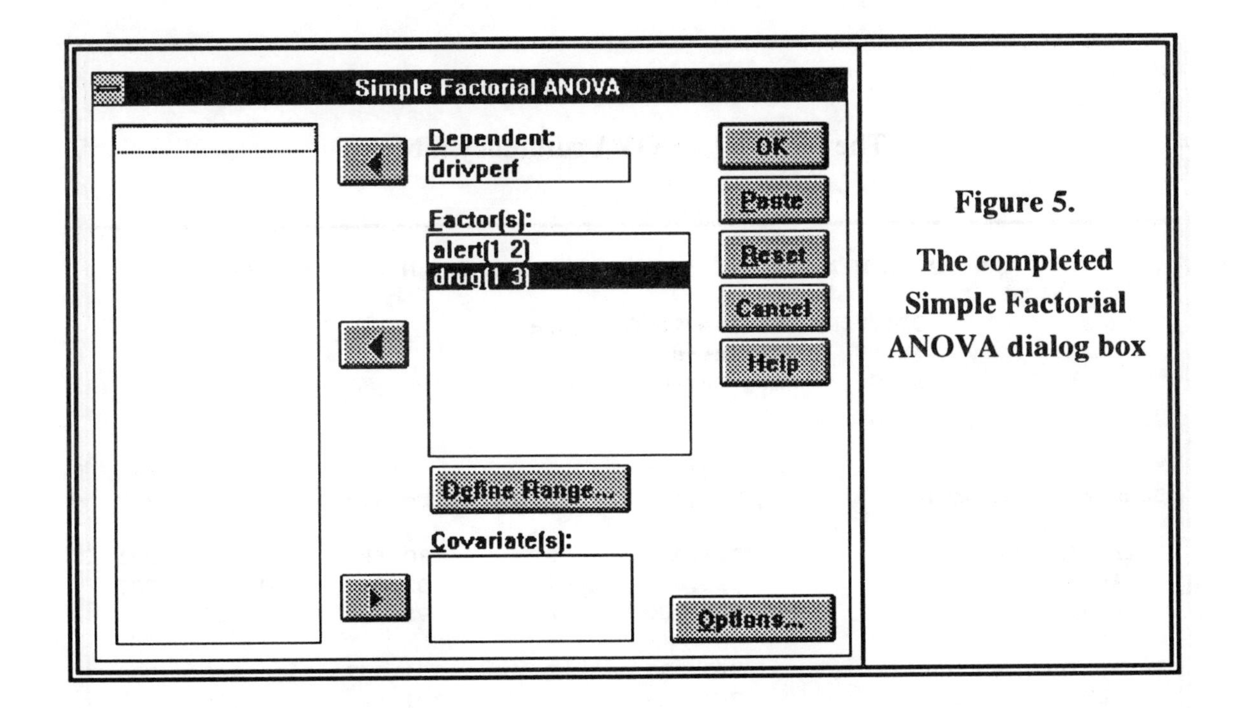

Figure 5.

The completed Simple Factorial ANOVA dialog box

8.2.4 Output listing for a factorial ANOVA

8.2.4.1 The factorial ANOVA summary table

The ANOVA table in Output Listing 2 (SPSS 6 and 7) tabulates the F ratios and their associated p-values for the main effects and the two-way interaction. The tables also include rows summing up all the **Main Effects**, all the **2-Way Interactions** (though here there is just one), and all the **Explained** variance (i.e. main effects plus interactions). Thus the remaining 'unexplained' variance is the row labelled **Residual** representing the error variance which is used as the denominator for each of the F ratios.

Note the **Signif of F** (i.e. p-value, or tail probability) value for each F ratio. There are significant main effects for both the *alert* and *drug* factors: the former is significant beyond the 0.01 level; the latter beyond the 0.05 level, but not beyond the 0.01 level. In addition to main effects of both treatment factors, there is a significant interaction. The p-value is given as *0.000*, which means that it is less than *0.0005*. Clearly, the *drug* factor has different effects upon Fresh and Tired subjects; but to ascertain the nature of these effects, we shall need to examine the pattern of the treatment means more closely.

Output Listing 2 (SPSS 6).

The factorial ANOVA summary table

```
* * *  A N A L Y S I S   O F   V A R I A N C E  * * *

         DRIVPERF Driving Performance
     by  ALERT    Alertness
         DRUG     Drug Treatment


                           Sum of                 Mean            Sig
Source of Variation        Squares      DF       Square       F   of F

Main Effects               391.667       3      130.556   5.640   .002
   ALERT                   201.667       1      201.667   8.712   .005
   DRUG                    190.000       2       95.000   4.104   .022

2-Way Interactions         763.333       2      381.667  16.488   .000
   ALERT     DRUG          763.333       2      381.667  16.488   .000

Explained                 1155.000       5      231.000   9.979   .000

Residual                  1250.000      54       23.148

Total                     2405.000      59       40.763

60 cases were processed.
```

Output Listing 2 (SPSS 7).

The factorial ANOVA summary table

ANOVA[a,b]

			Unique Method				
			Sum of Squares	df	Mean Square	F	Sig.
Driving Performance	Main Effects	(Combined)	391.667	3	130.556	5.640	.002
		Alertness	201.667	1	201.667	8.712	.005
		Drug Treatment	190.000	2	95.000	4.104	.022
	2-Way Interactions	Alertness * Drug Treatment	763.333	2	381.667	16.488	.000
	Model		1155.000	5	231.000	9.979	.000
	Residual		1250.000	54	23.148		
	Total		2405.000	59	40.763		

a. Driving Performance by Alertness, Drug Treatment

b. All effects entered simultaneously

8.2.4.2 Exploring the interaction by graphing the cell means

It is quite possible to account for the significant main effect and interaction in the ANOVA summary table by studying the patterns of the means in Output Listing 1 (SPSS 6 and 7). The overall situation will, however, emerge much more clearly from a graphical representation.

Select

Graphs

Line

which will bring the **Line Charts** dialog box into view (Figure 5).

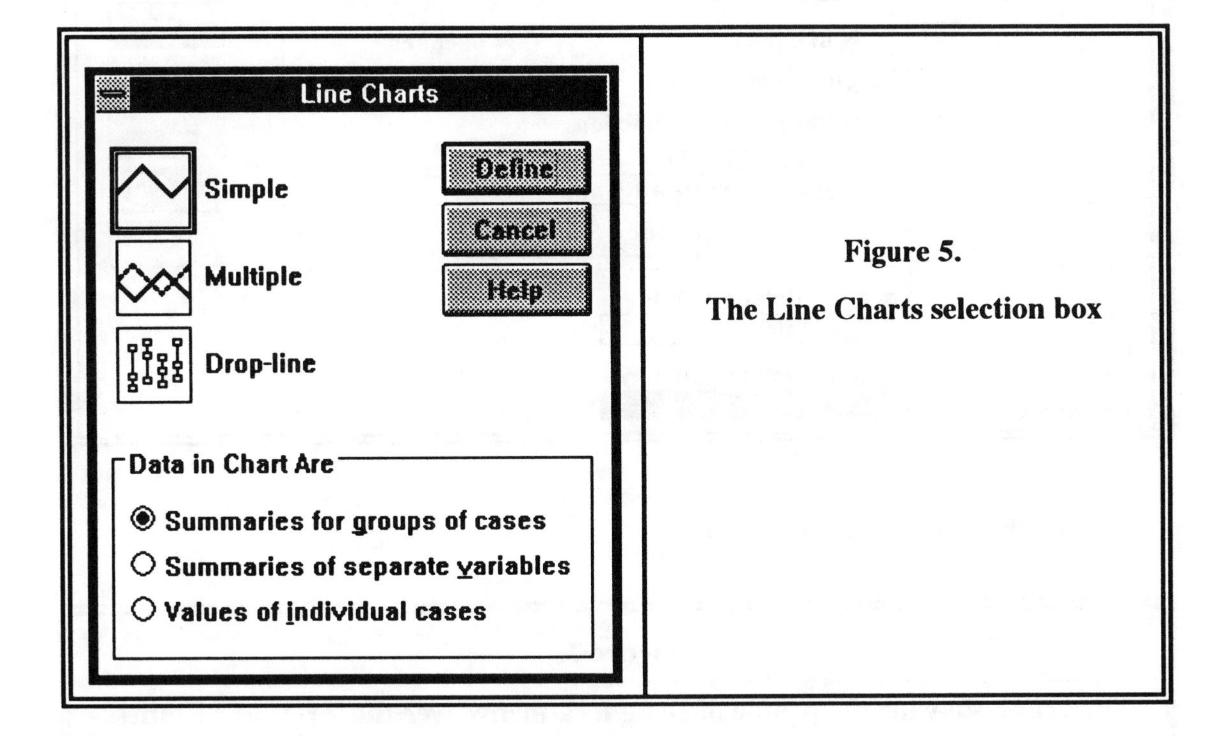

Figure 5.

The Line Charts selection box

Highlight the **Multiple** box and click on **Define** to open the **Define Multiple Line: Summaries for Groups of Cases** dialog box (the completed version is shown in Figure 6).

Within the **Lines Represent** box (Figure 6), mark the **Other Summary Function** radio button. By default, this choice selects the mean of whatever variable is entered into the **Variable** box (other functions, such as the median, can be selected by clicking on the **Change Summary** button.)

When the dialog box is first opened, the variable names are listed alphabetically by default in the panel on the left unless the **File** option for **Display Order for Variable Lists** within the **Preferences** dialog box has been previously selected (see Section 3.4.2). Since we want to plot the cell means on the dependent variable, highlight *drivperf*, click on the radio button **Other summary function** and then ▶ to make it the subject (i.e. the *argument* - the mathematical term for variable, constant or expression on which a function will be calculated) of the function **MEAN[ ]** in the **Variable** box. The entry in the **Variable** box will then appear as **MEAN[drivperf]**. Since we want to profile the three levels of the *drug* factor over the two conditions of the *alert* factor, we transfer the variable *alert* into the **Category Axis** box and the variable *drug* into the **Define Lines by** box.

Figure 6.

Part of the the Define Multiple Line: Summaries for Groups of Cases dialog box

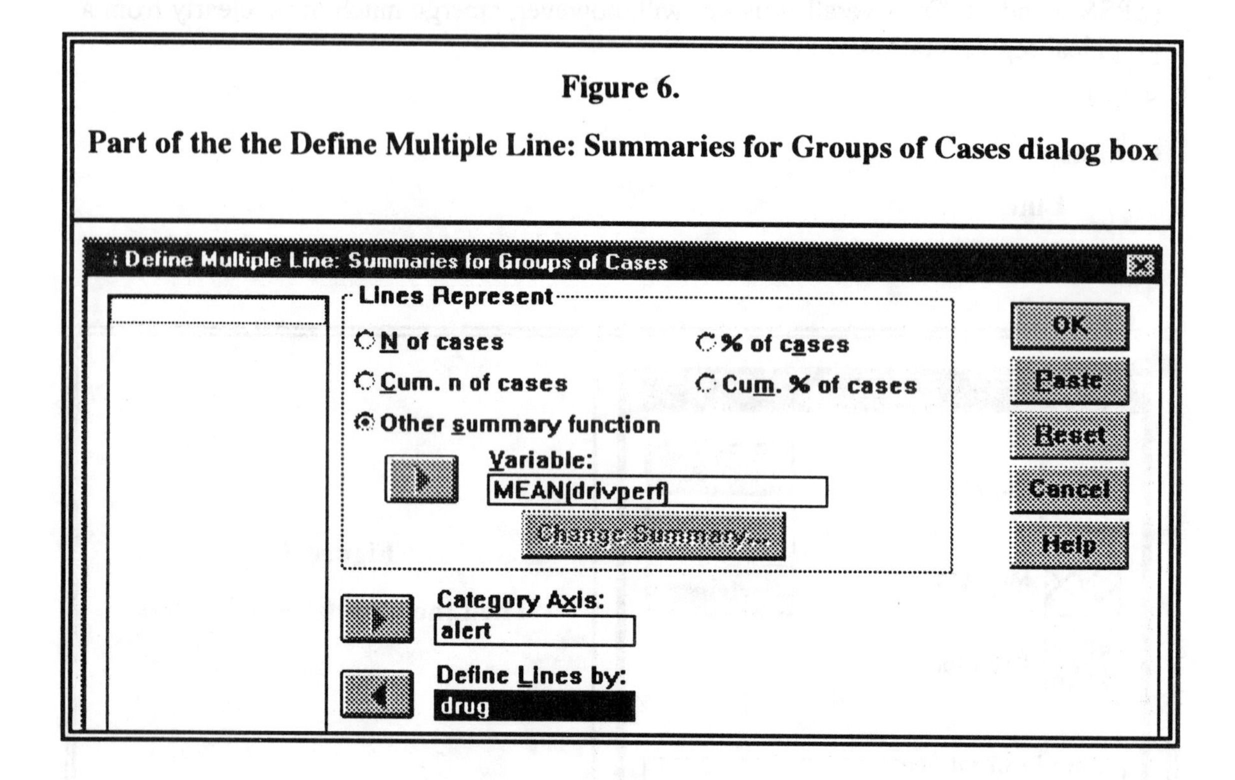

Click on **OK** to obtain the graph in Figure 7.

Figure 7.

The graph showing the profile of Drug treatments over the levels of Alertness

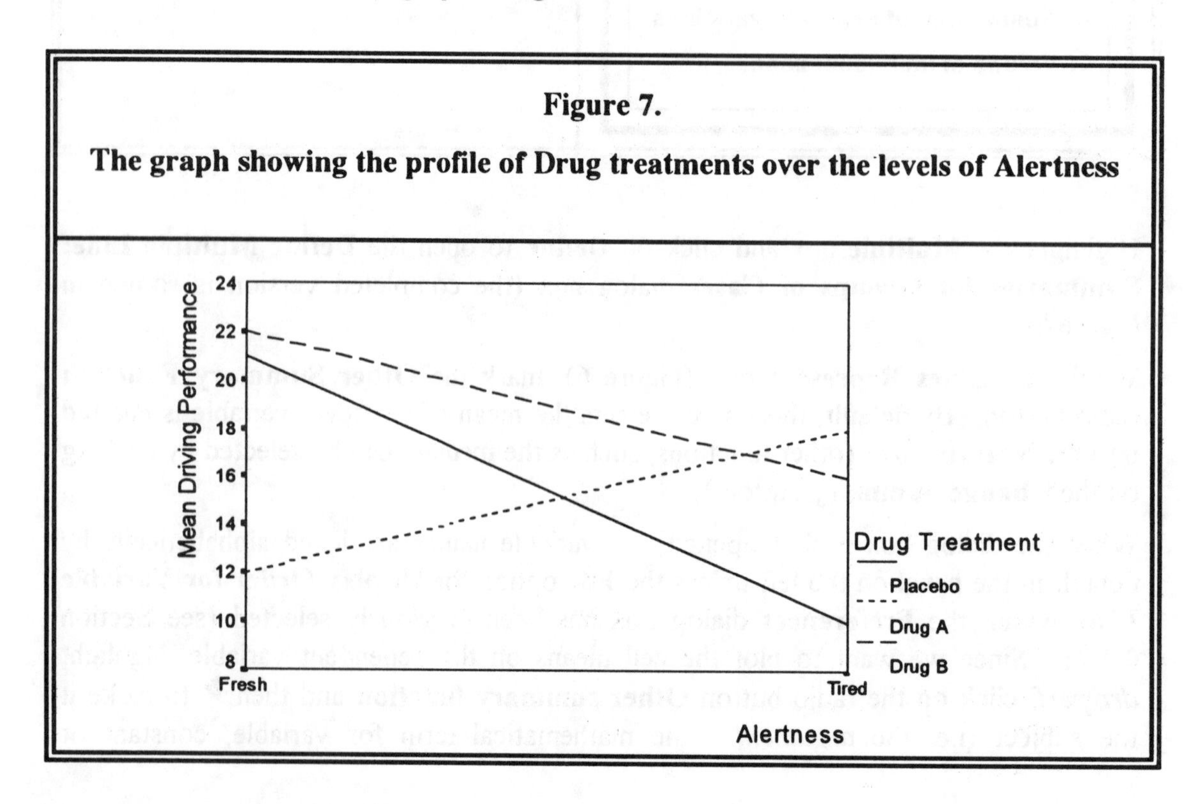

Figure 7 clearly shows several important experimental results.

(1) Alertness has a major effect on performance, as shown by the downward slope of the Placebo profile.

(2) Drug A does enhance the performance level of Tired subjects.

(3) But Drug A actually causes the performance of Fresh subjects to deteriorate.

(4) Drug B, while enhancing performance in both Fresh and Tired subjects, does not prevent performance from deteriorating as subjects become tired.

Notice that all the most interesting results from this experiment are to be found in the analysis of the cell means following the discovery of a significant interaction between the two factors Drug and Alertness. As is so often the case in factorial experiments, the presence of an interaction draws attention away from main effects (which, as we have seen, are apparent from considerations of the marginal means). In the present example, it is of relatively little interest to learn that the mean level of performance of drugged subjects is somewhat higher than that of undrugged subjects, because the three Drug profiles are so disparate. The finding that Fresh subjects outperform Tired subjects, while sensible, is hardly surprising.

Often, having made a preliminary graphical exploration of the cell means, the user will wish to make some unplanned pairwise comparisons among selected cell means to confirm the patterns evident in the graph. For example, Figure 7 suggests that the simple fact of tiredness led to a deterioration in performance. That would be confirmed should a comparison between the means for the combination (Placebo, Fresh) and (Placebo, Tired) prove significant. To confirm that Drug A actually has deleterious effect upon the performance of Fresh subjects, we should need to find a significant difference between the means for the (Placebo, Fresh) and (Drug A, Fresh) conditions. It is possible, too, that the improvement upon the performance of Fresh controls subjects achieved by Drug B may not be significant. That would be confirmed by a non-significant difference between the means for conditions (Placebo, Fresh) and (Drug B, Fresh).

Since the Alertness factor comprises only two conditions, the answer to the question of whether tiredness alone produces a significant decrement in performance is answered by a test for a **simple main effect** of Alertness at the Placebo level of the Drug factor. Tests for simple main effects are available on SPSS, but the user must know the syntax of the SPSS control language. Another approach is to perform an ANOVA only upon the data at the level of the qualifying factor concerned. If we go back to the **Data Editor**, select the data only from the Placebo condition and request a one-way ANOVA with Alertness as the single factor, we shall obtain an F of 23.99 (df = 1, 18); p = .0001. This confirms the simple main effect of Alertness at the Placebo level of the Drug factor and hence that the difference between the means for the (Placebo, Fresh) and (Placebo, Tired) conditions is indeed significant.

Some of the other questions mentioned can only be answered by directly making pairwise comparisons between specified treatment means. Since many such comparisons are possible, it is necessary to protect against inflation of the *per family* type I error rate by using a conservative method such as the **Tukey test**, described in the following section.

8.2.4.3 Unplanned multiple pairwise comparisons with Tukey's HSD test

Following a significant main effect or interaction, the user will often want to make unplanned comparisons either among the marginal means (for comparing levels in a main effect) or among the cell means (for investigating the source of an interaction).

In the present case, the ANOVA showed a significant main effect of the Drug factor, and the user would naturally wish to know which of the pairwise differences among the three treatment means are significant. Here the trick is to pretend that the experiment had only one treatment factor *drug*, and run a one-way ANOVA with the **Tukey HSD** test. Simply choose the one-way ANOVA procedure and specify the Drug factor as the independent variable, ignoring the Alertness factor.

Should an interaction prove significant (as in the present example), it will often be illuminating to make comparisons among the **cell means** rather than the marginal means. The **Tukey HSD** test can be used for inter-cell comparisons; but this time we must pretend the data are from a one-factor experiment with as many levels in its single factor as there are cell means in the original two-way table of results. To achieve this, we must construct a new coding variable *cellcode*, containing a code number for each of the combinations (*1, 1*), (*1, 2*), (*2, 1*), (*2, 2*), (*3, 1*), (*3, 2*) that coded the treatment combinations (Placebo, Fresh), (Placebo, Tired), (Drug A, Fresh), (Drug A, Tired), (Drug B, Fresh) and (Drug B, Tired).

To compute values 1 to 6 for each of these combinations in the variable *cellcode*, one method to use is the **Compute** procedure followed by the **Recode** procedure as follows:

(1) Click on **Transform** and **Compute** to obtain the **Compute Variable** dialog box (Chapter 4, Figure 27). In the **Target Variable** box, type the name of the new variable *cellcode*.

(2) Transfer *alert* with ▶ into the **Numeric Expression** box and type in *10 and +. Then transfer *drug* with ▶ into the box so that the whole expression is *alert**10 + *drug*. Click **OK** to create the new variable with values of 11, 12, 13, 21, 22 and 23.

(3) Click on **Transform, Recode** and **Into Same Variables** to obtain the **Recode into Same Variables** dialog box. Transfer cellcode with ▶ into the **Variables** box. Click on **Old and New Values** box and then build up a list of 11→1, 12→2, 13→3, 21→4, 22→5, 23→6 in the **Old→New** box using the procedure described in Section 4.4.3. Click **Continue** and then **OK** to effect these changes in the variable *cellcode*. You can check that this has been done by inspecting the **Data Editor** window.

Now simply run the **one-way ANOVA** procedure, with *drivperf* as the dependent variable and *cellcode* as the independent variable with levels 1 to 6, opting for the **Tukey HSD** test.

It is clear from the HSD Output Listing 3 (SPSS 6 and 7) that Group 4 (Tired, Placebo) differs significantly from Groups 1 (Fresh, Placebo), 3 (Fresh, Drug B) and 5 (Tired, Drug A), and that Group 2 (Fresh, Drug A) differs from Group 1 (Fresh, Placebo) and Group 3 (Fresh, Drug B).

```
                              G G G G G G
                              r r r r r r
                              p p p p p p

                              4 2 6 5 1 3
    Mean      CELLCODE

  10.0000     Grp 4
  12.0000     Grp 2
  16.0000     Grp 6
  18.0000     Grp 5           *
  21.0000     Grp 1           * *
  22.0000     Grp 3           * *
```

Output Listing 3 (SPSS 6).

Part of Tukey HSD listing for the interaction of *drug* and *alert*

Output Listing 3 (SPSS 7).

Part of Tukey HSD listing for the interaction of *drug* and *alert*

Multiple Comparisons

Dependent Variable: Driving Performance
Tukey HSD

(I) CELLCODE	(J) CELLCODE	Mean Difference (I-J)	Std. Error	Sig.	95% Confidence Interval Lower Bound	Upper Bound
1	2	9.00*	2.152	.001	2.64	15.36
	3	-1.00	2.152	.997	-7.36	5.36
	4	11.00*	2.152	.000	4.64	17.36
	5	3.00	2.152	.730	-3.36	9.36
	6	5.00	2.152	.203	-1.36	11.36
2	1	-9.00*	2.152	.001	-15.36	-2.64
	3	-10.00*	2.152	.000	-16.36	-3.64
	4	2.00	2.152	.937	-4.36	8.36
	5	-6.00	2.152	.075	-12.36	.36
	6	-4.00	2.152	.438	-10.36	2.36
3	1	1.00	2.152	.997	-5.36	7.36
	2	10.00*	2.152	.000	3.64	16.36
	4	12.00*	2.152	.000	5.64	18.36
	5	4.00	2.152	.438	-2.36	10.36
	6	6.00	2.152	.075	-.36	12.36
4	1	-11.00*	2.152	.000	-17.36	-4.64
	2	-2.00	2.152	.937	-8.36	4.36
	3	-12.00*	2.152	.000	-18.36	-5.64
	5	-8.00*	2.152	.006	-14.36	-1.64
	6	-6.00	2.152	.075	-12.36	.36
5	1	-3.00	2.152	.730	-9.36	3.36
	2	6.00	2.152	.075	-.36	12.36
	3	-4.00	2.152	.438	-10.36	2.36
	4	8.00*	2.152	.006	1.64	14.36
	6	2.00	2.152	.937	-4.36	8.36
6	1	-5.00	2.152	.203	-11.36	1.36
	2	4.00	2.152	.438	-2.36	10.36
	3	-6.00	2.152	.075	-12.36	.36
	4	6.00	2.152	.075	-.36	12.36
	5	-2.00	2.152	.937	-8.36	4.36

*. The mean difference is significant at the .05 level.

8.2.4.4 Unplanned multiple comparisons following the ANOVA of complex factorial experiments: Some cautions and caveats

In considering the making of unplanned multiple comparisons to explore a significant interaction, we have touched upon a difficult area, abounding in disagreement. The reader will look in vain, in the writings of the most respected statistical authorities, for a set of rules and procedures on which there is complete consensus. Few, however, would dispute the following statements.

(1) The making of unplanned multiple comparisons (and other *a posteriori* analyses following the initial ANOVA) carries a heightened risk of type I error, that is, obtaining a significant difference (or pattern) which has merely arisen through sampling variability. In factorial experiments, that is, there is a heightened risk of **capitalising upon chance**. Accordingly, the user must take precautions to prevent the *per family* (or experiment-wise) error rate from rising to unacceptable levels.

(2) The more complex the experiment (that is, the more factors there are and the more levels each factor has), the greater the risk of capitalising upon chance and so producing type I errors.

(3) The risks of capitalising upon chance are greatly increased if the researcher follows an indiscriminate dredging strategy, whereby every possible statistical test is automatically carried out: simple main effects of A at the various levels of B, simple effects of B at the different levels of A, comparisons between very possible pair of cell means, and so on. We have seen that only some comparisons are informative. In the present example, for instance, we should learn little from a comparison of (Placebo, Tired) with (Drug A, Fresh), because it would be impossible to say whether the Drug or the Alertness factor was responsible for the difference.

(4) Whatever strategy one adopts, formal testing should be driven by considerations of theory and the meaningfulness, rather than a desire to milk every data set to the maximum possible extent in the hope of finding significance somewhere.

The **Tukey test** (described in 8.2.4.3) assumes that every possible paired comparison will be made. Since, however, the discriminating user will only wish to make selected comparisons, it may be felt that the Tukey test is unduly conservative. Certainly, with more complex factorial designs, with many treatment combinations, the Tukey criterion for a significant difference is a very exacting one. For this reason, some authors (e.g. Keppel, 1973; p244) suggest that a preliminary test for a simple main effect can justify defining the comparison family more narrowly, and carrying out a Tukey test only on the means relating to the simple main effect concerned. For example, returning to our current example of the effects of drugs upon fresh and tired subjects, the significant ANOVA interaction could be followed by tests of the simple main effects of the Drug factor at the Fresh and Tired levels of the Alertness factor. Since there is a significant simple main effect of Drug at the Placebo level of Alertness, we can enter the table of critical values of the **Studentized Range Statistic** with (number of means) = 3, instead of 6.

8.3 EXPERIMENTS WITH MORE THAN TWO TREATMENT FACTORS

SPSS can readily be used to analyse data from more complex factorial experiments, with three or more treatment factors. We should warn the reader, however, that experiments with more than three factors should be avoided, because interpretation of complex interactions involving four or more factors is often extremely difficult.

The ANOVA of data from an experiment with three or more factors, however, is simple on SPSS: it is only necessary to remember that a grouping variable is needed for each factor.

SUMMARY

1) This chapter has considered the analysis of variance of data from a two-factor factorial experiment, with no repeated measures. The use of the technique assumes normality of distribution and homogeneity of cell variance.

2) The **factorial ANOVA** procedures test for the presence of a **main effect** of each factor considered separately and for an **interaction** between the factors. A factor is said to have a **main effect** if performance is not the same at all levels. Two factors are said to **interact** if the effect of either is heterogeneous across the levels of the other factor. The effect of one treatment factor at one particular level of another factor is known as a **simple main effect**.

3) For a factorial **ANOVA** with SPSS 6, choose

   Statistics

   ANOVA models

   Simple Factorial

   or with SPSS 7, choose

   Statistics

   General Linear Model

   Simple Factorial

4) Graphs of means can be drawn by choosing

   Graphs

   Line

   Multiple

5) **Simple main effects** can be explored by analysing one factor at just one level of another factor using

   Compare Means

   One-Way ANOVA.

CHAPTER 9

WITHIN SUBJECTS EXPERIMENTS

9.1 INTRODUCTION

In Chapter 7, a one-factor between subjects experiment was described, in which the recall of a text by three groups of subjects was compared, each group being tested at a different level of the treatment factor (Mnemonic Training History). In another type of experiment, however, it might be feasible to have just one sample of subjects, and to test each subject under all the conditions making up the treatment factor, assuming that there are no carry-over effects between the treatments. In that case, the experiment could be described as a **one-factor within subjects experiment** or as a **one-factor experiment with repeated measures**.

For example, suppose that in a study of performance, the independent variable is Task Complexity, with three levels: Simple, Medium and High. The experimental design is shown in Table 1.

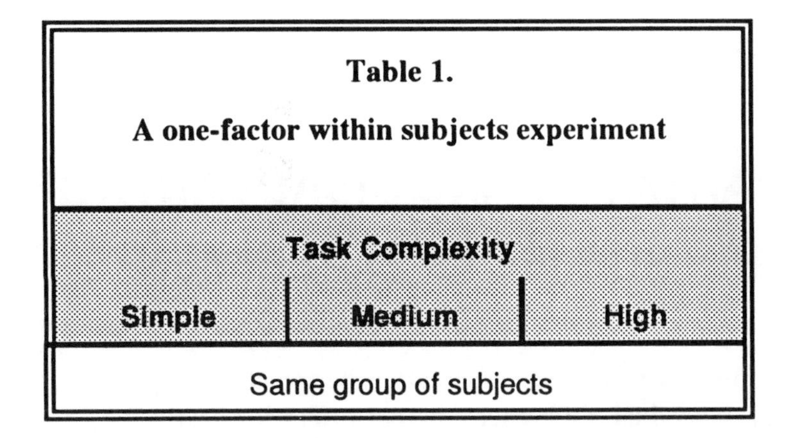

Table 1.

A one-factor within subjects experiment

Task Complexity		
Simple	Medium	High
Same group of subjects		

The same design, however, can be represented somewhat differently, as in Table 2.

Table 2.

Another representation of the design shown in Table 1

	Task Complexity		
	Simple	Medium	High
Subject 1	–	–	–
Subject 2	–	–	–
...	...	...	...
Subject 30	–	–	–

In each row, the dashes represent the scores that one particular subject achieves under the three conditions. It can be seen from Table 2 that, although there is just one treatment factor (Complexity), the design could be thought of as having two factors:

(1) the **Treatment factor** (with 3 levels);

(2) **subjects**, with 30 levels (if there are 30 subjects in the experiment).

Moreover, the two factors, Treatment and Subjects, **cross** each level of either factor is to be found in combination with every level of the other. The one-factor within subjects design, in fact, resembles a two-factor between subjects experiment (Chapter 8) with just one observation in each cell. For this reason, the one-factor within subjects experiment is sometimes termed a **subjects by treatments** experiment.In this chapter, we shall consider only the analysis of experiments that have repeated measures on **all** their treatment factors. In principle, as with between subjects experiments, there can be any number of treatment factors.

9.2 ADVANTAGES AND DISADVANTAGES OF WITHIN SUBJECTS EXPERIMENTS

A potential problem with between subjects experiments (Chapters 7 & 8) is that if there are large individual differences in performance, searching for a meaningful pattern in the data is like trying to listen to a radio programme against a background crackle of interference. For example, in the Mnemonics Methods experiment described in Chapter 7, some of the scores obtained by subjects in the control condition may well be higher than those of subjects who were trained to use a mnemonic. This is because there are some people who, when asked to read through a long list, can, **without any training at all**, reproduce most of the items accurately; whereas others, even after training, would recall very few items. Individual differences, therefore, can introduce considerable **noise** into the data from between subjects experiments.

Essentially, the within subjects experiment uses each subject as his/her own control; and the crossed nature of the design makes it possible to separate the variance that has resulted from the manipulation of the treatment factor from that arising from individual differences.

Another drawback with the between subjects experiment is that it is wasteful of subjects: if the experimental procedure is a short one, a subject may spend more time travelling to and from the place of testing than actually performing the experiment. The great appeal of the within subjects experiment is that much more extensive use can be made of the subject who has taken the trouble to attend.

In summary, therefore, the within subjects experiment has two advantages over the between subjects experiment:

(1) It cuts down data noise.

(2) It makes more efficient use of time and resources.

Nevertheless, the within subjects experiment also has disadvantages, which in some circumstances can outweigh considerations of convenience and maximising the signal-to-noise ratio. In designing an experiment, it is essential to try to ensure that the independent variable does not co-vary with an unwanted, or **extraneous** variable, so that the effects of the two are entangled, or **confounded**.

Suppose the mnemonics experiment had been of a within subjects design, and that each subject had first performed under the control condition, then under Mnemonic A and finally under Mnemonic B. Perhaps the improvement under mnemonic A was simply a **practice effect**: the more lists one learns, the better one becomes at learning lists. A practice effect is one kind of **carry-over effect**.

Carry-over effects do not always have a positive effect upon performance: recall of the items in a list is vulnerable to interference from items in previous lists. Carry-over effects may depend upon the sequence of conditions. For example, while performance under Mnemonic A may be unaffected by previous performance under the control condition, the converse may not be true: it may be difficult for subjects who have been trained in the use of a mnemonic to cease to use it on demand. This is an example of an **order effect**. Carry-over and order effects can act as extraneous, confounding variables, making it impossible to interpret the results of a within subjects experiment.

One approach to the problem of carry-over effects and order effects is the procedure known as **counterbalancing**, whereby the order of presentation of the conditions making up a within subjects factor is varied from subject to subject, in the hope that carry-over and order effects will balance out across conditions. Counterbalancing is not always sensible, however, as in the mnemonics experiment, where (as we have seen) it would make little sense to have the control condition coming last. These matters must be carefully considered before deciding to perform an experiment with repeated measures on its treatment factors.

An additional problem with a within subjects design is that if there is **heterogeneity of covariance** (see next section), there is a heightened risk of statistical error. Covariance is a measure of statistical association between two variables: the Pearson correlation discussed in Chapter 11 is the covariance between two variables that have been standardised (i.e. they have means of zero and standard deviations of unity).

9.3 WITHIN SUBJECTS ANOVA WITH SPSS

To perform a univariate within subjects ANOVA on SPSS, the user in SPSS 6 must turn to the **ANOVA Models** and select **Repeated Measures...** or in SPSS 7 to **General Linear Model** and select **GLM - Repeated Measures...** or **MANOVA - Repeated Measures...**.

The choice in SPSS 7 allows the user slightly different options. The GLM version does not have an option for suppressing the multivariate output (to be explained below) though the univariate tables in the Output Navigator are easily selected out from the rest of the output. The Output Navigator automatically presents the **Epsilon corrected averaged F** test (i.e. the **Greenhouse-Geisser epsilon)** and all the output is nicely tabulated. The MANOVA - Repeated Measures version has the same options and output layout as in the SPSS 6 version. On balance, we recommend the GLM version, mainly for the clarity of its output.

All these within subjects options are based on SPSS's MANOVA (Multivariate ANOVA) program, even though the experimental design is not technically a multivariate one (i.e. having more than one DV), because initially the program treats the responses to the levels of the within subjects IV as separate DVs. Provided the factor levels are all linked with the name of a within subjects factor, the output will include a univariate within subjects ANOVA. Unfortunately, however, the output contains other statistics pertaining to multivariate analysis which may be unfamiliar to readers used to the univariate F test in ANOVA. We strongly recommend readers who wish to deepen their understanding of the topic to study the readable text by Tabachnick & Fidell (1996).

It is important to be aware that the model underlying the use of the within subjects univariate ANOVA specifies certain additional requirements, over and above those required for between subjects experiments. The most important of these is that the correlations among the scores at the various levels of the within subjects factor are homogeneous (i.e. the off-diagonal elements of the variance-covariance matrix are constant). This requirement is known as the assumption of **homogeneity of covariance** (or **sphericity).** If this assumption is violated, the true type I error rate (i.e. the probability of rejecting H_0 when it is true) may be greatly inflated.

The SPSS MANOVA program tests for homogeneity of covariance with the **Mauchly sphericity test**. Should the data fail the sphericity test (i.e. p-value < 0.05), the ANOVA F test can be modified to make it more conservative. The **Greenhouse-Geisser** test, available as an option (referred to as the **Epsilon corrected averaged F)** within one of the dialog boxes, reduces the degrees of freedom of the numerator and denominator of the F test by multiplying the original degrees of freedom values by a factor **e**, the value of which is given in the SPSS output under **Greenhouse-Geisser epsilon**. (The value of F remains the same as before: only the degrees of freedom are reduced.) For a helpful discussion, see Howell (1997: Chapter 14).

9.4 A ONE-FACTOR WITHIN SUBJECTS ANOVA

9.4.1 Some experimental results

In an experiment on aesthetics, each subject was asked to produce three pictures using just one of three different materials for any one picture: Crayons, Paints or Felt-tip pens. The data are shown in Table 3.

The dependent variable was the Rating a picture received from a panel of judges. The independent variable was the type of implement used to produce the picture. Since the subjects would certainly vary in artistic ability, it was decided to ask each to produce three pictures, one with each type of implement. In an attempt to neutralise order effects, the order of implements was counterbalanced across subjects. This is a one-factor within subjects experiment. Alternatively, it could be described as a **one-factor experiment with repeated measures** or a **subjects by treatments** experiment.

Table 3.

Results of a one-factor within subjects experiment

	Implement		
	Crayon	Paint	Felt-tip
s1	10	12	14
s2	18	10	16
s3	20	15	16
s4	12	10	12
s5	19	20	21
s6	25	22	20
s7	18	16	17
s8	22	18	18
s9	17	14	12
s10	23	20	18

9.4.2 Entering the data

When entering the data of Table 3 into the SPSS Data Editor Grid, no grouping (code) variable is required, since the subject sample as a whole has not been divided into groups. Using the procedures described in Section 3.4, define the variables *crayon*, *paint*, and *felttip*, and enter the data of Table 3 into three columns.

9.4.3 Exploring the data: Boxplots for within subjects factors

To draw boxplots of within subjects factors, it is necessary to change the radio button option within the first **Boxplot** dialog box to **Summaries of separate variables** before clicking on the **Define** box (Figure 1).

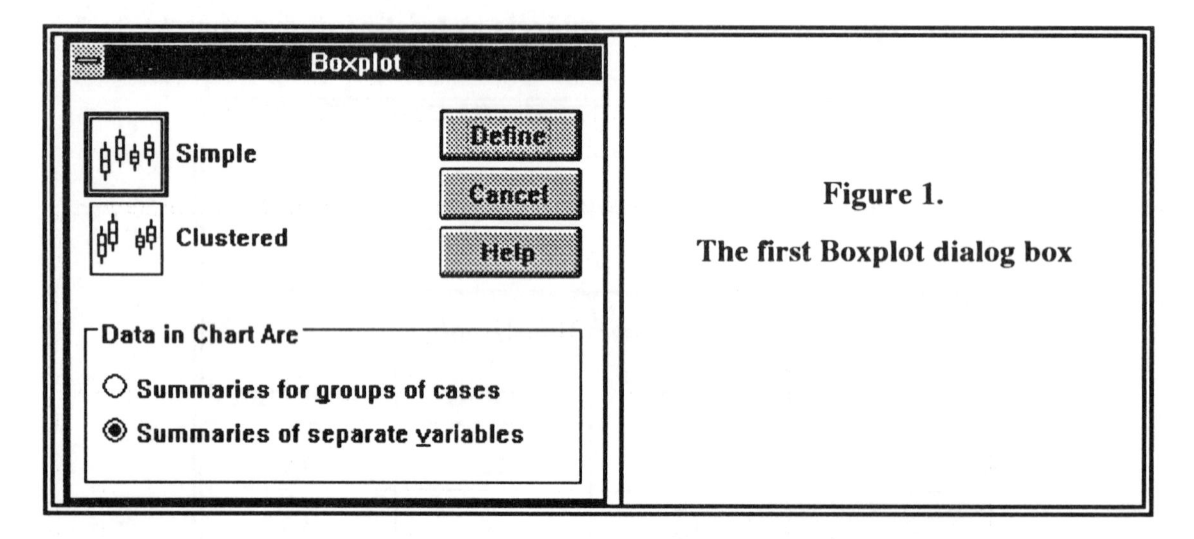

Figure 1.

The first Boxplot dialog box

Click on **Define** to open the **Define Simple Boxplot** dialog box (Figure 2).

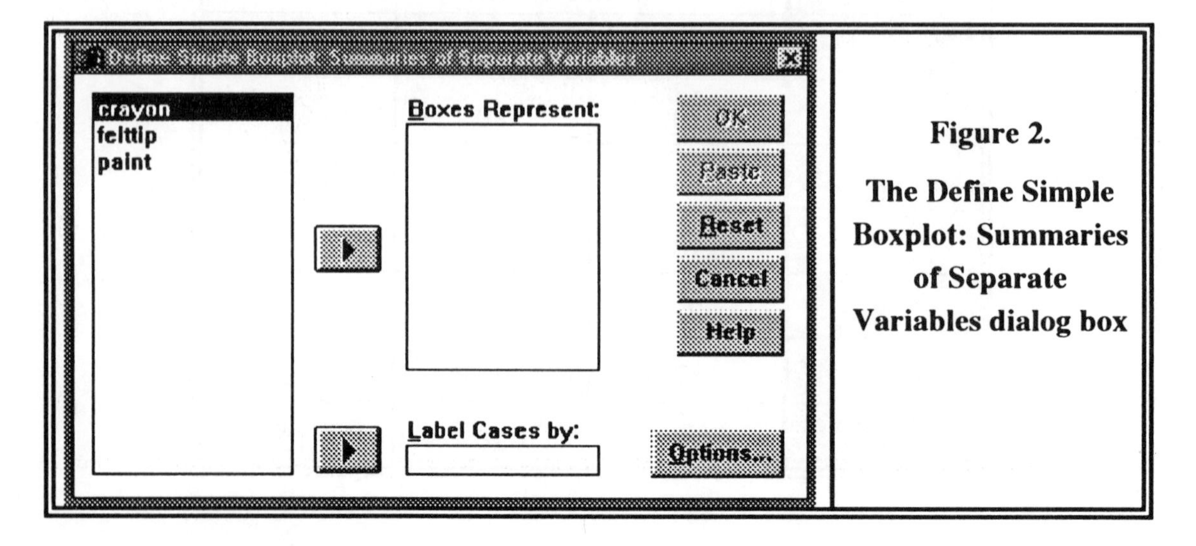

Figure 2.

The Define Simple Boxplot: Summaries of Separate Variables dialog box

When the **Define Simple Boxplot: Summaries of Separate Variables** dialog box appears (Figure 2), the variable names are normally listed in alphabetical order in the left-hand box (unless the default setting of **Alphabetical** has been changed to **File** in the **Display Order for Variable Lists** within the **Preferences** dialog box - see Section 3.4.2 - in which case they will appear in the order of the columns in the Data Editor). Transfer them one at a time in the sequence desired for the boxplot diagram.

The edited boxplot is shown in Figure 3. The figure was edited to improve reproduction clarity by replacing the default black shading of the boxes by white, making the box borders black, and adding a diagonal shading.

To make these changes, click on the **Edit** box, highlight the boxes by clicking on one of them so that each corner has little black squares, and click on the colour icon (a picture of a crayon) to open the **Colors** dialog box. By changing the **Fill** colour to white and the **Border** colour to black, and then clicking on the **Apply** box, the black boxes will change to white boxes surrounded by black borders. Finally click on **Close** to remove the **Colors** dialog box. With the boxes still selected, click on the shadings icon next to the colour icon to open the **Fill Patterns** dialog box, select the desired pattern, click on **Apply** and then on **Close**. After completing this alteration, click anywhere in the Chart window to turn off the box highlighting.

Remember that it is always necessary to select the aspect of a figure that is to be edited by clicking on the aspect before any of the editing options will work. Failure to do this will result in the **Apply** box of an editing dialog box remaining inoperative.

Figure 3.

Boxplots of within subjects data

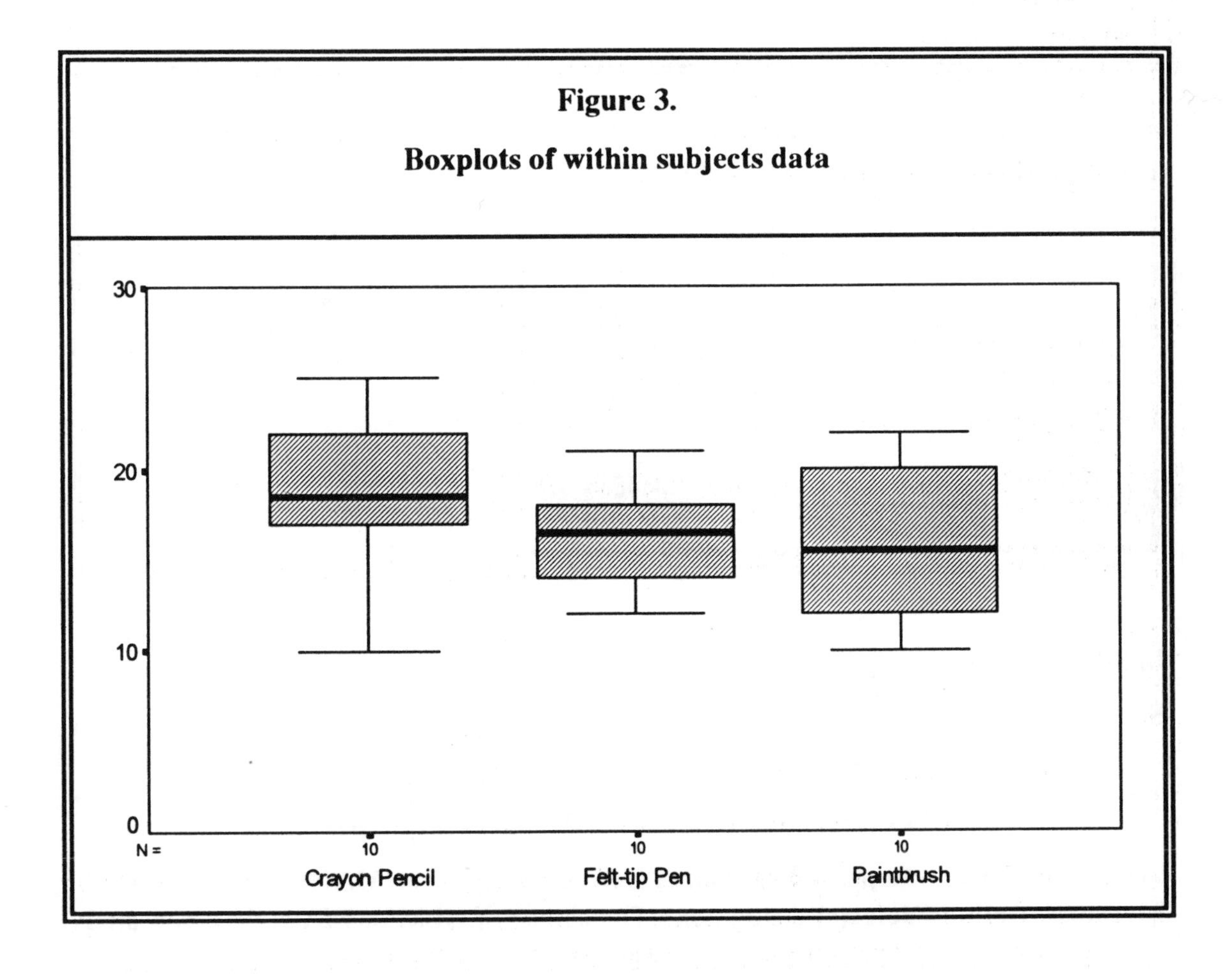

9.4.4 Running the within subjects ANOVA

In SPSS 6, select the **Repeated Measures** item from the **ANOVA Models** menu (Figure 4) by choosing

Statistics

    ANOVA Models

        Repeated Measures

to open the **Repeated Measures Define Factor(s)** dialog box (Figure 5).

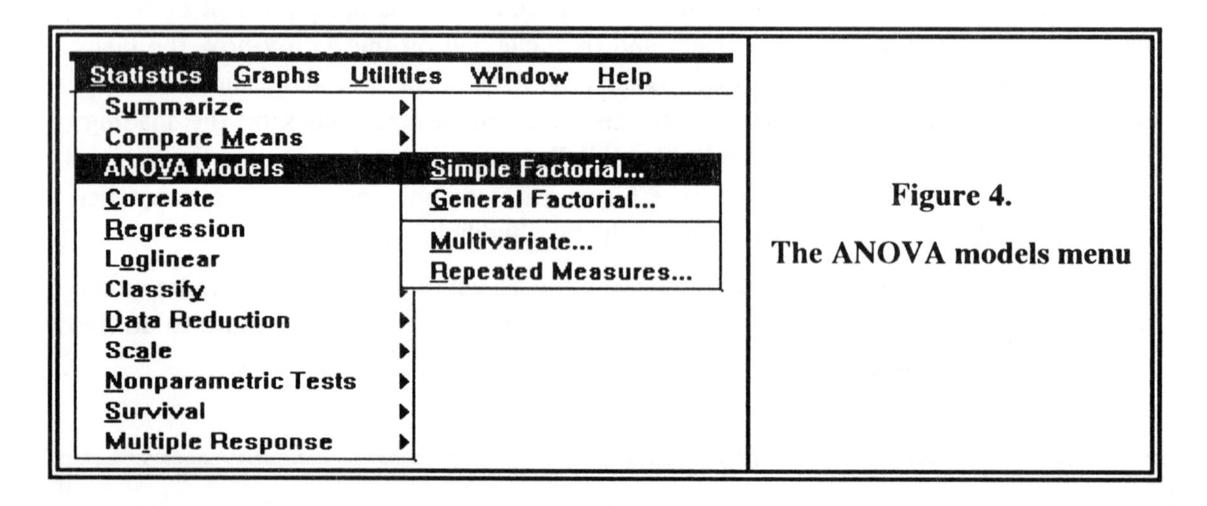

Figure 4.

The ANOVA models menu

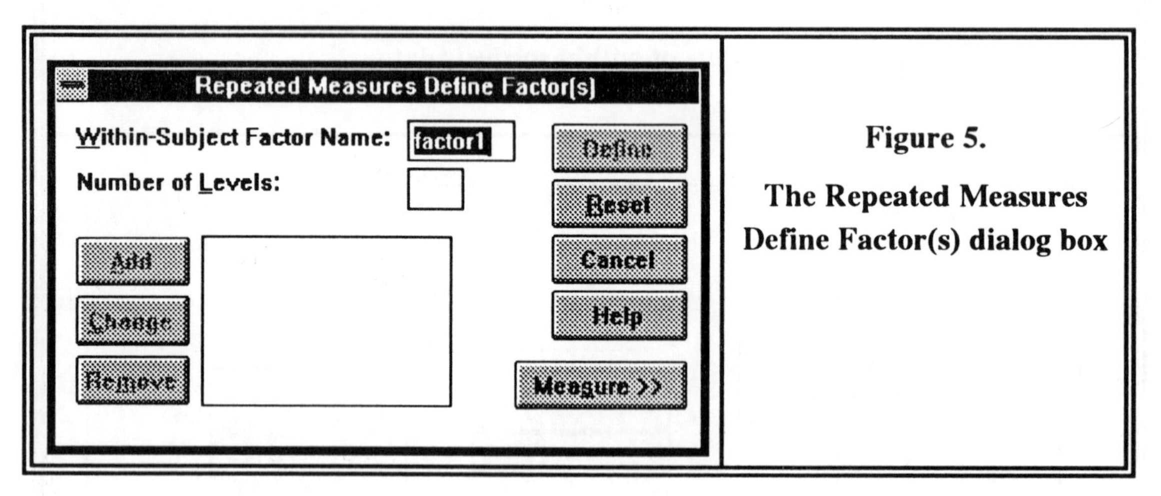

Figure 5.

The Repeated Measures Define Factor(s) dialog box

In SPSS 7, select

Statistics

    General Linear Model

        GLM - Repeated Measures or **MANOVA - Repeated Measures**

to open the **GLM - Repeated Measures Define Factor(s)** or **MANOVA - Repeated Measures Define Factor(s)** dialog box. The choice of GLM or MANOVA Repeated

Measures depends on the considerations outlined in Section 9.3, but we recommend the GLM version. The subsequent dialog boxes are similar to those for SPSS 6.

In the **Within-Subject Factor Name** box, delete *factor1* and type in a generic name (such as *implem*), bearing in mind that the new name must not be that of any of the variables in the data set; moreover, it must not exceed 8 characters in length. In the **Number of Levels** box, type the number of conditions (*3*) making up the Implement factor. Click on **Add** to paste the factor name and number of levels into the lowest box (Figure 6).

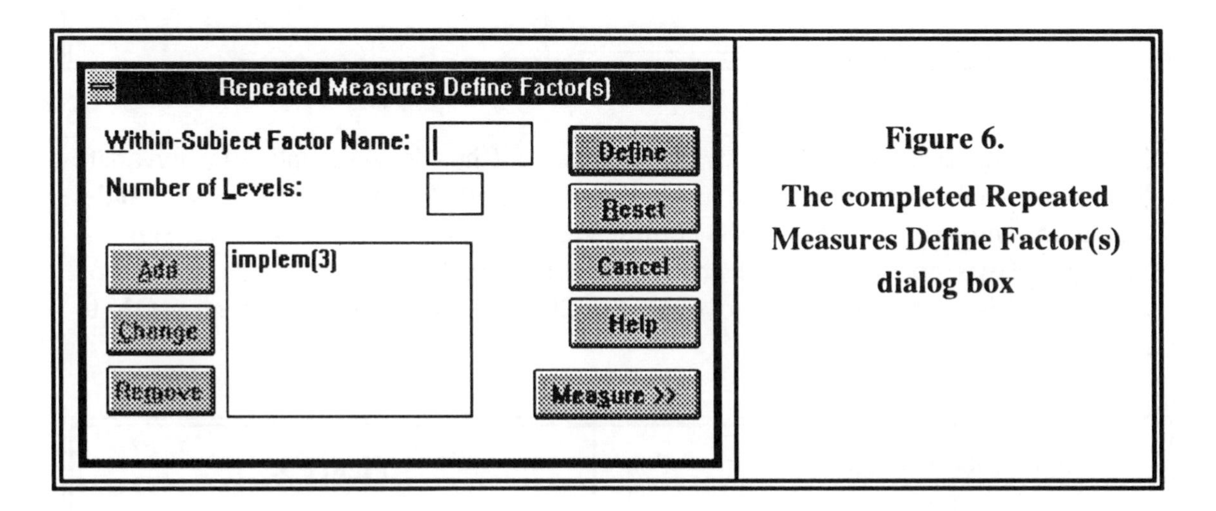

Figure 6.

The completed Repeated Measures Define Factor(s) dialog box

Click on **Define** to open the **Repeated Measures ANOVA** dialog box (Figure 7).

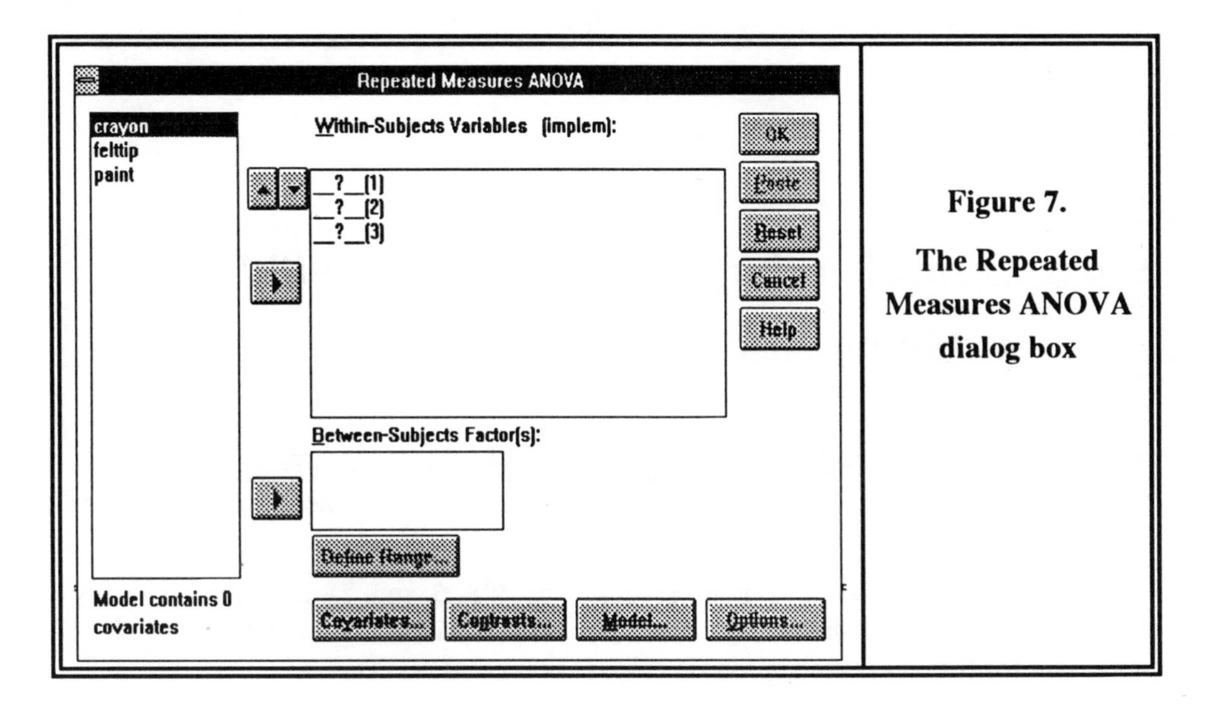

Figure 7.

The Repeated Measures ANOVA dialog box

Click-and-drag the arrowhead cursor down all three variables to select them and click on ▶ to transfer them into the box labelled **Within-Subjects Variables [implem]**. The question marks will be replaced by the variable names as shown in Figure 8.

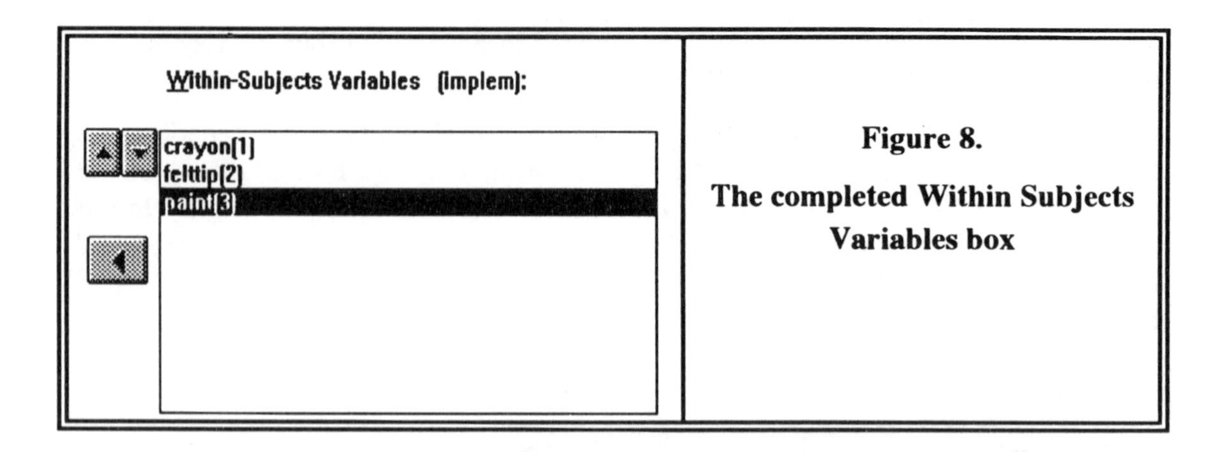

Figure 8.

The completed Within Subjects Variables box

Finally the multivariate listing can be suppressed (thus leaving only the univariate listing) by clicking on **Model** to open the **Repeated Measures ANOVA: Model** dialog box (not reproduced). In the bottom left-hand corner, is a box labelled **Within-Subjects Tests** containing three check boxes (Figure 9). Click on the check box beside **Multivariate tests to** remove the X. Click on **Continue**, and then on **OK** to run the analysis.

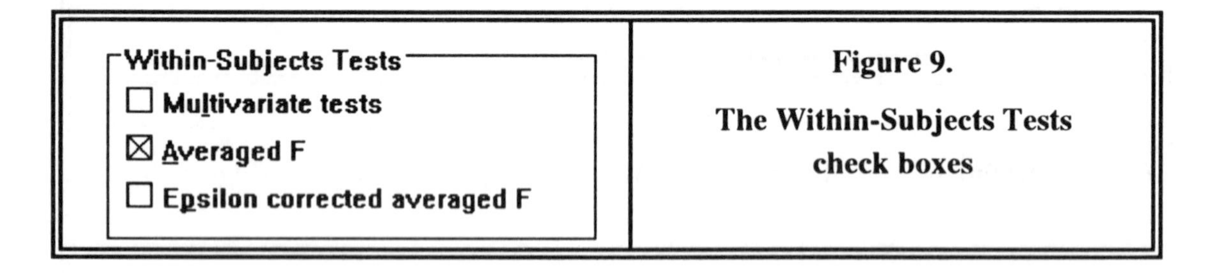

Figure 9.

The Within-Subjects Tests check boxes

9.4.5 Output listing for a one-factor within subjects ANOVA

The first part of the listing (not reproduced here) is subtitled **Tests of Between Subjects Effects** and can be ignored, since this example has no between subjects variable.

The next section shown in Output Listing 1 (SPSS 6 and 7) uses the **Mauchly Sphericity Test** to evaluate the homogeneity of covariance assumption, which is important for the univariate approach.

Output Listing 1 (SPSS 6).

The Mauchly sphericity test and epsilon

```
Tests involving 'IMPLEM' Within-Subject Effect.

 Mauchly sphericity test, W =       .90942
 Chi-square approx. =               .75963 with 2 D. F.
 Significance =                       .684

 Greenhouse-Geisser Epsilon =       .91694
 Huynh-Feldt Epsilon =             1.00000
 Lower-bound Epsilon =              .50000

AVERAGED Tests of Significance that follow multivariate
tests are equivalent to univariate or split-plot or
mixed-model approach to repeated measures.  Epsilons
may be used to adjust d.f. for the AVERAGED results.
```

Output Listing 1 (SPSS 7).

The Mauchly sphericity test and epsilon

Mauchly's Test of Sphericity[a]

Measure: MEASURE_1

Within Subjects Effect	Mauchly's W	Approx. Chi-Square	df	Sig.	Epsilon[b] Greenhouse-Geisser	Huynh-Feldt	Lower-bound
IMPLEM	.909	.760	2	.68	.917	1.000	.500

Tests the null hypothesis that the error covariance matrix of the orthonormalized transformed dependent variables is proportional to an identity matrix.

a. Design: Intercept
Within Subjects Design: IMPLEM

b. May be used to adjust the degrees of freedom for the averaged tests of significance. Corrected tests are displayed in the layers (by default) of the Tests of Within Subjects Effects table.

If the test is not significant (i.e. **Significance**, the p-value, has a value greater than 0.05), then the p-value given in the ANOVA summary table, which appears under the title **Averaged Tests of Significance**, can be accepted. If the test is significant (i.e. **Significance**, the p-value, has a value less than or equal to 0.05), then one can make a more conservative test, such as the Greenhouse-Geisser by returning to the **Within-Subjects Tests** check boxes (Figure 9), clicking on the **Epsilon corrected averaged F** check box and re-executing the analysis.

It is worth noting that even if the Mauchly test is significant, a value of F for the effect under consideration which, with the usual degrees of freedom values, has a small tail probability (say less than 0.03), will not become non-significant on the conservative test. The conservative F-test only makes a difference when:

(1) there is heterogeneity of covariance (i.e. Mauchly test is significant);

(2) the F with unadjusted degrees of freedom is barely significant beyond the 0.05 level.

Should F have a lower tail probability, the null hypothesis can safely be rejected without making a conservative test.

In the present case, the Mauchly test gives a p-value of 0.684, so there is no evidence of heterogeneity of covariance. Thus the usual ANOVA F test should be used because it is more powerful (i.e. more likely to reject H_0 if it is false) than MANOVA tests.

The ANOVA summary table is shown in Output Listing 2 (SPSS 6 and 7). Note the **Signif of F** value for the *implem* within-subject factor is *0.021* (i.e. the obtained value of F is significant beyond the 5 per cent level, but not beyond the 0.01 level). Thus the type of implement used does affect the ratings that a painting receives.

Output Listing 2 (SPSS 6).

The ANOVA summary table

```
* * * A n a l y s i s   o f   V a r i a n c e -- design   1 * * *

Tests involving 'IMPLEM' Within-Subject Effect.

 AVERAGED Tests of Significance for MEAS.1 using UNIQUE sums of squares
 Source of Variation           SS        DF         MS          F  Sig of F

 WITHIN+RESIDUAL            72.73        18       4.04
 IMPLEM                     39.27         2      19.63       4.86      .021
```

Output Listing 2 (SPSS 7).

The ANOVA summary table

Tests of Within-Subjects Effects

Measure: MEASURE_1

Sphericity Assumed

Source	Type III Sum of Squares	df	Mean Square	F	Sig.	Noncent. Parameter	Observed Power[a]
IMPLEM	39.267	2	19.633	4.859	.021	9.718	.729
Error(IMPLEM)	72.733	18	4.041				

a. Computed using alpha = .05

Output Listing 2 (SPSS 7) contains an item with the label 'Observed Power'. The **power (P)** of a statistical test is the probability that if the null hypothesis is false, it will be rejected. The complementary probability (β), namely, the failure to reject the same false null hypothesis, is known as the **beta-rate**, or the **type II error rate**, the two probabilities being related according to: $P = 1 - \beta$.

The power of a test depends on several factors, including the sample size and the size of the true differences, in the population, among the performance means for the different conditions in the experiment. The power of a test also depends upon the **significance level (α)**: if significance beyond the 0.01 level is insisted upon, the power of the test will be reduced. (On the other hand, the probability of a **type I error**, that is, rejection of the null hypothesis when it is true, is also reduced, because the type I error rate is simply the significance level decided upon before the experiment is carried out.)

In Output Listing 2 (SPSS 7), there is also the **noncentrality parameter** (see Howell, 1997; p.200, p.335) abbreviated to **Noncent. Parameter**. Its value reflects the magnitudes of the differences among the treatment population means. (In the present case it has been estimated from the data.) In general, the larger the differences, the greater the value of the noncentrality parameter and the more powerful the test. In this case, the power (.729) is reasonable, in that it is greater than that of many of the tests reported in the psychological literature.

If the Mauchly test had been significant, then after clicking on the **Epsilon corrected averaged F** check box, the output would have appeared as in Output Listing 3 (SPSS 6). The output from SPSS 7 Manova Repeated Measures is similar. It is apparent from the **Sig of F** column that these more conservative statistics in this case make no difference to the decision.

Output Listing 3 (SPSS 6).

More conservative statistics when Mauchly is significant

```
Tests involving 'IMPLEM' Within-Subject Effect.

 AVERAGED Tests of Significance for MEAS.1 using UNIQUE sums of squares
 Source of Variation            SS        DF          MS         F  Sig of F

 WITHIN+RESIDUAL             72.73        18        4.04
     (Greenhouse-Geisser)              16.50
     (Huynh-Feldt)                     18.00
     (Lower bound)                      9.00
 IMPLEM                      39.27         2       19.63      4.86      .021
     (Greenhouse-Geisser)               1.83                  4.86      .024
     (Huynh-Feldt)                      2.00                  4.86      .021
     (Lower bound)                      1.00                  4.86      .055
```

9.4.6 Unplanned multiple comparisons: Bonferroni method

There is some dubiety as to whether, following significant main effects of within subjects factors, the Tukey HSD test affords sufficient protection against inflation of the *per family* type I error rate. Other methods, therefore, have been recommended. Earlier, we distinguished between planned and unplanned tests. Suppose it is planned to make exactly *c* pairwise comparisons among a set of treatment means resulting from a one-factor experiment. It is desired to keep the *per family* error rate at 0.05. In the **Bonferroni method**, ordinary t-tests are used for the pairwise comparisons, but the *per family* error rate is divided by the number of planned comparisons. To achieve significance, therefore, each t-test must show significance beyond the 0.05 level.

The Bonferroni method can also be used to make *unplanned* pairwise multiple comparisons among a set of *k* treatment means following a one-factor ANOVA.

In this case, however, the *per family* type I error rate must be divided by the number of possible pairs (c) that can be drawn from an array of k means, which is given by

$$c = \frac{k!}{2!(k-2)!}$$

where the symbol ! means factorial (e.g. 4! is $4 \times 3 \times 2 \times 1 = 24$). For example, if there are five treatment means, $c = 5! / (2! \times 3!) = (5 \times 4 \times 3 \times 2)/(2 \times 3 \times 2) = 10$, and the test statistic will have to be significant beyond the $0.05/10 = 0.005$ level for a comparison to be deemed significant.

In the present example, the ANOVA has shown a significant main effect of the Implement factor. Here the number of treatment means (k) = 3, so $c = 3$. The Bonferroni t-tests, therefore, will have to show significance beyond the $0.05/3 = 0.02$ level, approximately.

To make the t-tests, we simply leave ANOVA and request **Paired-Sample T-Tests** for comparisons among the means of the *crayon, felttip* and *paint* columns in the Data Editor. When these are done with the present data, only the p-value for the difference between the means for the Paint and Crayon conditions is significant ($p = 0.0146$).

9.5 NONPARAMETRIC TESTS FOR A ONE-FACTOR WITHIN SUBJECTS EXPERIMENT

As with the one-factor completely randomised experiment, nonparametric methods are available for the analysis of ordinal and nominal data.

9.5.1 The Friedman test

Suppose that six people rank five objects in order of pleasingness. Their decisions might appear as in Table 4.

Table 4.

Six people's ranks of five objects in order of pleasingness

	Object 1	Object 2	Object 3	Object 4	Object 5
Person 1	2	1	5	4	3
Person 2	1	2	5	4	3
Person 3	1	3	4	2	5
Person 4	2	1	3	5	4
Person 5	2	1	5	4	3
Person 6	1	2	5	3	4

If we assume that the highest rank is given to the most pleasing object, it would appear, from inspection of Table 4, that Object 3 seems to be more pleasing to most of the raters than is Object 1. Since, however, each of the entries in Table 4 is not an independent measurement but a rank, the one-factor within subjects ANOVA cannot be used here. The Friedman test is suitable for ordinal data of the type shown in Table 4. Enter the data in the usual way in the **Data Editor** window, naming the variables *O1, O2, ... O5*. Choose

Statistics

Nonparametric Tests

K Related Samples

to obtain the **Tests for Several Related Samples** dialog box (not shown).

On the left, will appear a list of the variables in the **Data Editor** grid. This list should include the items *O1*, *O2*, ..., *O5*, which will contain the numbers shown in Table 4. Simply transfer these names to the **Test Variables** box in the usual way. Make sure the **Friedman** check box has been marked and click on **OK** to run the Friedman test.

The Friedman results (a list of average ranks for each object has been omitted) are shown in Output Listing 4. Clearly the rankings differ significantly across the objects since the p-value (**Significance** or **Asymp. Sig.**) is less than 0.01.

Output Listing 4 (SPSS 6 - left and SPSS 7 - right).

Friedman test results

```
              Friedman Two-Way Anova

Cases   Chi-Square  D.F.  Significance
  6       17.2000     4       .0018
```

Test Statistics[a]

N	6
Chi-Square	17.200
df	4
Asymp. Sig.	.002

a. Friedman Test

9.5.2 Cochran's Q test

Suppose that six children are asked to imagine they were in five different situations and had to choose between Course of Action *A* (coded *0*) and *B* (coded *1*). The results might appear as in Table 5.

Table 5.

Courses of action chosen by six children in five scenarios

	Scene 1	Scene 2	Scene 3	Scene 4	Scene 5
Child 1	0	0	1	1	1
Child 2	0	1	0	1	1
Child 3	1	1	1	1	1
Child 4	0	0	0	1	0
Child 5	0	0	0	0	0
Child 6	0	0	0	1	1

From inspection of Table 5, it would seem that *Course of Action B* (i.e. cells containing *1*) is chosen more often in some scenarios than in others. A suitable confirmatory test is **Cochran's Q** test, which was designed for use with related samples of dichotomous nominal data.

The **Cochran Q** test is run by bringing the **Test for Several Related Samples** dialog box to the screen (see previous section). Click off the **Friedman** check box and click on the **Cochran** check box.

The results are shown in Output Listing 5.

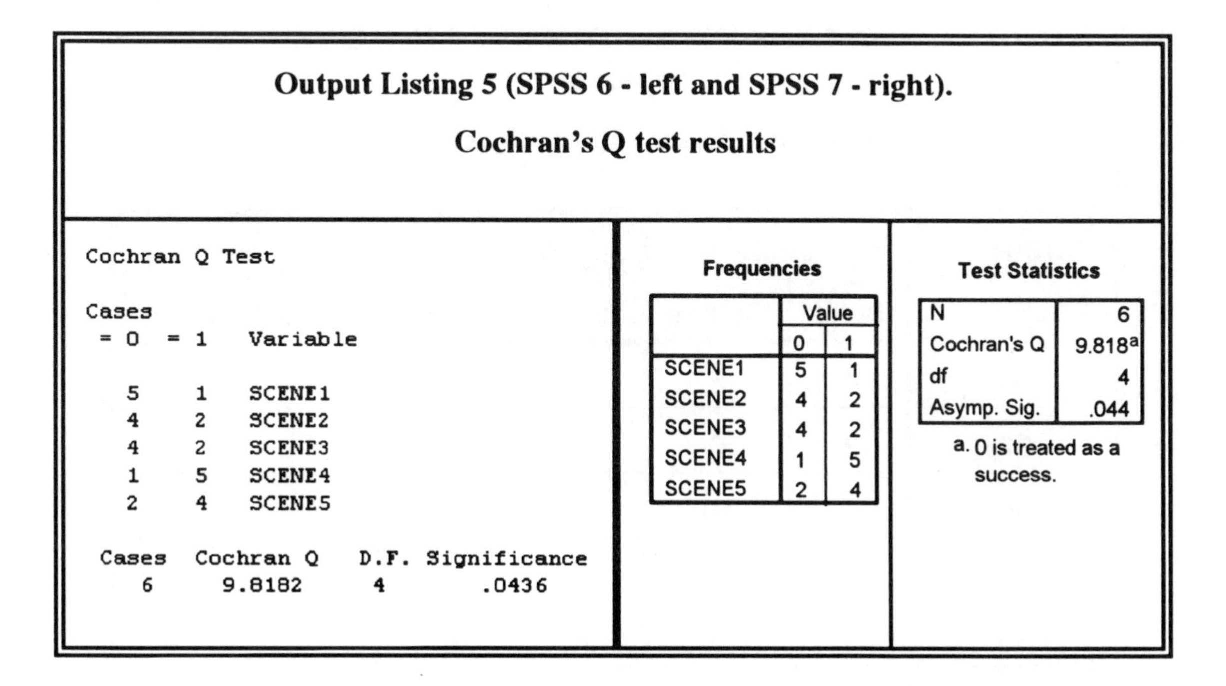

Output Listing 5 (SPSS 6 - left and SPSS 7 - right).

Cochran's Q test results

```
Cochran Q Test

Cases
 = 0   = 1    Variable

  5     1     SCENE1
  4     2     SCENE2
  4     2     SCENE3
  1     5     SCENE4
  2     4     SCENE5

  Cases   Cochran Q    D.F.  Significance
    6      9.8182       4        .0436
```

Frequencies

	Value	
	0	1
SCENE1	5	1
SCENE2	4	2
SCENE3	4	2
SCENE4	1	5
SCENE5	2	4

Test Statistics

N	6
Cochran's Q	9.818[a]
df	4
Asymp. Sig.	.044

a. 0 is treated as a success.

The output listings show that the differences in the courses of action taken by the children are just significant since the p-value (**Significance** or **Asymp. Sig.**) is marginally smaller than 0.05.

9.6 THE TWO-FACTOR WITHIN SUBJECTS ANOVA

9.6.1 Results of a two-factor within subjects experiment

An experiment is designed to investigate the detection of certain theoretically-important patterns on a screen. The patterns vary in shape and solidity. The dependent variable (DV) is the Number of Errors made in responding to the pattern, and the two factors are Shape (Circle, Square, or Triangle) and Solidity (Outline or Solid). The experimenter suspects that a shape's solidity affects whether it is perceived more readily than another shape. The same sample of subjects is used for all the possible treatment combinations, that is, there are repeated measures on both factors in the experiment. As with the one-factor within subjects experiment, the univariate ANOVA

Models menu. In this case, although each treatment combination will be treated as a separate dependent variable, the listing will contain a univariate ANOVA summary table with F tests of main effects and the interaction.

The results are shown in Table 6.

Table 6.

Results of a two-factor within subjects experiment

SHAPE:-	Circle		Square		Triangle	
SOLIDITY:-	Solid	Outline	Solid	Outline	Solid	Outline
S1	4	2	2	8	7	5
S2	3	6	2	6	8	9
S3	2	10	2	5	5	3
S4	1	8	5	5	2	9
S5	4	6	4	5	5	10
S6	3	6	4	6	9	12
S7	7	12	2	6	4	8
S8	6	10	9	5	0	10
S9	4	5	7	6	8	12
S10	2	12	12	8	10	12

Extra care is needed when analysing data from experiments with two or more within subjects factors. It is essential to ensure that SPSS understands which data were obtained under which combination of factors. In the present example, there are six data for each subject, each datum being a score achieved under a different combination of the two factors. We can label the data variables as *circsol*, *circlin*, *squarsol*, *squarlin*, *triansol* and *trianlin*, representing all possible combinations of the shape and solidity factors. Should there be many treatment combinations in the experiment, however, it would be very tedious to name the variables individually. In such cases, it is much more convenient to use the default variable names provided by the computer (e.g. *var00001*, *var00002*, *var00003* etc.), but a careful note must be kept about which combinations of levels of the within subjects factors are represented by which of these default variable names. This information must be borne in mind later in the naming of the within subjects factors within the **Repeated-Measures Define Variable(s)** dialog box (see below).

In the present example, remembering that the program initially treats each combination of levels of within subjects factors as a separate dependent variable, it can be seen that the sequence of names *circsol*, *circlin*, *squarsol*, *squarlin*, *triansol* and *trianlin*, represents successive columns of data in Table 6.

9.6.2 Preparing the data set

The data file (part of which is shown in Figure 10) is prepared as before, except that there are now six columns rather than three. Care must be taken with the ordering of the columns - see the previous section.

	circsol	circlin	squarsol	squarlin	triansol	trianlin
1	4	2	2	8	7	5
2	3	6	2	6	8	9
3	2	10	2	5	5	3
4	1	8	5	5	2	9

Figure 10. Part of the SPSS data file for the two-factor within subjects ANOVA

9.6.3 Running the two-factor within subjects analysis

In SPSS 6, select

Statistics

ANOVA Models

Repeated Measures

and then complete the various dialog boxes as in the previous example, except that there is an extra repeated-measures factor to be defined.

In SPSS 7, select

Statistics

General Linear Model

GLM - Repeated Measures or **MANOVA - Repeated Measures**

to open the **GLM - Repeated Measures Define Factor(s)** or **MANOVA - Repeated Measures Define Factor(s)** dialog box. The choice of GLM or MANOVA Repeated

Measures depends on the considerations outlined in Section 9.3, but we recommend the GLM version. The subsequent dialog boxes are similar to those for SPSS 6.

The completed **Repeated Measures Define Factor(s)** dialog box, with two generic names *shape* and *solidity* (together with their respective numbers of levels) is shown in Figure 11.

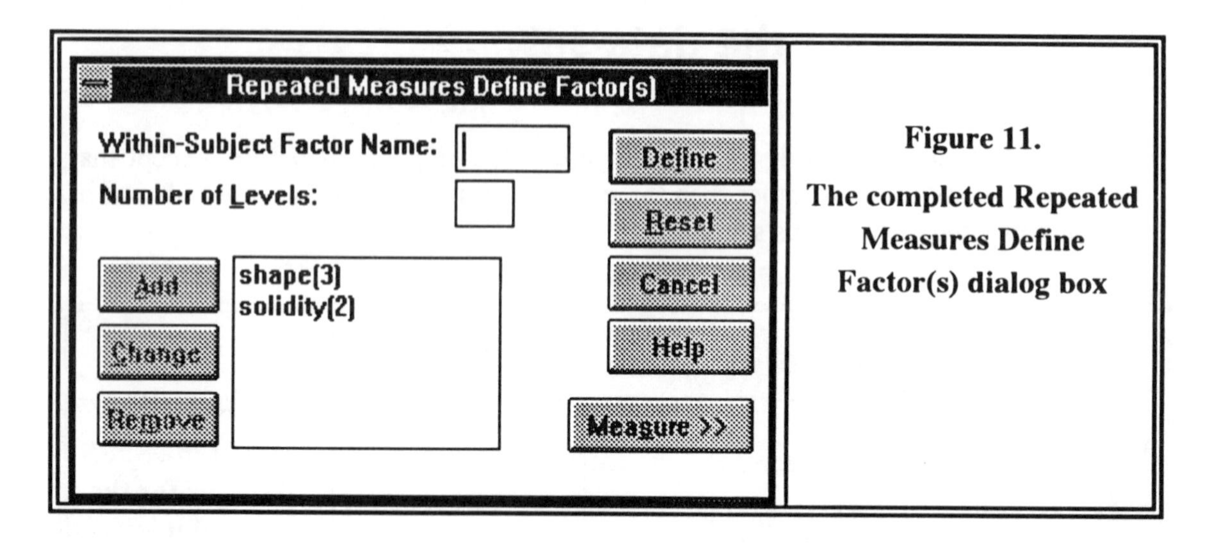

Figure 11.

The completed Repeated Measures Define Factor(s) dialog box

After the **Define** button has been clicked on, the **Repeated Measures ANOVA** dialog box appears (see Figure 12).

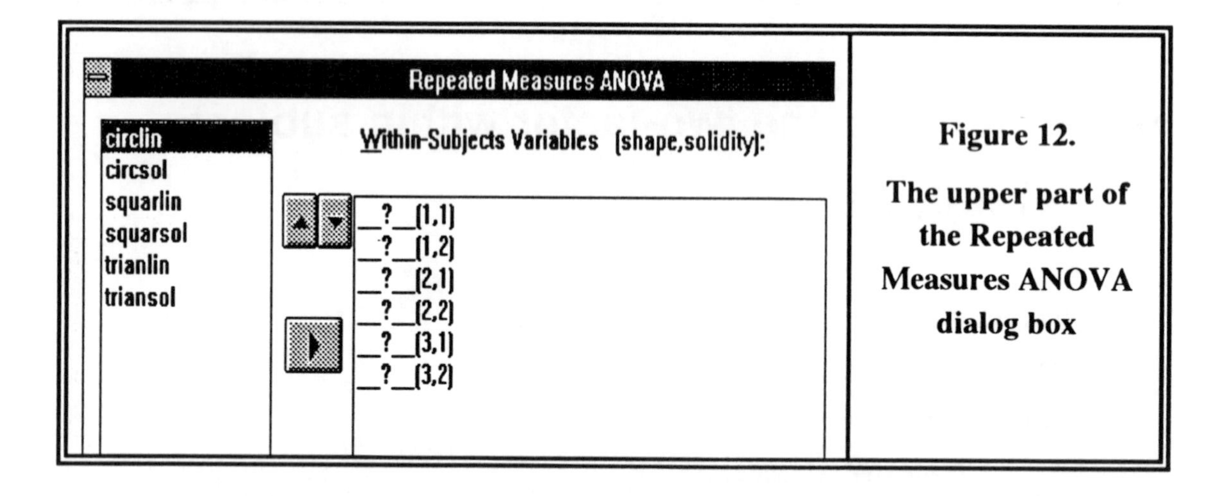

Figure 12.

The upper part of the Repeated Measures ANOVA dialog box

On the left, the six variables are listed in alphabetical order. On the right, in the box labelled **Within-Subjects Variables [shape,solidity]**, appears a list of the various combinations of the code numbers representing the levels of each of the two treatment factors. It will be noticed that, as one reads down the list, the first number in each pair changes more slowly than the second.

When there is more than one within subjects factor, it is not advisable to transfer the variable names in a block from the left-hand box to the **Within-Subjects Variables** box by a click-and-drag operation, as was done in the case of one within subjects factor. Care must be taken to ensure that the correct variable name is transferred to the correct slot; it is recommended that the variables are transferred one at a time, by noting the numbers in the square brackets and referring to the names of the defined within subjects factors within the square brackets at the head of the box (in Figure 12, it is Within-Subjects Variables [shape, solidity]).

Remember that the order of variables listed in the left-hand box is alphabetic, unless the default setting of **Alphabetical** has been changed to **File** in the **Display Order for Variable Lists** within the **Preferences** dialog box (see Section 3.4.2), in which case they will appear in the order of the columns in the Data Editor. A table such as Table 7 clarifies the numbering of the levels of within subjects variables. Thus the variable *circsol* is [shape 1, solidity 1] i.e. [1,1], *circol* is [1,2] and so on.

Table 7.

Numbering of levels in within subjects variables

Shape Factor	**Shape 1** (Circle)		**Shape 2** (Square)		**Shape 3** (Triangle)	
Solidity Factor	**Solidity 1** (Solid)	**Solidity 2** (Outline)	**Solidity 1** (Solid)	**Solidity 2** (Outline)	**Solidity 1** (Solid)	**Solidity 2** (Outline)
Variable name	***circsol***	***circlin***	***squarsol***	***squarlin***	***triansol***	***trianlin***

The upper section of the completed **Repeated Measures ANOVA** dialog box is shown in Figure 13.

Figure 13.

The upper section of the completed Repeated Measures ANOVA dialog box for two within subjects factors [shape and solidity]

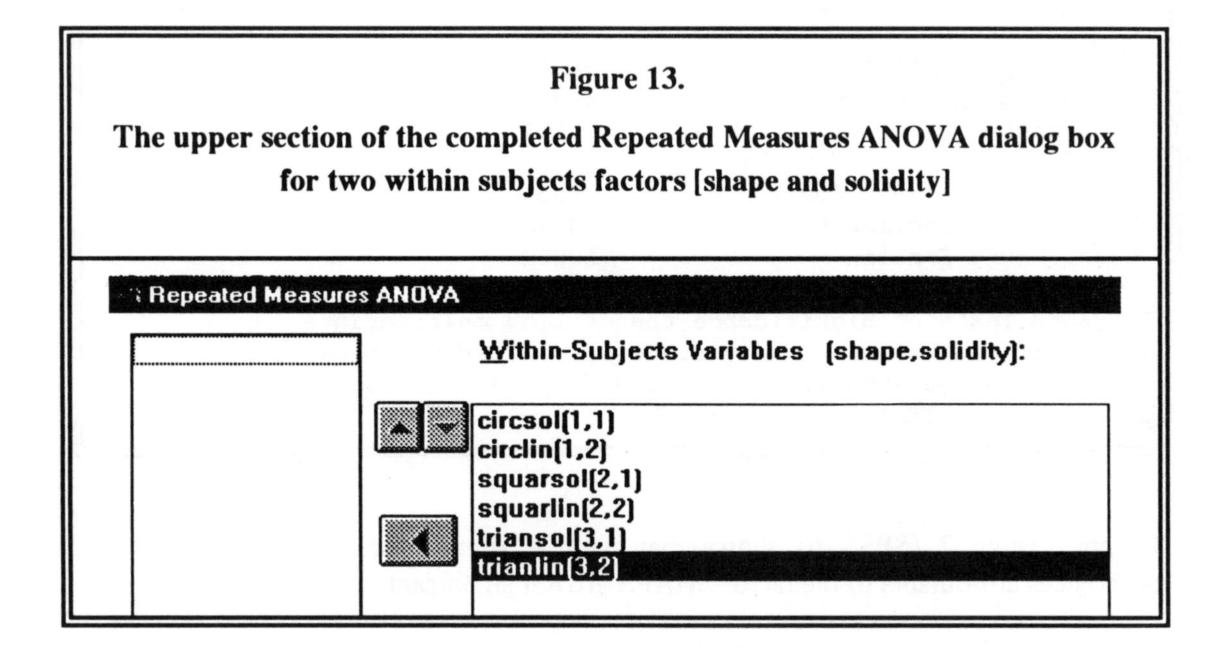

9.6.4 Output listing for a two-factor within subjects ANOVA

The SPSS 6 output is presented first. Since the SPSS 7 output from the GLM - Repeated Measures combines the Mauchly tests for the SHAPE and interaction terms in one table and all the F tests in another table, they will be reproduced in Output Listings 10 and 11 at the end. The section subtitled **Tests of Between-Subjects Effects** (not reproduced here) can be ignored: here we are interested only in within subjects effects.

9.6.4.1 Tests for main effects

Output Listing 6 (SPSS 6) contains the **Mauchly sphericity test**, which is used to check the homogeneity of covariance assumption for the SHAPE within subject effect. In this case it is not significant, because the p-value (0.197) is greater than 0.05. Accordingly, the **Averaged Tests of Significance** (the univariate ANOVA) for SHAPE can be accepted.

Output Listing 6 (SPSS 6).

Some statistics of the SHAPE factor

```
Tests involving 'SHAPE' Within-Subject Effect.

 Mauchly sphericity test, W =        .66634
 Chi-square approx. =               3.24763 with 2 D. F.
 Significance =                        .197

 Greenhouse-Geisser Epsilon =        .74982
 Huynh-Feldt Epsilon =               .86638
 Lower-bound Epsilon =               .50000

AVERAGED Tests of Significance that follow multivariate
tests are equivalent to univariate or split-plot or mixed-model
approach to repeated measures.  Epsilons may be used to adjust
d.f. for the AVERAGED results.
```

Output Listing 7 (SPSS 6) shows that with a **Significance of F** = 0.076, the differences attributable to the factor SHAPE are not significant.

Output Listing 7 (SPSS 6).

The ANOVA summary table for SHAPE

```
Tests involving 'SHAPE' Within-Subject Effect.

 AVERAGED Tests of Significance for MEAS.1 using UNIQUE sums of squares
 Source of Variation          SS        DF          MS          F  Sig of F

 WITHIN+RESIDUAL          138.97        18        7.72
 SHAPE                     46.03         2       23.02       2.98      .076
```

Output Listing 8 (SPSS 6) examines the within subject factor SOLIDITY.

Output Listing 8 (SPSS 6).

The ANOVA summary table for SOLIDITY

```
Tests involving 'SOLIDITY' Within-Subject Effect.

 Tests of Significance for T4 using UNIQUE sums of squares
 Source of Variation          SS        DF          MS          F  Sig of F

 WITHIN+RESIDUAL           19.40         9        2.16
 SOLIDITY                 117.60         1      117.60      54.56      .000
```

With only two levels in this factor, the multivariate and univariate approaches are identical, and no sphericity test is necessary. This factor is significant beyond the 1 per cent level, since the **Significance of F** is listed as 0.000 (meaning that the p-value is less than .0005).

9.6.4.2 Test for an interaction

The next sections of the listing examine the interaction of the two within subject factors (SHAPE BY SOLIDITY).

Since the **Mauchly sphericity test** is not significant (Significance = 0.663), the univariate test can be used as in Output Listing 9 (SPSS 6). The ANOVA summary table, however, shows that this interaction is not significant (**Significance of F** = 0.270).

In conclusion, the listing shows that only *solidity* is significant: the other systematic sources, namely, *shape* and its interaction with *solidity*, are not significant.

Output Listing 9 (SPSS 6).

Some statistics and the ANOVA summary table for the interaction

```
Tests involving 'SHAPE BY SOLIDITY' Within-Subject Effect.

 Mauchly sphericity test, W =       .90250
 Chi-square approx. =               .82067 with 2 D. F.
 Significance =                       .663

 Greenhouse-Geisser Epsilon =       .91116
 Huynh-Feldt Epsilon =             1.00000
 Lower-bound Epsilon =              .50000

AVERAGED Tests of Significance that follow multivariate tests are
equivalent to univariate or split-plot or mixed-model approach to
repeated measures.  Epsilons may be used to adjust d.f. for the
AVERAGED results.

Tests involving 'SHAPE BY SOLIDITY' Within-Subject Effect.

 AVERAGED Tests of Significance for MEAS.1 using UNIQUE sums of squares
 Source of Variation          SS       DF        MS         F  Sig of F

 WITHIN+RESIDUAL            151.30      18      8.41
 SHAPE BY SOLIDITY           23.70       2     11.85      1.41      .270
```

The relevant SPSS 7 GLM - Repeated Measures output is confined to two tables, Output Listing 10 (SPSS 7) combining Mauchly test results and Output Listing 11 (SPSS 7) combining all the univariate tests.

Output Listing 10 (SPSS 7).

Mauchly Test data

Mauchly's Test of Sphericity [a]

Measure: MEASURE_1

Within Subjects Effect	Mauchly's W	Approx. Chi-Square	df	Sig.	Epsilon [b]		
					Greenhouse-Geisser	Huynh -Feldt	Lower -bound
SHAPE	.666	3.248	2	.197	.750	.866	.500
SOLIDITY	1.000	.000	0	.	1.000	1.000	1.000
SHAPE * SOLIDITY	.903	.821	2	.663	.911	1.000	.500

Tests the null hypothesis that the error covariance matrix of the orthonormalized transformed dependent variables is proportional to an identity matrix.

a. Design: Intercept
Within Subjects Design: SHAPE+SOLIDITY+SHAPE*SOLIDITY

b. May be used to adjust the degrees of freedom for the averaged tests of significance. Corrected tests are displayed in the layers (by default) of the Tests of Within Subjects Effects table.

Output Listing 11 (SPSS 7).

F tests for Within Subjects effects

Tests of Within-Subjects Effects

Measure: MEASURE_1
Sphericity Assumed

Source	Type III Sum of Squares	df	Mean Square	F	Sig.	Noncent. Parameter	Observed Power[a]
SHAPE	46.033	2	23.017	2.981	.076	5.963	.507
Error(SHAPE)	138.967	18	7.720				
SOLIDITY	117.600	1	117.600	54.557	.000	54.557	1.000
Error(SOLIDITY)	19.400	9	2.156				
SHAPE * SOLIDITY	23.700	2	11.850	1.410	.270	2.820	.263
Error(SHAPE*SOLIDITY)	151.300	18	8.406				

a. Computed using alpha = .05

Notice that the Observed Power values in Output Listing 11 (SPSS 7) are low for rejecting H_0 in the cases of Shape and the interaction of Shape and Solidity.

9.6.5 Unplanned comparisons following a factorial within subjects experiment

In the example we have just considered, the question of unplanned multiple comparisons does not arise, because (1) there is no interaction and (2) the sole significant main effect involves a factor with only two levels, implying that the two means must be significantly different. Had there been a significant interaction, however, the approach already described in the context of the one-factor within subjects experiment would also have been applicable here. The problem with the **Bonferroni test**, however, is that even with only six cells, it is very difficult to get a difference sufficiently large to be significant. With six cells, $c = 15$ and each t-test has to have a p-value of 0.003 or less to be deemed significant. There is, therefore, a case to be made for testing initially for **simple main effects** of the principal experimental factor of interest at various levels of the other factor. A significant simple main effect may justify defining the comparison family more narrowly and improves the chances of finding significant differences. As in a between subjects factorial experiment, a simple main effect of a factor can be computed by carrying out a one-way ANOVA upon the data at only one level of the other factor. In the case of a within subjects factorial experiment, however, the data at different levels of either factor are not independent. It is wise, therefore, to adopt a stricter criterion for significance of a simple main effect in such cases, by applying the Bonferroni criterion and setting the significance level for each simple effect test at 0.05 divided by the number of tests that will be made.

SUMMARY

1) When an experiment has **within subjects factors**, the analysis can be obtained from the **repeated measures** option within the **ANOVA Models** menu. If the **Mauchly sphericity test** is significant, a **conservative F test** can be made by adjusting the degrees of freedom.

2) The procedure for within subjects factor(s) ANOVA is

   Statistics

   ANOVA Models (or General Linear Model in SPSS 7)

   Repeated Measures (either GLM or MANOVA in SPSS 7)

   In SPSS 7, we recommend the **GLM - Repeated Measures** alternative.

   Within subjects factors are defined in the **Repeated Measures Define Factor(s)** dialog box. After clicking on **Define**, the **Repeated Measures ANOVA** dialog box is opened. Here the variable names are arranged in alphabetical order within the left-hand box. The names of the within subjects levels (or when there is more than one factor, the combinations of within subjects levels) are transferred to the **Within-Subjects Variables** box, taking particular care, when there is more than one within subjects factor, to enter the correct name in the appropriate slot.

3) Multivariate output can be suppressed (except in SPSS 7 GLM - Repeated Measures) by clicking on **Model** and switching off the check box for **Multivariate tests**.

4) Nonparametric tests for a one-factor within subjects experiment include the **Friedman test** for ordinal data and **Cochran's Q test** for dichotomous nominal data. Choose

   Statistics

   Nonparametric Tests

   K Related Samples

   to open the **Tests for Several Related Samples** dialog box. Click on the **Friedman** or **Cochran** check box as required.

5) Unplanned pairwise comparisons can be made using the **Bonferroni** modification of the significance level of a t-test.

CHAPTER 10

EXPERIMENTS OF MIXED DESIGN

10.1 INTRODUCTION

10.1.1 Mixed (or split-plot) factorial experiments

It is very common for factorial designs to have within subjects (repeated measures) factors on **some** (but not all) of their treatment factors. Since such experiments have a mixture of between subjects and within subjects factors, they are often said to be of **mixed** design. The term **split-plot** is also used, reflecting the agronomic context in which this type of experiment was first employed.

In psychological and educational research, the researcher often selects two samples of subjects (e.g. male and female groups) and performs the same repeated measures experiment upon each group. Suppose, for example, that samples of male and female subjects are tested for recall of a written passage with three different line spacings, the order of presentation of the three levels of the spacing factor being counterbalanced across subjects to neutralise order effects. In this experiment, there are two factors:

(1) Gender (Male, Female);

(2) Spacing (Narrow, Medium, Wide).

The levels of Gender vary **between** subjects; whereas those of Spacing vary **within** subjects. The experiment has thus one between subjects and one within subjects factor.

10.1.2 A notational scheme for mixed factorial experiments

In the foregoing experiment on the effects of Gender and Spacing upon Recall of written passages, the Gender factor was between subjects and the Spacing factor was within subjects. We shall adopt the convention whereby within subjects factors are bracketed, so that if A is Gender and B is Spacing, the reading experiment is of type **A×(B)**, signifying a mixed design with repeated measures on factor B.

With three treatment factors, two mixed designs are possible: there may be one or two repeated measures factors, the former design being denoted by **A×B×(C)**, the latter by **A×(B×C)**.

10.2 THE TWO-FACTOR MIXED FACTORIAL ANOVA

10.2.1 Mixed factorial ANOVA with SPSS

The SPSS **Repeated Measures** program from either the **ANOVA Models** (SPSS 6) or **General Linear Model** (SPSS 7) menu is used for the analysis of data from experiments with treatment within subjects factors. The procedure for defining the within subjects factors was explained in Chapter 9. In experiments of mixed design, however, there are also between subjects factors. As in between subjects experiments, their levels are identified by means of a numerical code in the data file.

10.2.2 Results of a mixed A×(B) experiment

A researcher designs an experiment to explore the hypothesis that engineering students, because of their training in two-dimensional representation of three-dimensional structures, have a more strongly developed sense of shape and symmetry than do psychology students. Three theoretically-important types of shapes are presented to samples of Psychology and Engineering students under sub-optimal conditions on a monitor screen. All three types of shape are presented to each subject: hence Shape is a within subjects factor. The category of Student (Psychology or Engineering) on the other hand, is a between subjects factor. The dependent variable is the Number of Shapes correctly identified.

The results of the experiment are shown in Table 1.

Table 1.

Results of a two-factor mixed factorial experiment of type A×(B)

Category of Student	Subject	Shape		
		Triangle	Square	Rectangle
Psychology	s1	2	12	7
	s2	8	10	9
	s3	4	15	3
	s4	6	9	7
	s5	9	13	8
	s6	7	14	8
Engineering	s7	13	3	35
	s8	21	4	30
	s9	26	10	35
	s10	22	8	30
	s11	20	9	28
	s12	19	8	27

10.2.3 Preparing the SPSS data set

In Table 1, we chose to represent the experimental design with the levels of the within subjects factor arrayed horizontally and those of the between subjects factor stacked vertically, with the level Engineering under Psychology. We did so because this arrangement corresponds to the arrangement of the results in the SPSS data set.

The first column of the **Data Editor** grid will contain a single grouping variable Category representing the Psychologists (*1*) and the Engineers (*2*). The second, third and fourth columns will contain the results at the three levels of the Shape factor (i.e. Triangle, Square, and Rectangle).

Using the techniques described in Section 3.5, define four variables: *category* (the grouping variable), *triangle*, *square*, and *rectangl* (remember the variable names must not exceed 8 characters in length). Using the **Define Labels** procedure (Section 3.5.3.4), assign to the values of the *category* variable the value labels *Psychology Student* and *Engineering Student*. When the data of Table 1 have been entered into the **Data Editor** grid, the first five cases appear as shown in Figure 1.

	category	triangle	square	rectangl
1	1	2	12	7
2	1	8	10	9
3	1	4	15	3
4	1	6	9	7
5	1	9	13	8

Figure 1.

The first five cases of the SPSS data set from the results in Table 1

10.2.4 Exploring the results: Boxplots and tables of means and standard deviations

As always, the first step is to explore the data set. The boxplot was described in Section 4.3.2.4; here the clustered boxplot (for different levels of the between subjects variable) is appropriate. It can be obtained by selecting the **Clustered** option and the **Summaries of separate variables** radio button within the **Boxplot** dialog box. Transfer the variable names *triangle square rectangl* to the **Boxes Represent:** box and the variable name *category* to the **Category Axis** box and click on **OK**. The resulting boxplot will have the three boxes for Engineering on the left and the three boxes for Psychology on the right.

A table of cell means and standard deviations, together with the marginal means for the three different shapes, is desirable. Inspection of this table will indicate whether there has been a main effect of the within subjects factor *shape* or a *shape by category* interaction. The table can be obtained directly by using the **Means** procedure (see below).

We shall also want the marginal means for the between subjects factor to ascertain whether it had a main effect, too. These too can be obtained by running **Means**; but first it is necessary to use **Compute** to calculate the mean score over the three different shapes that each subject achieved (see below).

10.2.4.1 Obtaining the cell means and the marginal means for the within subjects factor

Choose
Statistics
  Compare Means
    Means

to open the **Means** dialog box. Detailed instructions are given in Section 4.3.3.3. Transfer the names of the three *shape* variables into the **Dependent List** box. Transfer *category* into the **Independent List** box. Click on **OK** to obtain a table showing the cell means and the marginal means for the *shape* factor. This table, however, does not include the marginal means for the between subjects factor, *category*. The next section describes a way of computing these remaining means.

10.2.4.2 Obtaining the marginal means for the between subjects factor

In order to use **Means** to calculate the marginal means for *category*, one must first define a new variable (e.g. *meancat*), which is the mean score that a subject achieves over the three different shapes.

Choose
Transform
  Compute

to open the **Compute Variable** dialog box. Detailed instructions are given in Section 4.4.2. Type *meancat* into the **Target Variable** box. In the **Functions** box, scroll down to, and highlight, the function **MEAN[numexpr, numexpr ....]** and click on ▲ to transfer the function to the **Numeric Expression** box, where question marks will replace **numexpr**, inviting specific variable names. Delete the question marks and then successively highlight and transfer the variable names *triangle*, *square*, and *rectangl*, taking care to ensure that there is a comma between each name. The final entry is now **MEAN[triangle, square, rectangl]**. Click on **OK** to run the procedure.

Note that in order to display the values of the *meancat* variable in the **Data Editor** window to, say, two places of decimals, it may be necessary to override the general format instruction specified in **Preferences**, which may have specified that all variables will be displayed as integers. Within the **Define Variable** dialog box (brought by double-clicking on the heading *meancat* column), click on **Type** and make the necessary adjustment to the value in the **Decimal Places** box. Now it is possible to compute the marginal means and standard deviations for *category* by returning to **Means** and transferring *meancat* to the **Dependent List** box, and *category* to the **Independent List** box. Click on **OK**.

10.2.4.3 The complete table of marginal and cell means and standard deviations

Table 2 combines the information from the computations described in the previous subsections.

Table 2.

Mean levels of performance by two groups of students with three different shapes (standard deviations are given in brackets)

	Shape			
Category	Triangle	Square	Rectangle	Means
Psychology	6.00 (2.61)	12.17 (2.32)	7.00 (2.10)	8.39
Engineering	20.20 (4.26)	7.00 (2.83)	30.83 (3.83)	19.33
Means	13.08	9.58	18.92	13.86

The values of the marginal means in Table 2 strongly suggest main effects of both the Shape and Category factors. Moreover, the markedly superior performance of the engineers on triangles and rectangles is reversed with squares, suggesting the presence of an interaction.

10.2.5 Procedure for a mixed A×(B) ANOVA

For SPSS 6 users, select the **Repeated Measures** item from the **ANOVA Models** menu by choosing
Statistics
    ANOVA Models
        Repeated Measures

to open the **Repeated Measures Define Factor(s)** dialog box (Chapter 9, Figure 5).

For SPSS 7 users, select
Statistics
  General Linear Model
    MANOVA - Repeated Measures or **GLM - Repeated Measures**

to open the **GLM - Repeated Measures Define Factor(s)** or **MANOVA - Repeated Measures Define Factor(s)** dialog box. The choice of GLM or MANOVA Repeated Measures depends on the considerations outlined at the end of Section 9.3.

In the **Within-Subject Factor Name** box, delete *factor1* and type a generic name (such as *shape*) for the repeated factor. This name must not be that of any of the three levels making up the factor and must also conform to the rules governing the assignment of variable names. In the **Number of Levels** box, type the number of levels (*3*) making up the repeated measures factor. Clicking on **Add** will result in the appearance of the entry *shape(3)* in the lowest box (Figure 2).

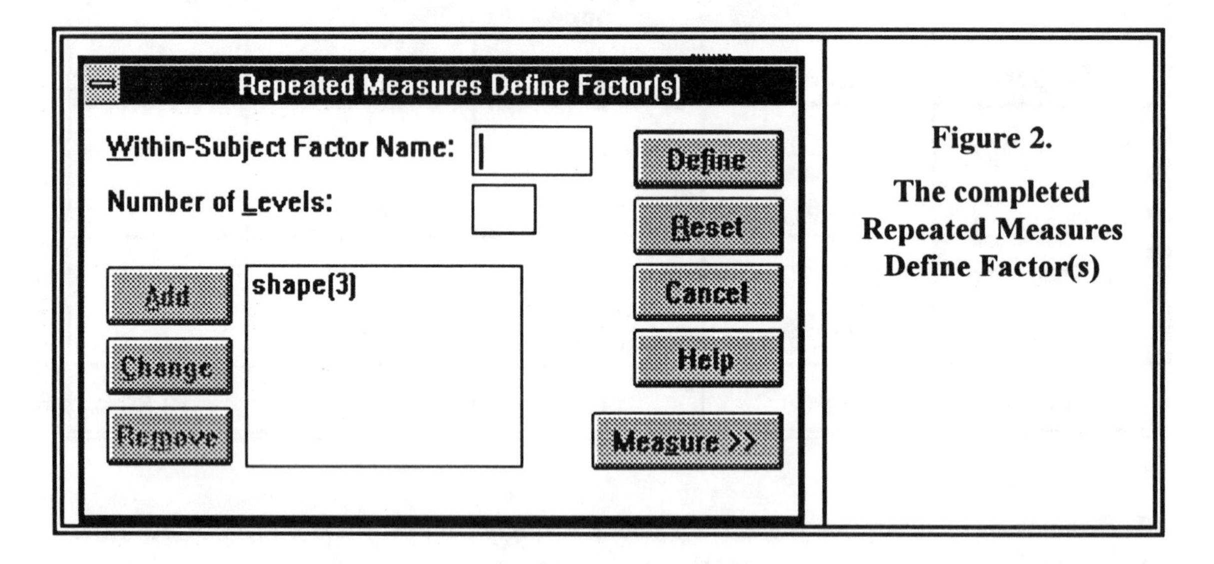

Figure 2.

The completed Repeated Measures Define Factor(s)

Click on **Define** to open the **Repeated Measures ANOVA** dialog box (part of which is shown in Figure 3).

Figure 3.

Part of the Repeated Measures ANOVA dialog box before entering the names of the levels

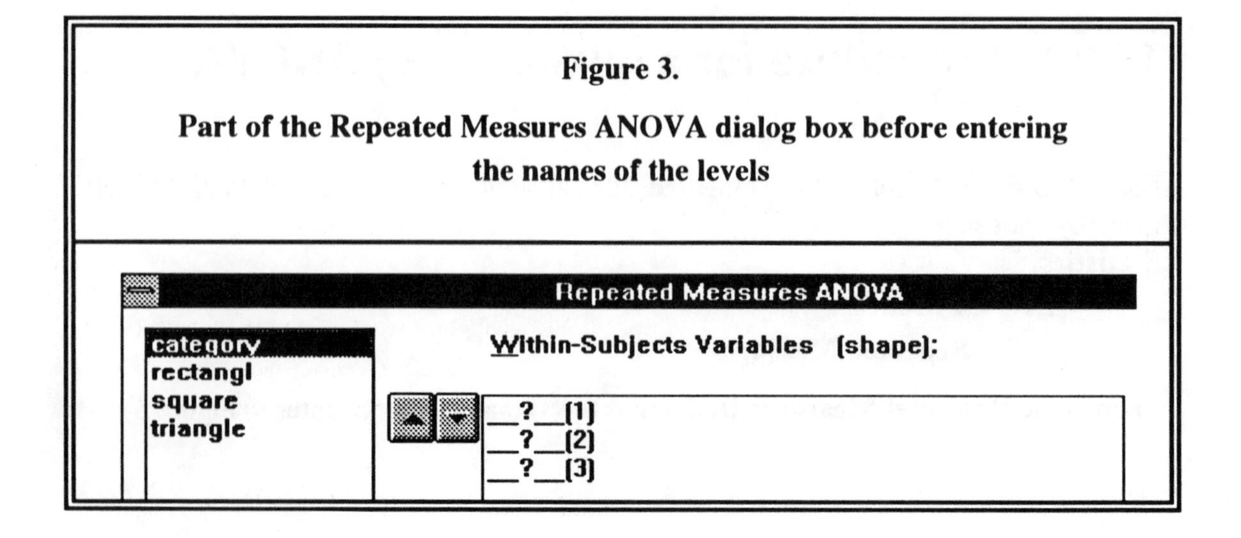

Click-and-drag the arrowhead down the variable names *rectangl, square, triangle* to highlight them, and click on ▶ to transfer them into the **Within-Subjects Variable(s) [shape]** box (Figure 4). So far, the procedure has been as described in Chapter 9.

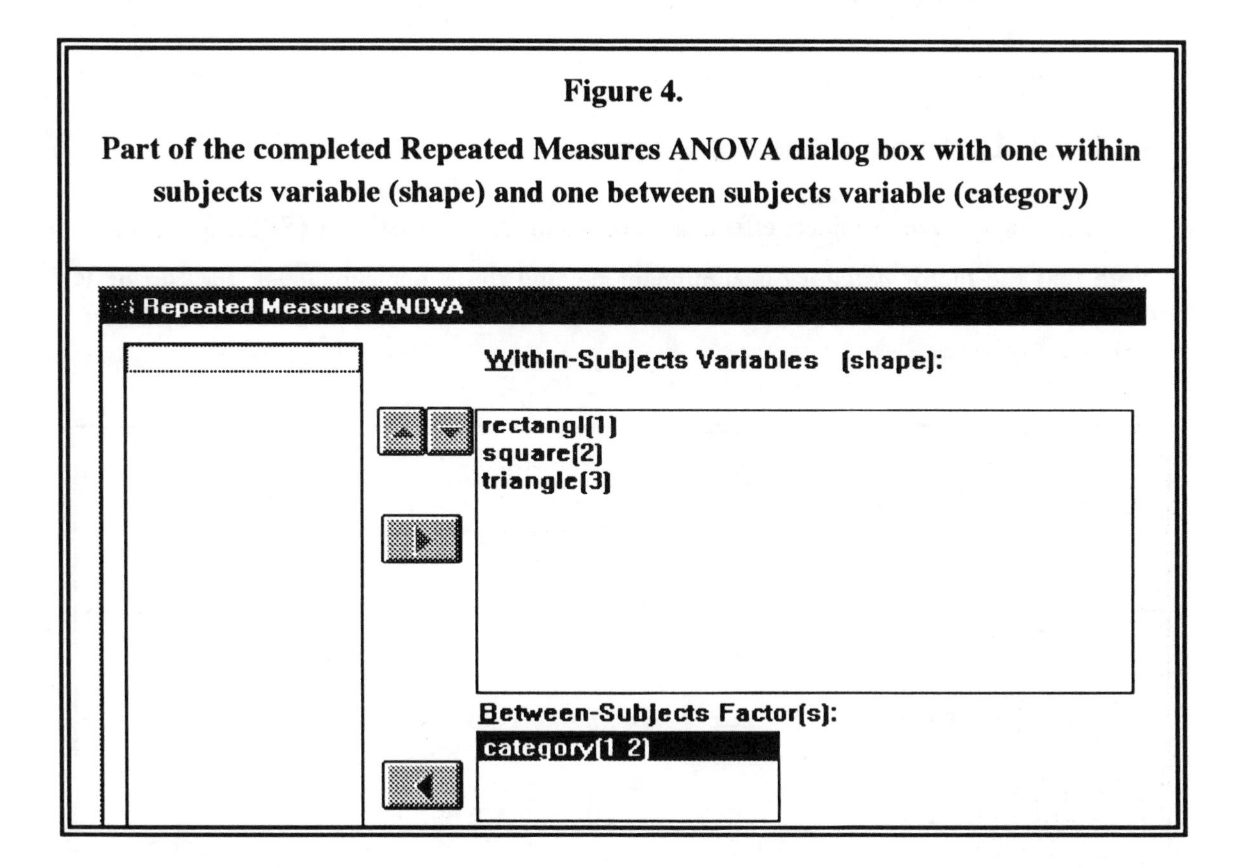

Figure 4.

Part of the completed Repeated Measures ANOVA dialog box with one within subjects variable (shape) and one between subjects variable (category)

The new element is the presence of the between subjects factor *category*. Click on that variable name and transfer it to the **Between-Subjects Factor(s)** box by clicking on ▶ to the left of that box. On transferral, click on **Define Range** and type the value *1* into the **Minimum** box and *2* into the **Maximum** box. Click on **Continue** to return to the **Repeated Measures ANOVA** dialog box which now appears as shown in Figure 4.

Finally, before running the ANOVA, we suggest that **Multivariate tests** should be turned off. Click on **Model** to open the **Within-Subjects Tests** dialog box, within which are the check boxes of the **Within-Subjects Tests** menu. Cancel the X beside **Multivariate tests** to disable that function (Figure 5).

Within-Subjects Tests
☐ Multivariate tests
☒ Averaged F
☐ Epsilon corrected averaged F

Figure 5.

The Within-Subjects Tests check boxes within the Repeated Measures ANOVA: Model dialog box

Click on **Continue** to return to the **Repeated Measures ANOVA** dialog box, and then on **OK** to run the ANOVA.

10.2.6 Output listing for the two-factor mixed ANOVA

10.2.6.1 Between subjects effects

The tests for between subjects effects are shown in Output Listing 1 (SPSS 6 and 7).

Note that the factor *category* is significant beyond the 1 per cent level: the **Sig of F** (0.000) is less than 0.0005. There is thus a difference in performance between the two groups of students.

Output Listing 1 (SPSS 6).

Tests for Between Subjects Effects

```
Tests of Between-Subjects Effects.

 Tests of Significance for T1 using UNIQUE sums of squares
 Source of Variation          SS      DF        MS        F  Sig of F

 WITHIN+RESIDUAL          108.94      10     10.89
 CATEGORY                1078.03       1   1078.03    98.95      .000
```

Output Listing 1 (SPSS 7).

Tests for Between Subjects Effects

Tests of Between-Subjects Effects

Measure: MEASURE_1
Transformed Variable: Average

Source	Type III Sum of Squares	df	Mean Square	F	Sig.	Noncent. Parameter	Observed Power[a]
Intercept	916.694	1	916.694	634.883	.000	634.883	1.000
CATEGORY	078.028	1	078.028	98.952	.000	98.952	1.000
Error	108.944	10	10.894				

a. Computed using alpha = .05

10.2.6.2 Tests for within subjects and interaction effects

Output Listing 2 (SPSS 6) shows the **Mauchly sphericity test** test for homogeneity of covariance in the within subjects *shape* factor. Since the statistic is not significant (**Significance** is greater than 0.05), it can be assumed that the covariance matrix is homogeneous. Had the Mauchly test shown significance, it would have been necessary to make a conservative Greenhouse-Geisser test with fewer degrees of freedom (obtained by multiplying the original numerator and denominator degrees of freedom by the value of **epsilon**, which is given in the output). This could also be done by clicking on the **Epsilon corrected averaged F** test in the **Within-Subjects Tests** box (Figure 5).

Output Listing 2 (SPSS 6).

Statistics of the Within Subjects shape factor

```
Tests involving 'SHAPE' Within-Subject Effect.

 Mauchly sphericity test, W =        .90277
 Chi-square approx. =                .92059 with 2 D. F.
 Significance =                        .631

 Greenhouse-Geisser Epsilon =        .91139
 Huynh-Feldt Epsilon =              1.00000
 Lower-bound Epsilon =               .50000

AVERAGED Tests of Significance that follow multivariate
tests are equivalent to univariate or split-plot or
mixed-model approach to repeated measures.  Epsilons may
be used to adjust d.f. for the AVERAGED results.
```

Output Listing 3 (SPSS 6 and 7) shows the ANOVA summary table for the within subjects factor *shape* and the *category by shape* interaction.

Output Listing 3 (SPSS 6).

ANOVA summary table for shape main effect and for category by shape interaction

```
Tests involving 'SHAPE' Within-Subject Effect.

 AVERAGED Tests of Significance for MEAS.1 using UNIQUE sums of squares
 Source of Variation          SS      DF         MS          F  Sig of F

 WITHIN+RESIDUAL          163.56      20       8.18
 SHAPE                    533.56       2     266.78      32.62      .000
 CATEGORY BY SHAPE       1308.22       2     654.11      79.99      .000
```

Output Listing 3 (SPSS 7).

ANOVA summary table for shape main effect and for category by shape interaction

Tests of Within-Subjects Effects

Measure: MEASURE_1
Sphericity Assumed

Source	Type III Sum of Squares	df	Mean Square	F	Sig.	Noncent. Parameter	Observed Power[a]
SHAPE	533.556	2	266.778	32.622	.000	65.245	1.000
SHAPE * CATEGORY	1308.222	2	654.111	79.986	.000	159.973	1.000
Error(SHAPE)	163.556	20	8.178				

a. Computed using alpha = .05

The ANOVA strongly confirms the patterns that were discernible in Table 2: the Shape and Category factors both have significant main effects and the interaction between the factors is also significant.

10.2.6.3 Unplanned comparisons following a significant interaction

The procedures described in the previous chapter can readily be applied to the analysis of data from experiments with a mixture of between and within subjects factors. In mixed experiments, it is the within subjects factors that are generally of principal interest. Following a significant interaction, therefore, one could proceed to test for **simple main effects of the within subjects factor** at the various levels of the between subjects factor. Following a significant simple main effect in the data from one group of subjects, **Bonferroni t-tests** could then be applied to make pairwise comparisons among the different levels of the within subjects factor.

Simple effects of between factors can readily be tested by performing **one-way ANOVAs** on the data at selected levels of within-subjects factors. (Since each test for a main effect uses a fresh set of data, there is no need to use the Bonferroni method to make the tests specially conservative. Should a simple effect prove significant, the **Tukey HSD test** can be used to make unplanned pairwise multiple comparisons among a set of means comprising only those relevant to the main effect concerned.

10.3 THE THREE-FACTOR MIXED ANOVA

The procedures described in Section 10.2 can readily be extended to the analysis of data from mixed factorial experiments with three treatment factors. In Section 10.1.2, we introduced a notation for specifying a particular mixed design, whereby a within subjects factor is written in brackets, so that the designation **A×(B)** denotes a mixed, two-factor factorial experiment, where factor A is between subjects and factor B is within subjects. Here we consider the two possible mixed three-factor factorial designs:

(1) the **A×(B×C)** experiment, with two within subjects factors;

(2) the **A×B×(C)** experiment, with one within subjects factor.

10.3.1 The mixed A×(B×C) experiment

Suppose that to the A×(B) experiment described in Section 10.2.2 we were to add an additional within subjects factor C, such as the Solidity of the shape with two levels, either Solid or Outline. Thus the subjects (either Psychology or Engineering students) have to try to recognise either Solid or Outline Triangles, Squares, or Rectangles. We now have an A×(B×C) experiment, with 3×2 = 6 within subjects variables in the **Data Editor** window, each variable containing the data for a combination of Shape and Solidity. It is convenient (though not essential) to prepare these columns in the **Data Editor** window systematically by taking the first level of one variable and combining it in turn with each of the levels of the second variable, followed by the second level of the first variable combined with each level of the second variable, and so on. Thus for this experiment the **Data Editor** window might appear as in Figure 6.

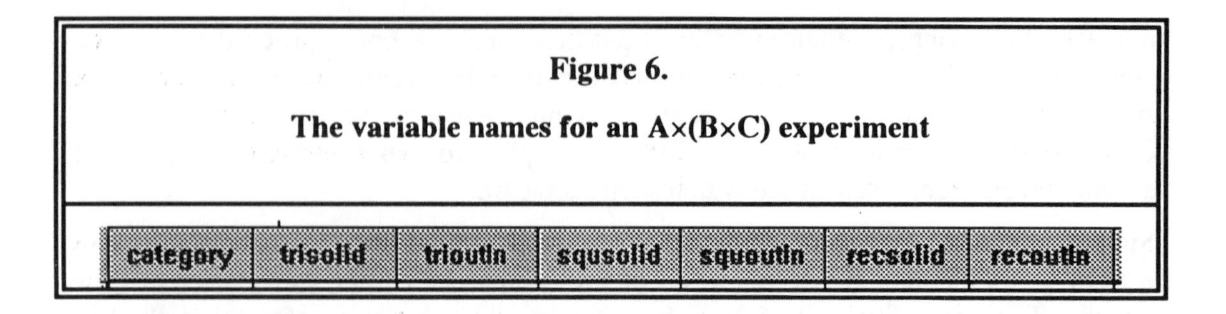

Figure 6.

The variable names for an A×(B×C) experiment

Care must be taken in transferring variable names within the **Repeated Measures ANOVA** dialog box. Remember that the order of variables listed in the left-hand box is alphabetic unless the default setting of **Alphabetical** has been changed to **File** in the **Display Order for Variable Lists** within the **Preferences** dialog box (see Section 3.4.2) in which case they will appear in the order of the columns in the Data Editor. It may, therefore, be necessary to transfer the variable names one at a time to the **Within-Subjects Variables** box to ensure that the correct names are fitted into the various slots, bearing in mind that the order of the defined factors is shown in square brackets above the box. Part of the completed dialog box is shown in Figure 7.

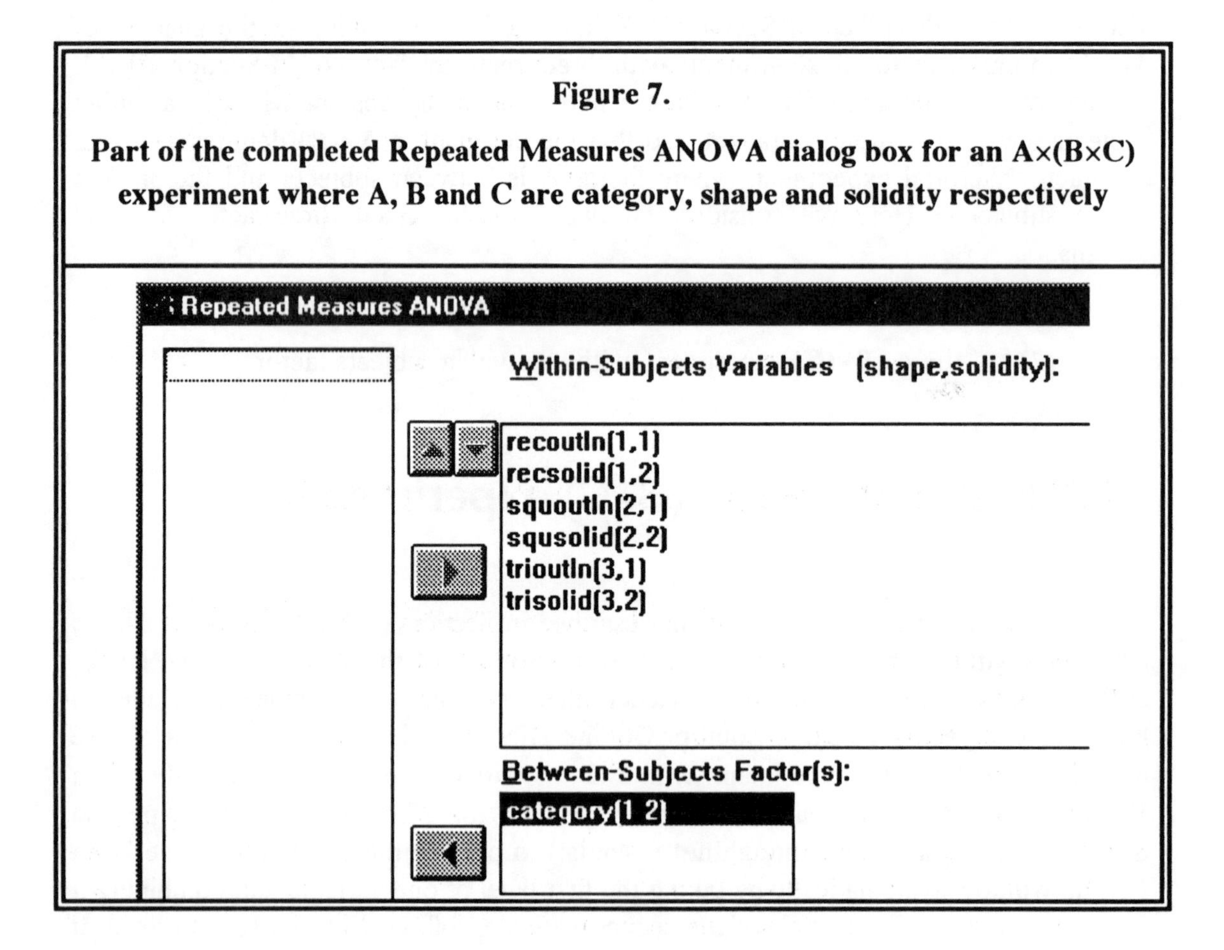

Figure 7.

Part of the completed Repeated Measures ANOVA dialog box for an A×(B×C) experiment where A, B and C are category, shape and solidity respectively

10.3.2 The mixed A×B×(C) experiment

This experiment has two between subjects factors (A and B) and one within subjects factor (C). Suppose the A×(B) experiment described in Section 10.2.2 were to have an additional between subjects factor added, such as the Sex of the subjects. This variable has two levels Male and Female. Thus the subjects (either Psychology or Engineering students, and either Male or Female) have to try to recognise shapes (either Triangles, Squares, or Rectangles). The experiment is now of the A×B×(C) type.

There will now be two coding variables *category* and *sex*, and the three levels of the within subjects variable *rectangl*, *square*, and *triangle*. Thus for this experiment the **Data Editor** window might appear as in Figure 8.

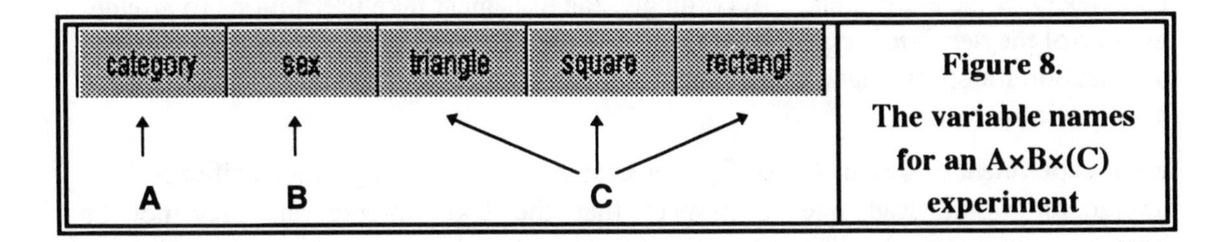

Figure 8.
The variable names for an A×B×(C) experiment

Part of the completed **Repeated Measures ANOVA** dialog box would then be as shown in Figure 9.

Figure 9.
Part of the completed Repeated Measures ANOVA dialog box for an A×B×(C) experiment with category as A, sex as B, and shape as C

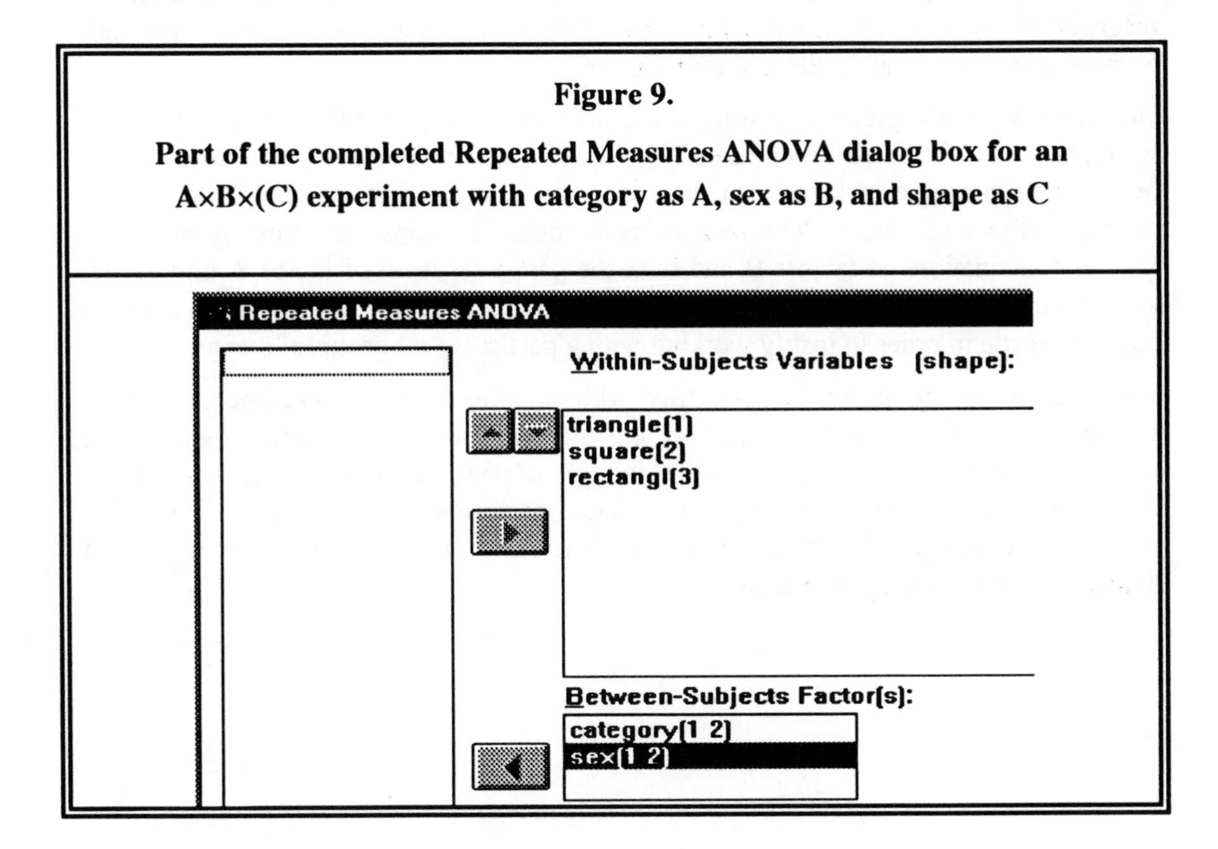

10.4 FURTHER ANALYSIS: SIMPLE EFFECTS AND MULTIPLE COMPARISONS

The analysis of variance is a large topic in statistics, and there are available many more techniques than we can mention in this book, which is primarily concerned with computing, rather than statistics as such. For example, following the confirmation that an interaction is significant, it is often useful to follow up the initial ANOVA with additional tests of the effects of one factor at specific levels of another. Such analyses of **simple effects** can be combined with both planned and unplanned multiple comparisons. We urge the reader who is unfamiliar with such methods to read the relevant chapters in a lucid textbook such as Howell (1997).

At this point, it may be worth reminding the reader that the dangers of committing a type I error in unplanned multiple comparisons increase enormously with the complexity of the experiment. Accordingly, the user must take precautions to attempt to control the *per family* type I error rate. The use of simple effects tests may give one justification for specifying a smaller subgroup of treatment means and so increasing the power of each test.

In an experiment of design A×(B×C), for example, the obtaining of a significant ABC interaction would lead one to suspect that the B×C interactions may not be homogeneous across the different levels of factor A (the between subjects factor).

By analogy with simple main effects, a **simple two-way interaction** is one considered only *at a particular level* of a third factor: thus there are simple BC interactions at A_1, A_2, ..., A_a, simple AB interactions at C_1, C_2, ..., C_c, and so on. A **three-factor interaction** is said to occur when the simple two-factor interactions are not homogeneous across all levels of a third factor.

One can test for the presence of simple BC interactions at particular levels of factor A by running two-factor (BC) within subjects ANOVAs on the data from those groups only. Then, having established that there is a simple interaction, one could proceed to use the methods of Chapter 9 to make pairwise multiple comparisons among the means for the combinations of factors B and C at the particular level of factor A concerned. As before, tests of simple effects (in this case, actually **simple simple main effects**) could be made in order to justify working with a particular subgroup of means.

We should warn the reader, however, that with complex factorial experiments, there is a heightened risk that some interaction or other will be found significant by chance alone. Should a particular interaction be thought crucial, it would be highly advisable to design another experiment to focus upon performance under those particular conditions, to see whether the pattern really is robust. Otherwise, the user is in great danger of capitalizing upon chance.

SUMMARY

1) An ANOVA design that includes both between subjects and within subjects factors is called a **mixed,** or **split-plot**, design. In SPSS, the results of such an experiment are analysed with the **Repeated Measures** item from the **ANOVA Models** menu.

2) The data can be explored with boxplots and tables of means and standard deviations, the latter using the **Means** procedure. The mean scores at different levels of between subjects factors are obtained by computing a new variable of means across all levels of the within subjects factors using the **Compute** procedure, and then applying the **Means** procedure to this new variable.

3) The procedure for mixed designs is

   Statistics

   ANOVA Models (or General Linear Model in SPSS 7)

   Repeated Measures (either GLM or MANOVA in SPSS 7)

   Generic names for repeated measures are defined in the **Repeated Measures Define Factor(s)** dialog box. After each within subjects factor name has been entered, the number of levels it contains is typed into the **Number of Levels** box. Click on **Add** to transfer the factor name and its levels into the **Factor Name** box.

   The variable names are then entered in the **Repeated Measures ANOVA** dialog box, taking care if there is more than one within subjects factor to ensure that the correct name is transferred to the appropriate slot in the **Within-Subjects Variables [*factor1*, *factor2*]** box. Between subjects factor names, along with their ranges of levels, are entered in the **Between-Subjects Factor(s)** box. Multivariate output can be suppressed (except in the case of SPSS 7 GLM - Repeated Measures) by clicking on the **Model** box and clicking off the **Multivariate tests** check box.

CHAPTER 11

MEASURING STATISTICAL ASSOCIATION

11.1 INTRODUCTION

11.1.1 Statistical association in interval data

So far, this book has been concerned with statistical methods devised for the purpose of comparing averages between or among samples of data that might be expected to differ in general level: for example, right-handed people might be compared with left-handed people; the trained might be compared with the untrained; males might be compared with females.

Consider, however, a set of paired data of the sort that might be produced if one were to weigh each of a sample of one hundred men before and after they had taken a fitness course. Previously, our concern would have been with the **comparison** of the men's average weight before the course with their average weight afterwards. One would expect these data to show another feature, however: the person who was heaviest before the course is likely to be among the heaviest in the group afterwards; the lightest person before the course should be among the lightest afterwards; and one with an intermediate score before the course is likely to be in the middle of the group afterwards. In other words, there should be a statistical **association** or **correlation** between people's weights before and after the course.

11.1.2 Depicting an association: Scatterplot

The existence of a statistical association between two variables is most apparent in the appearance of a diagram called a **scatterplot** (see Section 4.3.3.7) which, in the foregoing example, would be constructed by representing each person as a point in space, using as co-ordinates that person's weights before and after taking the course. The cloud of points would take the shape of an ellipse (see bottom right scatterplot in Figure 1 in Section 11.1.4), whose longer axis slopes upwards from left to right across the page. An elliptical scatterplot indicates the existence of a **linear relationship** between two variables. If the slope of the major axis is positive, the variables are said to be **positively correlated**; if it is negative, they are **negatively correlated**. The thinner the ellipse, the stronger the degree of linear relationship; the fatter the ellipse, the weaker the relationship. A circular scatterplot indicates the absence of any relationship between the two variables.

11.1.3 Linear association

The term **linear** means 'of the nature of a straight line'. In our current example, a straight line (known as a **regression line**) can be drawn through the points in the elliptical scatterplot so that it is rather close to most of the points (though there may be one or two atypical scores, or **outliers** as they are termed). We can use the regression line to make quite a good **estimate** of a particular man's weight after the course from a knowledge of his weight before the course: if we have Weight Before on the horizontal axis and Weight After on the vertical axis, we need only move up to the point on the regression line vertically above his first weight, and then move across to the vertical scale to estimate his second weight. If we do that, we shall probably be in error, the difference between his true weight after the course and his estimated weight from the regression line being known as a **residual.** The value of the residual, however, is likely to be small in comparison with the man's true weight after the course.

11.1.4 Measuring the strength of a linear association: Pearson correlation

A **correlation coefficient** is a statistic devised for the purpose of measuring the strength, or degree, of a supposed linear association between two variables, each of which has been measured on a scale with units. The most familiar correlation coefficient is the **Pearson correlation (r)**. The Pearson correlation is so defined that it can take values only within the range from -1 to $+1$, inclusive. The larger the absolute value (i.e. ignoring the sign), the narrower the ellipse, and the closer to the regression line the points in the scatterplot will fall. A perfect correlation arises when the values of one variable are exactly predictable from those of the other and the Pearson correlation takes a value of ± 1, in which case all the points in the scatterplot lie on the regression line. In other cases, the narrower the elliptical cloud of points, the stronger the association, and the greater the absolute value of the Pearson correlation. When there is no association whatever between two variables, their scatterplot should be a roughly circular cloud, in which case the Pearson correlation will be about zero and the regression line will be horizontal, i.e. have a slope of zero (see Figure 1).

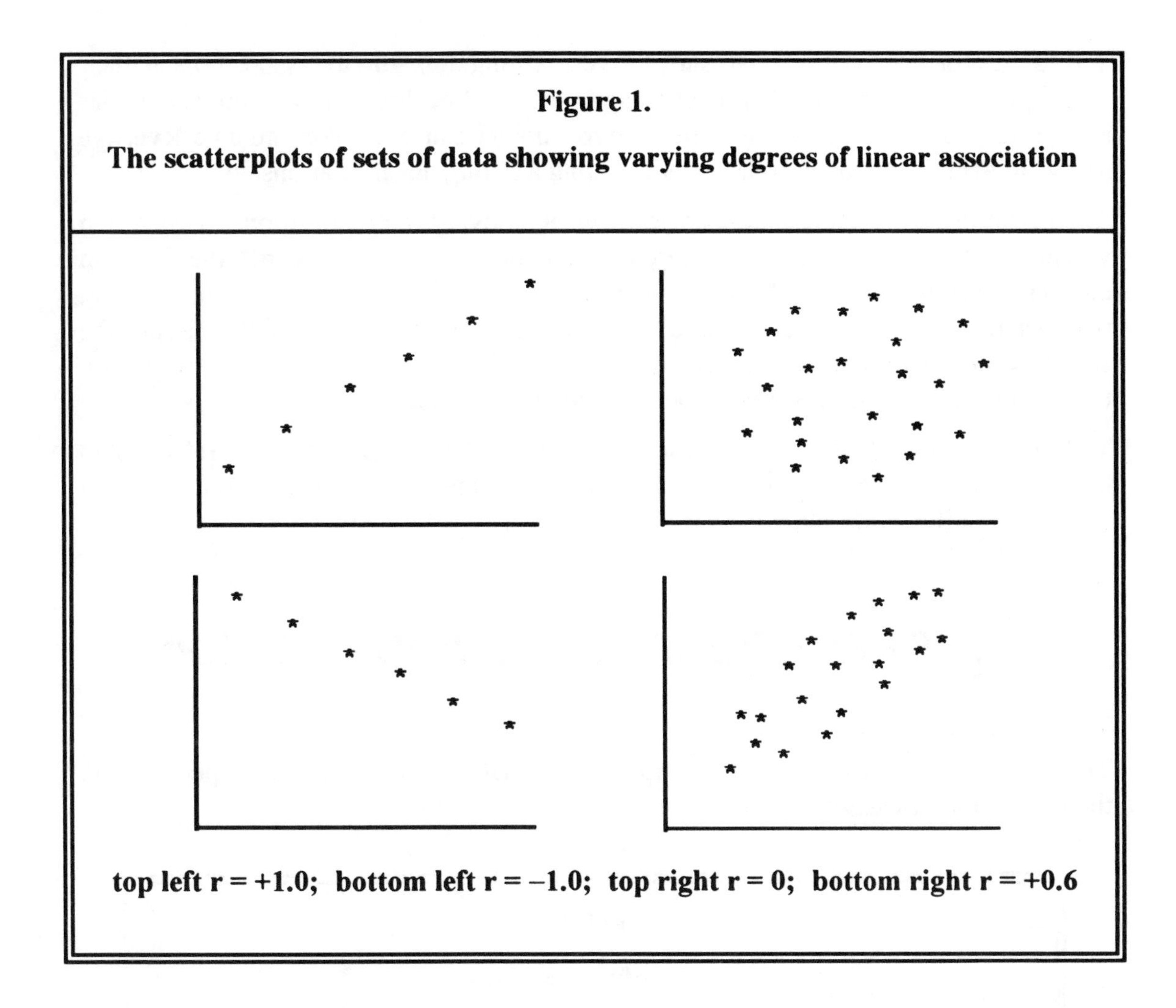

Figure 1.

The scatterplots of sets of data showing varying degrees of linear association

top left r = +1.0; bottom left r = –1.0; top right r = 0; bottom right r = +0.6

11.1.5 A word of warning

It is quite possible, from inspection of a scatterplot, to do two things:

(1) see whether there is indeed a linear relationship between the variables, in which case the Pearson correlation would be a meaningful statistic to use;

(2) guess fairly accurately what the value of the Pearson correlation would be if calculated.

In other words, from inspection of their scatterplot alone, one can discern all the essential features of the true relationship (if any) between two variables. So if we reason from the scatterplot to the statistics, we shall not go seriously wrong.

The converse, however, is not true: **given only the value of a Pearson correlation, one can say nothing whatsoever about the relationship between two variables**. In a famous paper, the statistician Anscombe (1973) presents data which illustrate how misleading the value of the Pearson correlation can be. Basically, he shows that, wherever the scatterplot is neither elliptical nor circular (i.e. the variables are neither in a linear relationship nor independent), the value of the Pearson correlation is misleading. (Exercise 18 uses Anscombe's data to show this.) For example, data giving a zero Pearson correlation may show a very strong **non-linear** association in their scatterplot. Two variables may be unrelated (and most of the data may show a circular scatterplot), but the presence of one or two outliers can exert considerable **leverage** and yield a high Pearson correlation, suggesting a strong linear relationship.

The moral of this cautionary tale is clear: when studying the association between two variables, always construct a scatterplot, and interpret (or disregard) the Pearson correlation accordingly. In the same paper, Anscombe gives a useful rule for deciding whether there really is a robust linear relationship between two variables: should the shape of the scatterplot be unaltered by the removal of a few observations at random, there is probably a real relationship between the two variables.

To sum up, the **Pearson correlation** is a measure of a **supposed** linear relationship between two variables; and the supposition of linearity must be confirmed by inspection of the scatterplot.

11.2 CORRELATIONAL ANALYSIS WITH SPSS

The principal of a tennis coaching school thinks that tennis proficiency depends upon the possession of a degree of general hand-eye co-ordination.

Table 1.

A set of paired data

Pupil	Initial Co-ordination	Final Tennis Proficiency
1	4	4
2	4	5
3	5	6
4	2	2
5	10	6
6	4	2
7	7	5
8	8	6
9	9	9
10	5	3

To confirm this hunch, she measures the hand-eye co-ordination (Initial Co-ordination) of some pupils who are beginning the course and their proficiency in tennis at the end of the course (Final Tennis Proficiency). The data are shown in Table 1.

11.2.1 Preparing the SPSS data set

Using the techniques described in Section 3.5, define the variables *coordin* and *proficy* (fuller names, such as *Initial Co-ordination* and *Final Tennis Proficiency*, can be assigned by using the **Define Labels** procedure).

11.2.2 Obtaining a scatterplot

Choose
Graphs
    Scatter

When the **Scatterplot** selection box (Figure 2) appears, click on **Define** (with a **Simple** scatterplot selected by default).

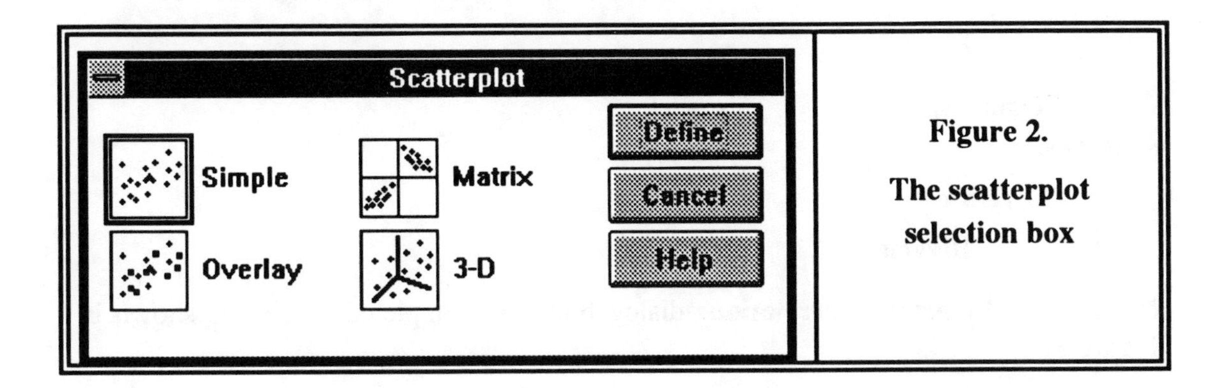

Figure 2.
The scatterplot selection box

Enter the variable names *proficy* and *coordin* into the **y-axis** and the **x-axis** box, respectively. Click on **OK**.

The scatterplot is shown in Figure 3. The plot shows a consistent trend, with no outliers.

It is possible to categorise points on a scatterplot by the levels of a grouping variable (e.g. sex) by inserting the grouping variable name in the **Set Markers by:** box. The points for males and females will be plotted in different colours.

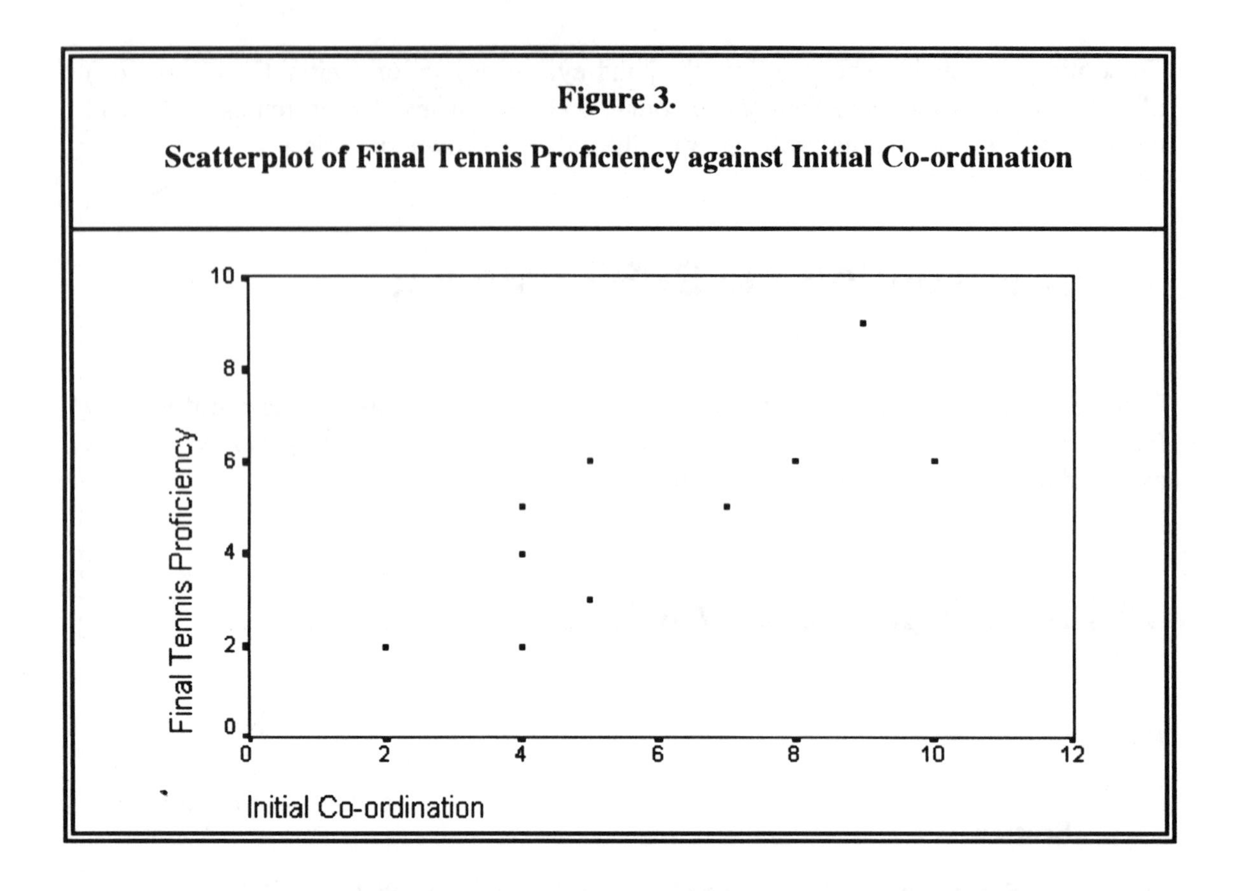

Figure 3.

Scatterplot of Final Tennis Proficiency against Initial Co-ordination

11.2.3 Procedure for the Pearson correlation

Choose (Figure 4)
Statistics

Correlate

Bivariate

to open the **Bivariate Correlations** dialog box (the completed version is shown in Figure 5).

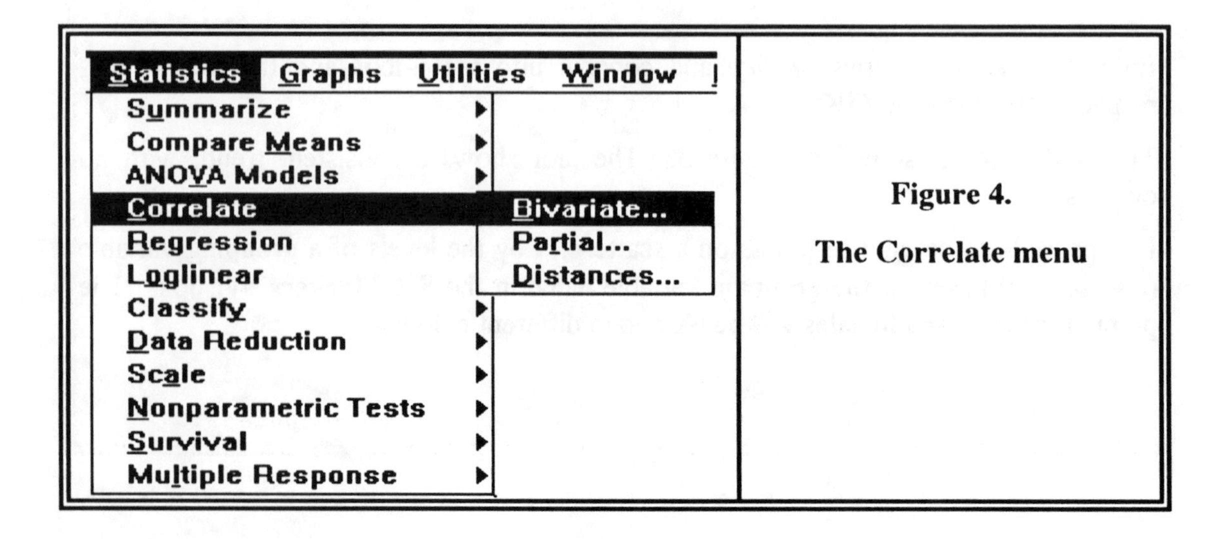

Figure 4.

The Correlate menu

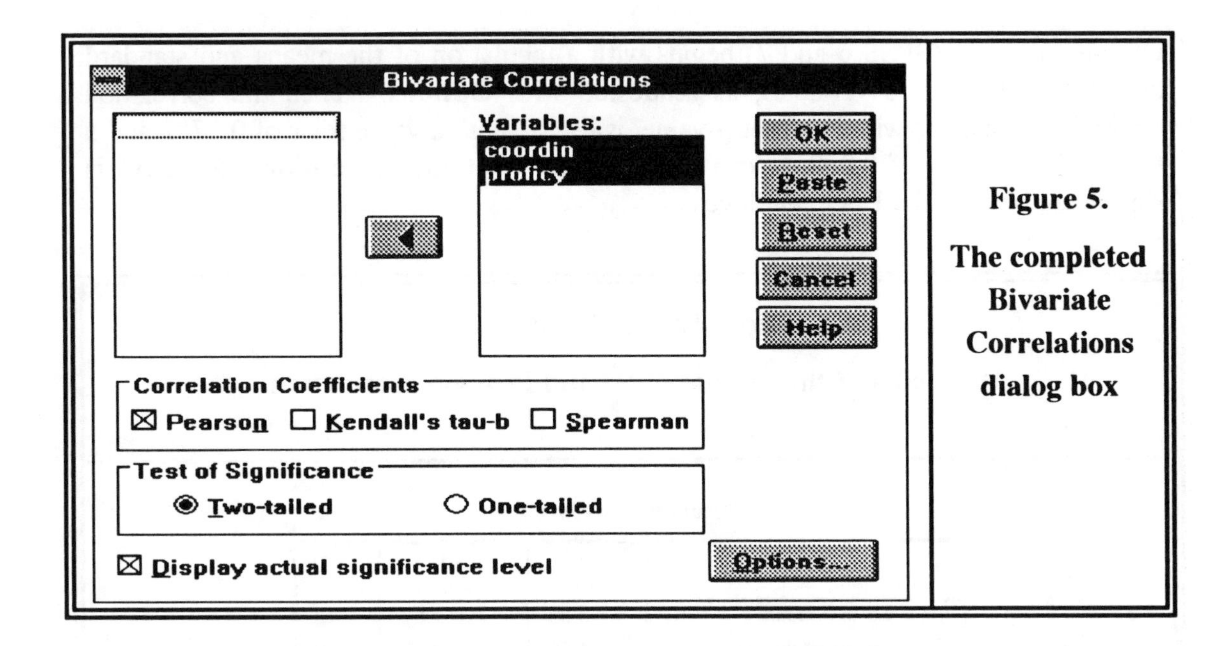

Figure 5.

The completed Bivariate Correlations dialog box

Highlight both variables and click on ▶ to transfer the names to the **Variables** box. Click on **Options** and then click on the **Means and Standard Deviations** check box. Click on **Continue** and then on **OK** to run the correlation coefficient and the optional additional statistics.

11.2.4 Output listing for the Pearson correlation

Output Listing 1 (SPSS 6).

Statistics of the two variables and Pearson correlation

```
Variable      Cases         Mean         Std Dev

COORDIN          10       5.8000          2.5734
PROFICY          10       4.8000          2.1499

   - -  Correlation Coefficients   - -

              COORDIN     PROFICY

COORDIN       1.0000       .7752
             (    10)    (    10)
             P= .        P= .008

PROFICY        .7752      1.0000
             (    10)    (    10)
             P= .008     P= .

(Coefficient / (Cases) / 2-tailed Significance)
" . " is printed if a coefficient cannot be computed
```

Output Listing 1 (SPSS 6 and 7) begins with a tabulation of the means and standard deviations of the two variables, as requested with **Options**. Then the correlation coefficient, together with its exact p-value, is listed. With a value for r of 0.7752 and a two-tailed p-value of 0.008, it can be concluded that the correlation coefficient is significant beyond the 1 per cent level.

Output Listing 1 (SPSS 7).

Statistics of the two variables and Pearson correlation

Descriptive Statistics

	Mean	Std. Deviation	N
Initial Co-ordination	5.80	2.57	10
Final Tennis Proficiency	4.80	2.15	10

Correlations

		Initial Co-ordination	Final Tennis Proficiency
Pearson Correlation	Initial Co-ordination	1.000	.775**
	Final Tennis Proficiency	.775**	1.000
Sig. (2-tailed)	Initial Co-ordination	.	.008
	Final Tennis Proficiency	.008	.
N	Initial Co-ordination	10	10
	Final Tennis Proficiency	10	10

**. Correlation is significant at the 0.01 level (2-tailed).

If the **Display actual significance level** check box at the bottom left of the SPSS 6 **Bivariate Correlations** dialog box is turned off (see Figure 5), the correlation is displayed as in Output Listing 2 (SPSS 6).

```
  - -  Correlation Coefficients  - -

             COORDIN      PROFICY

COORDIN      1.0000        .7752**
PROFICY       .7752**     1.0000

* - Signif. LE .05    ** - Signif. LE .01   (2-tailed)
```

Output Listing 2 (SPSS 6).

Brief display of the significance of r

11.2.5 Obtaining a correlation matrix

When there are more than two variables, SPSS can be commanded to construct a **correlation matrix**, a rectangular array whose entries are the correlations between each variable and every other variable. This is done by entering as many variable names as required into the **Variables** box within the **Bivariate Correlations** dialog box (Figure 5).

11.2.6 Point-biserial correlation

When one of the variables is a dichotomy such as male/female or pass/fail, and the other is measured on a continuous scale and assumed to be distributed normally in the population, then the Pearson correlation can still be used though in this situation it is usually referred to as **point-biserial correlation** (r_{pb}). Thus in our example, a Pearson correlation (alias point-biserial) could have been calculated for Final Tennis Proficiency and Gender (assuming the genders of the subjects were known).

11.3 OTHER MEASURES OF ASSOCIATION

The Pearson correlation is suitable only for interval data. With nominal or ordinal data, other measures must be used. (**Ordinal** data are either ranks or records of **ordered** category membership; **nominal** data are records of **qualitative** category membership.)

11.3.1 Measures of association strength for ordinal data

The term ordinal data embraces all data relating to quantitative variables that are not measures on an independent scale with units. For example, if we rank a group of 10 people with respect to height, giving 10 to the tallest and 1 to the shortest, the resulting set of ranks is an ordinal data set, because an individual rank does not signify so many inches, centimetres (or some other unit of height): a rank merely expresses an individual's height in relation to the heights of the other people in that particular group.

If two judges are asked to rank, say, ten paintings in order of preference, they may well disagree in their orderings, especially if each judge is required to assign a different rank to each object and avoid 'ties'. (This stricture, however, is not always enforced and one or two ties may be tolerated.) The result of such an exercise would be a set of paired ordinal data.

In a rather different procedural paradigm, however, ties, rather than being, at best, tolerable may actually be built into the judgmental process. Judges may be asked to assign objects to a pre-specified set of ordered categories. If, as is usual, there are more objects than categories, tied observations are inevitable. Rating scales yield data in the form of assignments to ordered categories.

The term **ordinal data** includes both ranks and assignments to ordered categories. When, as in the case of the two judges, ordinal data are paired, the question arises as to the extent to which the two sets of ranks of category assignments agree. This is a question about the strength of association between two variables which, although quantitative, are measured at the ordinal, rather than the interval level.

11.3.1.1 The Spearman rank correlation

Suppose that the ranks assigned to the ten paintings by the two judges are as in Table 2.

It is obvious from Table 2 that the judges generally agree closely in their rankings: at most, the ranks they assign to a painting differ by a single rank. One way of measuring the level of agreement between the two judges is by calculating the Pearson correlation between the two sets of ranks. This correlation is known as the **Spearman rank correlation** (or as **Spearman's rho**). The Spearman rank correlation is usually presented in terms of a formula which, although it looks very different from that of the Pearson correlation, is actually equivalent, provided that no ties are allowed.

Table 2.

Ranks assigned by two judges to each of ten paintings

Painting	A	B	C	D	E	F	G	H	I	J
First Judge	1	2	3	4	5	6	7	8	9	10
Second Judge	1	3	2	4	6	5	8	7	10	9

The use of the Spearman rank correlation is not confined to ordinal data. Should a scatterplot show that the Pearson correlation is unsuitable as a measure of the strength of association between two quantitative variables which have been measured at the interval level, the scores on both variables can be converted to ranks and the Spearman rank correlation calculated instead.

With small samples, it is difficult to obtain an accurate p-value for a Spearman correlation, especially when there are tied ranks. When there are no tied ranks, one can obtain critical values for the Spearman rank correlation from tables in textbooks such as Neave & Worthington (1988). When ties are present, they must reduce one's confidence in the critical values given in the tables. The user can but hope that when there is only a tie or two here and there, the tables will still give serviceable p-values.

11.3.1.2 Kendall's tau statistics

Kendall's tau statistics provide an alternative to the Spearman rank correlation as measures of agreement between rankings, or assignments to ordered categories. The basic idea is that one set of ranks can be converted into another by a succession of reversals of pairs of ranks in one set: the fewer the reversals needed (in relation to the total number of possible reversals), the larger the value of tau. The numerator of Kendall's tau is the difference between the number of pairs of objects whose ranks are concordant (i.e. they go in the same direction) and the number of discordant pairs. If the former predominate, the sign of tau is positive; if the latter predominate, tau is negative.

There are three different versions of Kendall's tau: **tau-a**, **tau-b** and **tau-c**. All three measures have the same numerator, the difference between the numbers of concordant and discordant pairs. It is in their denominators that they differ, the difference lying in the way they handle tied observations. The denominator of tau-a is simply the total number of pairs. The problem with tau-a is that when there are ties, its range quickly becomes restricted, to the point where it becomes difficult to interpret. The correlation tau-b has terms in the denominator that consider, in either variable, pairs that are tied on one variable but not on the other. (When there are no ties, the values of tau-a and tau-b are identical.) The correlation tau-c was designed for situations where one wishes to measure agreement between assignments to unequal-sized sets of ordered categories. Provided the data meet certain requirements, the appropriate tau correlation can vary throughout the complete range from −1 to +1.

Kendall's tau correlations have advantages over the Spearman correlation, especially with small data sets, in which there are tied assignments, where serviceable p-values can still be obtained.

11.3.1.3 Obtaining the Spearman and Kendall rank correlations

In the **Data Editor** grid, define two variables, *judge1* and *judge2*. From Table 2, enter the ranks assigned by the first judge into the *judge1* column and those assigned by the second judge into the *judge2* column.

Choose

Statistics

    Correlate

        Bivariate

to obtain the **Bivariate Correlations** dialog box (Figure 5).

By default, the **Pearson** check box will be marked. Mark also the **Kendall's tau-b** and the **Spearman** check boxes and click on **OK** to obtain all three statistics, shown in Output Listing 3 (SPSS 6 and 7).

Output Listing 3 (SPSS 6).

Correlations between two sets of ranks

```
- -  Correlation Coefficients  - -

               JUDGE1      JUDGE2
JUDGE1         1.0000       .9515
              (   10)     (   10)
              P= .        P= .000
JUDGE2          .9515      1.0000
              (   10)     (   10)
              P= .000     P= .

(Coefficient / (Cases) / 2-tailed Significance)
" . " is printed if a coefficient cannot be computed

K E N D A L L   C O R R E L A T I O N  C O E F F I C I E N T S

JUDGE2            .8222
               N(    10)
               Sig .001
                 JUDGE1

S P E A R M A N   C O R R E L A T I O N  C O E F F I C I E N T S

JUDGE2            .9515
               N(    10)
               Sig .000
                 JUDGE1
```

Correlations

			JUDGE1	JUDGE2
Kendall's tau_b	Correlation Coefficient	JUDGE1	1.000	.822*
		JUDGE2	.822*	1.000
	Sig. (2-tailed)	JUDGE1	.	.001
		JUDGE2	.001	.
	N	JUDGE1	10	10
		JUDGE2	10	10
Spearman's rho	Correlation Coefficient	JUDGE1	1.000	.952*
		JUDGE2	.952*	1.000
	Sig. (2-tailed)	JUDGE1	.	.000
		JUDGE2	.000	.
	N	JUDGE1	10	10
		JUDGE2	10	10

**. Correlation is significant at the .01 level (2-tailed).

Output Listing 3 (SPSS 7).

Correlations between two sets of ranks

Note that the calculation of Kendall's statistics with **categorial** data, in the form of assignments of target objects to ordered categories, is best handled by the **Crosstabs** procedure (see next section); indeed, tau-c can only be obtained in **Crosstabs**.

Output Listing 3 (SPSS 6 and 7) show the Pearson correlation between the two sets of ranks as *0.9515*, and the Kendall correlation as *0.8222*. This value is different from that of the Pearson correlation, but there is nothing untoward in this: the two statistics are based on quite different theoretical foundations and often take noticeably different values. Finally the Spearman rank correlation is *0.9515*, which is exactly the value given for the Pearson correlation.

11.3.2 Measures of association strength for categorial data

When people's membership of two sets of mutually exclusive and exhaustive categories (such as sex or blood group) is recorded, it is possible to construct a **crosstabulation**, or **contingency table** (see Section 3.9.2). In the analysis of categorial data, the crosstabulation is the analogue of the scatterplot. Note that the categories of each variable must be mutually exclusive, that is no individual or case can fall into more than one combination of categories.

In SPSS, crosstabulations are handled by **Crosstabs**, which is found in the **Summarize** menu. Within the **Crosstabs** dialog box, there is a **Statistics** subdialog box (this chapter, Figure 11) containing check boxes for several measures of association. Many of these are based on the familiar **chi-square** statistic, which is used for determining the presence of an association between two qualitative variables. The rejection of H_0 by means of chi-square, however, only establishes the **existence** of a statistical association: it does not measure its **strength**. In fact, the chi-square statistic is unsuitable as a **measure** of association, because it is affected by the total frequency.

A word of warning about the misuse of chi-square should be given here. It is important to realise that the calculated statistic is only **approximately** distributed as the theoretical chi-square distribution: the greater the expected frequencies, the better the approximation, hence the rule about minimum expected frequencies, which is stated in Section 11.3.2.2. It is also important to note that the use of the chi-square statistic requires that **each individual studied contributes to the count in only one cell in the crosstabulation**. There are several other potential problems the user should be aware of. A lucid account of the rationale and assumptions of the chi-square test is given by Howell (1997), and a survey of the errors and misconceptions about chi-square that abound in the research literature is given by Delucchi (1983).

Several measures of strength of association for nominal data have been proposed (see Reynolds, 1984). An ideal measure should mimic the correlation coefficient by having a maximum absolute value of 1 for perfect association, and a value of 0 for no association. The choice of the appropriate statistic depends on whether the variables are ordinal or nominal, and whether the contingency (crosstabulation) table is 2×2 (each variable has two categories) or larger. Guidance can be found by clicking on the **Help** box and choosing the various statistics in turn to find the most appropriate one.

One such statistic, for example, is the **phi coefficient**, obtained by dividing the value of chi-square by the total frequency and taking the square root. For two-way contingency tables involving variables with more than two categories, however, another statistic, known as **Cramér's V**, is preferred because with more complex tables, Cramér's measure can still, as in the 2×2 case, achieve its maximum value of unity. Other measures of association, such as **Goodman & Kruskal's lambda**, measure the proportional reduction in error achieved when membership of a category on one attribute is used to predict category membership on the other. If the categories in the cross-tabulation are **ordered**, we have ordinal, not nominal, data and Kendall's statistics **tau-b** and **tau-c** are appropriate.

11.3.2.1 A 2 × 2 contingency table

Suppose that 50 boys and 50 girls are individually asked to select toys from a cupboard. The available toys have previously been categorised as mechanical or non-mechanical. The hypothesis is that the boys should prefer mechanical toys, and the girls non-mechanical toys. There are two nominal variables here: Group (Boys or Girls); and Children's Choice (Mechanical or Non-Mechanical). The null hypothesis (H_0) is that there is no association between the variables. Table 3 shows the children's choices.

Table 3. A contingency table

	Children's Choice		
Group	Mechanical	Non-Mechanical	Total
Boys	30	20	50
Girls	15	35	50
Total	45	55	100

From inspection of this 2×2 contingency table, it would appear that there is an association between the Group and Choice variables: the majority of the Boys did, in fact, choose Mechanical toys; whereas the majority of the Girls chose Non-Mechanical toys.

11.3.2.2 Procedure for crosstabulation and associated statistics (chi-square, phi and Cramér's V)

The SPSS data set for a contingency table must include two coding variables to identify the various cell counts, one representing the rows (*group*), the other the columns (*choice*). Using the techniques described in Section 3.5, define the variables *group*, *choice*, and *count*. In the *group* variable, the code numbers *1* and *2* can represent Boys and Girls, respectively; in the *choice* variable, the values *1* and *2* can represent Mechanical and Non-Mechanical, respectively. Type the data into the three columns, as shown in Figure 6.

	group	choice	count
1	1	1	30
2	1	2	20
3	2	1	15
4	2	2	35

Figure 6.

Part of the Data Editor window showing the coding of the children's choices

The next step is essential. Since the data in the *count* column represent cell frequencies of a variable (not values), SPSS must be apprised of this by means of the **Weight Cases** item within the **Data** menu (Figure 7).

Choose

Data

  Weight Cases

to open the **Weight Cases** dialog box (Figure 8).

Click on the name of the variable that is to be weighted (*count*), then on the item **Weight cases by** (which cancels the default item **Do not weight cases**), and finally on ▶ to enter *count* into the **Frequency Variable** box. Click on **OK.** The completed dialog box is shown in Figure 8.

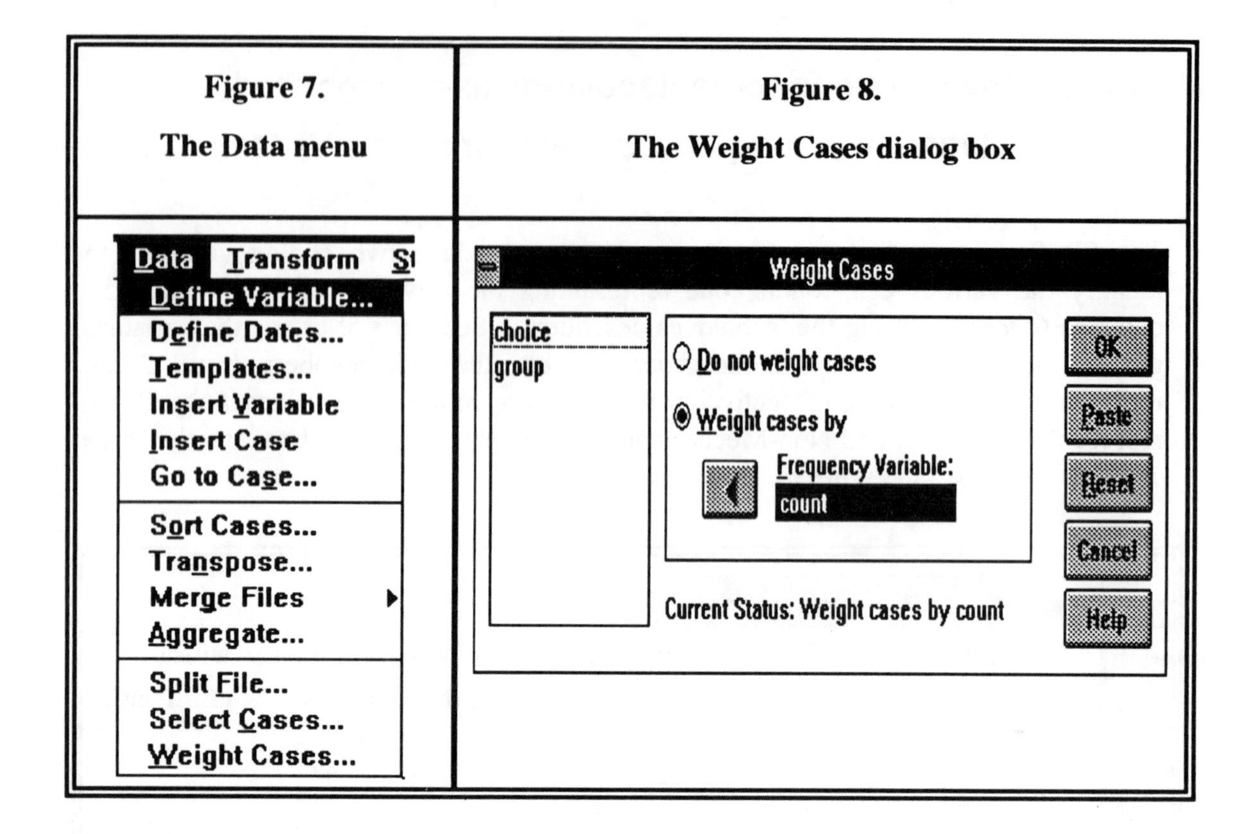

Figure 7.
The Data menu

Figure 8.
The Weight Cases dialog box

To analyse the contingency table data, choose
Statistics

  Summarize

and then click on **Crosstabs** (Figure 9). This will open the **Crosstabs** dialog box (Figure 10).

Statistics Graphs Utilities Window Help
Summarize | Frequencies...
Compare Means | Descriptives...
ANOVA Models | Explore...
Correlate | Crosstabs...
Regression | List Cases...
Loglinear | Report Summaries in Rows...
Classify | Report Summaries in Columns...
Data Reduction
Scale
Nonparametric Tests
Survival
Multiple Response

Figure 9.
Finding Crosstabs in the Statistics menu

Within the **Crosstabs** dialog box, click on *group* and then on ▶ to transfer the name into the **Row(s)** box. Click on *choice* and then on ▶ to transfer the name into the **Column(s)** box (Figure 10).

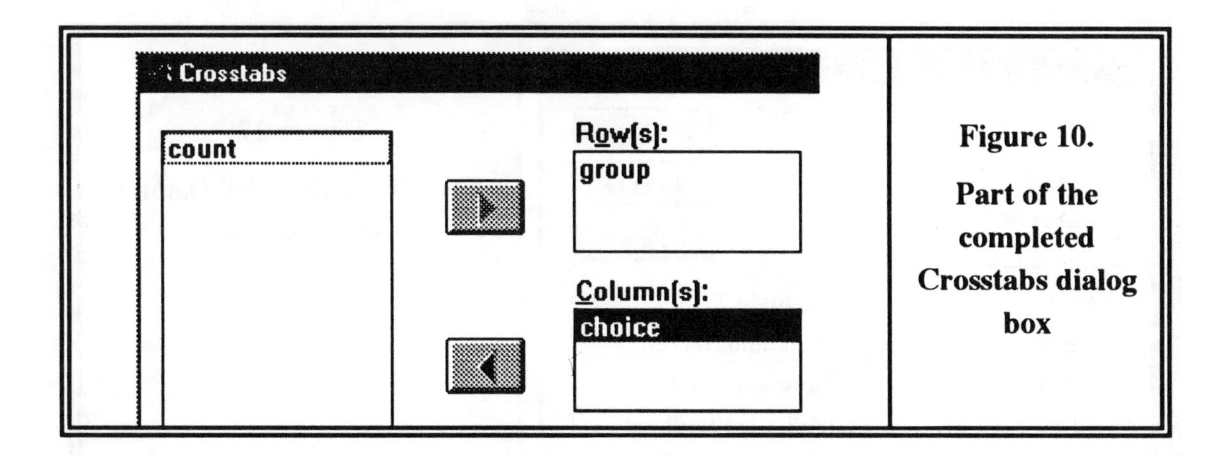

Figure 10. Part of the completed Crosstabs dialog box

Click on **Statistics** to open the **Crosstabs: Statistics** dialog box (Figure 11).

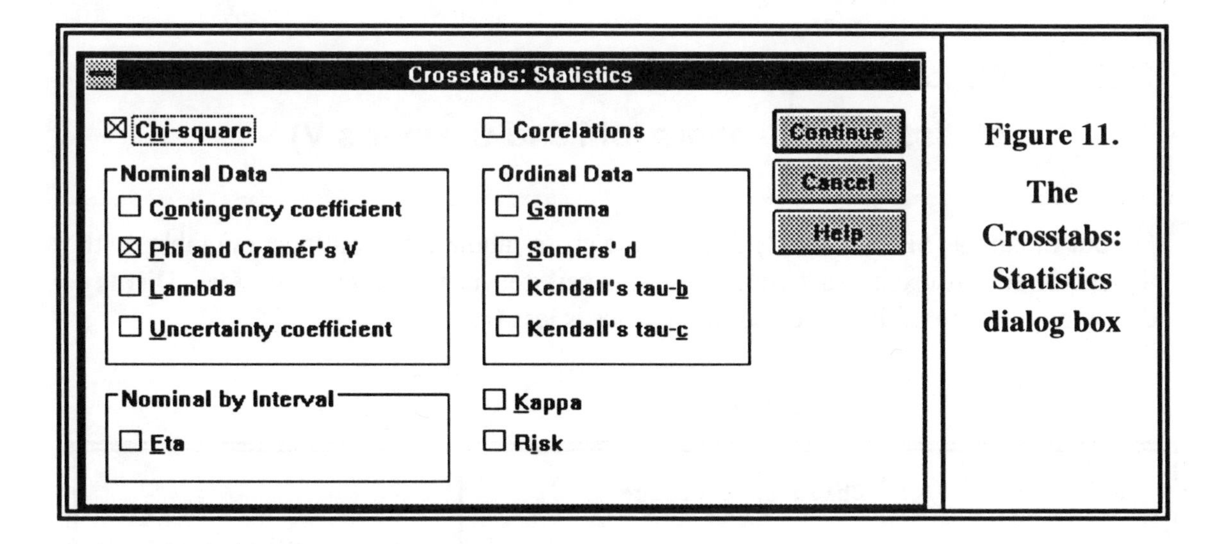

Figure 11. The Crosstabs: Statistics dialog box

Within the **Nominal Data** list of check boxes, select **Chi-square** and **Phi and Cramér's V**. Click on **Continue** to return to the **Crosstabs** dialog box.

We recommend an additional option for computing the expected cell frequencies. This enables the user to check that the prescribed minimum requirements for the valid use of chi-square have been fulfilled.

Although there has been much debate about these, the practice of leading authorities has been to proscribe the use of chi-square when:

(a) in 2 × 2 tables, any of the expected frequencies is less than 5;

(b) in larger tables, any of the expected frequencies is less than 1 or more than 20% are less than 5.

Click on **Cells** at the foot of the **Crosstabs** dialog box (Figure 10) to open the **Crosstabs: Cell Display** selection box (Figure 12).

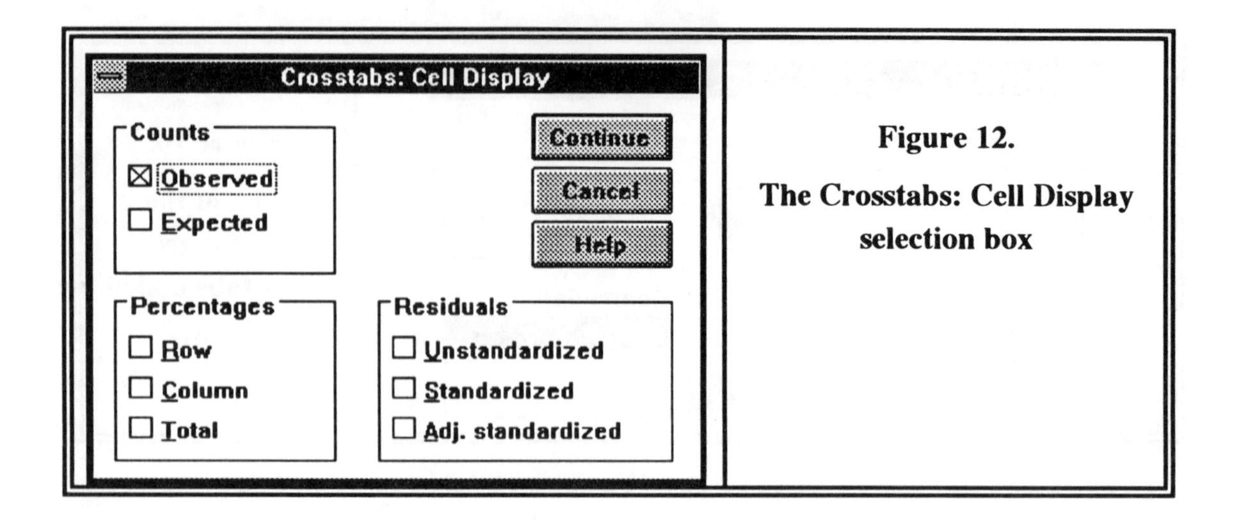

Figure 12.

The Crosstabs: Cell Display selection box

11.3.2.3 Output listing for crosstabulation and associated statistics (chi-square, phi and Cramér's V)

Output Listing 4 (SPSS 6 and 7) displays the cross-tabulation (contingency) table, with the observed and expected frequencies, as requested in the **Crosstabs: Cell Display** dialog box. None of the expected frequencies is less than 5.

```
GROUP  by  CHOICE  Children's Choice

                       CHOICE
              Count   |
              Exp Val |Mechanic Non-mech
                      |al       anical    Row
                      |       1|       2| Total
GROUP         --------+--------+--------+
                 1    |    30  |    20  |    50
  Boys                |  22.5  |  27.5  |  50.0%
                      +--------+--------+
                 2    |    15  |    35  |    50
  Girls               |  22.5  |  27.5  |  50.0%
                      +--------+--------+
               Column      45       55      100
                Total   45.0%    55.0%   100.0%
```

Output Listing 4 (SPSS 6).

A contingency table including the optional expected values

Output Listing 4 (SPSS 7).

A contingency table including the optional expected values

GROUP * Children's Choice Crosstabulation

			Children's Choice		Total
			Mechanical	Non-mechanical	
GROUP	Boys	Count	30	20	50
		Expected Count	22.5	27.5	50.0
	Girls	Count	15	35	50
		Expected Count	22.5	27.5	50.0
Total		Count	45	55	100
		Expected Count	45.0	55.0	100.0

Output Listing 5 (SPSS 6 and 7) shows the requested statistics.

Output Listing 5 (SPSS 6).

Statistics of a contingency table

```
        Chi-Square                    Value        DF      Significance
--------------------------        -----------    ----     ------------

Pearson                             9.09091        1          .00257
Continuity Correction               7.91919        1          .00489
Likelihood Ratio                    9.24017        1          .00237
Linear-by-Linear                    9.00000        1          .00270
        Association
Fisher's Exact Test:
    One-Tail                                                  .00232
    Two-Tail                                                  .00464

Minimum Expected Frequency -    22.500

                                                  Approximate
      Statistic                  Value           Significance
--------------------          ---------          ------------

Phi                             .30151             .00257
Cramer's V                      .30151             .00257
```

Output Listing 5 (SPSS 7).

Statistics of a contingency table

Chi-Square Tests

	Value	df	Asymp. Sig. (2-tailed)	Exact Sig. (2-tailed)	Exact Sig. (1-tailed)
Pearson Chi-Square	9.091[b]	1	.003		
Continuity Correction [a]	7.919	1	.005		
Likelihood Ratio	9.240	1	.002		
Fisher's Exact Test				.005	.002
Linear-by-Linear Association	9.000	1	.003		
N of Valid Cases	100				

a. Computed only for a 2x2 table

b. 0 cells (.0%) have expected count less than 5. The minimum expected count is 22.50.

The row labelled **Pearson** in Output Listing 5 (SPSS 6 and 7) lists the conventional chi-square statistic, along with its tail probability under H_0 (labelled **Significance** or **Asymp. Sig.**). Ignore the other rows in the Chi-Square section. It can be concluded that there is a significant association between the variables *group* and *choice*, as shown by the p-value (less than 0.01) for chi-square.

Beneath the Chi-Square section in Output Listing 5 (SPSS 6) and in a separate table labelled **Symmetric Measures** in the Output Navigator in SPSS 7 (reproduced here in Output Listing 6 (SPSS 7)), are the values of the extra requested statistics, the **phi coefficient** and **Cramér's V**. These provide a measure of the strength of the association rather like that of the Pearson correlation coefficient.

Output Listing 6 (SPSS 7).

Values of Phi and Cramér's V

Symmetric Measures

		Value	Approx. Sig.
Nominal by Nominal	Phi	.302	.003
	Cramer's V	.302	.003
N of Valid Cases		100	

SUMMARY

1) The **degree of association** between two quantitative interval variables level can be measured by a **correlation coefficient**. The most well-known correlation coefficient is the **Pearson correlation**.

   Choose

   Statistics

   Correlate

   Bivariate

2) It is recommended that a **scatterplot** should always be requested. Choose

   Graphs

   Scatter

   Simple

3) For **ordinal data in the form of ranks**, measures of association strength are provided by the **Spearman rank correlation** and **Kendall's tau-a** and **tau-b** statistics. These can be found by choosing

   Statistics

   Correlate

   Bivariate

4) Various statistics for **categorial data** are available in the **Crosstabs** menu, which analyses contingency tables. When the data are in the form of counts of category membership, coding variables are needed to identify the cells of the table.

5) If the contingency table contains a variable representing cell frequencies, then it is necessary to show SPSS that they are frequencies and not just score values by using the **Weight Cases** procedure.

   Choose

   Data

   Weight Cases.

(continued)

5) (continued)

Select the appropriate variable name for the frequency data, click on the **Weight Cases by** option, and then on ▶ to insert the name in the **Frequency Variable** box.

6) To run the cross-tabulation statistical procedures, choose

Statistics

Summarize

Crosstabs

Select the row and column variables using the **Row(s)** and **Column(s)** boxes. Choose the appropriate statistics by clicking on **Statistics** within the **Crosstabs** dialog box and then clicking on check boxes in the **Crosstabs: Statistics** selection box. It is also recommended that expected cell frequencies are selected by clicking on **Cells** within the **Crosstabs** dialog box and then clicking on the **Expected** check box.

CHAPTER 12

REGRESSION

12.1 INTRODUCTION

Much of Chapter 11 was devoted to the use of the **Pearson correlation** to measure the strength of the association between two quantitative variables, each of which has been measured on an interval scale.

But the associative coin has two sides. On the one hand, a single number can be calculated (a correlation coefficient) which expresses the **strength** of the association. On the other, however, there is a set of techniques, known as **regression methods**, which utilise the presence of an association between two variables to predict the values of one (the dependent variable) from those of another (the independent variable). It is with this predictive aspect that the present chapter is concerned.

To sum up, in **correlation**, the **degree of statistical association** between variables is expressed as a single number known as a **correlation coefficient**. In **regression**, the purpose is to **estimate** or **predict** some characteristic from a knowledge of others by constructing a **regression equation**.

12.1.1 Simple, two-variable regression

In **simple, two-variable regression**, the values of one variable (the dependent variable, y) are estimated from those of another (the independent variable, x) by a linear (straight line) equation of the general form

$$y' = b_0 + b_1(x)$$

where y' is the estimated value of y, b_1 is the slope (known as the **regression coefficient**), and b_0 is the intercept (known as the **regression constant**).

12.1.2 Multiple regression

In **multiple regression**, the values of one variable (the dependent variable y) are estimated from those of two or more other variables (the independent variables x_1 , x_2 , ... , x_p).

This is achieved by the construction of a linear equation of the general form

$$y' = b_0 + b_1(x_1) + b_2(x_2) + \dots + b_p(x_p)$$

where the parameters b_1, b_2, ..., b_p are the partial **regression coefficients** and the intercept b_0 is the **regression constant**. This equation is known as the **multiple linear regression equation of y upon x_1 , ... , x_p .**

12.1.3 Residuals

When a regression equation is used to estimate the values of a variable y from those of one or more independent variables x, the estimates y' will usually fall short of complete accuracy. Geometrically speaking, the data points will not fall precisely upon the straight line, plane or hyperplane specified by the regression equation. The discrepancies ($y - y'$) on the predicted variable are known as **residuals**. When using regression methods, the study of the residuals is of great importance, because they form the basis for measures of the accuracy of the estimates and of the extent to which the **regression model** gives a good account of the data in question. (See Lovie, 1991, for an account of the analysis of residuals, a topic known as **regression diagnostics**.)

12.1.4 The multiple correlation coefficient

One simple (though rather limited) measure of the efficacy of regression for the prediction of y is the Pearson correlation between the true values of the target variable y and the estimates y' obtained by substituting the corresponding values of x into the regression equation. The correlation between y and y' is known as the **multiple correlation coefficient *R***. Notice that the upper case is used for the multiple correlation coefficient, to distinguish it from the correlation between the target variable and any one independent variable considered separately. In simple, two-variable regression, the multiple correlation coefficient takes the **absolute** value of the Pearson correlation between the target variable and the independent variable: so if $r = -0.90$, $R = 0.90$. It can be shown algebraically that the multiple correlation coefficient cannot have a negative value.

12.2 SIMPLE REGRESSION

To illustrate the use of this technique, consider that among university authorities, there is much concern about the methods used to select students for entry. The following example concerns a study of the association between students' marks on the initial academic selection examinations and performance in their university examinations.

Given data on people's final examination marks y and their performance x on the entrance examination, a Pearson correlation can be used to measure the degree of statistical association between the former and the latter. It is also possible to use simple regression to predict examination performance at university from marks in the entrance examination. It can be shown by mathematical proof, however, that when two or more independent variables are used to predict the target variable y, the predictions will, on average, be **at least as accurate** as when any one of the same independent variables is used: in other words, the multiple correlation coefficient *R* must be at least as great as any single Pearson correlation *r*. For the moment, however, we shall be considering the simple regression of university examination performance upon the marks in one entrance examination.

12.2.1 Procedure for simple regression

12.2.1.1 Some data

In Table 1, the first score *x* in each (*x*, *y*) pair is a student's mark in the final university examination, and the second *y* is the same student's mark in the entrance examination.

Table 1.

Table of the final university exam (y) and the selection exam (x) scores

y	x	y	x	y	x	y	x	y	x
38	44	76	37	98	40	112	49	145	60
49	40	78	41	100	37	114	46	150	55
61	43	81	53	100	48	114	41	152	54
65	42	86	47	103	48	117	49	164	58
69	44	91	45	105	43	125	63	169	62
73	46	94	41	106	55	140	52	195	49
74	34	95	39	107	48	142	56		

12.2.1.2 Preparing the SPSS data set

Using the techniques described in Section 3.5, define the variables *finalex* and *selectex*, using the labelling procedure to assign the more informative names *University Exam* and *Selection Exam*. Type the data into the columns.

12.2.1.3 Accessing the simple regression procedure

Choose (in both SPSS 6 and 7)
Statistics
　　Regression

(Figure 1) and click on **Linear** to open the **Linear Regression** dialog box (Figure 2).

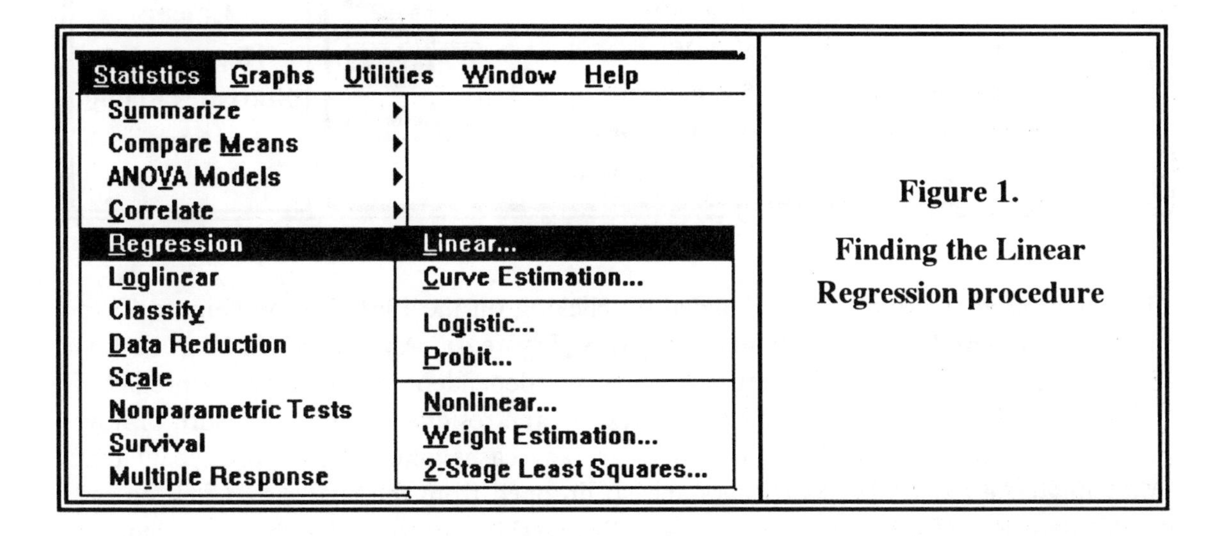

Figure 1.
Finding the Linear Regression procedure

The two variable names *finalex* and *selectex* will appear in the left-hand box. It is important to be clear about which variable is the dependent variable and which is the independent variable - in this example the dependent variable is the final university examination *finalex* and the independent variable is the selection exam *selectex*. Transfer these variable names into the appropriate boxes in the dialog box by clicking on the variable name and then on ▶ (Figure 2).

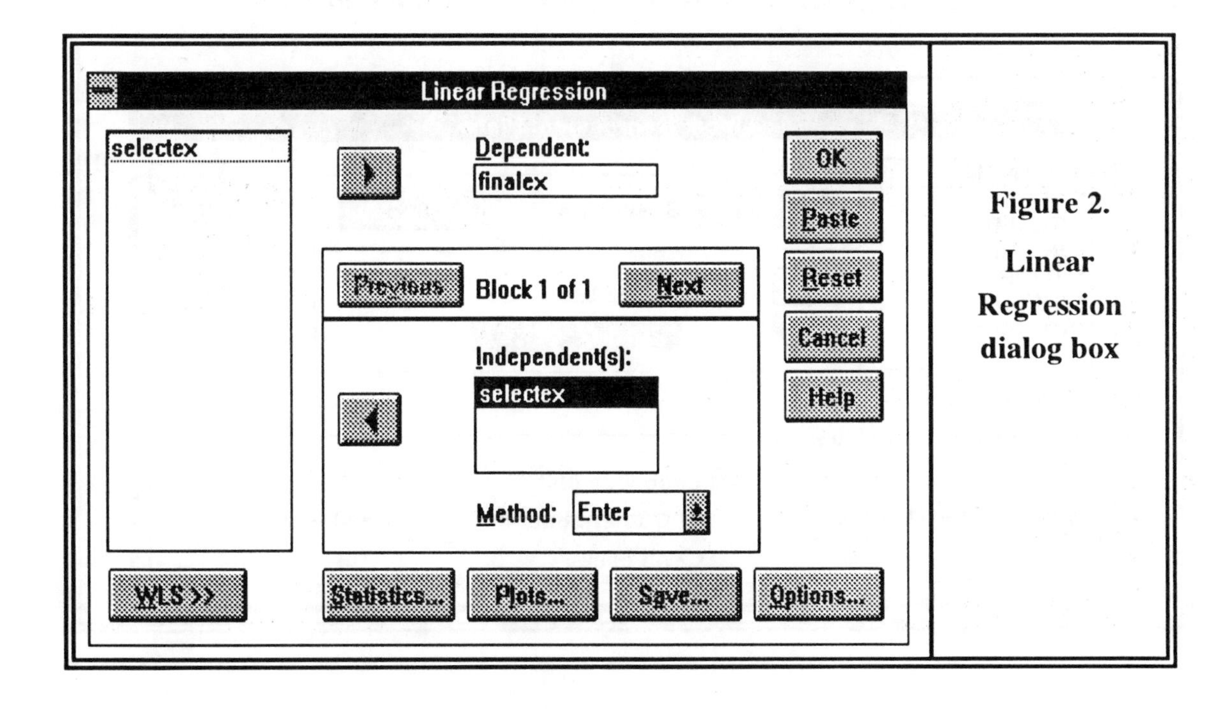

Figure 2.
Linear Regression dialog box

The user is urged to request additional descriptive statistics and a residuals analysis. To obtain descriptive statistics, click on the **Statistics** button (Figure 2) to open the **Linear Regression: Statistics** dialog box (Figure 3). Click on the **Descriptives** check box and then on **Continue** to return to the **Linear Regression** dialog box.

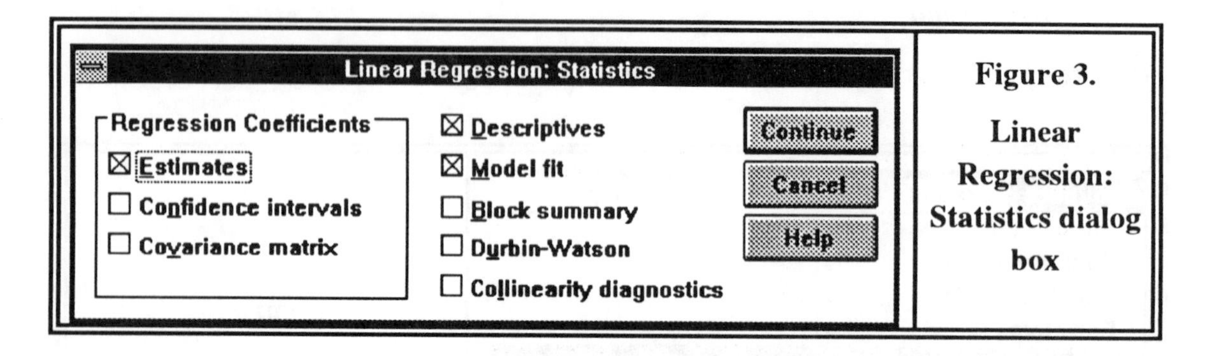

Figure 3. Linear Regression: Statistics dialog box

Information about residuals is obtained by clicking on the **Plots** button (Figure 2) to open the **Linear Regression: Plots** dialog box (Figure 4). A **residual** (Section 12.1.3) is the difference between the actual value of the dependent variable and its predicted value using the regression equation. Analysis of the residuals gives a measure of how good the prediction is and whether there are any cases which are so discrepant that they might be considered as outliers and so dropped from the analysis. Click on the **Casewise plot** check box in the **Linear Regression: Plots** dialog box to obtain a listing of any exceptionally large residuals. We recommend that this is done for an initial run of the procedure. Click **Continue** and then on **OK** to run the regression for the first time.

Figure 4.

Linear Regression: Plots dialog box for residuals analysis

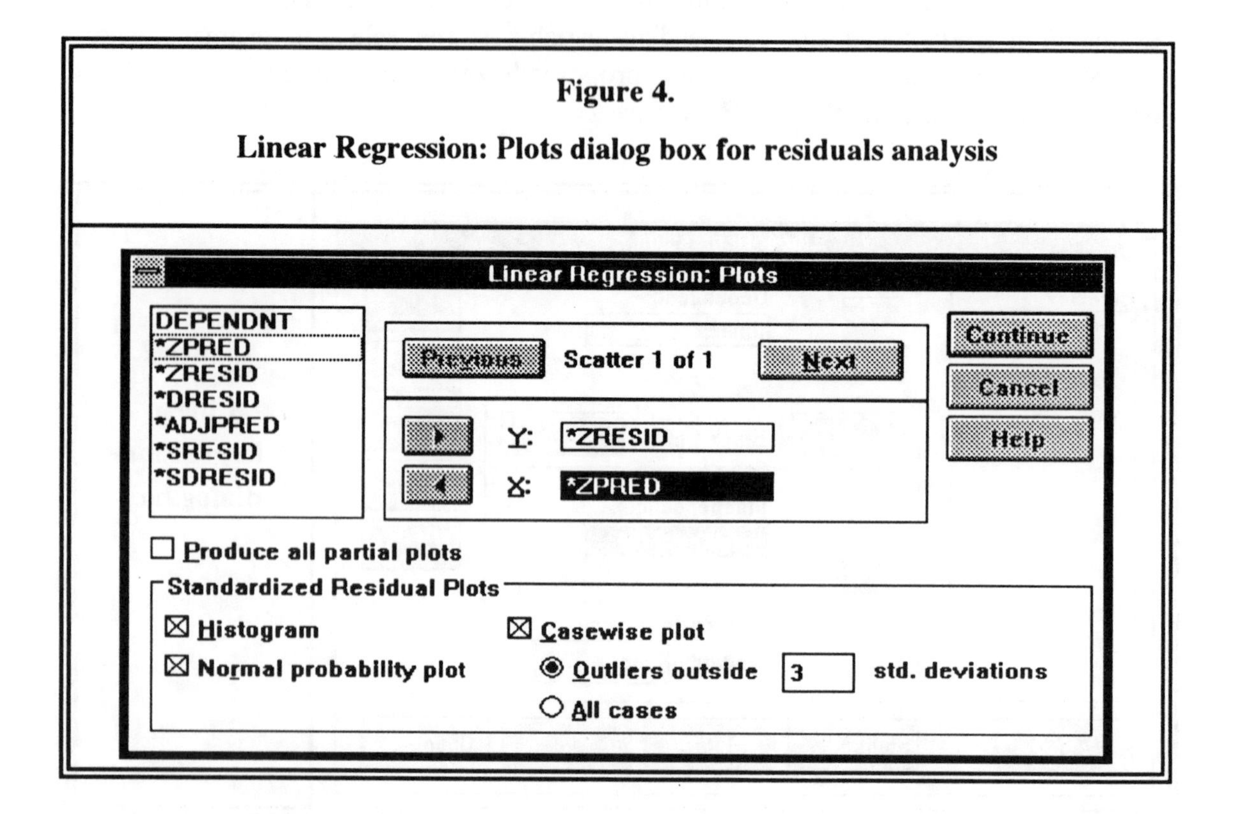

Once any outliers have been detected (and possibly excluded from the analysis), we recommend that the other **Standardized Residual Plots** are added by clicking on the remaining check boxes (labelled **Histogram** and **Normal probability plot**). The normal probability plot shows how well the residuals lie along a straight line (as they should do if the relationship between the dependent and the independent variable is basically a linear one).

12.2.2 Output listing for simple regression

12.2.2.1 Indication of residual outliers

The **Casewise plot of standardized Residual** output in Output Listing 1 (SPSS 6) occurs after the following four items (these will be reproduced in a later section):

(1) means and standard deviations;

(2) the correlation coefficient;

(3) multiple R and regression ANOVA;

(4) the regression equation.

The corresponding information in SPSS 7 is presented in a table labelled **Casewise Diagnostics** as shown in Output Listing 1 (SPSS 7).

Output Listing 1 (SPSS 6 and 7) shows that Case 1 with a score of *195* for *finalex* (University Examination) is the only outlier. The next section describes how to eliminate this outlier and run the subsequent regression analysis.

SPSS 6 Output Listing 1.

The casewise plot of standardized residual showing which outliers are greater than ± 3 standard deviations

```
Casewise Plot of Standardized Residual

Outliers = 3.     *: Selected    M: Missing

          -6.      -3.  3.       6.
  Case #   O:.......:   :.......:O    FINALEX        *PRED        *RESID
       1   .           ..*        .        195     110.9517      84.0483


       1 Outliers found.
```

Casewise Diagnostics[a]

Case Number	Std. Residual	University Examination	Predicted Value	Residual
1	3.117	195	110.95	84.05

a. Dependent Variable: University Examination

Output Listing 1 (SPSS 7).

The casewise diagnostics showing which outliers are greater than ± 3 standard deviations

12.2.2.2 Elimination of outliers

A more reliable regression analysis can be obtained by eliminating any outliers using the **Select Cases** procedure described in Section 3.9.1. Click on the **If condition is satisfied** radio button within the **Select Cases** dialog box and define the condition as *finalex ~=195*. (The symbol ~= means 'not equal to'.) Click on **Continue** and then on **OK** to deselect this case.

If there is more than one outlier, they can be deselected by defining the condition with an inequality operator (e.g. *finalex* < 150). Sometimes it is convenient to re-order by value the critical variable in the Data Editor window using the **Sort Cases** option within the **Data** drop-down menu in order to see what value to use in the inequality expression.

12.2.2.3 Output listing for simple regression after eliminating the outlier

Re-run the regression after eliminating the outlier by returning to the **Linear Regression** dialog box and click on **Plots** to open the **Linear Regression: Plots** dialog box (Figure 4). Click on the remaining two check boxes to turn them on within the **Standardised Residual Plots** box (Figure 4). Click **Continue** and then **OK**.

Output Listing 2 (SPSS 6 and 7) shows the descriptive statistics and the correlation coefficient for the remaining 33 cases.

```
                Mean   Std Dev   Label

FINALEX     102.818    32.633   University Examination
SELECTEX     47.273     7.539   Selection Exam

N of Cases =      33

Correlation, 1-tailed Sig:

              FINALEX    SELECTEX

FINALEX         1.000        .729
                  .          .000

SELECTEX         .729       1.000
                 .000          .
```

Output Listing 2 (SPSS 6).

The descriptive statistics and correlation coefficient

Output Listing 2 (SPSS 7).

The descriptive statistics and correlation coefficient

Descriptive Statistics

	Mean	Std. Deviation	N
University Examination	102.82	32.63	33
Selection Exam	47.27	7.54	33

Correlations

		University Examination	Selection Exam
Pearson Correlation	University Examination	1.000	.729
	Selection Exam	.729	1.000
Sig. (1-tailed)	University Examination		.000
	Selection Exam	.000	
N	University Examination	33	33
	Selection Exam	33	33

Output Listing 3 (SPSS 6 and 7) contains a value for **Multiple R** which in the case of just one independent variable has the same absolute value as the correlation coefficient ***r*** listed in Output Listing 2. There is also an ANOVA, which is intended to test whether there really is a linear relationship between the variables by forming an F ratio of the mean square for regression to the residual mean square.

Output Listing 3 (SPSS 6).

Multiple R and the regression ANOVA

```
          * * * *   M U L T I P L E   R E G R E S S I O N   * * * *

Equation Number 1    Dependent Variable..   FINALEX   University Examination

Block Number  1.  Method:  Enter      SELECTEX

Variable(s) Entered on Step Number
   1..     SELECTEX  Selection Exam

Multiple R            .72873
R Square              .53104
Adjusted R Square     .51592
Standard Error      22.70468

Analysis of Variance
                      DF       Sum of Squares        Mean Square
Regression             1          18096.32896        18096.32896
Residual              31          15980.58013          515.50258

F =       35.10424        Signif F =  .0000
```

Output Listing 3 (SPSS 7).

Multiple R and the regression ANOVA

Model Summary[a,b]

Model	Variables		R	R Square	Adjusted R Square	Std. Error of the Estimate
	Entered	Removed				
1	Selection Exam[c,d]	.	.729	.531	.516	22.70

a. Dependent Variable: University Examination

b. Method: Enter

c. Independent Variables: (Constant), Selection Exam

d. All requested variables entered.

ANOVA[a]

Model		Sum of Squares	df	Mean Square	F	Sig.
1	Regression	18096.3	1	18096.3	35.104	.000[b]
	Residual	15980.6	31	515.503		
	Total	34076.9	32			

a. Dependent Variable: University Examination

b. Independent Variables: (Constant), Selection Exam

In this example, the value of F in the ANOVA Table is highly significant. **It should be noted, however, that only an examination of the scatterplot of the variables can ensure that the relationship between two variables is genuinely linear.**

The other statistics listed are **R Square** which is a positively biased estimate of the proportion of the variance of the dependent variable accounted for by regression, **Adjusted R Square** which corrects this bias and therefore has a lower value, and **Standard Error** or **Std. Error of the Estimate** which is the standard deviation of the residuals.

Output Listing 4 (SPSS 6 and 7) is the kernel of the regression analysis, because it contains the regression equation. The values of the **regression coefficient** and **constant** are given in column **B** of the table. The equation is, therefore,

***Predicted Final Exam Mark* = 3.15 × (*Selection Exam Mark*) - 46.30**

Thus a person with a Selection Exam Mark of 60 would be predicted to score

$$3.15 \times 60 - 46.30 = 142.7 \qquad \text{(i.e. 143).}$$

Notice from the data that the person who did score 60 on the selection examination actually scored 145 on the final examination. The residual is, therefore, 145-143 = +2.

Other statistics listed are **SE B** or **Std. Error** which is the standard error of the regression coefficient **B**, **Beta** which is the beta weight showing the change in the dependent variable (expressed in standard deviation units) that would be produced by a positive increment of one standard deviation in the independent variable, **T** or **t** which tests the regression coefficient for significance, and **Sig T** or **Sig.** which is the p-value of **t** (here it is listed as .000 meaning it is <0.00005 i.e. highly significant).

Output Listing 4 (SPSS 6).

The regression equation and associated statistics

```
------------------ Variables in the Equation ------------------

Variable              B          SE B        Beta          T  Sig T

SELECTEX       3.154519       .532419     .728727      5.925  .0000
(Constant)   -46.304539     25.477326                 -1.817  .0788
```

Output Listing 4 (SPSS 7).

The regression equation and associated statistics

Coefficients[a]

Model		Unstandardized Coefficients		Standardized Coefficients		
		B	Std. Error	Beta	t	Sig.
1	(Constant)	-46.305	25.477		-1.817	.079
	Selection Exam	3.155	.532	.729	5.925	.000

a. Dependent Variable: University Examination

The remaining parts of the listing relate to the optional residuals analysis requested from the* Linear Regression: Plots *subdialog box.

The first item is the **Casewise plot** but since we have already deselected the only outlier among the data, no plot is produced. The listing states: **No outliers found. No casewise plot produced.**

The next item is a table of statistics relating to the residuals in Output Listing 5 (SPSS 6 and 7). **PRED* comprises the unstandardised predicted values, **RESID* is the set of unstandardised residuals, **ZPRED* contains the standardised predicted values (i.e. **PRED* has been transformed to a scale with mean 0 and SD 1), and **ZRESID* comprises the standardised residuals (i.e. **RESID* standardised to a scale with mean 0 and SD 1).

Output Listing 5 (SPSS 6).

Table of statistics relating to the residuals

```
Residuals Statistics:

                 Min        Max       Mean   Std Dev    N

*PRED        60.9491  152.4302  102.8182   23.7805   33
*RESID      -54.4943   30.9693      .0000   22.3471   33
*ZPRED       -1.7607    2.0862      .0000    1.0000   33
*ZRESID      -2.4001    1.3640      .0000     .9843   33

Total Cases =         33
```

Output Listing 5 (SPSS 7).

Table of statistics relating to the residuals

Residuals Statistics[a]

	Minimum	Maximum	Mean	Std. Deviation	N
Predicted Value	60.95	152.43	102.82	23.78	33
Residual	-54.49	30.97	3.9E-15	22.35	33
Std. Predicted Value	-1.761	2.086	.000	1.000	33
Std. Residual	-2.400	1.364	.000	.984	33

a. Dependent Variable: University Examination

The remaining items in the output are the extra requested plots. In SPSS 6, they are reproduced in the **Charts Carousel** as indicated by the message in Output Listing 6 (SPSS 6). In SPSS 7, they follow on in the **Output Navigator**. To see the plots in SPSS 6, it is necessary to click on the **Carousel** icon (if it is visible) or to click on the **Window** pull-down menu and select **Chart Carousel**.

Hi-Res Chart # 1:Histogram of *zresid Hi-Res Chart # 3:Normal p-p plot of *zresid Hi-Res Chart # 2:Scatterplot of *zpred with *zresid	**Output Listing 6 (SPSS 6).** **List of charts in the Chart Carousel**

The histogram of **ZRESID* is shown in Figure 5. The grey bars show the frequencies. The superimposed curve is the ideal normal distribution for the residuals.

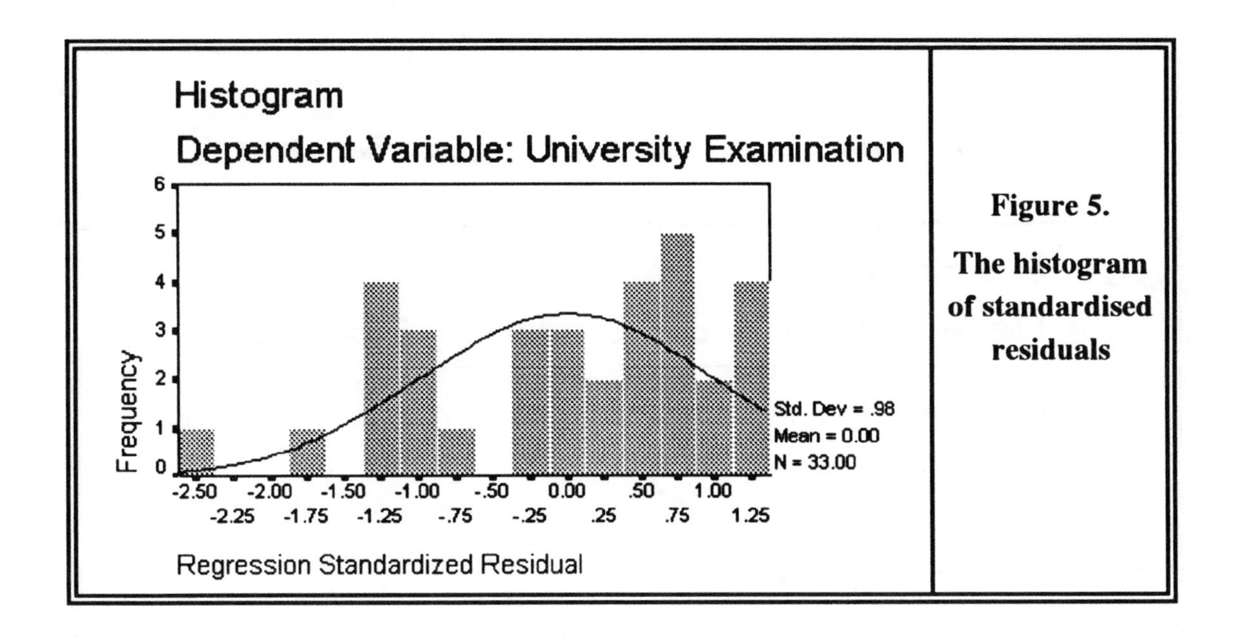

Figure 5.

The histogram of standardised residuals

The next plot is a cumulative probability plot of *ZRESID (Figure 6). Ideally, the points should lie along or adjacent to the diagonal. If they do not, the residuals are not normally distributed and it may be necessary to apply a transformation to the data. (For a discussion of the rationale of transformations, see Howell, 1997, pp323-329.)

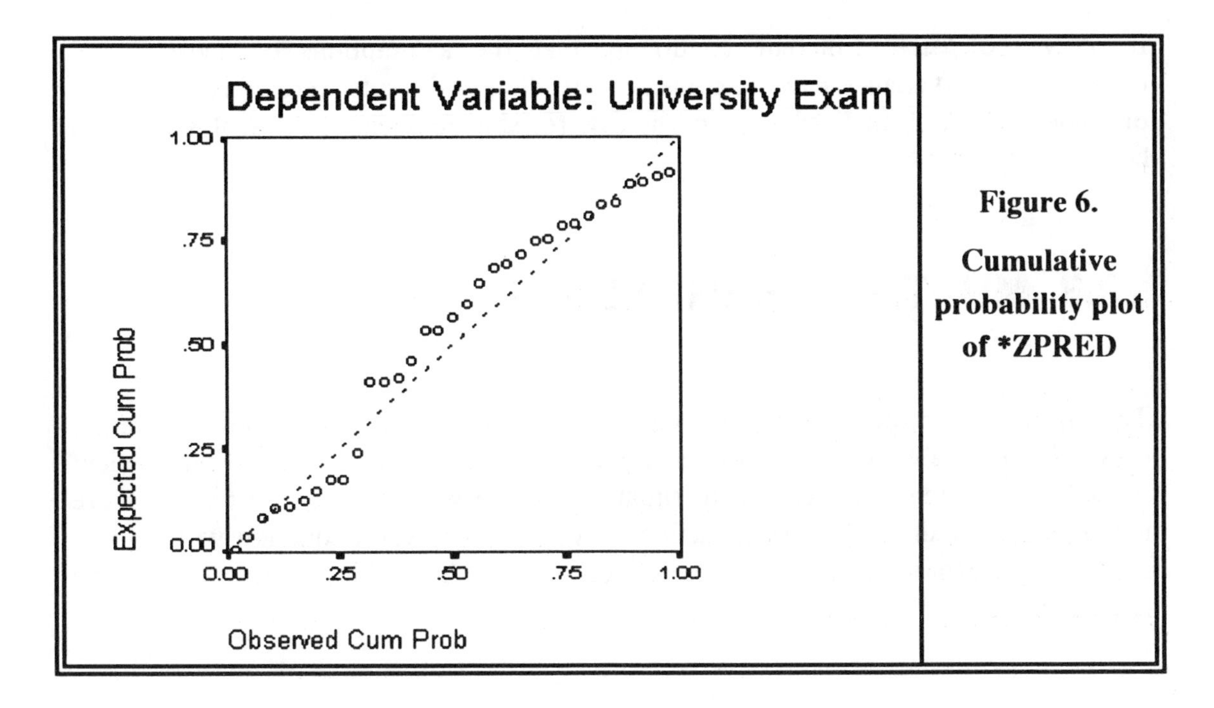

Figure 6.

Cumulative probability plot of *ZPRED

The final plot is the scatterplot of predicted scores against residuals (Figure 7).

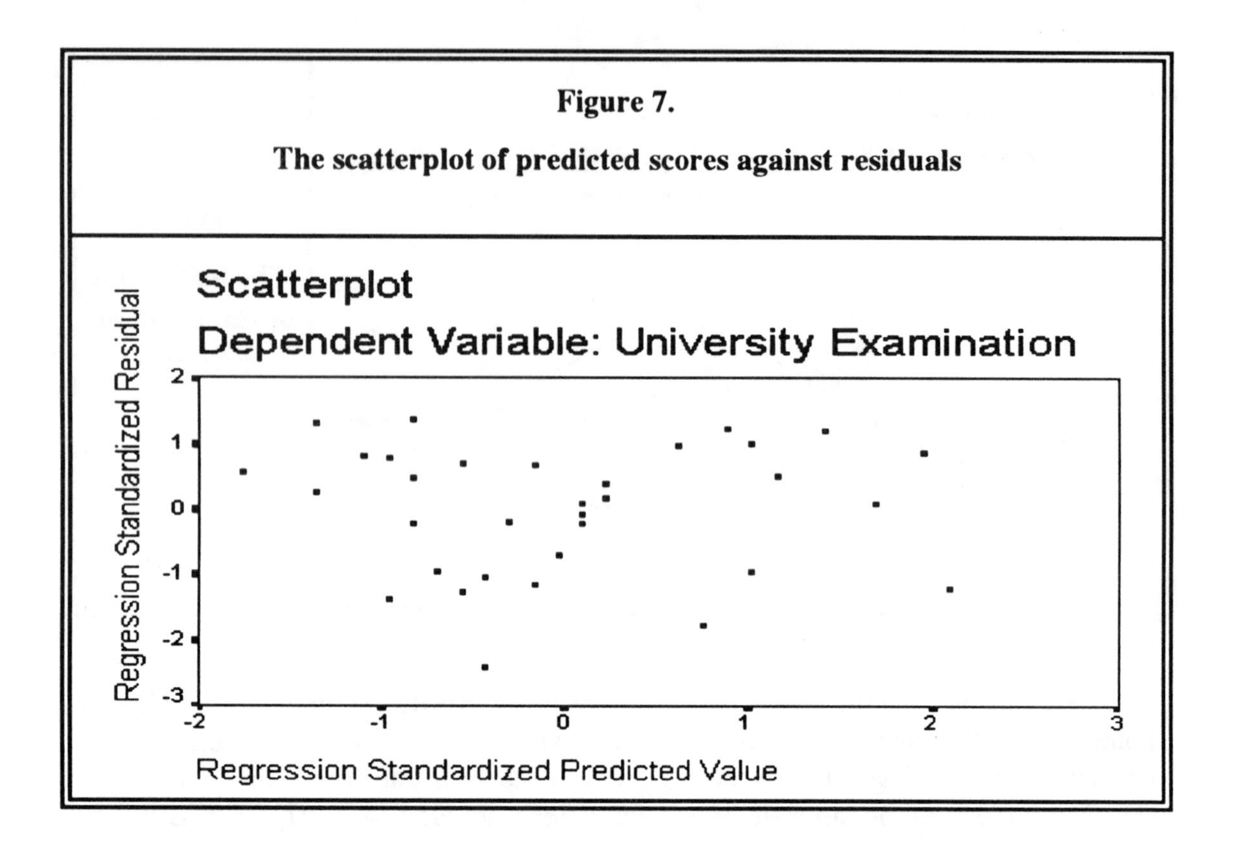

Figure 7.

The scatterplot of predicted scores against residuals

It shows no pattern, thereby confirming that the assumptions of linearity and homogeneity of variance have been met. If the cloud of points were crescent-shaped or funnel-shaped, further screening of the data (or abandonment of the analysis) would be necessary.

12.3 MULTIPLE REGRESSION

The process of constructing a linear equation that will predict the values of a target (dependent) variable from knowledge of specified values of a regressor (independent variable) can readily be extended to situations where we have data on two or more independent variables. The construction of a linear regression equation with two or more independent variables (or regressors) on the right hand side is known as multiple regression.

12.3.1 Some more data

Two extra variables, the subjects' ages and their scores obtained on a relevant academic project, have been added (Table 2) to the original variables *finalex* and *selectex* listed in Table 1 except the outlier has been omitted.

Table 2.

An extension of Table 1, with data on two additional independent variables (outlier omitted)

Finalex	Selectex	Age	Project	Finalex	Selectex	Age	Project
38	44	21.9	50	103	48	22.3	53
49	40	22.6	75	105	43	21.8	72
61	43	21.8	54	106	55	21.4	69
65	42	22.5	60	107	48	21.6	50
69	44	21.9	82	112	49	22.8	68
73	46	21.8	65	114	46	22.1	72
74	34	22.2	61	114	41	21.9	60
76	37	22.5	68	117	49	22.5	74
78	41	21.5	60	125	63	21.9	70
81	53	22.4	69	140	52	22.2	77
86	47	21.9	64	142	56	21.4	79
91	45	22.0	78	145	60	21.6	84
94	41	22.2	68	150	55	22.1	60
95	39	21.7	70	152	54	21.9	76
98	40	22.2	65	164	58	23.0	84
100	37	39.3	75	169	62	21.2	65
100	48	21.0	65				

In the following discussion, we shall be concerned with two main questions:

(1) does the addition of more independent variables improve the accuracy of predictions of *finalex*?

(2) of these new variables, are some more useful than others for prediction of the dependent variable?

We shall see that the answer to the first question is 'Yes'. The second question, however, is deeply problematic, and none of the available approaches to it is entirely satisfactory.

Many years ago, Darlington (1968) drew attention to some widespread misunderstandings among users of multiple regression; in fact, he was trying to do for regression what Lewis & Burke (1949) had done some years earlier for chi-square analysis. Darlington placed special emphasis upon the thorny problem of how to say which of the independent variables in a multiple regression equation is the most 'important', or 'useful' in accounting for variability in the dependent variable. (Of more recent non-technical treatments, the most lucid we have been able to find is by Cohen & Cohen, 1983.)

There are many problems; but most of them may be summed up in a well-known aphorism: **Correlation does not imply causation**. In a situation where everything correlates with everything else, **it is quite impossible to attribute variance in the dependent variable unequivocally to any one independent variable**. It is certainly true, for example, that the amount of damage done by a fire is strongly correlated with the number of firemen on the scene. But both variables are a direct consequence of the severity of the fire, and the correlation between them is, in this sense, an artificial one.

This fundamental dubiety is belied by considerations of some of the terms in the multiple regression equation, and by the availability of methods that have been specifically designed to evaluate the relative importance of the independent variables in the equation.

In a multiple regression equation, the coefficients of the independent variables are known as **partial regression coefficients**, meaning that they express the increase in the dependent variable that would be produced by a positive increase of one unit in the independent variable concerned, the effects of the other independent variables, both on the independent variable and the dependent variable, being supposedly held constant. Such **statistical control**, however, is no substitute for true **experimental** control, where the independent variable, having been manipulated by the experimenter, really is independent of the dependent variable.

If scores on all the variables in a multiple regression equation are standardised, the intercept of the regression equation disappears and each regression coefficient, referred to as a **beta weight**, expresses the change in the dependent variable, expressed in standard deviation units, that would be produced by a positive increment of one standard deviation in the independent variable concerned.

In this section, we shall consider two approaches to multiple regression, neither of which is entirely satisfactory. In **simultaneous** multiple regression, all the available independent variables are entered in the equation directly. In **stepwise** multiple regression, the independent variables are added to (or taken away from) the equation one at a time, the order of entry (or removal) being determined by statistical considerations. Despite the appeal of the second approach, however, there is the disconcerting fact that the addition of another 'independent' variable can completely change the apparent contributions of the other regressors to the variance of scores on the dependent variable.

12.3.2 Constructing the SPSS data set

Using the techniques described in Section 3.5, restore the original data set to the **Data Editor** window (removing the outlier), define the two new variables and type in the new data.

12.3.3 Procedure for simultaneous multiple regression

In the **Linear Regression** dialog box, transfer the variable names *selectex, age* and *project* into the **Independent Variables** box by highlighting them and clicking on the appropriate button. The **Dependent Variable** box must contain the variable name *finalex*. For the **Method**, select **Enter** (for the simultaneous regression procedure) and click on **OK** to run the regression.

12.3.4 Output listing for simultaneous multiple regression

Output Listing 7 (SPSS 6 and 7) shows that the multiple correlation coefficient (**R**) is 0.77.

Recalling that, when one independent variable *selectex* is used to predict *finalex*, the value of R was 0.73, we see that the answer to the question of whether adding more independent variables improves the predictive power of the regression equation is certainly 'Yes'.

Output Listing 7 (SPSS 6).

The simultaneous regression of finalex upon three regressors: selectex, age and project (ANOVA omitted)

```
Equation Number 1    Dependent Variable..   FINALEX   University Exam

Block Number  1.  Method:  Enter      SELECTEX AGE      PROJECT

Variable(s) Entered on Step Number
   1..     PROJECT   Project Mark
   2..     AGE
   3..     SELECTEX  Entrance Exam

Multiple R          .76609

------------------ Variables in the Equation ------------------

Variable              B          SE B        Beta          T  Sig T

SELECTEX       3.088891       .573397     .713567      5.387  .0000
AGE            1.423078      1.375600     .132812      1.035  .3094
PROJECT         .628040       .460888     .175991      1.363  .1835
(Constant)  -117.915892     46.421126                 -2.540  .0167
```

Output Listing 7 (SPSS 7).

The simultaneous regression of finalex upon three regressors: selectex, age and project (ANOVA omitted) - Model Summary

Model Summary[a,b]

Model	Variables Entered	Variables Removed	R	R Square	Adjusted R Square	Std. Error of the Estimate
1	Entrance Exam, AGE, Project Mark[c]	.	.766	.587	.544	22.03

a. Dependent Variable: University Exam

b. Method: Enter

c. Independent Variables: (Constant), Entrance Exam, AGE, Project Mark

d. All requested variables entered.

But what about the second question? Do both new variables contribute substantially to the predictive power of the regression equation, or is one a passenger in the equation? From column **B** in the section headed **Variables in the Equation** in Output Listing 7 (SPSS 6) and column **B** in **Unstandardized Coefficients** in Output Listing 8 (SPSS 7), we learn that the multiple regression equation of *finalex* upon *selectex*, *age* and *project* is:

$$\textbf{\textit{finalex}}' = \textbf{3.08} \times (\textbf{\textit{selectex}}) + \textbf{0.63} \times (\textbf{\textit{project}}) + \textbf{1.42} \times (\textbf{\textit{age}}) - \textbf{117.71}$$

This, however, tells us nothing about the relative importance of the independent variables, because the **values of the partial regression coefficients reflect the original units in which the variables were measured**. From the fact that the coefficient for age is larger than that for project, therefore, one cannot conclude that age is the more important regressor.

Output Listing 8 (SPSS 7).

The simultaneous regression of finalex upon three regressors: selectex, age and project (ANOVA omitted) - Coefficients

Coefficients[a]

Model		Unstandardized Coefficients		Standardized Coefficients	t	Sig.
		B	Std. Error	Beta		
1	(Constant)	-117.916	46.421		-2.540	.017
	AGE	1.423	1.376	.133	1.035	.309
	Project Mark	.628	.461	.176	1.363	.183
	Entrance Exam	3.089	.573	.714	5.387	.000

a. Dependent Variable: University Exam

The **beta** weights (in the column headed **Beta** in both SPSS 6 and 7) tell us rather more, because each gives the number of standard deviations change on the dependent variable that will be produced by a change of one standard deviation on the independent variable concerned. On this count, *selectex* still makes by far the greatest contribution, because a change of one standard deviation on that variable produces a change of 0.71 standard deviations on *finalex*, whereas a change of one standard deviation in *project* produces an increase of only 0.18 of a standard deviation in *finalex*. A change of one standard deviation in age produces a change of only 0.13 of a standard deviation in *finalex*. This ordering of the standardised beta weights is supported by consideration of the correlations between the dependent variable and each of the three regressors: the correlations between *finalex* and *project*, *selectex* and *age* are 0.40, 0.73 and −0.03, respectively. (These values are easily obtained by running the **bivariate correlations** procedure.) It is not surprising that the regressor with the largest beta weight also has the largest correlation with the dependent variable.

12.3.5 Procedure for stepwise multiple regression

If, in the **Linear Regression** dialog box, the choice of **Method** is **Stepwise**, rather than **Enter**, a **forward** stepwise regression will be run, whereby regressors are added to the equation one at a time. (In the **backward elimination** method, which is also available in SPSS, they are subtracted one at a time.) Selected portions of the results are shown in Output Listing 9 (SPSS 6 and 7). Only the final model is included in Output Listing 9 (SPSS 7) since in this example it is the same as the first model or step.

Output Listing 9 (SPSS 6).

Forward stepwise multiple regression

```
Equation Number 1    Dependent Variable..   FINALEX   University Exam

Block Number  1.  Method:  Stepwise    Criteria   PIN  .0500   POUT  .1000
   SELECTEX AGE       PROJECT

Variable(s) Entered on Step Number
   1..     SELECTEX  Entrance Exam

Multiple R             .72873

------------------ Variables in the Equation ------------------

Variable                B          SE B         Beta          T  Sig T

SELECTEX        3.154519      .532419      .728727      5.925  .0000
(Constant)    -46.304539    25.477326                  -1.817  .0788

------------- Variables not in the Equation -------------

Variable      Beta In  Partial  Min Toler          T  Sig T

AGE           .178115  .250347    .926438      1.416  .1670
PROJECT       .210591  .294227    .915421      1.686  .1021

End Block Number   1   PIN =     .050 Limits reached.
```

Output Listing 9 (SPSS 7).

Forward stepwise multiple regression - only variable remaining in the regression equation (i.e. *selectex* - the Entrance Exam)

Model Summary[a,b]

Model	Variables		R	R Square	Adjusted R Square	Std. Error of the Estimate
	Entered	Removed				
2	Entrance Exam[d]	.	.729	.531	.516	22.70

a. Dependent Variable: University Exam

b. Method: Stepwise (Criteria: Probability-of-F-to-enter <= .050, Probability-of-F-to-remove >= .100).

d. Probability of F-to-enter = .050 limits reached.

Coefficients[a]

Model		Unstandardized Coefficients		Standardized Coefficients	t	Sig.
		B	Std. Error	Beta		
2	(Constant)	-46.305	25.477		-1.817	.079
	Entrance Exam	3.155	.532	.729	5.925	.000

a. Dependent Variable: University Exam

Excluded Variables[a]

Model		Beta In	t	Sig.	Partial Correlation	Collinearity Statistics
						Tolerance
2	AGE	.178	1.416	.167	.250	.926
	Project Mark	.211	1.686	.102	.294	.915[c]

a. Dependent Variable: University Exam

c. This variable is not added to the model because PIN = .050 limits reached.

The most obvious feature of the output is the multiple correlation coefficient which is given as 0.729. This is smaller than the value given for simultaneous regression of *finalex* upon *selectex*, *project* and *age* (0.77). Nevertheless, the decision of the stepwise program is that the increment in R with the inclusion of the variables *project* and *age* is not robust, and so those variables are dropped from the final equation. Only *selectex* (the Entrance Exam) is a worthwhile predictor of *finalex* (the University Exam).

12.3.6 Adding another variable

Why should *selectex* be a better predictor of *finalex* than is *project*? The researcher suspects that both the university degree examination and the selection examination tap the candidate's verbal ability, as well as motivation for the material of the curriculum. Adding the candidates' verbal IQs to the regression equation, therefore, should improve the accuracy of predictions from the multiple regression equation. To test this hypothesis, the researcher obtains the verbal IQs of the same students who provided the data on the other variables.

These scores are given in Table 3.

Table 3.

The data from Table 2 plus IQs

F	S	Age	Proj	IQ	F	S	Age	Proj	IQ
38	44	21.9	50	110	103	48	22.3	53	134
49	40	22.6	75	120	105	43	21.8	72	140
61	43	21.8	54	119	106	55	21.4	69	127
65	42	22.5	60	125	107	48	21.6	50	135
69	44	21.9	82	121	112	49	22.8	68	132
73	46	21.8	65	140	114	46	22.1	72	135
74	34	22.2	61	122	114	41	21.9	60	135
76	37	22.5	68	123	117	49	22.5	74	129
78	41	21.5	60	133	125	63	21.9	70	140
81	53	22.4	69	100	140	52	22.2	77	134
86	47	21.9	64	120	142	56	21.4	79	134
91	45	22.0	78	115	145	60	21.6	84	132
94	41	22.2	68	124	150	55	22.1	60	135
95	39	21.7	70	135	152	54	21.9	76	135
98	40	22.2	65	132	164	58	23.0	84	149
100	37	39.3	75	128	169	62	21.2	65	135
100	48	21.0	65	130					

As an exercise, the reader may wish to add the variable *iq* to the data set and re-run both the simultaneous and the stepwise regressions. Selected parts of the results of the simultaneous regression of *finalex* upon *iq*, *age*, *projectex* and *selectex* are shown in Output Listing 10 (SPSS 6 and 7).

It can be seen from these Listings that the addition of *iq* improves the predictive power of the regression equation: the value of multiple R is now 0.87, which is noticeably larger than it was when there were only three regressors (0.77).

Looking at the standardised **beta** weights (column labelled **Beta**), we see that a change of one standard deviation in *selectex* produces a change of 0.58 of a standard deviation in *finalex* and the same change in *iq* increases *finalex* by 0.45 of a standard deviation. These appear to be substantial contributions, in comparison with those of *project* (0.14) and *age* (0.11).

Output Listing 10 (SPSS 6).

The simultaneous regression of finalex upon selectex, age, IQ and project

```
Equation Number 1     Dependent Variable..    FINALEX    University Exam
Block Number  1.  Method:  Enter        AGE         IQ         PROJECT  SELECTEX

Variable(s) Entered on Step Number
   1..      SELECTEX  Entrance Exam
   2..      AGE
   3..      IQ
   4..      PROJECT   Project Mark

Multiple R            .87449

------------------ Variables in the Equation ------------------

Variable                B          SE B         Beta          T  Sig T

AGE              1.244163      1.057195      .116114      1.177  .2492
IQ               1.509827       .328181      .447155      4.601  .0001
PROJECT           .503658       .354999      .141136      1.419  .1670
SELECTEX         2.494034       .458966      .576148      5.434  .0000
(Constant)    -272.129581     48.935525                  -5.561  .0000
```

Output Listing 10 (SPSS 7).

The simultaneous regression of finalex upon selectex, age, IQ and project

Model Summary[a,b]

Model	Variables Entered	Variables Removed	R	R Square	Adjusted R Square	Std. Error of the Estimate
1	Entrance Exam, AGE, IQ, Project Mark[c,d]	.	.874	.765	.731	16.92

a. Dependent Variable: University Exam

b. Method: Enter

c. Independent Variables: (Constant), Entrance Exam, AGE, IQ, Project Mark

d. All requested variables entered.

Coefficients[a]

Model		Unstandardized Coefficients B	Unstandardized Coefficients Std. Error	Standardized Coefficients Beta	t	Sig.
1	(Constant)	-272.130	48.936		-5.561	.000
	AGE	1.244	1.057	.116	1.177	.249
	IQ	1.510	.328	.447	4.601	.000
	Project Mark	.504	.355	.141	1.419	.167
	Entrance Exam	2.494	.459	.576	5.434	.000

a. Dependent Variable: University Exam

Output Listings 11 and 12 (SPSS 6) show selected parts of the output for the **forward stepwise** regression of *finalex* upon all four regressors.

The first step in Output Listing 11 (SPSS 6) enters *selectex* into the equation, the second step and final step in Output Listing 12 (SPSS 6) adds *iq* into the equation. The stepwise regression stops after it has added these variables to the equation. Notice that the final value of R is 0.85, which is close to the value of R when all four regressors are included in the regression equation (0.87). The decision of the regression procedure, therefore, is that the variables *project* and *age* do not contribute reliably to the regression equation.

Output Listing 11 (SPSS 6).

The first step in the forward stepwise regression of finalex upon IQ, age, project and selectex

```
Equation Number 1    Dependent Variable..   FINALEX   University Exam
Method:  Stepwise
   AGE       IQ        PROJECT  SELECTEX
Variable(s) Entered on Step Number
   1..    SELECTEX   Entrance Exam

Multiple R           .72873

------------------ Variables in the Equation ------------------

Variable                 B          SE B        Beta          T  Sig T

SELECTEX         3.154519       .532419     .728727      5.925  .0000
(Constant)     -46.304539     25.477326                 -1.817  .0788

------------- Variables not in the Equation -------------

Variable      Beta In  Partial  Min Toler         T  Sig T

AGE           .178115  .250347    .926438     1.416  .1670
IQ            .466653  .645641    .897691     4.631  .0001
PROJECT       .210591  .294227    .915421     1.686  .1021
```

Output Listing 12 (SPSS 6).

The second (and final) step in the forward stepwise regression of finalex upon IQ, age, project and selectex

```
Variable(s) Entered on Step Number
   2..    IQ
Multiple R           .85237

------------------ Variables in the Equation ------------------

Variable                 B          SE B        Beta          T  Sig T

IQ                1.575662       .340252     .466653      4.631  .0001
SELECTEX          2.508390       .436214     .579465      5.750  .0000
(Constant)     -219.068451     42.224992                 -5.188  .0000

------------- Variables not in the Equation -------------

Variable      Beta In  Partial  Min Toler         T  Sig T

AGE           .151842  .279001    .829761     1.565  .1285
PROJECT       .171017  .311663    .840563     1.766  .0879

End Block Number   1   PIN =      .050 Limits reached.
```

The first and final steps (called Models in SPSS 7) are shown together in Output Listing 13 (SPSS 7).

Output Listing 13 (SPSS 7).

The first step (Model 1) and final step (Model 3) in the forward stepwise regression of finalex upon IQ, age, project and selectex

Coefficients[a]

Model		Unstandardized Coefficients		Standardized Coefficients		
		B	Std. Error	Beta	t	Sig.
1	(Constant)	-46.305	25.477		-1.817	.079
	Entrance Exam	3.155	.532	.729	5.925	.000
3	(Constant)	-219.068	42.225		-5.188	.000
	Entrance Exam	2.508	.436	.579	5.750	.000
	IQ	1.576	.340	.467	4.631	.000

a. Dependent Variable: University Exam

Excluded Variables[a]

Model		Beta In	t	Sig.	Partial Correlation	Collinearity Statistics
						Tolerance
3	AGE	.152	1.565	.129	.279	.923
	Project Mark	.171	1.766	.088	.312	.908[d]

a. Dependent Variable: University Exam

d. This variable is not added to the model because PIN = .050 limits reached.

12.3.7 The need for a substantive model of causation

These results highlight an important consideration for the use of multiple regression as a research tool. The addition of new regressors can radically affect the relative contributions of those variables already in the equation. To select new regressors, the researcher must be guided by a substantive theoretical rationale. A statistical model, therefore, cannot by itself yield an unequivocal interpretation of regression results: the user must also be guided by a substantive model of causation.

12.4 SCATTERPLOTS AND REGRESSION LINES

A regression line can be added to a scatterplot such as Figure 3 in Chapter 11. After plotting the scatterplot in the usual way, click on the **Edit** box (SPSS 6) or double-click on the plot (SPSS 7), and then the **Options** item within the **Chart** drop-down menu to open the **Scatterplot Options** dialog box (Figure 8).

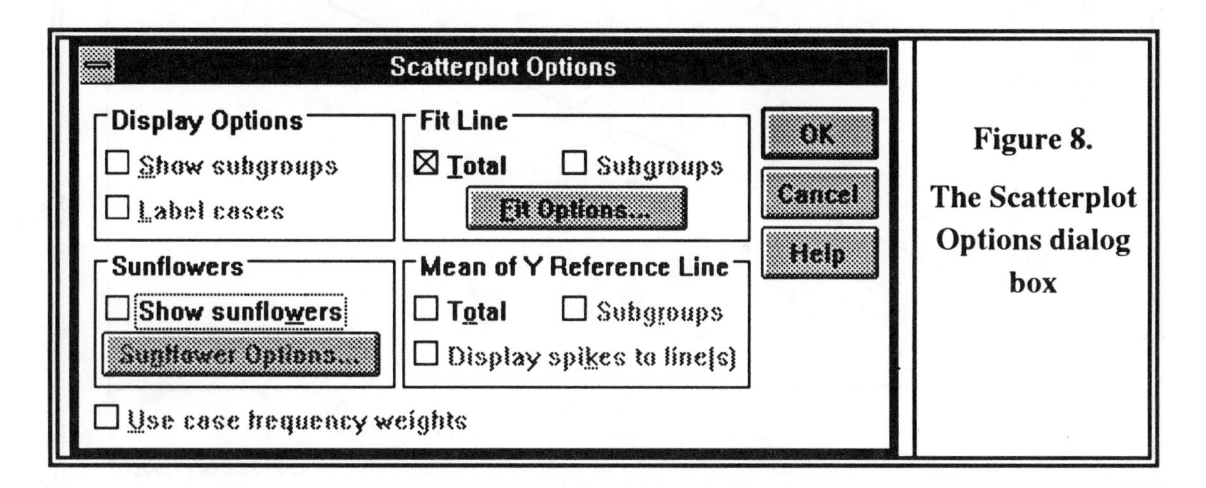

Figure 8. **The Scatterplot Options dialog box**

Within the **Fit Line** box click on the **Total** box and then click on the **OK** box to plot the default linear regression line. If other regression lines (e.g. quadratic, cubic) are desired, click on the **Fit Options** box to open the **Scatterplot Options: Fit Line** dialog box (Figure 9).

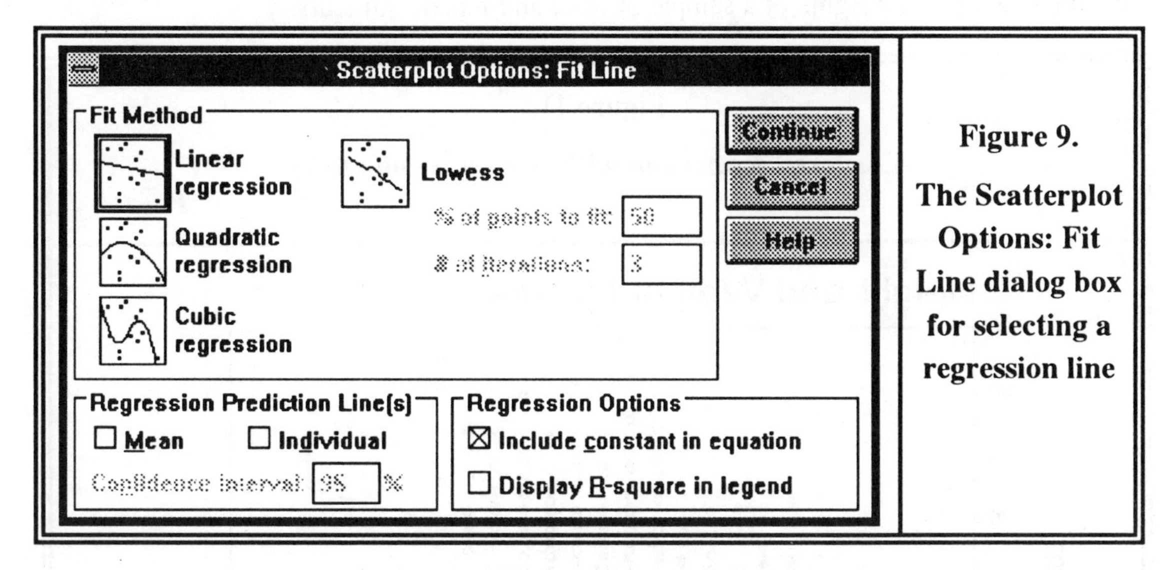

Figure 9. **The Scatterplot Options: Fit Line dialog box for selecting a regression line**

Here it is possible to select higher powered regression lines within the **Fit Method** box and also the confidence limits (95% is the default level) within the **Regression Prediction Line(s)** box. The value of R^2 can be displayed beside the scatterplot by clicking on the **Display R-squared in legend** box. The resulting plot is shown in Figure 10.

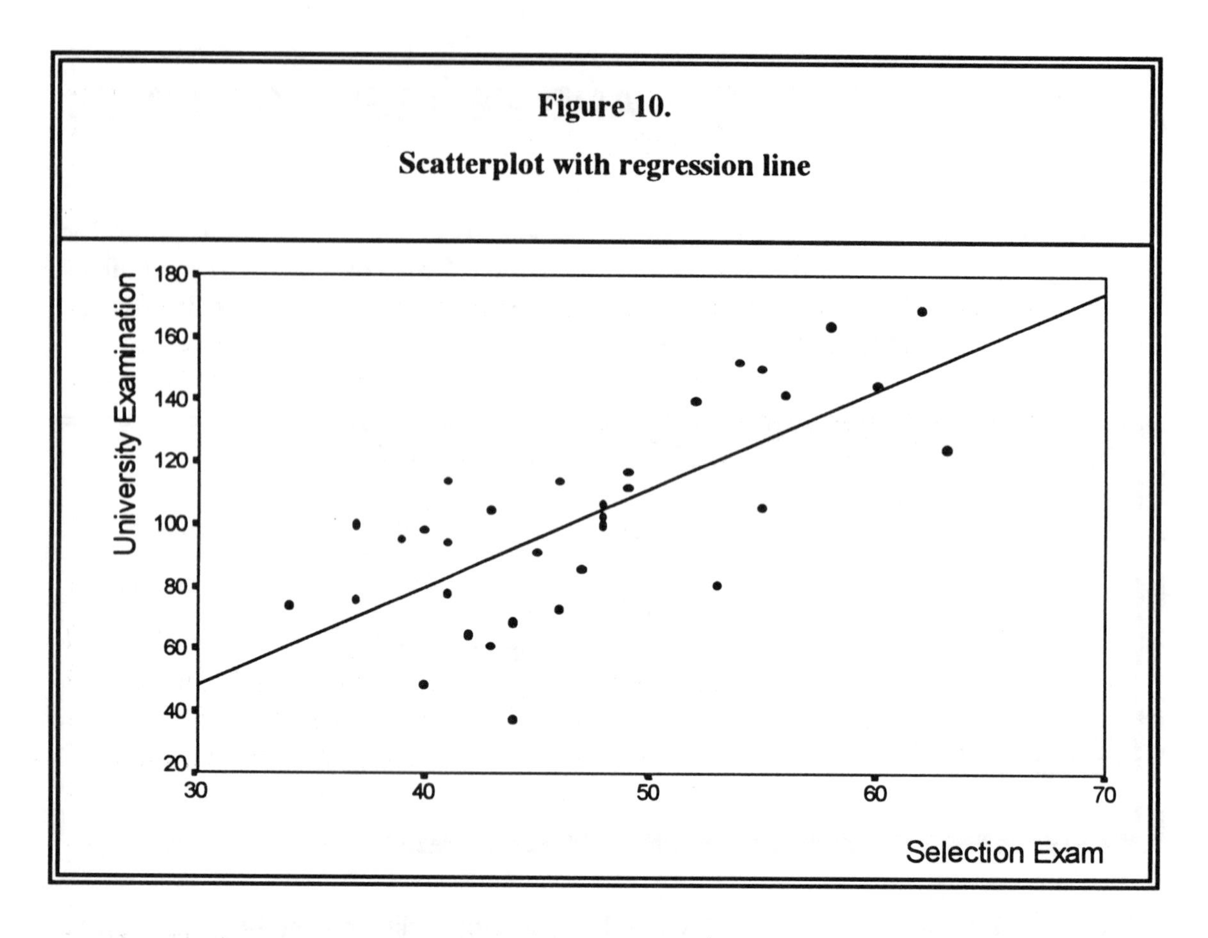

Figure 10.

Scatterplot with regression line

If a clustered scatterplot has been drawn by including a category variable in the **Set Markers by** box (here it is *sex*) within the **Simple Scatterplot** dialog box, it is possible to plot regression lines for each category of the cluster as shown in Figure 11 for the heights and weights of a sample of male and female students.

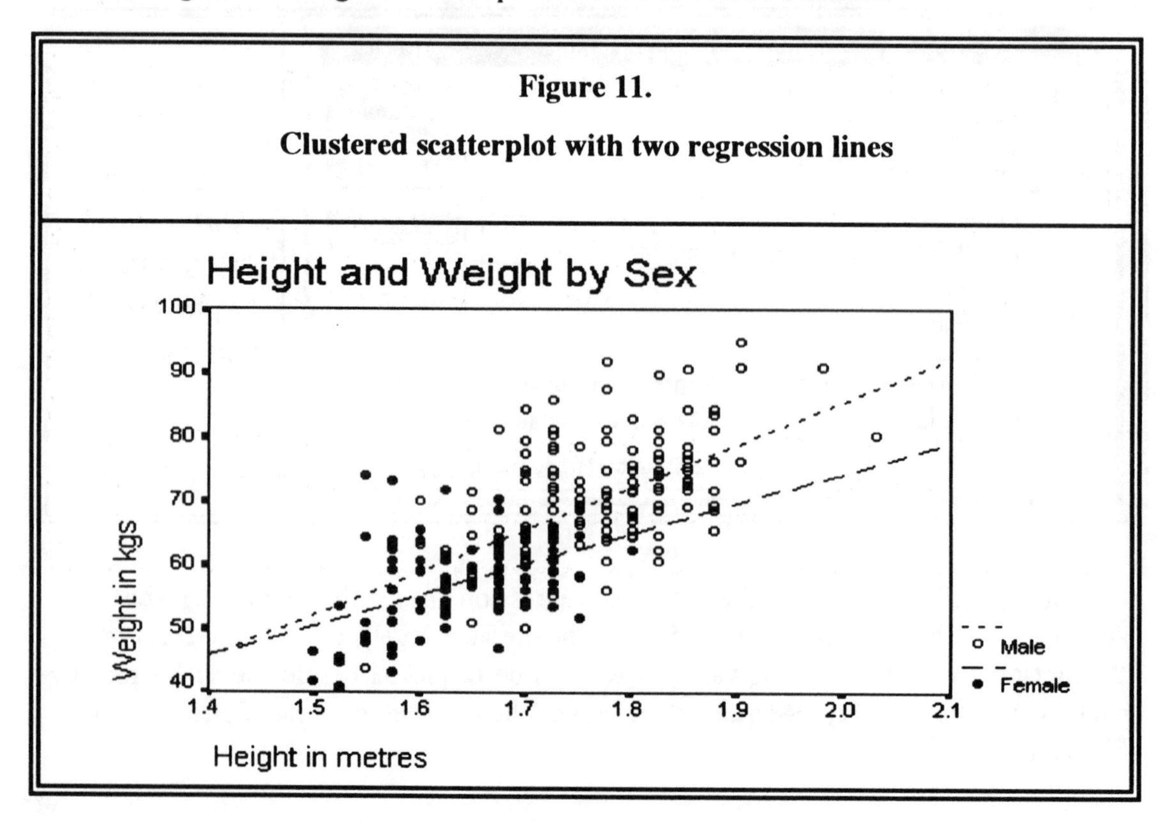

Figure 11.

Clustered scatterplot with two regression lines

SUMMARY

1) Regression generates an equation for predicting a value on a target variable from specified values of one or more other variables (the independent variables). In **simple regression**, there is only one independent variable; in **multiple regression**, there may be many.

2) The procedure for a regression analysis is

   Statistics

   Regression

   and click on **Linear**. Enter the name of the dependent variable into the **Dependent:** box, and the name(s) of the independent variable(s) into the **Independent:** box. When there is only one independent variable, the **Method:** is **Enter**. When there are two or more independent variables, the recommended method is **Stepwise**.

3) Options include selecting **Descriptives** within the **Linear Regression: Statistics** dialog box, which is obtained by clicking on **Statistics**. This causes the means and standard deviations of all the variables to be listed. It is also recommended that residuals are scrutinised by clicking on **Plots** and selecting the three options within **Standardized Residual Plots**. These provide extra information about outliers and checks for violation of the assumptions of the linear regression model. Finally a plot of ***zpred** and ***zresid** should also be included.

4) In the listing of the output, the regression equation appears in column **B** of the section subheaded **Variables in the Equation.** In multiple regression, there may be more than one equation, in which case the final equation is the appropriate one.

5) Regression lines can be added to scatterplots by clicking on **Edit** (SPSS 6) or double-click on the plot (SPSS 7) and then **Options** within the **Charts** menu to open the **Scatterplot Options** dialog box.

CHAPTER 13

LOGLINEAR ANALYSIS

13.1 INTRODUCTION

The starting point for the analysis of nominal data on two or more attributes is a contingency table, each cell of which is the frequency of occurrence of individuals in various combinations of categories. In an earlier chapter (Chapter 11), we described the use of the chi-square test to test for the presence of an association between qualitative variables in a two-way contingency table.

In a two-way contingency table, the presence (or absence) of an association between the attributes is often very apparent from inspection alone: the formal statistical analysis merely confirms (or fails to confirm) a readily discernible pattern. It is quite possible, however, to have more complex contingency tables, in which individuals are classified with respect to several qualitative variables. In such multi-way contingency tables, it is often very difficult to discern associations; and indeed, it is only too easy to misinterpret what one does see. Recent years have seen great advances in the analysis of multi-way contingency tables (Everitt, 1977; Upton, 1978, 1986), and these new methods, collectively known as **loglinear analysis**, are now available in computing packages such as SPSS.

13.1.1 Comparison with ANOVA

To understand how loglinear analysis works, it may be helpful to recall some aspects of the completely randomised factorial analysis of variance, because there are some striking parallels between the two sets of techniques. In the ANOVA, it is possible to test for **main effects** and for **interactions**. Suppose that, following a three-factor experiment, all systematic sources are found to be significant. That would imply that the correct model for the experimental data must contain a term for each and every possible effect thus:

score = systematic effects* + error effects

(* 3 main effect terms + 3 two-way interaction terms + 1 three-way interaction term)

If, on the other hand, only one main effect and one of the possible two-way interactions were to prove significant, a much simpler model would account for a subject's score. This simplified model would contain, in addition to the error term, only one main effect term and one two-way interaction term thus:

score = systematic effects* + error effects

(* 1 main effect term + 1 two-way interaction term)

In the analysis of variance, the presence of an interaction often necessitates the re-interpretation of a significant main effect. Examination of the interaction may show that an experimental treatment has a strong effect at some levels (or combinations of levels) of other factors in the experiment, but no effect at other levels; in fact, the simple main effects of a factor may be in opposite directions at different levels of another factor..

Graphs of two-way tables of means are often very illuminating: if the factor profiles are non-parallel, a two-way interaction is indicated. Graphs of three-way tables, however, are more difficult to interpret visually, because, just as graphs of two-way tables reflect the presence of main effects as well as the two-way interaction, graphs of three-way tables reflect two-way interactions as well as the three-way interaction.

There are many parallels between the foregoing considerations and the loglinear analysis of multi-way contingency tables. Just as in the context of ANOVA, it is meaningful to speak of 'main effects' and of 'interactions'. Moreover, in interpreting multi-way tables by inspection alone, it is only too easy to confuse one effect for another. Loglinear analysis, however, like ANOVA, offers methods of testing the various effects separately. As in ANOVA, the presence of an interaction often necessitates the re-interpretation of a main effect; indeed, main effects, when considered on their own, can be highly deceptive. That is why the common procedure of 'collapsing', i.e. combining the frequencies at all levels of some factors to exclude those factors from the classification, can produce misleading patterns in the data. As with ANOVA, a loglinear analysis tries to find the model that best accounts for the data available. It contains both main effect terms and interaction terms, so that the values in the contingency table are expressed as the sum of main effects and interaction components.

There are, however, also important differences between loglinear and ANOVA models. In ANOVA, the target of the model is the **individual score** of a subject in the experiment. In loglinear analysis, the target is the **total frequency of observations in a cell.** The ANOVA model cannot predict the individual scores with perfect accuracy, because of the inevitable presence of errors of measurement, individual differences and experimental error. In contrast, as we shall see, it is **always** possible, by including all the possible terms in the loglinear model, to predict perfectly the cell frequencies in a contingency table. A model that contains all the possible effect terms is known as a **saturated model**. The purpose of a loglinear analysis is to see whether the cell frequencies may be adequately approximated by a model that contains **fewer** than the full set of possible treatment effects.

13.1.2 Why 'loglinear' analysis?

Recall that in the simple chi-square test of association in a two-by-two contingency table, the **expected frequencies** are obtained by **multiplying** marginal total frequencies and dividing the product by the total frequency. This is because the null hypothesis of independence of the variables implies that the probability of an individual occupying a cell of the classification is the **product** of the relevant main effect probabilities, the latter being estimated from the marginal totals. (Recall that the probability of the joint occurrence of independent events is the **product** of their separate probabilities.) Loglinear analysis exploits the fact that the logarithm (log) of a product is the **sum** of the logs of the terms in the product. Thus the **log** of the cell frequencies may be expressed as a **linear** (i.e. additive) function of the **logs** of the components. If one were to work directly with the cell frequencies, rather than their logs, one would require a **multiplicative** model for the data. While that is feasible, the simplicity of a summative, ANOVA-type model is lost.

13.1.3 Constructing a loglinear model

The purpose of a loglinear analysis is to construct a model such that the cell frequencies in a contingency table are accounted for in terms of a minimum number of terms. Several strategies can be followed in the construction of such a model, but the **backward hierarchical method** is perhaps the easiest to understand. The first step is to construct a saturated model for the cell frequencies, in which all the component effects are present. This model, as we have seen, will predict the cell frequencies perfectly. The next step is to remove the highest-order interaction, to determine the effect this would have upon the closeness with which the model predicts the cell frequencies. It may be that this interaction can be removed without affecting appreciably the accuracy of estimation of the target frequencies. The process of progressive elimination is continued, and each time a term is removed, a statistical test is carried out to determine whether the accuracy of prediction falls to a sufficient extent to show that the component most recently excluded should indeed be one of the components in the final model. The assessment of the goodness-of-fit at each stage of the procedure is made by means of a statistic known as the **likelihood ratio** (called **L.R. Chisq** by SPSS), which has a known distribution.

The evaluation of the final model is made by comparing the observed and expected frequencies for each cell using the likelihood ratio as described above; but it is also advisable to examine the distribution of **residuals** (the differences between the observed and expected frequencies), or more conveniently, the **standardised residuals** (the residuals expressed in standardised form) in a manner similar to that described for regression in the last chapter.

13.1.4 Small expected frequencies

Just as in the case of the chi-square test, the size of the **expected frequency** (not the observed frequency) in each cell must be adequate for the analysis to be worthwhile. Small expected frequencies can lead to a drastic loss of power.

Problems with low expected cell frequencies should not arise provided:

(i) there are not too many variables in comparison with the size of the sample;

(ii) there are no categories with very few cases.

Tabachnick and Fidell (1996) recommend examining the expected cell frequencies for all **two-way associations** to ensure that all **expected frequencies** are greater than 1 and that no more than 20% are less than 5. If there is any doubt about the assumption of adequate expected cell frequencies, they can be checked out by using the **Crosstabs** procedure.

13.2 AN EXAMPLE OF A LOGLINEAR ANALYSIS

13.2.1 A three-way contingency table

In an investigation of the relationships between success on a second year university psychology statistics course and a number of possibly relevant background variables, researchers collected a body of information on a number of students, including whether or not they had taken an advanced school mathematics course and whether they had passed a data-processing examination in their first year at university. On each student's record, it was also noted whether he or she had passed the second year psychology statistics examination. (It will be noted that these yes/no variables are not true dichotomies, but artificial ones created from interval data. For present purposes, however, we shall assume that they are true qualitative variables.)

The data are presented in Table 1.

Table 1.

A three-way contingency table

Advanced Maths	Yes				No			
Data Processing	Pass		Fail		Pass		Fail	
Psychology Statistics	Pass	Fail	Pass	Fail	Pass	Fail	Pass	Fail
CELL FREQUENCIES	47	10	4	10	58	17	10	20

It is useful to summarise the cell frequencies for categories of single variables as shown in Table 2.

Table 2.

Summary of cell frequencies for each variable

Advanced Maths	Yes	71	No	105	Total	176
Data Processing	Pass	132	Fail	44	Total	176
Psych Statistics	Pass	119	Fail	57	Total	176

It can be seen from Table 2 that of the 176 students in the study, 71 had taken advanced mathematics, and 105 had not. From Table 1, it can be seen that of those who had taken advanced mathematics, 57 passed first year data-processing and 14 did not, compared with 75 passes and 30 failures in the non-mathematical group. Relatively speaking, therefore, more of the mathematical group passed first year data-processing. Turning now to the statistics examination, it can be seen that of the mathematical group, the pass ratio was 51:20, compared with 68:37 in the non-mathematical group; and among those who had passed data-processing, the success ratio was 105:27, compared with 14:30 in the group that had failed data processing.

First, let us consider the (very unlikely) null hypothesis that there are **no links whatsoever** among the three variables studied. Suppose there is no tendency for those who have taken school mathematics to pass first year data-processing, no tendency for those who have passed data-processing to pass second year statistics and so on. It is a relatively simple matter, using a pocket calculator, to use the appropriate marginal totals to obtain the expected cell frequencies in a calculation similar to that appropriate for a two-way contingency table. Since there are three dichotomous (or pseudo-dichotomous) variables, there are 8 expected cell frequencies, the values of which are shown in Table 3. A way of computing these expected frequencies with SPSS will be described in Section 13.2.4.

Table 3.

Observed (O) and expected (E) cell frequencies for Table 1

Advanced Maths	Yes				No			
Data Processing	Pass		Fail		Pass		Fail	
Psychology Statistics	Pass	Fail	Pass	Fail	Pass	Fail	Pass	Fail
Cell Freq O	47	10	4	10	58	17	10	20
E	36.00	17.25	12.00	5.75	53.25	25.50	17.75	8.50

In several cells, the observed frequencies differ markedly from the expected values, suggesting that the complete independence model gives a poor account of the data. Clearly at least some associations are present among the three variables; but where exactly are they?

A loglinear analysis on SPSS can answer that question very easily. SPSS offers a hierarchical loglinear procedure within the **loglinear** menu. This procedure begins by constructing a fully saturated model for the cell frequencies, and works backwards in the manner described above, in order to arrive at a model with a minimum number of terms. Some of these are of little interest: for example, there are fewer subjects in the advanced mathematics group than there are in the non-mathematical group, so we can expect a main effect term for this variable in the final model. Main effects are usually unimportant in loglinear analysis. In the terms of ANOVA, we are seeking **interactions**, rather than **main effects**: the presence of associations among the three variables will necessitate the inclusion of interaction terms in the model.

13.2.2 Procedure for a loglinear analysis

Using the procedures described in Section 3.5, define three coding variables: *maths*, *dataproc* and *psystats*. A fourth variable, *count* will contain the cell frequencies. Type in the data and save the set in the usual way. The complete SPSS data set is shown in Figure 1.

	maths	dataproc	psystats	count
1	1	1	1	47
2	1	1	2	10
3	1	2	1	4
4	1	2	2	10
5	2	1	1	58
6	2	1	2	17
7	2	2	1	10
8	2	2	2	20

Figure 1.

The data grid showing the SPSS data set

It is now necessary to inform SPSS that the variable *count* contains frequencies and not simply scores. The procedure is described in Section 3.9.2.

Choose

Data

Weight Cases

to open the **Weight Cases** dialog box (Chapter 3, Figure 19), and transfer the variable *count* to the **Frequency Variable** box. Click on **OK**.

The next stage is to check whether the expected frequencies are sufficiently large using the **Crosstabs** procedure (Section 11.3.2.2).

Choose
Statistics
  Summarize
    Crosstabs

and then complete the **Crosstabs** dialog box (Figure 2) by transferring *dataproc* to the **Row(s)** box, *psystats* to the **Column(s)** box, and *maths* to the lowest box. Click on the **Cells** button to bring to the screen the **Crosstabs: Cell Display** dialog box (See Chapter 11, Figure 12). Within the **Counts** box, mark the **Expected** check box and click on **Continue**.

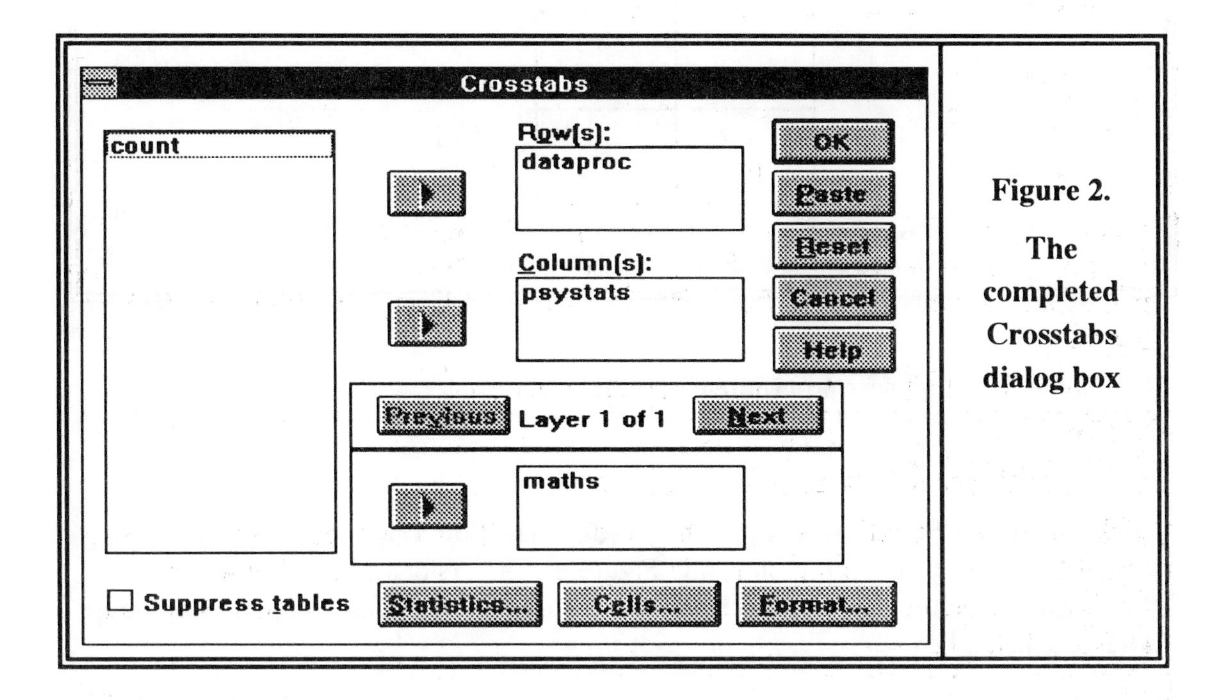

Figure 2. The completed Crosstabs dialog box

The **Crosstabs** procedure presents two-way contingency tables for each layer of *maths*, because that was chosen as the layering variable. The table for the first level of *maths* is shown in Output Listing 1 (SPSS 6). Provided the expected frequencies meet the criteria described in Section 13.1.4, the loglinear analysis can proceed and in this case they clearly do (the Maths = 2 expected frequencies are also adequate).

Output Listing 1 (SPSS 6).

Observed and expected frequencies for a three-way contingency table (Maths = 1 only)

```
DATAPROC  Data Processing Exam  by  PSYSTATS  Psych Stats Exam
Controlling for..
MATHS  Advanced Maths Course  Value = 1  Yes

                     PSYSTATS     Page 1 of 1
             Count  |
           Exp Val  |Pass      Fail
                    |                   Row
                    |       1|       2| Total
DATAPROC   ---------+--------+--------+
                 1  |    47  |    10  |    57
  Pass              |  40.9  |  16.1  | 80.3%
                    +--------+--------+
                 2  |     4  |    10  |    14
  Fail              |  10.1  |   3.9  | 19.7%
                    +--------+--------+
            Column      51       20       71
             Total    71.8%    28.2%   100.0%
```

The hierarchical loglinear procedure is started by choosing
Statistics

Loglinear (Figure 3)

Click on **Model Selection** to open the **Model Selection Loglinear Analysis** dialog box (the completed version is shown in Figure 4). In versions of SPSS prior to 6.1.3, the loglinear option is **Hierarchical** which opens the **Hierarchical Loglinear Analysis** dialog box.

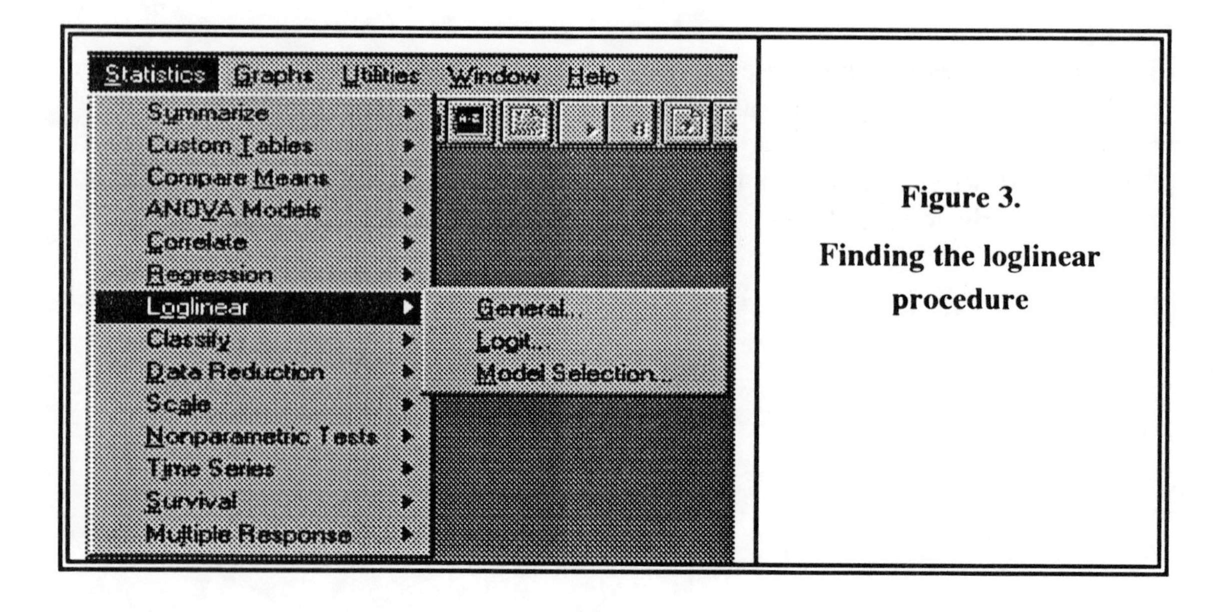

Figure 3.

Finding the loglinear procedure

Drag the cursor down the variable names *dataproc maths psystats* to highlight them, and click on ▶ to the left of the **Factor(s)** box to transfer these names into it. Click on **Define Range** and enter *1* into the **Minimum** box and *2* into the **Maximum** box. Click on **Continue**. The names will then appear with [1,2] after each of them (see Figure 4).

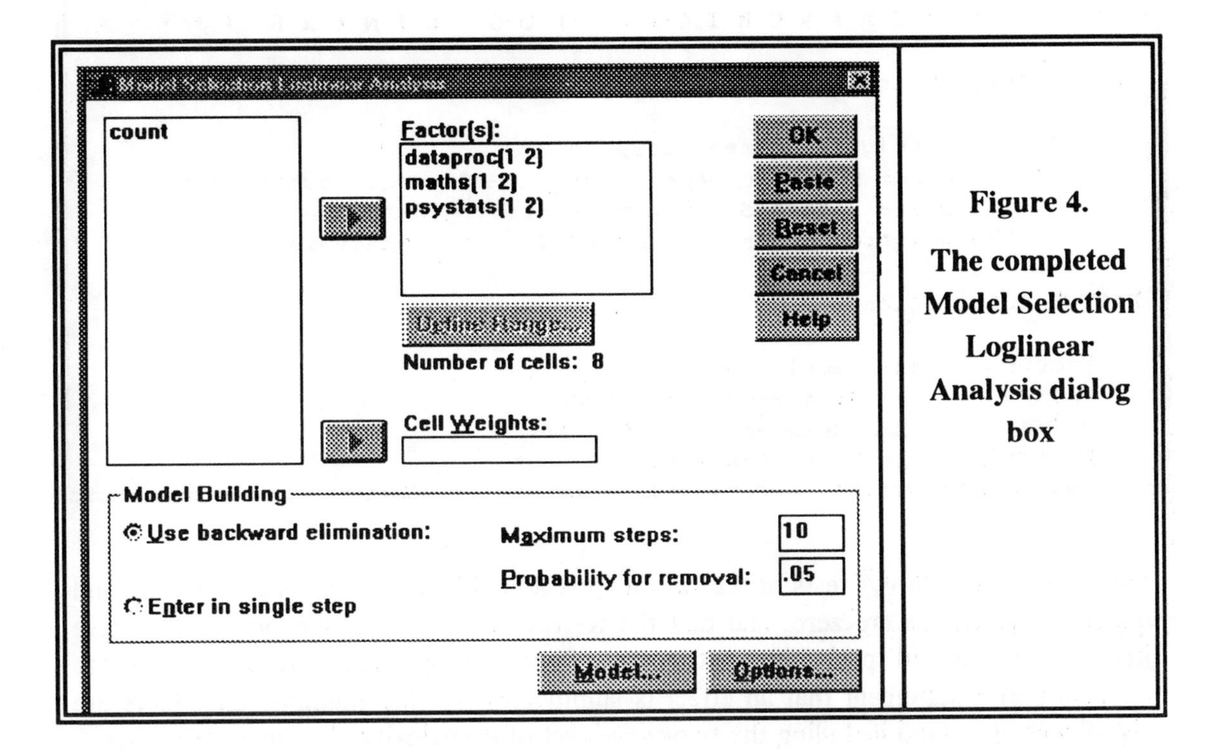

Figure 4.

The completed Model Selection Loglinear Analysis dialog box

Check that the radio button for the default model **Use backward elimination** is on and then click on **OK**.

13.2.3 Output listing for a loglinear analysis

The current SPSS 7 output is the same as that for SPSS 6.

Output Listing 2 contains information about the data and the factors.

This is followed by a table (not reproduced here) listing the counts (OBS count) for the combinations of the three factors. At this stage, SPSS is fitting a **saturated model**, MATHS*DATAPROC*PSYSTATS, to the cell frequencies. The table is useful for checking the accuracy of the data transcription.

Output Listing 2.

Basic design information

```
* * * * *  H I E R A R C H I C A L   L O G   L I N E A R  * * * * *

DATA    Information

          8 unweighted cases accepted.
          0 cases rejected because of out-of-range factor values.
          0 cases rejected because of missing data.
        176 weighted cases will be used in the analysis.

FACTOR Information

   Factor  Level  Label
   DATAPROC    2  Data Processing Exam
   MATHS       2  Advanced Maths Course
   PSYSTATS    2  Psych Stats Exam
```

Output Listing 3 shows tests of the various possible effects. It shows that K-way and higher order effects are zero, and that the K-way effects themselves are zero. These items give the tail probabilities for the effects of specified order and (where appropriate) a statement that an effect is significant. In this example, all effects are significant up to and including the two-way level of complexity. The three-way effect, however, is not significant.

Output Listing 3.

Tests of effects

```
* * * * *  H I E R A R C H I C A L   L O G   L I N E A R  * * * * *

Tests that K-way and higher order effects are zero.

         K     DF   L.R. Chisq    Prob  Pearson Chisq    Prob   Iteration

         3      1         .431   .5116           .426   .5141           3
         2      4       35.310   .0000         37.077   .0000           2
         1      7      110.282   .0000        123.000   .0000           0

Tests that K-way effects are zero.

         K     DF   L.R. Chisq    Prob  Pearson Chisq    Prob   Iteration

         1      3       74.972   .0000         85.923   .0000           0
         2      3       34.879   .0000         36.651   .0000           0
         3      1         .431   .5116           .426   .5141           0
```

Output Listings 4-7 show the most interesting part of the listing headed:

'Backward Elimination (p = .050) for Design 1 with generating class . . .'

The purpose of the analysis is to find the unsaturated model that gives the best fit to the observed data. This is achieved by checking that the model currently being tested does not give a significantly worse fit than its predecessor in the hierarchy.

Recall that in the hierarchical backward elimination method, the procedure starts with the most complex model (which in the present case contains all three factors, together with all their possible interactions), and progresses down the hierarchy of complexity, eliminating each effect from the model in turn and determining which decrement in accuracy is less than the **least-significant change in the chi-square value.** At each step, such an effect would be eliminated, leaving the remaining effects for inclusion:

'The best model has generating class . . . '

The procedure continues until no elimination produces a decrement with a probability greater than 0.05. The model containing the remaining effects is then adopted as 'The final model'. In this example, the final model is reached after four steps.

Output Listing 4.

Step 1 of the loglinear analysis

```
* * * * *  H I E R A R C H I C A L   L O G   L I N E A R  * * * * *

Backward Elimination (p = .050) for DESIGN 1 with generating class

  DATAPROC*MATHS*PSYSTATS

 Likelihood ratio chi square =      .00000     DF = 0  P = 1.000
- - - - - - - - - - - - - - - - - - - - - - - - - - - - - - - - - - -
If Deleted Simple Effect is             DF   L.R. Chisq Change    Prob  Iter

 DATAPROC*MATHS*PSYSTATS                 1                .431   .5116     3

Step 1

  The best model has generating class

      DATAPROC*MATHS
      DATAPROC*PSYSTATS
      MATHS*PSYSTATS

  Likelihood ratio chi square =      .43089     DF = 1  P =  .512
```

At Step 2, MATHS*PSYSTATS is eliminated, because it has the largest probability (.6564).

Output Listing 5.

Step 2 of the loglinear analysis

```
If Deleted Simple Effect is          DF   L.R. Chisq Change    Prob  Iter

 DATAPROC*MATHS                       1              1.029    .3104     2
 DATAPROC*PSYSTATS                    1             32.098    .0000     2
 MATHS*PSYSTATS                       1               .198    .6564     2

Step 2

  The best model has generating class

      DATAPROC*MATHS
      DATAPROC*PSYSTATS

  Likelihood ratio chi square =      .62884     DF = 2  P =  .730
```

At Step 3, DATAPROC*MATHS is eliminated, because it has the larger probability (and it is greater than the criterion level of 0.05). Having processed all the interactions, it remains for any main effect which is not part of the remaining 2-way interaction to be included. In this case, MATHS is such a variable.

Output Listing 6.

Step 3 of the loglinear analysis

```
If Deleted Simple Effect is          DF   L.R. Chisq Change    Prob  Iter

 DATAPROC*MATHS                       1              1.806    .1790     2
 DATAPROC*PSYSTATS                    1             32.875    .0000     2

Step 3

  The best model has generating class

      DATAPROC*PSYSTATS
      MATHS

  Likelihood ratio chi square =     2.43511     DF = 3  P =  .487
```

At Step 4, neither of these effects can be eliminated, because both probabilities are less than 0.05. This, therefore, is adopted as the final model.

Output Listing 7.

The final step of the loglinear analysis

```
If Deleted Simple Effect is          DF   L.R. Chisq Change    Prob   Iter

 DATAPROC*PSYSTATS                    1              32.875   .0000      2
 MATHS                                1               6.610   .0101      2

Step 4

  The best model has generating class

      DATAPROC*PSYSTATS
      MATHS

  Likelihood ratio chi square =     2.43511    DF = 3  P =  .487

- - - - - - - - - - - - - - - - - - - - - - - - - - - - - - - - - - - - -

The final model has generating class

    DATAPROC*PSYSTATS
    MATHS
```

The final model includes the interaction between the variables representing the data processing exam and the psychology statistics exam, plus a main effect of maths. Note that there are no interactions involving the maths variable. Thus the most interesting finding is the interaction between the two examinations.

Finally, the computer lists the table of observed frequencies and the expected frequencies **as estimated by the final model** (Output Listing 8). The final chi-square test shows that these expected frequencies do **not** differ significantly from the observed frequencies (chi-square is not significant). This Table also lists the residuals and standardised residuals.

Output Listing 8.

Observed frequencies, expected frequencies and residuals estimated by the final mode

```
Observed, Expected Frequencies and Residuals.

      Factor          Code           OBS count   EXP count   Residual   Std Resid

  DATAPROC           Pass
   MATHS              Yes
    PSYSTATS           Pass            47.0        42.4        4.64        .71
    PSYSTATS           Fail            10.0        10.9        -.89       -.27
   MATHS              No
    PSYSTATS           Pass            58.0        62.6       -4.64       -.59
    PSYSTATS           Fail            17.0        16.1         .89        .22

  DATAPROC           Fail
   MATHS              Yes
    PSYSTATS           Pass             4.0         5.6       -1.65       -.69
    PSYSTATS           Fail            10.0        12.1       -2.10       -.60
   MATHS              No
    PSYSTATS           Pass            10.0         8.4        1.65        .57
    PSYSTATS           Fail            20.0        17.9        2.10        .50

Goodness-of-fit test statistics

    Likelihood ratio chi square =    2.43511    DF = 3  P =  .487
              Pearson chi square =    2.39308    DF = 3  P =  .495
```

13.2.4 Comparison with the total independence model

Notice that the expected frequencies estimated by the final model are much closer to the observed counts than those for the total independence model, whose values were listed in Table 3, and are reproduced in Table 4 for the purposes of comparison.

The reader might wish to use the loglinear procedure to check these values. After inserting the factor names and values in the **Factor(s)** box as before, click on the **Model** box. Within the **Specify model** box, select **Custom**. Enter the three factor names into the **Generating Class** box by clicking on each of *dataproc*, *maths* and *psystats*, following each variable name with ▸. Within the **Build Term(s)** box, click on **Interaction** and select **all 3-way**. Within the **Model Building** box, click on the **Enter in single step** option. The completed dialog box is shown in Figure 5. Click on **Continue** and then on **OK**.

Figure 5.

The completed dialog box for determining the expected frequencies assuming the total independence model

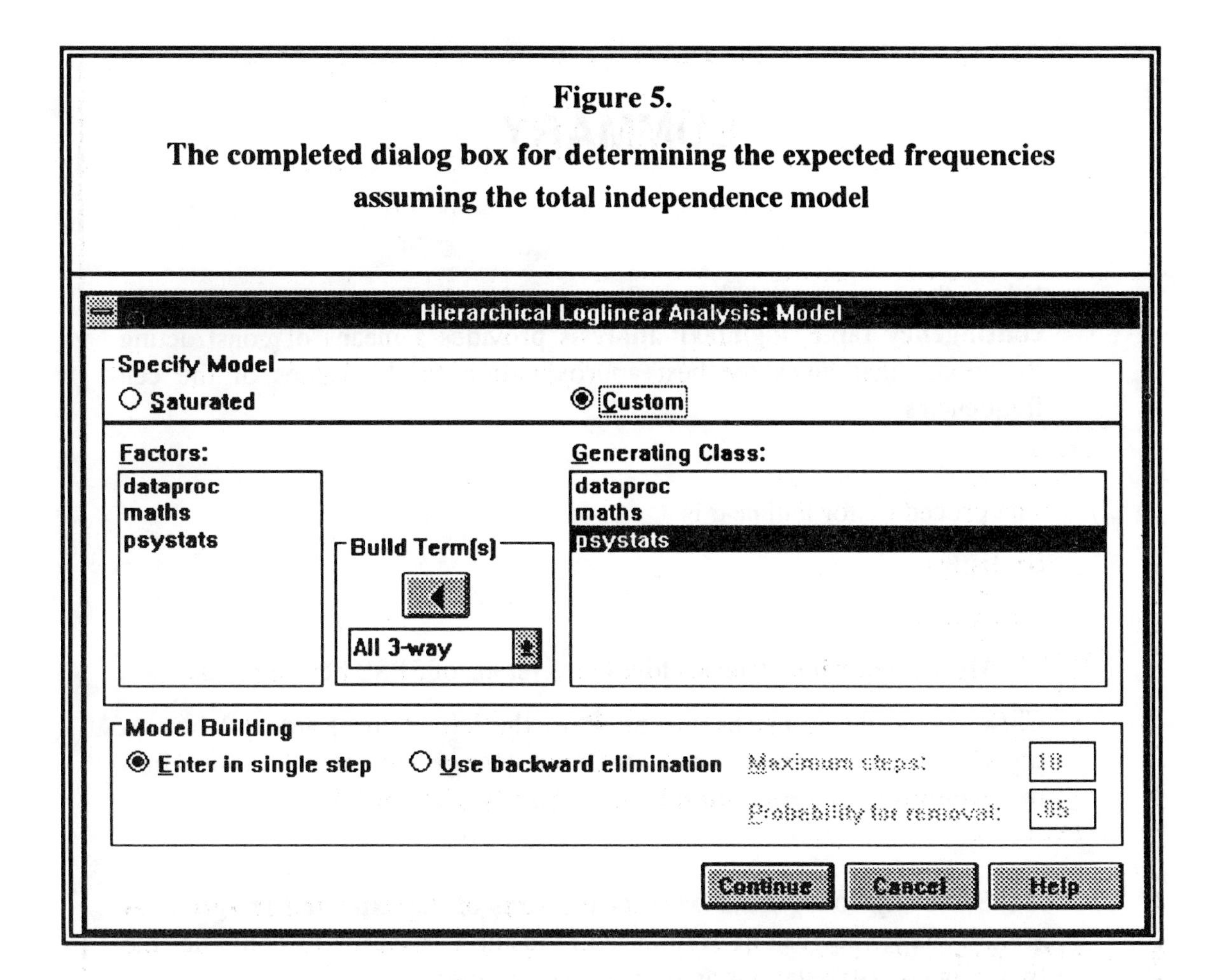

Table 4 contrasts the observed and expected cell frequencies under the assumptions of the 'best model' generated by the loglinear procedure with the corresponding discrepancies under the total independence model.

Table 4.

Expected frequencies under the final loglinear model E(loglinear) and the total independence model E(independent)

Advanced Maths	Yes				No			
Data Processing	Pass		Fail		Pass		Fail	
Psychology Statistics	Pass	Fail	Pass	Fail	Pass	Fail	Pass	Fail
Cell Freq:								
Observed	47	10	4	10	58	17	10	20
E (loglinear)	42.4	10.9	5.6	12.1	62.6	16.1	8.4	17.9
E (independent)	36.0	17.3	12.0	5.8	53.3	25.5	17.8	8.5

SUMMARY

1) When data are in the form of **counts in the cells of a multi-way contingency table**, **loglinear analysis** provides a means of constructing the model that gives the best approximation to the values of the cell frequencies.

2) The procedure for loglinear is

   Statistics

   Loglinear

   Model Selection (**Hierarchical** in versions of SPSS before 6.1.3)

   Click on the factor names and on ▶ to the left of the **Factor(s)** box to transfer the factor names. Click on **Define Range** and enter the values into the **Minimum** and **Maximum** boxes. Finally click on **OK**.

3) If there is any doubt about whether the sizes of the **expected frequencies** are adequate, they can be scrutinised by using **Crosstabs** to construct the two-way cross-tabulations among all the variables.

4) The output listing includes tables indicating the level of complexity of interaction at which the effects are significant, the various steps of the backward elimination of insignificant effects, and the identification of the **final optimal model**. The output listing concludes with a table contrasting the observed frequencies with the expected frequencies, assuming the final model.

CHAPTER 14

DISCRIMINANT ANALYSIS

14.1 INTRODUCTION

14.1.1 Discriminant analysis

In Section 5.2.1, the rationale of multivariate analysis of variance (MANOVA) was outlined. Essentially, the multivariate technique known as **discriminant analysis** is the obverse of MANOVA. In the MANOVA situation, you know which categories the subjects belong to and you want to explore the possibility of identifying a composite variable which shows up differences among the groups. In other circumstances, however, one might wish to ascertain **category membership** on the basis of subjects' performance on the DVs. It would be of considerable value, for example, on the basis of records of children on a number of variables recorded during the earlier school years, to predict which children go on to further education, which secure immediate employment on leaving school, and which join the ranks of the unemployed. Discriminant analysis offers answers to such questions.

The composite variable obtained in MANOVA is known as a **discriminant function**, because it is a weighted sum of the DVs, with the weightings chosen such that the distributions for the various groups are separated to the greatest possible extent. In discriminant analysis, the very same composite variable is constructed, so that category membership can be predicted to the greatest possible extent. Mathematically, therefore, the techniques of MANOVA and discriminant analysis have much in common. In the latter, however, the attempt is made to predict category membership using the discriminant function. There are other important differences between MANOVA and discriminant analysis (see Tabachnick & Fidell, 1996). For present purposes, however, their similarities are more notable than their differences, and it is worth noting that MANOVA computing programs can be used to perform discriminant analysis.

The reader will have noted that in the present book, having defined the terms **dependent variable** and **independent variable** in the context of experimental, as opposed to correlational, research, - see Section 3.2.3, we are now following the convention favoured by several other authors, such as Tabachnick & Fidell (1996) and Kerlinger (1986), whereby an independent variable is any variable that is supposed to have a causal effect upon another, irrespective of whether one is manipulating it directly, or merely measuring it as it occurs with other variables in the subjects studied. As a consequence of this, it is important to observe that in performing a discriminant analysis on data from an experiment with two or more DVs, the former DVs now become the **independent variables**, and the group variable is now the **dependent variable**.

The purpose of discriminant analysis is, given the independent variables IV_1, IV_2, . . ., IV_p, to find a linear function (D) of the IVs such that when a **one-way ANOVA** is carried out to compare the categories of the qualitative dependent variable with respect to D, the ratio $SS_{between}/SS_{total}$ is as large as possible. The function D will be of the general form:

$$D = b_0 + b_1(IV_1) + b_2(IV_2) + ... + b_p(IV_p)$$

As in multiple regression, it is possible to identify those variables that make significant contributions to the predictive process and drop the others from the final function. There are many other parallels between the two statistical techniques.

Recall that in one-way ANOVA, the total sum of squares (SS_{total}), which is a measure of the total dispersion of the scores around the grand mean, can be partitioned into two components:

(1) $SS_{between}$

(2) SS_{within}

The first of these components is the dispersion of the group means around the grand mean; the second is the dispersion of the scores around their group means. The three sums of squares are related according to the identity:

$$SS_{total} = SS_{between} + SS_{within}$$

ANOVA will show a smaller p-value as the ratio of $SS_{between}$ to SS_{within} becomes greater, or equally, as the ratio of $SS_{between}$ to SS_{total} becomes nearer to unity (i.e. the group means show large dispersion, whereas the individual scores lie close to their group means). This second ratio (i.e. $SS_{between}/SS_{total}$) is sometimes known as **eta squared (η^2)** or the correlation ratio, and is one of the oldest measures of the strength of an experimental effect.

Ratios of variances are formed to test main effects and interactions using the familiar statistic ***F***. This can be expressed in another way. In the univariate case (i.e. where there is just one dependent variable), the ratio SS_{within}/SS_{total} is the value of a statistic known as **Wilks' lambda (Λ)**. Hence

$$\eta^2 + \Lambda = \frac{SS_{between}}{SS_{total}} + \frac{SS_{within}}{SS_{total}} = \frac{SS_{between} + SS_{within}}{SS_{total}} = 1$$

Thus in the univariate case, Λ is $\mathbf{1 - \eta^2}$. Because the relatively small dispersion of the individual scores around their group means implies a relatively large dispersion among the group means, *smaller* values of Λ are more likely to be significant.

In the multivariate case (i.e. where there is more than one dependent variable) as in discriminant analysis, Λ becomes a ratio of determinants of matrices of sums of squares and cross-products. It is used to assess whether a function of the independent variables (the discriminating variables) reliably discriminates among the categories of the dependent variable. Since the sampling distribution of Λ is very complex, its significance is more conveniently found from a chi-square approximation.

For each of the categories of the dependent variable, there will be a (supposedly normal) distribution of D for the members of that category. The distributions will usually overlap, of course; but the goal of discriminant analysis is to find values for the constants ($b_0, b_1, \ldots, b_p$) in the discriminant function such that the overlap among the distributions of D is minimised. In other words, the idea is to spread out the distributions of D to the greatest possible extent. If there are only two categories in the dependent variable, only one discriminant function can be constructed.

14.1.2 Types of discriminant analysis

There are three types of discriminant analysis (DA): **direct**, **hierarchical**, and **stepwise**. In **direct** DA, all the variables enter the equations at once; in **hierarchical** DA, they enter according to a schedule set by the researcher; and in **stepwise** DA, statistical criteria alone determine the order of entry. In most analyses, the researcher has no reason for giving some predictors higher priority than others. The third (stepwise) method, therefore, is the most generally applicable and is the only one discussed in this chapter.

14.1.3 Stepwise discriminant analysis

The statistical procedure for stepwise discriminant analysis is similar to that for multiple regression, in that the effect of the addition or removal of an IV is monitored by a statistical test and the result used as a basis for the inclusion of that IV in the final analysis. When there are only two groups, there is just one discriminant function. With more than two groups, however, there can be several functions; though it is unusual for more than the first three to be useful.

Various statistics are available for weighing up the addition or removal of variables from the analysis, but the most commonly used is **Wilks' Lambda (Λ)**. The significance of the change in Λ when a variable is entered or removed is obtained from an **F test**. At each step of adding a variable to the analysis, the variable with the largest F (**F TO ENTER**) is included. This process is repeated until there are no further variables with an F value greater than the critical minimum threshold value. At the same time, any variable which had been added earlier, but which no longer contributes to maximising the assignment of cases to the correct groups because other variables in concert have taken over its role, is removed when its F value (**F TO REMOVE**) drops below the critical maximum threshold value. These critical values are listed in Output Listing 3.

Eventually, the process of adding and subtracting variables is completed, and a summary table is listed showing which variables were added or subtracted at each step. The variables remaining in the analysis are those used in the discriminant function(s). The first table thereafter shows which functions are statistically reliable. The first function provides the best means of predicting membership of the groups: later functions may or may not contribute reliably to the prediction process. Additional tables for listing the functions and their success rate for correct prediction can be requested. Plots can also be specified.

14.2 DISCRIMINANT ANALYSIS WITH SPSS

14.2.1 A problem in vocational guidance

A school's vocational guidance officer would like to be able to help senior pupils to choose which subjects to study at university. Fortunately, some data are available from a project on the background interests and school-leaving examination results of samples of architectural, engineering and psychology students. The students also filled in a questionnaire about their extra-curricular interests, including outdoor pursuits, drawing, painting, computing, and kit construction. The problem is this. Can knowledge of the pupils' scores on a number of variables be used to predict their subject category at university? In this study, then, subject category at university (psychologists, architects or engineers) is the dependent variable, and all the other variables are the independent variables.

14.2.2 Procedure for discriminant analysis

14.2.2.1 Preparing the SPSS data set

Since the data for this example consists of the results of 118 persons over ten variables, it would be extremely tedious for readers to enter the data themselves into the Data Editor but the data are available for anyone interested on WWW (http://www.psyc.abdn.ac.uk/teaching/spss/spssbook.htm).

Similar data would be entered in the following manner. Using the techniques described in Section 3.5, define the coding variable *studsubj* (full variable label: *Study Subject*), comprising three values: *1 = Architects, 2 = Psychologists, 3 = Engineers*. This is the dependent variable. Define the independent variables *sex* (which, like *studsubj*, is also a grouping variable), *conkit*, *model*, *draw*, *paint*, *outdoor*, *comput*, *vismod*, and *quals* (see Figure 2). Type in the data in the usual way. To specify the user-missing values, follow the procedure described in Section 3.5.8. For example, since the values of the independent variable *qual* cannot be negative, an appropriate user-missing value would be a negative number, such as –9 (see Figure 1).

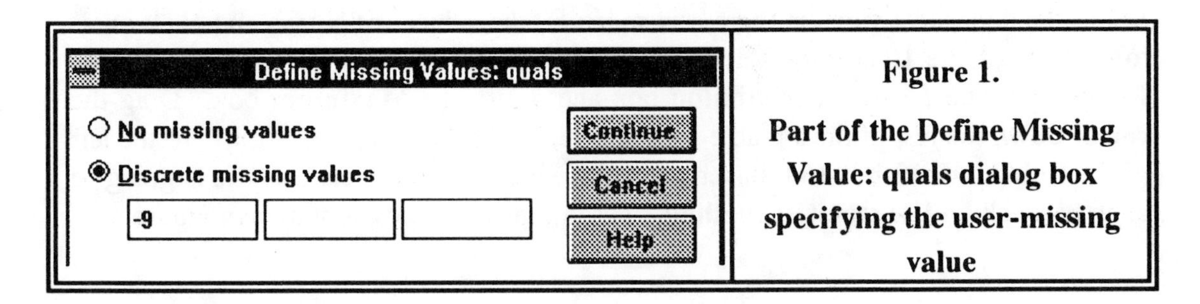

Figure 1.

Part of the Define Missing Value: quals dialog box specifying the user-missing value

Figure 2 shows the first four cases in the completed SPSS data set.

Figure 2.

The first four cases in the SPSS data set

	studsubj	sex	conkit	model	draw	paint	outdoor	comput	vismod	quals
1	1	1	2	3	2	0	1	0	5	99
2	1	1	3	2	6	2	2	0	6	10
3	1	2	5	5	6	7	0	3	4	8
4	1	1	5	6	7	1	4	3	6	99

14.2.2.2 Finding and running discriminant analysis

Discriminant analysis is found by choosing
Statistics

Classify (see Figure 3)

Discriminant...

to open the **Discriminant Analysis** dialog box (Figure 4).

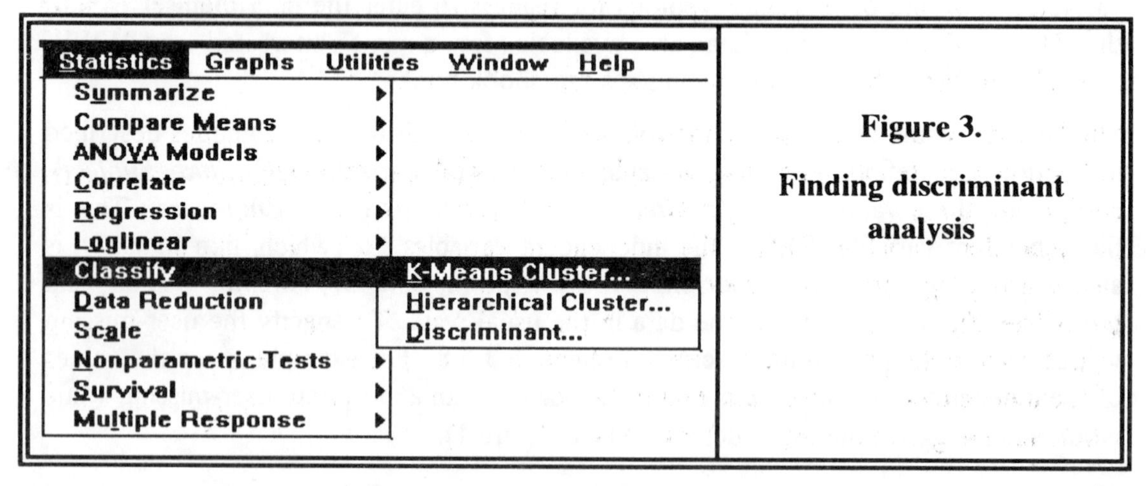

Figure 3.

Finding discriminant analysis

Select the dependent variable (here it is *studsubj*, the subject of study) and click on ▶ to the left of the **Grouping Variable** box to transfer the name. Click on **Define Range** and type *1* into the **Minimum** box and *3* into the **Maximum** box. Drag the cursor down the rest of the variable names to highlight them, and click on ▶ to the left of the **Independents** box to transfer them all. Since a hierarchical analysis is going to be used, click on **Use stepwise method**. The completed dialog is shown in Figure 4.

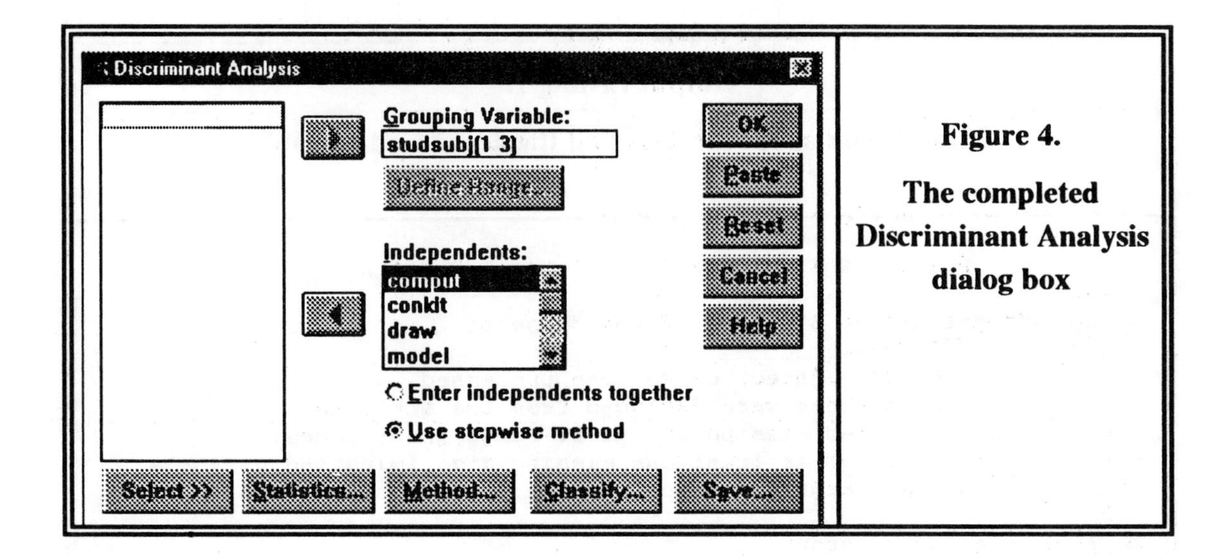

Figure 4.

The completed Discriminant Analysis dialog box

Recommended options include one-way ANOVAs for each of the variables across the three levels of the independent variable and a final summary table showing the success or failure of the analysis. To obtain the ANOVAs, click on **Statistics** and within the **Descriptives** box, select **Univariate ANOVAs**. Click on **Continue**. To obtain the success/failure table, click on **Classify** and within the **Display** box, select **Summary table**. Click on **Continue** and then on **OK**.

14.2.3 Output listing for discriminant analysis

14.2.3.1 Information about the data and the number of cases in each category of the grouping variable

The current SPSS 7 output is the same as that for SPSS 6. The information about the data is shown in Output Listing 1.

Output Listing 1.

Information about the data and the dependent variable

```
 - - - -    D I S C R I M I N A N T    A N A L Y S I S    - - - -

On groups defined by STUDSUBJ  Study Subject

          118 (Unweighted) cases were processed.
           10 of these were excluded from the analysis.
               0 had missing or out-of-range group codes.
              10 had at least one missing discriminating variable.
          108 (Unweighted) cases will be used in the analysis.

Number of cases by group

                Number of cases
  STUDSUBJ  Unweighted      Weighted  Label
         1          30          30.0  Architects
         2          37          37.0  Psychologists
         3          41          41.0  Engineers

     Total         108         108.0
```

14.2.3.2 Statistics

The optional **Univariate ANOVAs** selection is shown in Output Listing 2.

Output Listing 2.

Univariate ANOVAs

```
    Wilks' Lambda (U-statistic) and univariate F-ratio
    with 2 and 105 degrees of freedom

      Variable    Wilks' Lambda            F          Significance
      --------    -------------    -------------      ------------
      COMPUT          .99997             .0013             .9987
      CONKIT          .84396            9.7064             .0001
      DRAW            .89612            6.0862             .0032
      MODEL           .96136            2.1099             .1264
      OUTDOOR         .94183            3.2427             .0430
      PAINT           .83454           10.4086             .0001
      QUALS           .87670            7.3838             .0010
      SEX             .76652           15.9914             .0000
      VISMOD          .84351            9.7397             .0001
```

This indicates whether there is a statistically significant difference among the dependent variable means (*studsubj*) for each independent variable. All these differences are significant except *comput* and *model*.

14.2.3.3 Selection of variables

Details of Stepwise variable selection (Output Listing 3) and Canonical Discriminant Functions (not reproduced here) are listed. Notice the value of **Minimum F to enter** is 3.84 - this critical value is the minimum value for entering variables in a stepwise analysis.

Output Listing 3.

Rules for stepwise variable selection

```
Stepwise variable selection
     Selection rule:  minimize Wilks' Lambda
     Maximum number of steps..................     18
     Minimum tolerance level..................  .00100
     Minimum F to enter...................... 3.84000
     Maximum F to remove..................... 2.71000
```

14.2.3.4 Entering and removing variables step-by-step

The output listing starts with a table of variables and their **F to Enter** values (not reproduced) showing that *sex* has the highest **F to Enter** value. It is, therefore, selected as the first variable to enter at Step 1 (Output Listing 4).

At Step 2, the next variable with the highest **F-to-enter** value (*paint*) is entered.

This process of entering (and possibly removing) variables one at a time continues for a further five steps until Step 7 when the criteria shown in Output Listing 3 preclude any further steps.

Output Listing 4.

Entering and removing variables step-by-step

```
At step 1, SEX       was included in the analysis.

                              Degrees of Freedom  Signif. Betw Groups
Wilks' Lambda        .76652    1     2         105.0
Equivalent F       15.9914           2         105.0    .0000

---------- Variables in the Analysis after Step 1 ----------

Variable  Tolerance  F to Remove   Wilks' Lambda

SEX       1.0000000       15.9914

---------- Variables not in the Analysis after Step 1 --------

                     Minimum
Variable  Tolerance  Tolerance  F to Enter    Wilks' Lambda

COMPUT     .7450074   .7450074     4.2028382     .7091994
CONKIT     .9287215   .9287215     3.4285574     .7191062
DRAW       .9950388   .9950388     6.0381945     .6867722
MODEL      .9414225   .9414225     2.1991574     .7354177
OUTDOOR    .9826969   .9826969     1.4938129     .7451145
PAINT      .8832568   .8832568    10.1872805     .6409513
QUALS      .9834662   .9834662     7.6903191     .6677635
VISMOD     .9977884   .9977884     8.8257836     .6552981


At step 2, PAINT     was included in the analysis.

                              Degrees of Freedom  Signif.  Betw Groups
Wilks' Lambda            .64095 2    2         105.0
Equivalent F           12.95175      4         208.0    .0000

---------- Variables in the Analysis after Step 2 --------

Variable  Tolerance  F to Remove   Wilks' Lambda

PAINT      .8832568       10.1873      .7665196
SEX        .8832568       15.7061      .8345440
```

Finally at Step 7:

Output Listing 4 (continued).

Entering and removing variables step-by-step

```
At step 7, COMPUT   was included in the analysis.

                                Degrees of Freedom  Signif. Betw Groups
Wilks' Lambda          .37391  7    2        105.0
Equivalent F          8.98587      14        198.0    .0000

--------- Variables in the Analysis after Step 7 --------

Variable  Tolerance  F to Remove   Wilks' Lambda

COMPUT     .6995932       3.8543      .4030275
CONKIT     .8006370       4.3322      .4066375
OUTDOOR    .8426921       3.9592      .4038200
PAINT      .7344426      10.9168      .4563764
QUALS      .9145207      10.8321      .4557366
SEX        .5923199       7.4714      .4303510
VISMOD     .8998970       7.9591      .4340345

--------- Variables not in the Analysis after Step 7 ------

                      Minimum
Variable  Tolerance  Tolerance  F to Enter    Wilks' Lambda

DRAW       .6280746   .5205052      .9114370      .3670851
MODEL      .7160546   .5718517      .3562813      .3712141

F level or tolerance or VIN insufficient for further computation.
```

The analysis stops at this point because neither of the **F to enter** values exceeds the critical value of 3.84. Thus two variables *draw* and *model* are excluded from the analysis.

14.2.3.5 The summary table

The stepwise variable selection section concludes with a **Summary Table** (Output Listing 5) showing the order in which the variables were entered or removed (though in this analysis none was removed), along with values of Wilks' Lambda and the associated probability levels.

Output Listing 5.

The summary table

Summary Table

Step	Action Entered	Action Removed	Vars in	Wilks' Lambda	Sig.	Label
1	SEX		1	.76652	.0000	Sex of Student
2	PAINT		2	.64095	.0000	Interest in Painting
3	QUALS		3	.53865	.0000	School Qualifications
4	VISMOD		4	.48073	.0000	Ability to Visualise Model
5	OUTDOOR		5	.43903	.0000	Interest in Outdoor Pursuits
6	CONKIT		6	.40303	.0000	Interest in Construction Kits
7	COMPUT		7	.37391	.0000	Interest in Computing

14.2.3.6 Statistics of the discriminant functions

Output Listing 6 shows the percentage (**Pct**) of the variance accounted for by each discriminant function and how many of them (if any) are significant. It also shows that both functions (**Fcn**) are highly significant (see the **Sig** column on the right).

Output Listing 6.

Statistics of the discriminant functions

Canonical Discriminant Functions

Fcn	Eigenvalue	Pct of Variance	Cum Pct	Canonical Corr		After Fcn	Wilks' Lambda	Chi-square	df	Sig
					:	0	.373913	100.341	14	.0000
1*	.6980	54.83	54.83	.6412	:	1	.634921	46.334	6	.0000
2*	.5750	45.17	100.00	.6042	:					

* Marks the 2 canonical discriminant functions remaining in the analysis.

14.2.3.7 Standardised coefficients and within groups correlations with discriminants

Two tables follow in the listing, the first (not reproduced here) being the standardised function coefficients, and the second (Output Listing 7) the pooled within groups correlations between the discriminating variables and the functions. It is clear from the output in Output Listing 7 that the first function is based on subjects' interests in painting, drawing, and visualising models, while the second is based on the sex of the subjects and their interest in kit construction. The asterisks mark the correlation with the higher value for each variable.

Output Listing 7.

The structure matrix

```
Structure matrix:

Pooled within-groups correlations between discriminating
variables and canonical discriminant functions
(Variables ordered by size of correlation within function)

                Func  1     Func  2

VISMOD          -.50787*    -.09751
QUALS            .42584*    -.15639
PAINT           -.41858*     .36345
DRAW            -.21738*     .11537
MODEL           -.11505*     .07006
COMPUT           .00603*     .00007

SEX              .19409      .69570*
CONKIT          -.14833     -.54298*
OUTDOOR          .19267      .24970*

* denotes largest absolute correlation between each variable
and any discriminant function.
```

14.2.3.8 Success of predictions of group membership

The optional selection of **Summary table** from the **Classify** options in the **Discriminant Analysis** dialog box provides an indication of the success rate for predictions of membership of the grouping variable's categories using the discriminant functions developed in the analysis (see Output Listing 8). The table indicates that the overall success rate is 72.2%.

Output Listing 8 also shows that Engineers are the most accurately classified, with 75.6% of the cases correct. Architects are next with 73.3%, and Psychologists are last, with 67.6%. Notice that incorrectly classified Architects are more likely to be classified as Engineers than as Psychologists, and that incorrectly classified Psychologists are more likely to be classified as Engineers than as Architects!

Output Listing 8.

Classification results

Classification results -

Actual Group	No. of Cases	Predicted Group Membership 1	2	3
Group 1 Architects	30	22 73.3%	2 6.7%	6 20.0%
Group 2 Psychologists	37	4 10.8%	25 67.6%	8 21.6%
Group 3 Engineers	41	5 12.2%	5 12.2%	31 75.6%

Percent of "grouped" cases correctly classified: 72.22%

14.2.4 Predicting group membership

Sectional 14.2.1 posed the problem whether a knowledge of pupils' scores on a number of variables could be used to predict their subjects of study at university. The analysis has demonstrated that two discriminant functions can be generated using all the variables except *draw and model* and that these can predict 72% of the cases correctly. Furthermore, it is clear from Output Listing 7 that *sex*, *vismod* and *conkit* are the major contributors to the functions. However what about future students for whom only the data for predicting variables are known? Can the program be used to predict which subject they should study? The answer is yes.

Proceed as follows:

1) enter the data for the new students at the end of the data in the Data Editor window. Leave the grouping variable blank or enter an out-of-range number so that the analysis does not include these cases when it is computing the discriminant functions;

2) complete the **Discriminant Analysis** dialog box as before but, in addition, click the **Save** option and then click the radio button for **Predicted group membership**. Click **Continue** and then **OK** to run the analysis;

3) the predicted group membership will appear in a new column labelled **Dis_1**.

SUMMARY

1) Discriminant analysis is used to predict **category membership** (the DV) from data on several other variables (the IVs). The procedure generates **discriminant functions**, which are weighted sums of IVs, in which the weightings are chosen to maximise the differences, on the new variables, among the categories.

2) The independent variables (IVs) should generally be quantitative and satisfy the usual assumption of normality of distribution, though some authorities allow qualitative binary IVs to be included.

3) The procedure for discriminant analysis is found by choosing

   Statistics

   Classify

   and then clicking on **Discriminant** to open the dialog box.

   The grouping variable name is entered in the **Grouping Variable** box and its levels defined with the **Define Range** option. The remaining variables are entered into the **Independents** box. If the recommended stepwise method is being adopted, click on the **Use stepwise method** option. Other options include **Univariate ANOVAs** selected from the **Descriptives** box, and **Summary table**, selected from the **Display** box.

4) The listing includes details of which variables are included in the functions, and which functions are significant.

5) Predictions of category membership for new cases can be made by using the **Save** option and specifying **Predicted group membership**. Leave blank or enter an out-range value for the grouping variable. The predicted memberships will appear in a new variable called Dis_1.

CHAPTER 15

FACTOR ANALYSIS

15.1 INTRODUCTION

15.1.1 The nature of factors

Suppose that the subjects in a sample are each tested on several variables, perhaps an assortment of tests of intellectual ability, such as vocabulary, short term memory, reaction speed and so on. The correlations of performance on each test with every other test in the battery can be arranged in a rectangular array known as a **correlation matrix**, or **R-matrix**. Each row (or column) of R would contain all the correlations involving one particular test in the battery. The cells along the **principal diagonal** (running from the top left to the bottom right of the matrix) would remain empty (or contain the entry *1*), since each cell on that diagonal represents the combination of a particular test with itself; but each off-diagonal cell would be occupied by the correlation between the tests whose row and column intersect at that particular cell. The R-matrix is the starting point for several statistical procedures, but in this chapter we shall consider just one: **factor analysis.**

The presence, in the R-matrix, of clusters of sizeable correlations among subsets of the tests in the battery would suggest that the tests in a subset may be measuring the same underlying psychological dimension, or ability. If the traditional British theories in the psychology of intelligence are correct, there should be fewer (far fewer) dimensions than there are tests in the battery. The purpose of factor analysis is to discern and to quantify the dimensions supposed to underlie performance on a variety of tasks. The **factors** produced by factor analysis are mathematical entities, which can be thought of as classificatory axes, with respect to which the tests in a battery can be 'plotted'. The greater the value of a test's co-ordinate, or **loading**, on a factor, the more important is that factor in accounting for the correlations between that test and others in the battery.

A factor, then, has the geometric interpretation as a classificatory axis in an axial reference system with respect to which the tests in the battery are represented as points in space.

But the term **factor** also has an equivalent algebraic, or arithmetical interpretation as a linear function of the observed scores that people achieve on the tests in a battery. For example, if a battery comprises 8 tests, and each testee were also to be assigned a ninth score consisting of the sum of the 8 test scores, that ninth, artificial, score would be a **factor score**, and it would make sense to speak of correlations between the factor and the real test scores. We have seen that the loading of a test on a factor is, geometrically speaking, the co-ordinate of the test point on the factor axis. But that axis represents a 'factor' in the second, algebraic sense, and the loading is the correlation between the test scores and those on the factor.

In factor analysis, a major assumption is that the mathematical factors represent **latent variables** (i.e. psychological dimensions), the nature of which can only be guessed at by examining the nature of tests that have sizeable co-ordinates on any particular axis. It should perhaps be said at the outset that this claim is controversial, and there are notable psychologists who hold that the factors of factor analysis are statistical realities, but psychological fictions.

The topic of factor analysis is not elementary, and the SPSS output bristles with highly technical terms. If you are unfamiliar with factor analysis, we suggest you read the lucid texts by Kim and Mueller (1978a, 1978b) and by Tabachnick and Fidell (1996), which contain relatively painless introductions to the technical jargon.

15.1.2 Stages in a factor analysis

A factor analysis usually takes place in three stages:

(1) a **matrix of correlation coefficients** is generated for all the variable combinations;

(2) from the correlation matrix, **factors** are extracted. The most common method is called **principal factors** (often wrongly referred to as **principal components** extraction, hence the abbreviation **PC**);

(3) the factors (axes) are **rotated** to maximise the relationships between the variables and some of the factors. The most common method is **varimax**, a rotation method which maintains independence among the mathematical factors. Geometrically, this means that during rotation, the axes remain **orthogonal** (i.e. they are kept at right angles).

A fourth stage can be added at which the scores of each subject on each of the factors emerging from the analysis are calculated. It should be stressed that these **factor scores** are not the results of any actual test taken by the subjects: they are estimates of the subjects' standing on the **supposed** latent variables that have emerged as mathematical axes from the factor analysis of the data set. Factor scores are very useful, however, because they can subsequently be used as input for further statistical analysis.

It is advisable to carry out only Stage 1 initially, in order to be able to inspect the correlation coefficients in the correlation matrix R. Since the purpose of the analysis is to link variables together into factors, those variables must be related to one another and therefore have correlation coefficients larger than about 0.3. Should any variables show no substantial correlation with any of the others, they would be removed from R in subsequent analysis. It is also advisable to check that the correlation matrix does not possess the highly undesirable properties of **multicollinearity** and **singularity**. The former is the condition where the variables are very highly (though imperfectly) correlated; the latter arises when some of the variables are exact linear functions of others in the battery, as when the variable *C* is constructed by adding together the subjects' scores on variables *A* and *B*. Should either multicollinearity or singularity be present, it would be necessary to drop some of the variables from the analysis.

15.1.3 The extraction of factors

The factors (or axes) in a factor analysis are **extracted** (or, pursuing the geometric analogy, **constructed**) one at a time, the process being repeated until it is possible, from the loadings of the tests on the factors so far extracted, to generate good approximations to the correlations in the original R matrix. Factor analysis tells us how many factors (or axes) are necessary to achieve a reconstruction of R that is sufficiently good to account satisfactorily for the correlations it contains.

15.1.4 The rationale of rotation

If we think of the tests in the battery and the origin of the axis (factor) set as stationary points and rotate the axes around the origin, the values of all the loadings will change. Nevertheless, the new set of loadings on the axes, *whatever their new position*, can still be used to produce exactly the same estimates of the correlations in the R-matrix. In this sense, the position of the axes is quite arbitrary: the factor matrix (or **F-matrix**) only tells us *how many* axes are necessary to classify the data adequately; but it does not thereby establish that the initial position of the axes is the appropriate one.

In **rotation**, the factor axes are rotated around the fixed origin until the loadings meet a certain criterion. The set of loadings that satisfies the criterion is known as the **rotated factor matrix**. The purpose of any rotation is to achieve a configuration of loadings having the qualities collectively known as **simple structure** which, loosely conceived, is the set of loadings that shows the maximum number of tests loading on the minimum number of factors. The idea is that the fewer the factors that are involved in accounting for the correlations among a group of tests, the easier it is to invest those factors with psychological meaning. In fact, simple structure is an ideal never achieved in practice, partly because the concept, in its original form, is actually rather vague and embodies contradictory properties. Modern computing packages such as SPSS offer a selection of rotation methods, each based upon a different (but reasonable) interpretation of simple structure. The most commonly used method of rotation is known as **varimax**.

15.2 A FACTOR ANALYSIS OF DATA ON SEVEN VARIABLES

Suppose a researcher has available the scores, on seven variables, of 120 applicants for a place on a course on cartography. In order to identify the psychological dimensions tapped by the seven variables, it is decided to carry out a factor analysis on the correlation matrix. The variable set comprises the following tests: **Mapping**;

Engineering; **Spatial ability**; **Mathematics**; **English**; **Art**; **Intelligence**. Section 15.2.1 outlines the procedure for a factor analysis using the scores directly. Sometimes, however, it is convenient to use previously computed correlations in the form of a correlation matrix as the input for a factor analysis; the procedure for this is given in Section 15.2.3.

15.2.1 Procedure for factor analysis with raw scores

15.2.1.1 Preparing the SPSS data set

Using the techniques described in Section 3.5, define the seven variables *artwork*, *engineer*, *english*, *intellig*, *mapping*, *maths* and *spacerel*, using the variable labels procedure to assign the fuller labels *Mapping*, *Engineering*, *Spatial Ability* and so on to the rather cryptic variable names.

Each of these variables will comprise the raw scores that the 120 applicants achieved on that particular test. Note that there are no grouping variables in this data set: this is a purely correlational (as opposed to experimental) study. Inasmuch as there can be said to be an 'independent' variable, it is one whose existence must be inferred from whatever patterns may exist in the correlation matrix. It is the *raison d'être* of factor analysis to make such an inference credible.

Type in the data and save the SPSS data set in the usual way.

15.2.1.2 Running the factor analysis

Find factor analysis by choosing
Statistics
    Data Reduction

(Figure 1). Click on **Factor** to open the **Factor** dialog box (Figure 2).

Highlight all the variable names in the **Factor** dialog box and click on ▶ to transfer them to the **Variables** box.

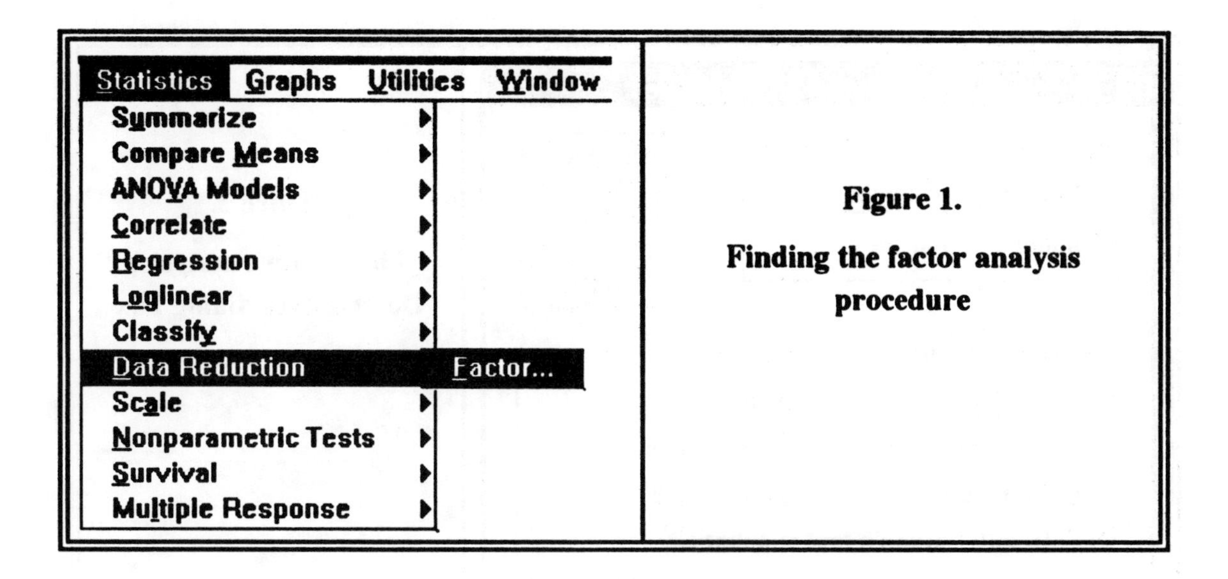

Figure 1.

Finding the factor analysis procedure

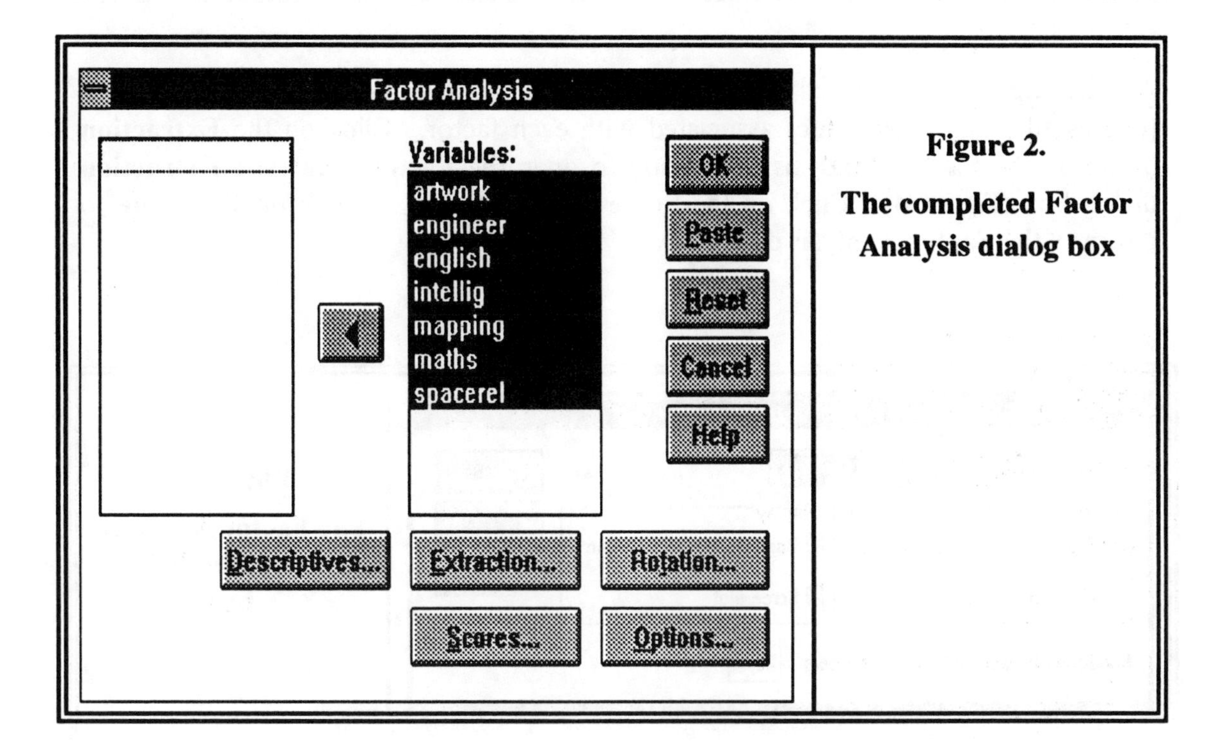

Figure 2.

The completed Factor Analysis dialog box

It only remains to select some options which regulate the manner in which the analysis takes place and produce some extra items of output. Click on the **Descriptives** button to open the **Factor Analysis: Descriptives** dialog box (Figure 3). Click on the following check boxes: **Coefficients, Determinant, KMO and Bartlett's test of sphericity,** and **Reproduced**. (KMO is the **Kaiser-Meyer-Olkin measure of sampling adequacy**, explained later in Section 15.2.2.) This will produce a range of matrices and diagnostics indicating the adequacy of the factor analysis. Click on **Continue** to return to the **Factor Analysis** dialog box.

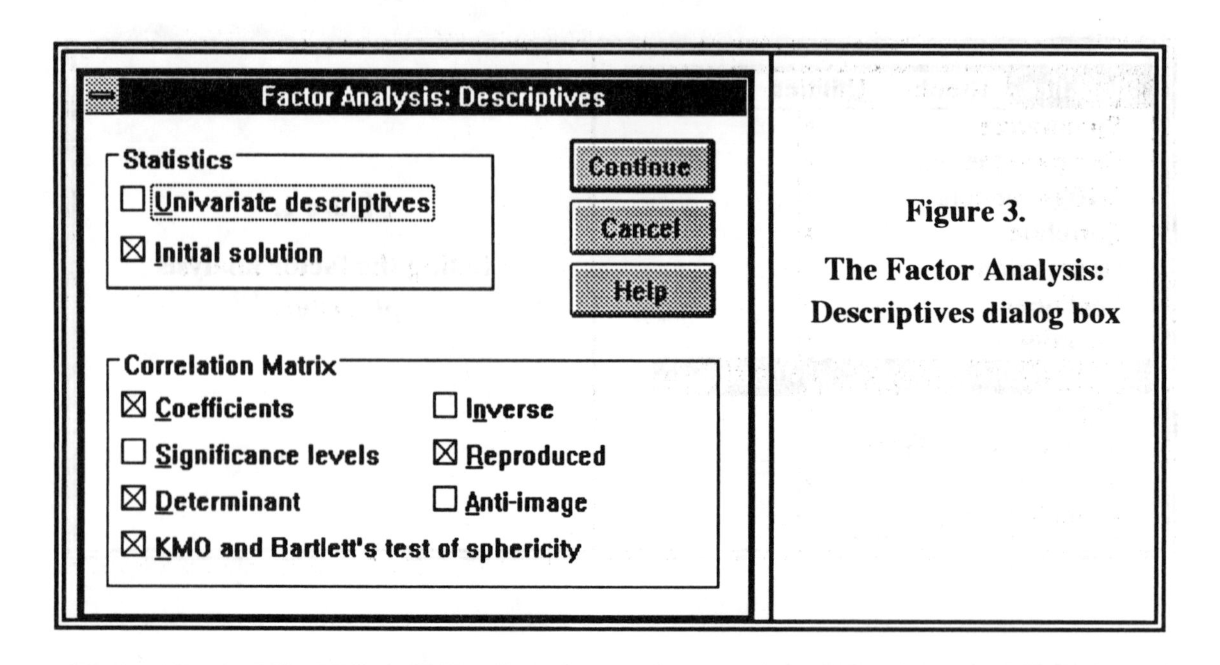

Figure 3.

The Factor Analysis: Descriptives dialog box

Another option is a special graph called a **scree plot**, which shows the variance (expressed as an **eigenvalue**) associated with each factor. Click on the **Extraction** button in the **Factor Analysis** dialog box to open the **Factor Analysis: Extraction** dialog box (Figure 4). Click on the **Scree plot** check box. Click on **Continue** to return to the **Factor Analysis** dialog box.

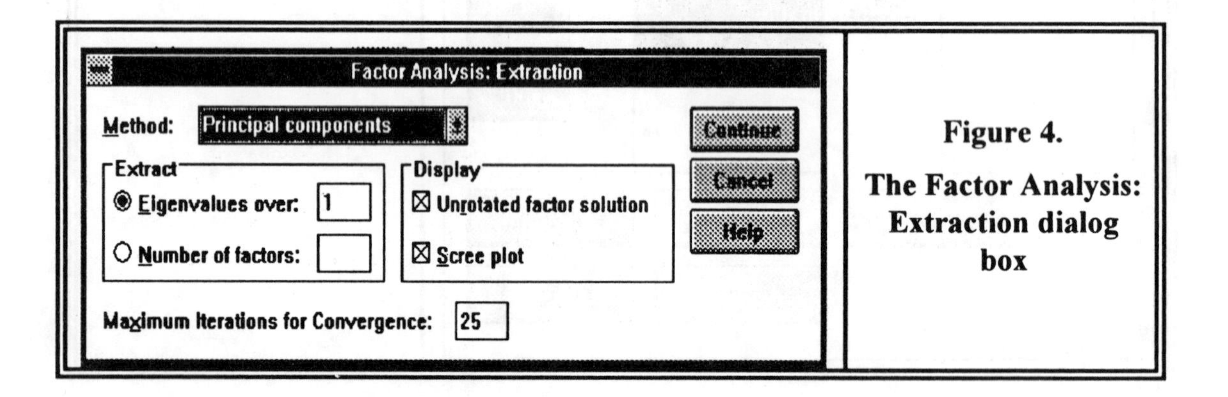

Figure 4.

The Factor Analysis: Extraction dialog box

To obtain the rotated F-matrix, click on the **Rotation** button in the **Factor Analysis** dialog box to obtain the **Factor Analysis: Rotation** dialog box (Figure 5). In the **Method** box, mark the **Varimax** radio button. Click on **Continue** to return to the **Factor Analysis** dialog box.

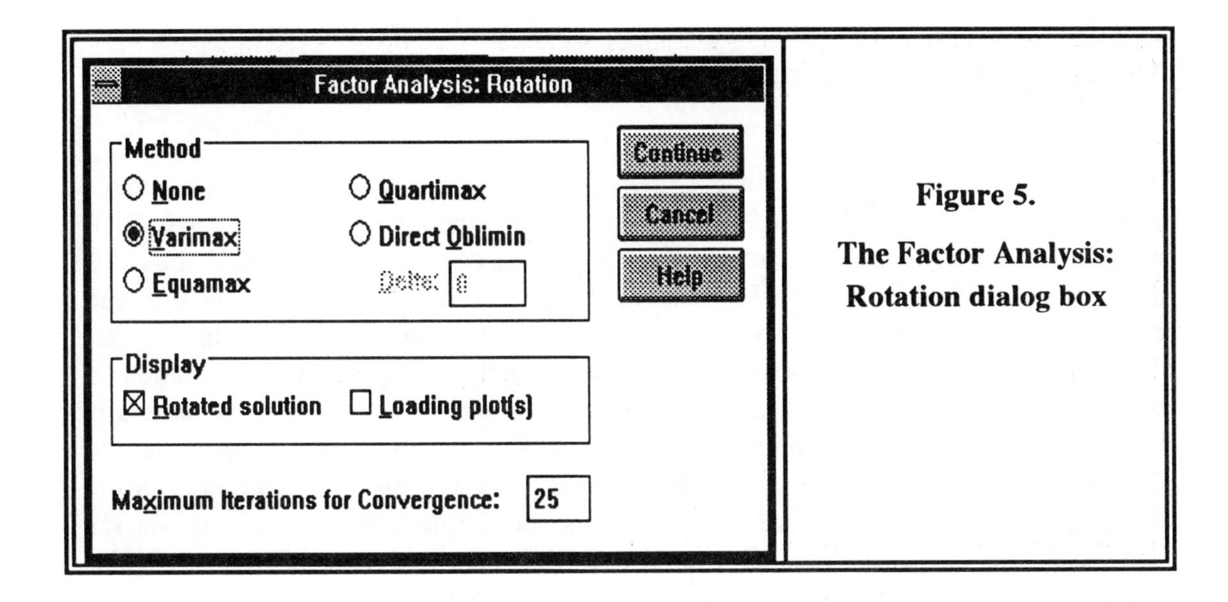

Figure 5.

The Factor Analysis: Rotation dialog box

Finally, to make the F-matrix easier to interpret, it is possible to suppress small factor loadings. Click on the **Options** button in the **Factor Analysis** dialog box to obtain the **Factor Analysis: Options** dialog box (Figure 6). In the box labelled **Coefficient Display Format**, click on the **Suppress absolute values less than:** check box and type the value *0.50* into the text box. This will have the effect of removing all loadings less than 0.5 from the F-matrix. Click on **Continue** and then on **OK** to execute the factor analysis.

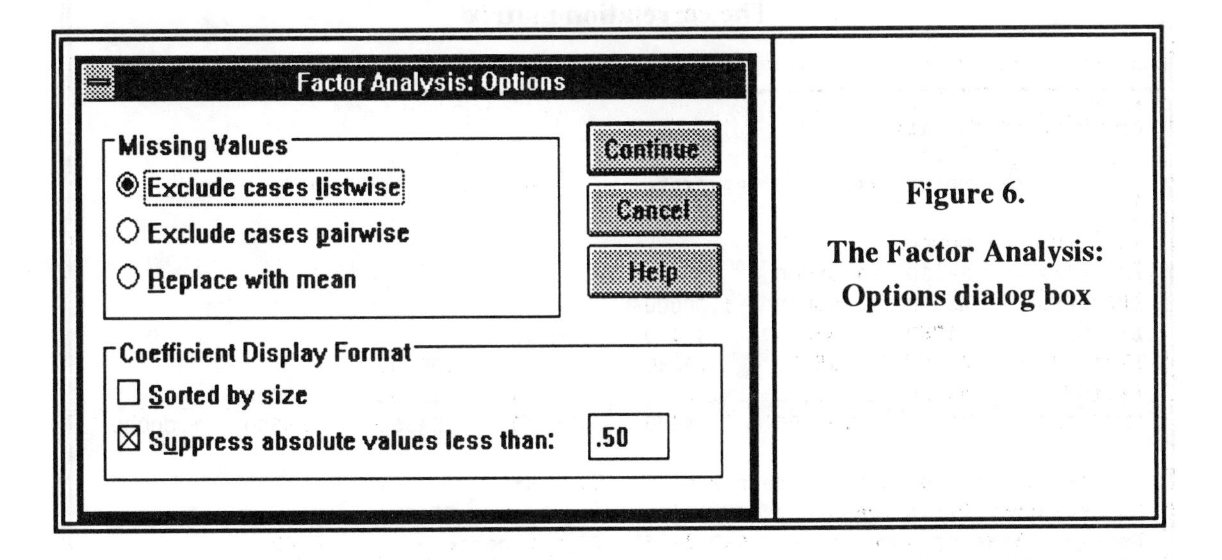

Figure 6.

The Factor Analysis: Options dialog box

15.2.2 Output listing for factor analysis

The current SPSS 7 output is the same as that for SPSS 6.

15.2.2.1 The correlation matrix

A correlation matrix is *square*, that is, there are as many rows as there are columns. The diagonal of cells running from top left to bottom right is known as the **principal diagonal** of the matrix. Since the variables are labelled in the same order in the rows and columns of **R,** each of the cells along the principal diagonal contains the correlation of one of the variables with itself (i.e. *1*). The correlations in the off-diagonal cells are the same above and below the principal diagonal (the correlation of *maths* with *english* is the same as that of *english* with *maths*). A **triangular matrix** is that part of a square matrix comprising the entries along the principal diagonal and the off-diagonal entries either above or below the diagonal: the **upper triangular matrix** comprises the principal diagonal plus the entries above; the **lower triangular matrix** comprises the principal diagonal plus the entries below. Either of the triangular versions of **R** contains all the information in the square matrix.

The **correlation matrix** derived from all the variables (in lower triangular form), together with the value of its **determinant** is shown in Output Listing 1. Provided the determinant is larger than 0.00001, the matrix can be assumed not to suffer from multicollinearity or singularity.

Output Listing 1.

The correlation matrix

Correlation Matrix:

	MAPPING	ENGINEER	SPACEREL	MATHS	ENGLISH	ARTWORK	INTELLIG
MAPPING	1.00000						
ENGINEER	.38230	1.00000					
SPACEREL	.65020	.40830	1.00000				
MATHS	.51750	.65560	.44190	1.00000			
ENGLISH	.23840	.35870	.15540	.41170	1.00000		
ARTWORK	.54320	.35300	.72220	.23040	.19900	1.00000	
INTELLIG	.45540	.62200	.54440	.65720	.54350	.35550	1.00000

Determinant of Correlation Matrix = .0272545
Kaiser-Meyer-Olkin Measure of Sampling Adequacy = .75160
Bartlett Test of Sphericity = 417.29363, Significance = .00000

15.2.2.2 Measure of sampling adequacy and Bartlett's test of sphericity

The items below the correlation matrix in Output Listing 1 are the **Kaiser-Meyer-Olkin (KMO) measure of sampling adequacy** (which should be greater than about 0.5 for a satisfactory factor analysis to proceed) and the **Bartlett test of sphericity**. If the Bartlett test is **not** significant (i.e. its associated probability is greater than 0.05), then there is the danger that the correlation matrix is an identity matrix (i.e. the diagonal elements are 1 and the off-diagonal elements are 0) and is therefore unsuitable for further analysis. In the present example, both statistics reassure us that we can continue with the analysis.

15.2.2.3 A table of initial statistics for principal components analysis

The initial statistics are tabulated in Output Listing 2. To the right of the column of asterisks, there is a column of **factors**, together with a corresponding column of **eigenvalues**, the **percent of variance** attributable to each factor, and the **cumulative variance** for the factor and the previous factors.

An **eigenvalue** is a measure of standardised variance with a mean of 0 and a standard deviation of 1. Because the variance that each standardised variable contributes to a principal components extraction is 1, a component with an eigenvalue of less than 1 is less important than an observed variable, and can therefore be ignored. For this reason, the program subsequently drops any factors with an eigenvalue of less than 1.

Notice that the first factor accounts for 53.5% of the variance and the second factor for the next 17.8% of the variance. The remaining factors are insignificant.

Output Listing 2.

Initial statistics from the analysis

Initial Statistics:

Variable	Communality	*	Factor	Eigenvalue	Pct of Var	Cum Pct
		*				
MAPPING	1.00000	*	1	3.74728	53.5	53.5
ENGINEER	1.00000	*	2	1.24626	17.8	71.3
SPACEREL	1.00000	*	3	.69019	9.9	81.2
MATHS	1.00000	*	4	.51560	7.4	88.6
ENGLISH	1.00000	*	5	.37528	5.4	93.9
ARTWORK	1.00000	*	6	.25194	3.6	97.5
INTELLIG	1.00000	*	7	.17345	2.5	100.0

15.2.2.4 The unrotated factor matrix

Output Listing 3 shows the loadings of the seven tests on the two factors extracted. When the factors are **orthogonal** (i.e. uncorrelated with each other), these factor loadings are the correlation coefficients between the variables and the factors. Thus the higher the absolute value of the loading (which can never exceed a maximum of 1), the more the factor contributes to the variable.

Note that the gaps in the Table represent factor loadings with values less than 0.5, because the option of suppressing coefficients below a stipulated level (we selected 0.5) was taken in order to make the table easier to read.

Output Listing 3.

The unrotated factor matrix

```
PC extracted 2 factors.
Factor Matrix:

               Factor  1      Factor  2

INTELLIG          .82647
SPACEREL          .78187
MATHS             .77899
MAPPING           .75007
ENGINEER          .74840
ARTWORK           .66104       -.57307

ENGLISH           .53515        .53830
```

15.2.2.5 A table of final statistics

Output Listing 4 tabulates the final statistics.

Output Listing 4.

Some final statistics from the analysis

```
Final Statistics:

Variable      Communality  *  Factor   Eigenvalue   Pct of Var   Cum Pct
                           *
MAPPING           .67226   *    1       3.74728       53.5        53.5
ENGINEER          .64117   *    2       1.24626       17.8        71.3
SPACEREL          .84794   *
MATHS             .72105   *
ENGLISH           .57615   *
ARTWORK           .76538   *
INTELLIG          .76957   *
```

In the left half, before the column of asterisks, the variable names are tabulated with their **communalities**, which show how much of the variance in the variables has been accounted for by the two factors that have been extracted: for example, nearly 85% of the variance in Space Relations is accounted for, whereas only 57% of the variance in

English is accounted for. The right half after the column of asterisks shows the two factors and their associated variances.

15.2.2.6 Reproduced correlation matrix and residuals

Output Listing 5 shows the **reproduced correlation matrix** of coefficients, computed from the extracted factors. The elements of this matrix are subtracted from those of the original correlation matrix to produce a matrix of **residuals**, the properties of which indicate the adequacy of the factor model.

Output Listing 5.

A reproduction of R from the loadings in the F matrix, and residuals

Reproduced Correlation Matrix:

	MAPPING	ENGINEER	SPACEREL	MATHS	ENGLISH
MAPPING	.67226*	-.08477	-.09733	.04512	.01525
ENGINEER	.46707	.64117*	-.03835	-.02363	-.19508
SPACEREL	.74753	.44665	.84794*	-.00276	-.00117
MATHS	.47238	.67923	.44466	.72105*	-.18711
ENGLISH	.22315	.55378	.15657	.59881	.57615*
ARTWORK	.68559	.33156	.79561	.32127	.04528
INTELLIG	.52251	.70228	.50311	.74322	.60062

	ARTWORK	INTELLIG
MAPPING	-.14239	-.06711
ENGINEER	.02144	-.08028
SPACEREL	-.07341	.04129
MATHS	-.09087	-.08602
ENGLISH	.15372	-.05712
ARTWORK	.76538*	-.02228
INTELLIG	.37778	.76957*

The lower left triangle contains the reproduced correlation matrix; the diagonal, reproduced communalities; and the upper right triangle residuals between the observed correlations and the reproduced correlations.

There are 12 (57.0%) residuals (above diagonal) with absolute values > 0.05.

This table lists both the correlations (the values in the columns below the asterisks) and the residuals (the values in the columns above the asterisks). A good factor model should be a good fit; the sentence at the foot of Output Listing 5 states the number and proportion of residuals (i.e. the differences) that are greater than 0.05. Sometimes what appears to be an unsatisfactory factor analysis can be saved by dropping a variable that correlates too highly with the others. A new analysis without the offending variable can easily be performed by returning to the **Factor Analysis** dialog box and removing the unwanted variable (e.g. *artwork*) from the list of variables.

15.2.2.7 The rotated factor matrix

Output Listing 6 shows the effect of trying to simplify the previous Factor Matrix by minimising the number of factors on which variables have high loadings. *Space Relations*, *Artwork*, and *Mapping* are now loaded substantially only on Factor 2, whereas *Maths*, *English*, and *Engineering* are now loaded only on Factor 1, the matrix is much easier to interpret psychologically. Compare this table with the unrotated matrix in Output Listing 3. Again, loadings with a value of less than 0.5 have been suppressed.

```
Rotated Factor Matrix:

              Factor  1     Factor  2

INTELLIG        .80332
MATHS           .79881
ENGLISH         .75864
ENGINEER        .74003

SPACEREL                      .89017
ARTWORK                       .87039
MAPPING                       .75530
```

Output Listing 6.

The rotated factor matrix

15.2.2.8 Factor transformation matrix

This matrix, which is not reproduced here, specifies the rotation applied to the factors, and for our purposes can be ignored.

15.2.2.9 Scree plot

This optional plot (Figure 7) graphs the eigenvalues of all the factors. To see it on the screen in SPSS 6, it is necessary to click on the **Carousel** icon at the foot of the screen or to click on the **Windows** drop-down menu and select **Chart Carousel**. The plot is useful for deciding how many factors to retain. The point of interest is where the curve connecting the asterisks starts to flatten out. This region of the curve has been likened to the rubble or scree on a mountain side. It can be seen that the curve begins to flatten out between the second and third factors. Note also that Factor 3 has an eigenvalue of less than 1, so only two factors have been retained.

In the event of more factors remaining in an analysis than are desired, the user can return to the original **Factor Analysis** dialog box and alter the specifications. Within the **Factor Analysis: Extraction** dialog box (Figure 4), specify how many factors are to be retained, and re-run the analysis.

Figure 7.

The factor scree plot

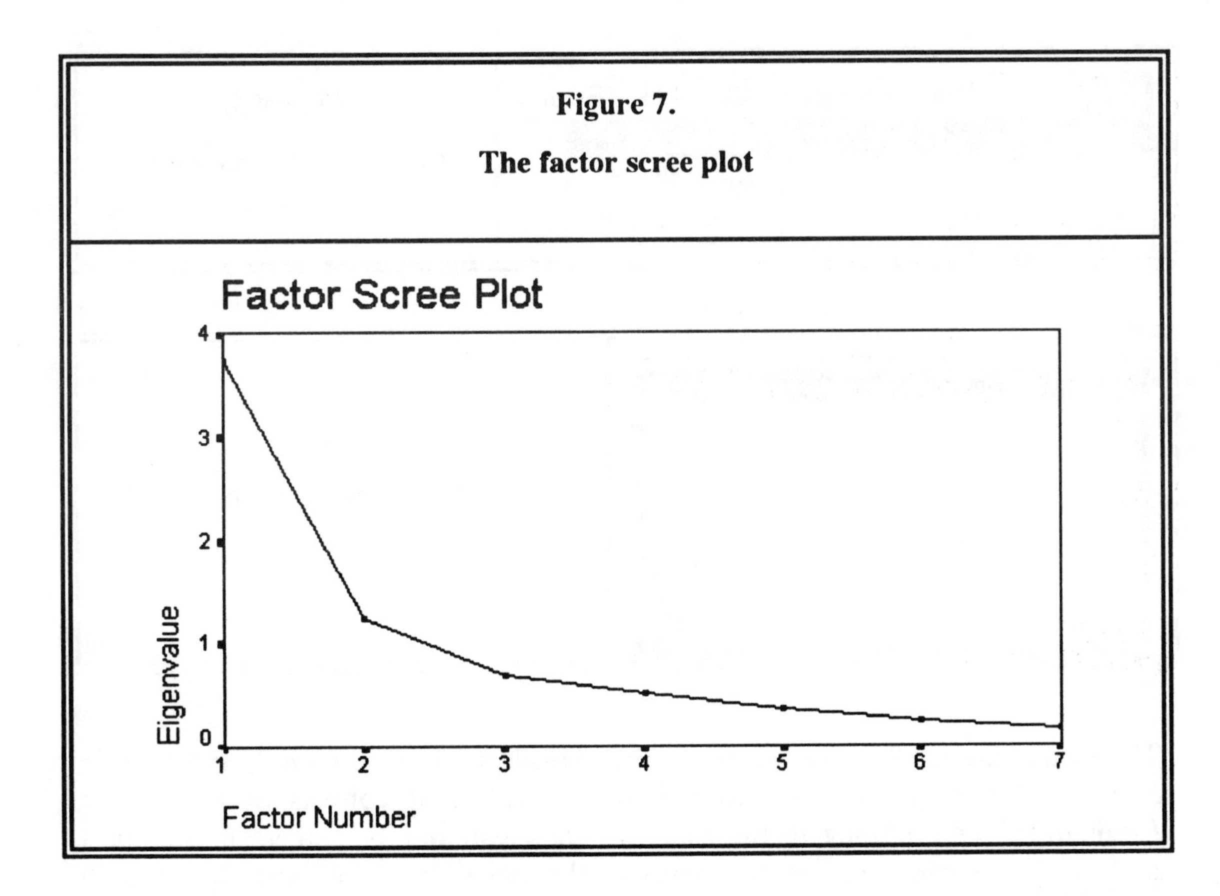

15.2.3 Using a correlation matrix as input for factor analysis

Sometimes it may be more convenient to use correlations rather than raw scores as the input for a factor analysis. Unfortunately this cannot be done by using the dialog box interface: instead the user has to resort to **SPSS Command Syntax**. There are two stages:

(1) preparing the correlation matrix;

(2) preparing the factor analysis command.

15.2.3.1 Preparation of the correlation matrix

Choose
File
New

(Figure 8). Click on **SPSS Syntax** to open the syntax window (Figure 9). In older versions of SPSS 6, the syntax window is slightly different.

File Edit Data Transform Statistics Graphs
New Data
Open SPSS Syntax
Read ASCII Data... SPSS Output

Figure 8.

Finding the syntax window

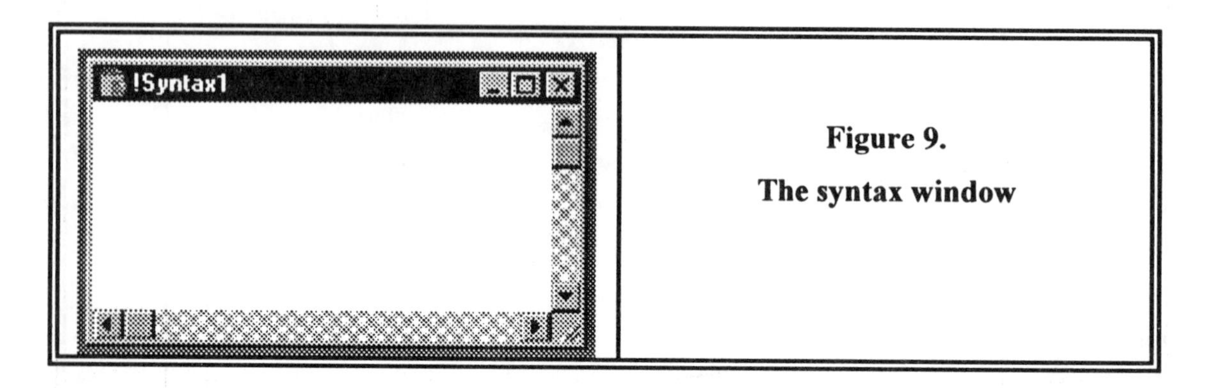

Figure 9.

The syntax window

The form of the SPSS syntax will be familiar to readers who have used SPSS/PC+ (see ***SPSS/PC+ Made Simple, Kinnear & Gray, 1992)***. It consists of a series of **commands**, some relating to the data (the **data commands**), others to statistical procedures. A command can have several **subcommands**; but it must always finish with a full stop (.) .

The syntax for inputting a data matrix is relatively simple. If the user wants to inspect the format of the syntax, this can be done by typing **Matrix data** in the syntax window and then clicking on the icon  in the toolbar (or in older versions of SPSS 6, click on the box labelled **Syntax**) to open the **Matrix Data Syntax** help window (Figure 10). Optional subcommands are shown in square brackets. Relevant parts can either be typed in the syntax window or, if desired, the whole block of syntax can be copied over for editing from the help window to the syntax window using **Copy** and **Paste** in the usual way.

The variable names must be entered in place of *varlist* and the rest of the correlation matrix entered as shown in Figure 11. Notice the variable *ROWTYPE_* which is a special string variable used to identify the type of data for each record. Thus *CORR* indicates a record of correlation coefficients, *N* is a record of counts (with a value for each of the experimental variables). The default structure of a correlation matrix is a lower triangular matrix. If an upper triangular or rectangular matrix is to be used, an additional */FORMAT* subcommand is required. The value of *N* is not needed for a factor analysis, but it is needed for tests of significance and for assessing the sampling adequacy of the data. The correlation matrix and value of *N* are then entered (preceded in each row with *CORR* or *N*, as appropriate) between the usual *BEGIN DATA* and *END DATA* commands. The full stops after the list of variable names, *BEGIN DATA* and *END DATA* **must not be omitted**. (See ***SPSS/PC+ Made Simple, Kinnear & Gray, 1992***; Chapter 2, Section 2.4.1.)

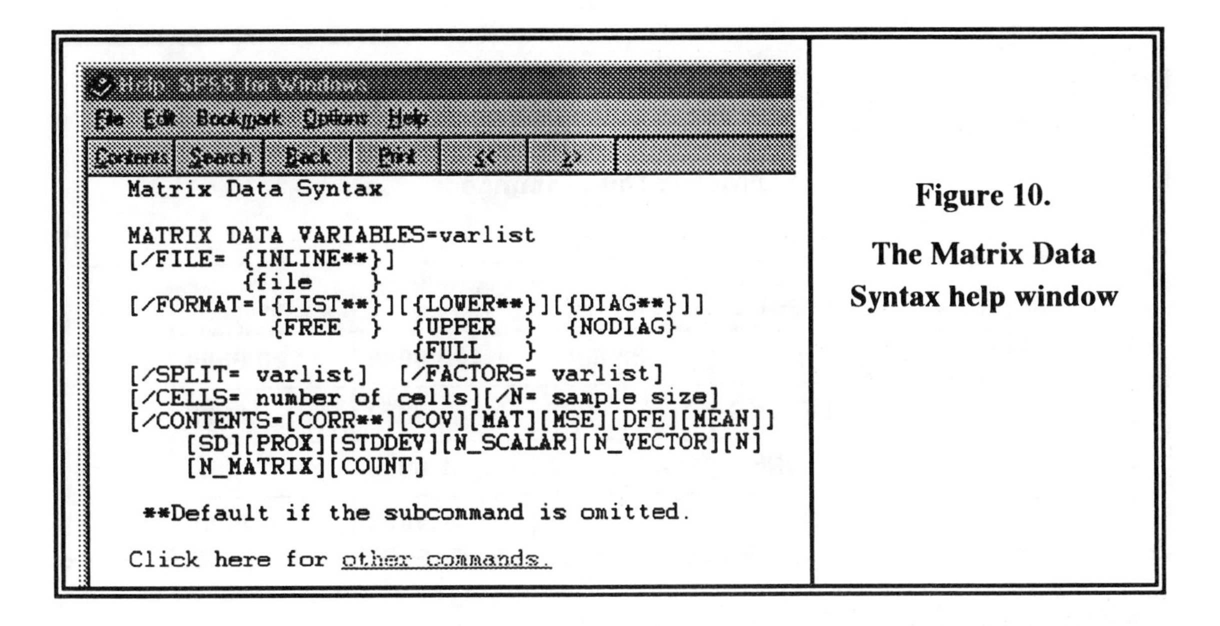

```
Matrix Data Syntax

MATRIX DATA VARIABLES=varlist
[/FILE= {INLINE**}]
        {file    }
[/FORMAT=[{LIST**}][{LOWER**}][{DIAG**}]]
          {FREE  }  {UPPER  }  {NODIAG}
                    {FULL   }
[/SPLIT= varlist]  [/FACTORS= varlist]
[/CELLS= number of cells][/N= sample size]
[/CONTENTS=[CORR**][COV][MAT][MSE][DFE][MEAN]]
    [SD][PROX][STDDEV][N_SCALAR][N_VECTOR][N]
    [N_MATRIX][COUNT]

 **Default if the subcommand is omitted.

Click here for other commands.
```

Figure 10.

The Matrix Data Syntax help window

Figure 11.

The matrix data command and data in the syntax window

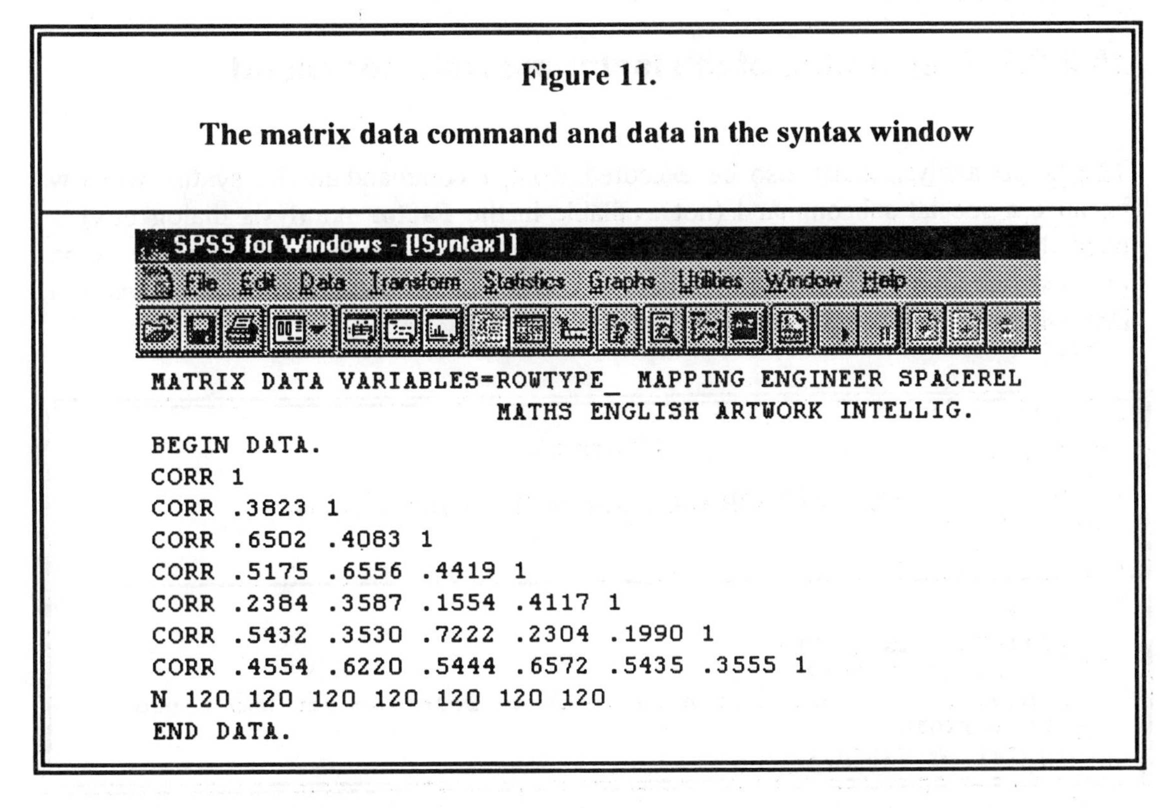

```
MATRIX DATA VARIABLES=ROWTYPE_ MAPPING ENGINEER SPACEREL
                      MATHS ENGLISH ARTWORK INTELLIG.
BEGIN DATA.
CORR 1
CORR .3823 1
CORR .6502 .4083 1
CORR .5175 .6556 .4419 1
CORR .2384 .3587 .1554 .4117 1
CORR .5432 .3530 .7222 .2304 .1990 1
CORR .4554 .6220 .5444 .6572 .5435 .3555 1
N 120 120 120 120 120 120 120
END DATA.
```

Run the **Matrix Data** commands by dragging the cursor over all the syntax in Figure 11, and then clicking on icon in the toolbar at the top of the syntax window (or on the box labelled **Run** in older versions of SPSS 6).

If all is well, no error messages should appear in the **Output** window. The matrix of correlations and the vector of counts can be inspected in the **Data Editor** window by clicking on the **Window** menu and selecting **Newdata**. Part of the **Data Editor** window is shown in Figure 12.

Figure 12.

Part of the data set in the Data Editor window after running the Matrix Data commands

	rowtype_	varname_	mapping	engineer	spacerel
1	N		120.0000	120.0000	120.0000
2	CORR	MAPPING	1.0000	.3823	.6502
3	CORR	ENGINEE	.3823	1.0000	.4083
4	CORR	SPACERE	.6502	.4083	1.0000

15.2.3.2 Preparation of the factor analysis command

The factor analysis must also be executed from a command in the syntax window because a special subcommand (not available in the **Factor Analysis** dialog box) is needed to read a correlation matrix. Return to the syntax window and type **Factor** on the next line after *END DATA*. As before, the complete syntax can be inspected in a help window. The completed command is shown in Figure 13.

Figure 13.

The FACTOR command in the syntax window

```
FACTOR
/MATRIX = IN (CORR=*)
/FORMAT SORT BLANK (0.5)
/PRINT initial extraction rotation correlation det kmo repro
/PLOT EIGEN
/ROTATION VARIMAX.
```

Notice the identification of the source of the matrix in the */MATRIX =IN* subcommand is given as (*CORR*=*). This shows that it is a correlation matrix (and not, say, a factor matrix), and that it is in the current data file (represented by *) as shown in the **Data Editor** window. The */FORMAT* option is the same as that selected in the **Options** dialog box, the */PRINT* options are those selected in the **Descriptives** dialog box, the */PLOT* option is that selected in the **Extraction** dialog box, and the */ROTATION* option is also that in the **Rotation** dialog box. Run the **Factor** command by highlighting the whole command with the cursor and then clicking on the icon in the toolbar at the top of the syntax window (or on the box labelled **Run** in older versions of SPSS 6). The output listing for the factor analysis will be identical to that previously described.

SUMMARY

1) **Factor analysis** is a set of techniques designed to account for the correlations among a set of variables in terms of relatively few underlying dimensions, or **factors**.

2) Several different kinds of factor analysis have been devised. The most common is the **principal factors** method (which SPSS terms **principal components** (PC)).

3) The relationships between the variables and **some** of the factors are maximised by a process called **rotation**. The most common method of rotation is **varimax.**

4) To run a factor analysis from raw data, choose

   Statistics

   Data Reduction

   and click on **Factor**. Select the variables to be used in the analysis by dragging the cursor down the list of variable names in the **Factor Analysis** dialog box and clicking on ▶ to transfer them to the **Variables** box.

5) Options available in the **Descriptives**, **Extraction**, **Rotation**, and **Options** dialog boxes include the plotting of the **scree slope** showing the variance accounted for by each factor, suppressing factor loadings with a value of less than a defined number (**0.5** is recommended), selecting the method of factor rotation (**varimax** is recommended), and printing various matrices and statistics (the **correlation matrix** and its **determinant**, **KMO** and **Bartlett's test of sphericity**, and the **reproduced correlation matrix** are recommended).

6) If the data are in the form of a correlation matrix rather than raw scores, the command syntax must be used instead of the dialog boxes.

EXERCISES

These Exercises have been prepared for SPSS 6.

They may need slight adaptation for use with SPSS 7

EXERCISE 1

SOME BASIC WINDOWS OPERATIONS

BEFORE YOU START

Before you begin the first exercise, there are one or two preliminaries which require your attention.

Know the material of Chapter 1

An essential prerequisite is a knowledge of the material in Chapter 1. If you are already an experienced computer user, however, you might well omit the elementary outline of computer basics that Chapter 1 contains.

Read Chapter 2

Even if you already have some experience of computing, we strongly recommend that you study Chapter 2 closely before proceeding with this practical.

Arrange access to a network

We assume that most of our readers will be users of a network, rather than owners (or exclusive users) of a PC. Assuming you have access to a network, there may be an identification, or logging in, procedure. If so, make sure you have organised your number and password.

Floppy disk

If you require to use a floppy disk for storing files, or as back-up for files saved on a hard disk, ensure that you have one available.

IF YOU HAVE NOT USED A COMPUTER BEFORE

If you are already an experienced user of a PC, you can ignore this section and pass on to the next.

Boot up the machine if necessary (Section 1.3.1)

The details of using a computer in a network vary enormously. If your machine is not already up and running, first establish whether a special booting-up disk is to be inserted in the disk drive. Now turn on the power, remembering that there may also be a crucial switch at the end of the bench.

Logging in (Section 1.3.2)

Log in to the computer in the required manner.

Learn to find your way around the keyboard (Section 1.2)

If you are a newcomer to computing (and a non-typist), a major obstacle to progress can be unfamiliarity with the PC keyboard. To overcome this difficulty, turn to Section 1.2 and systematically work through the keys described, identifying each on the real keyboard from the illustration or the description. It may be worth repeating this exercise when beginning the next two or three sessions.

GETTING INTO WINDOWS (Section 2.1)

As we explained in Section 1.3.1, you may or may not be transferred directly to **Windows** on booting up the machine: a menu may appear on the screen, or the **DOS** prompt, to which you must respond by typing **win** and pressing ↵. Read about the Windows operating system in Section 2.1.

The Program Manager window: look at the pointer (Section 2.2)

As the first window, the **Program Manager**, appears, watch out for the hour-glass and wait for it to disappear before experimenting with the mouse pointer.

The parts of a window

You have already read the descriptions of the various parts of a window. Now look for the various features in the display before you. Do not be surprised if, at first, things look very different from the illustration in Chapter 2, Figure 1. Much depends on which applications are loaded into your computer. Moreover, **Windows** offers the user a very flexible environment, and windows may be sized, shaped and positioned in an infinite variety of ways.

Title bar

The **title bar** is always the top structure in a window.

Menu bar

Notice the white **menu bar**, just underneath the **title bar**. With the mouse, click on the **File** caption and obtain the **File** drop-down menu. Having noted the choices it offers, remove it by clicking with the mouse on any point outside the menu boundaries.

Control-Menu box

At the left-hand end of the title bar is the **Control-Menu** box, consisting of a small square containing a horizontal bar. This is used to close a window.

Maximise and Minimise buttons

Identify the **Maximise** and **Minimise** buttons (see Figure 1 and read the description in Section 2.2.2).

Reducing a window to an icon

Click on the **Minimise** button. The effect is dramatic: the **Program Manager** is now a tiny icon in the bottom left corner of the screen, which now appears as a huge area known as the **desktop**. Restore the **Program Manager** window by double-clicking on the icon. At the level of the title bar, in a square to the right of the one containing the **Minimise** button, are two arrows: the upper arrow, the **Maximise** button, has the effect of making the window occupy the entire screen; the lower button restores the window to its original size.

Click-and-drag operations

Notice what happens when the screen pointer touches a border or corner of a window: the pointer changes from a diagonally upward-pointing single arrow to a double-headed arrow. Only when the double-headed arrow appears, can the window by re-sized by clicking-and-dragging on the border (or corner) with the mouse.

Open and close the Clipboard Viewer window

Notice that, in addition to the **File Manager**, there are other windows, one of which has the caption **Accessories** in its title bar. In the **Accessories** window is the icon of the **Clipboard Viewer**. Double-click on this to open the **Clipboard** window. Explore this window, comparing it with that of the **Program Manager**. Close it by clicking on the **Control-Menu** box.

THE FILE MANAGER WINDOW (Section 2.3)

Within the **Program Manager** window is the window of the **Main** group of applications. The **File Manager** icon is a drawing of a filing cabinet. Double-click on this to bring to the screen the **File Manager** window. You will see the directories (arranged in a **directory tree**) on the left. One of these, probably **spsswin**, will be highlighted.

The path name of the SPSSWIN directory

Notice the path name in the title bar: C:\SPSSWIN*.*. These terms are explained in Section 2.3.1. On the right of the directory tree are icons of all the files that this directory contains. See what happens to the path name when you click on another directory. Notice also that all the file icons change, since the new directory contains different files.

Format your disk (Section 2.4)

If you need to format a floppy disk (nowadays disks are usually supplied already formatted), read Section 2.4 carefully and follow the instructions for formatting your floppy disk, noting carefully the features of the **Format Disk** dialog box (Figure 8) and of the confirmation dialogs that appear at various stages in the proceedings.

Copying a file

Following the instructions in Section 2.4.3, copy the file *bank.sav* to your hard disk data storage location or to your floppy disk, taking care to enter the correct path in the **To** box within the **Copy** dialog box. Return to the **File Manager** window, and by clicking on the appropriate drive and filename, confirm that a copy of *bank.sav* really has been saved there.

Deleting a file

Following the instructions in Section 2.4.4, delete the file *bank.sav* from wherever you saved it. Return to the **File Manager** window, and by clicking on the appropriate drive, confirm that the file is no longer there.

FINISHING THE SESSION

Close the **File Manager** window by clicking on the **Control-Menu** box and (if this is appropriate on your network) leave Windows by clicking on the **Control-Menu** box of the **Program Manager**.

EXERCISE 2

QUESTIONNAIRE DATA

BEFORE YOU START

We urge you to read Chapter 3 carefully before starting this exercise.

THE PROJECT

Please complete the questionnaire below by entering the values or circling the appropriate option. Afterwards, you will enter your data in SPSS's **Data Editor** window and eventually you will access data collected from many other people to form a large data set.

QUESTIONNAIRE

Question	Option	Response
What is your age in years?		
What is your sex?		M F
What is your Faculty of study?	Arts	1
	Science	2
	Medicine	3
	Other	4
What is your status?	Undergraduate	1
	MSc postgraduate	2
	PhD postgraduate	3
	Other	4
What is your approximate weight?	Use British or metric measures	
	Stones	
	Pounds	
	Kilograms	
What is your approximate height?	Use British or metric measures	
	Feet	
	Inches	
	Metres (include two decimal places)	
Do you smoke?		Y N
	If so, how many a day?	

Entering the data

You will need to refer in detail to Sections 3.4 and 3.5.

The first task is to name the variables (i.e. the columns) with suitable and legal variable names (see Section 3.4.3.2 for the rules about variable names). Use numeric format (the default type) for all the variables except *sex* and *smoker* for which a string (i.e. alphanumeric - meaning letters and numbers) format is more appropriate. Remember to assign values and value labels when dealing with the numeric categorial variables *faculty* and *status*. Incidentally, the assignation of value labels is not mandatory but it makes the interpretation of output tables, charts and graphs much easier, because items will be identified with the labels you have assigned. Labelling is also advantageous when you have a large data file, with many values assigned to a single variable. Use string format for the two variables *sex* and *smoker*: to do this, you must click on **Type** within the **Define Variable** dialog box and change the radio button to **String**.

When you reach the height and weight data, you must set up three variables for each (*feet, inches* and *metres* for the height data, *stones, pounds* and *kilos* for the weight data) because some people will fill in their heights and weights in metric measures and some in the old British measures. This will then allow you to enter the data in whatever form it is entered on the questionnaire. Remember even if you enter your data in metric form, other people may not.

After naming all the variables and assigning values and value labels when appropriate, enter your data (Section 3.4.4) along the first row. Note that if you select **Value Labels** from the **Utilities** drop-down menu in the Toolbar at the top of the screen, you can alternate between the actual values you have entered into the Data Editor window and the value labels you have assigned to them. Since your data will be merged with other people's data in the next exercise, please use M and F for male and female respectively, and Y and N for smoker and non-smoker respectively.

Saving the data

Once you have entered the data set and checked it for accuracy (edit it if necessary - see Section 3.5), save the data by means of the **Save As** command within the **File** drop-down menu (Section 3.9.1) to your personal file space on a hard disk or on a floppy disk by selecting the appropriate disk drive and naming the file with a name that is meaningful to you within the constraints of file names - see Section 1.1.5. A possible name would be *myquest.sav* to remind you that it stores your own data from the questionnaire. Notice that data files in SPSS are saved with the file extension *.sav* and the computer will prompt you for a name with **.sav*, in which you should replace the * with the name you have chosen for the file.

FINISHING THE SESSION

Close down SPSS and any other open windows before logging out of the computer.

EXERCISE 3

QUESTIONNAIRE DATA (continued)

BEFORE YOU START

This exercise shows you how to open a saved file, how to merge your data with those of others, how to obtain information about the structure of a data file, and how to print out a file. The relevant sections are 3.9.2 (opening a file), 3.10.2 (displaying data file information) and 3.11 (printing in SPSS).

OPENING YOUR SAVED FILE

First of all open the file that you saved from the previous exercise, remembering in which hard disk drive it was located or whether it was on a floppy disk (usually drive a).

Do this by selecting (Section 3.9.2)

File

Open

Data

and then select the appropriate drive, highlight the name of the file and click on **OK.**

Examine the Data Editor window and check that all is well.

MERGING YOUR DATA

There are various ways of combining data from different cases into the same file. One way is to use SPSS's **Merge Files** procedure, which enables cases from two files with the same variables (though not necessarily in the same order) to be combined. Since you may not have named your variables exactly as those in the file containing other people's data, it may be necessary for you to change the name of one or more of your variables. This is easily done by double-clicking on the variable name at the top of the column in the Data Editor window and amending the name in the **Define Variable** dialog box. The names required are as follows (ignore any upper-case or lower-case letter differences):

age; sex; faculty; status; stones; pounds; kilos; feet; inches; metres; smoker; npday.

To merge the data, ensure that your own data is in the Data Editor window. Then choose

Data

Merge Files

Add Cases

and select the file containing the other people's data from wherever it is located. Your instructor may have downloaded it from WWW (http://www.psyc.abdn.ac.uk/teaching/spss/spssbook.htm) and placed it in a more accessible locus. Click **OK** to effect the merge. In the event of a mismatch in variable names, a message indicating this will appear in the **Add cases from ...** dialog box.

Check that your own data are in the first row and those on over 300 other people are in the succeeding rows. Save this merged file as your original file by clicking on **Save Data** within the **File** drop-down menu.

DISPLAYING DATA FILE INFORMATION

Clearing the Data Editor window

It is often useful to be able to see a list of variable names, formats, values and value labels for a particular file. Unfortunately SPSS does not allow you to do this for a file currently displayed in the Data Editor window. You must therefore clear the window by selecting **New** from the **File** drop-down menu.

Displaying data information

Choose

File

Display Data Info

and then select the file for which you wish to see the data details - in this case the data file you have just saved. Then select **OK**.

Inspect the output listing on the screen (see also Section 3.10.2) and notice how each variable is named along with any expanded variable names, the format, values and value labels.

Editing the output listing for printing

SPSS adds extra information and page throws to the output listing which the user may not always want, especially if there is a charge for each printed page!

- **Deleting material: You may wish to delete some of the preliminary material about the file (but leave the file name) and also each page throw. A new page is created on the printer when there is a small solid black rectangle located at the left-hand edge of the text followed by a line of text including the date and a page number. To delete material, use the cursor and the left-hand mouse button to highlight the sections of the text to be deleted and then press the Delete key. After removing a page throw, you can remove some of the extra blank lines by placing the cursor at the left-hand end of a blank line and pressing Delete.**
- **Adding material: You can insert any extra material such as the date and details of the file simply by moving the cursor to the desired point of insertion and then typing in the material.**

Saving the output listing

Save the edited output file as a listing file with a file extension *.lst* which is an abbreviated form of the word *list* (e.g. use the file name *datainfo.lst*) Note that the first symbol of the file extension is the letter l not the digit 1.

Choose

File

Save SPSS Output

and then select the appropriate disk drive to save the listing file to your personal file space on a hard disk or on a floppy disk. Type in the file name and click on **OK**. (Note that all SPSS output files should be saved with the file extension *.lst*. You will see that SPSS provides you with the option **.lst*; you need to type in a name to replace the wild-card character *.)

Printing the output listing file

Finally, to print a copy of this listing file, select

File

Print

You may need to change the printer set-up by clicking on **Setup...** and changing the printing arrangements according to local circumstances.

FINISHING THE SESSION

Close down SPSS and any other windows before logging out of the computer.

EXERCISE 4

EXPLORATORY DATA ANALYSIS (EDA)

BEFORE YOU START

This exercise explores the data in your saved file of merged data.

EDA

Restoring the data file in the Data Editor window

Open the data file saved from the previous exercise in the usual manner.

Describing categorial data: frequency distribution

First we shall look at some frequency distributions.

Use the **Frequencies** procedure described in **4.3.1.1** to obtain a frequency listing for the variable *smoker* in the Output window, remembering to click on the **Charts...** box in order to be able to select **Bar Chart(s)** within the **Frequencies: Charts** dialog box. If you cannot see the complete listing on the screen, change the font size by selecting

Utilities

Fonts

and then changing the font size to 10.

Inspect the frequency table. Is it what you expected? Before taking any steps to remedy the situation, inspect the bar chart in the **Chart Carousel.**

Describing categorial data: bar chart

Click on the icon to open the **Chart Carousel** window. There you will notice that you seem to have a category T as well as a category labelled with a dot. Why do you think these may have occurred?

Compare the bar chart and the frequency table. Obviously two things have happened:

1. A letter T has been entered by mistake somewhere (perhaps it should have been a Y, since T is next to Y on the keyboard?).
2. There is a missing entry (shown as a dot in the data table) - perhaps because a subject did not enter a response on the form.

Go back to your data file and see if you can find these anomalous entries (both are located in the first 20 cases). Errors in data entry may easily occur when entering large amounts of data, and will show up as soon as you start to analyse your data.

To remedy the situation:

1. Change the T to a Y. (**Note:** In normal circumstances you would always check your original data before making any corrections to the database but in this case it must be Y since this person smokes 5 cigarettes a day.)
2. It is more satisfactory to enter a specially defined code or value for a missing datum rather than leave the cell blank. In this way you can be sure that you have not just overlooked the cell when entering the data. When a code for a missing value is declared, SPSS ignores it when drawing a bar chart. The following procedure will define a missing value (Section 3.8).

Editing a data set; defining missing data

Double-click on the variable name *smoker* in the Data Editor window to open the **Define Variable** dialog box and click on **Missing Values** to open the **Define Missing Values: smoker** dialog box. Click on the **Discrete missing values** radio button, type in 999, and then click on **Continue** to return to the **Define Variable** dialog box. Click on **Labels** to open the **Define Labels** dialog box, enter the value 999 and a value label such as *Missing*, click on **Add** and then on **Continue**. Finally click on **OK**.

It remains to find the cell with a dot and replace the dot with 999. Highlight the cell, type 999 and then move the highlighting to an adjacent cell with one of the cursor keys in order to enter the value in the cell. If the **Values Labels** option is on, the 999 will appear as *Missing* provided the cell is wide enough to show the full label (you can widen the cells of a variable by moving the cursor up to the right-hand edge of the variable name box where it will turn into a left-and-right arrow: press the left-hand mouse button and slide the boundary to the right to widen the column to include the full *Not known* label).

Save the corrected data file, using the **Save Data** item within the **File** drop-down menu.

Now re-run the **Frequencies** command, but cancel the **Bar Chart** option: notice the difference in the listing table. The message is that EDA is useful for detecting any false data before more extensive statistical analyses are conducted.

Bar chart from the Graphs drop-down menu

If it is desired to plot a bar chart without a frequency table, then it can be requested directly by means of the **Bar** item within the **Graphs** drop-down menu. This facility also allows more complex bar charts to be drawn as illustrated in Section 4.3.3.4.

We shall use this procedure to obtain the corrected bar chart for *smoker*.

Choose

Graphs

Bar

By default the **Simple** and **Summaries for Groups of Cases** are already selected within the **Bar Charts** dialog box.

Click **Define** to open the **Define Simple Bar: Summaries for Groups of Cases** dialog box. Check that in the **Bars Represent** box the **N of cases** option is selected, and then enter the variable name *smoker* into the **Category Axis** box. If you want to add a title, select the **Titles** box and type in a suitable title. If you want to exclude the missing cases, click **Options** and deselect **Display groups defined by missing values.**

Click **OK** to execute the bar chart and then save it using the **Save chart** or **Save as** item within the **File** drop-down menu. Notice that this time you will be cued to name a file with a *.cht* extension.

- **Print the bar chart for *smoker.***

Describing categorial data: crosstabulation

Next we are going to produce some contingency tables, using the **Crosstabs** procedure (Section 4.3.1.2). Crosstabulation means tabulating the number of cases within each combination of values of two variables; here we shall crosstabulate *sex* and *faculty* of the cases.

Choose

Statistics

  Summarize

    Crosstabs

to open the **Crosstabs** dialog box.

Enter one of the variables into the **Row(s)** box by clicking on its name and then on ▶. Enter the other variable into the **Column(s)** box. Click on **OK**.

To save the crosstabulation output, highlight the relevant parts and then save to a suitable file using the **Save** command and answering **Yes** to the **Save selected area only?** question.

- **Print the highlighted portion of the output window (i.e. the crosstabulation) by specifying Selection within the Print command.**

FINISHING THE SESSION

Close down SPSS and any other windows before logging out of the computer.

EXERCISE 5

EDA (continued)

BEFORE YOU START

This exercise continues exploratory data analysis and also involves the transformation of variables. Open, in the usual way, the data file which you saved in Exercise 3.

EDA

Describing interval data

Use the **Frequencies** procedure outlined in Section 4.3.2.1 to obtain a histogram with a superimposed normal curve and a table showing the mean, standard deviation and quartiles for *age*. Select the same options as in the **Frequencies: Statistics** dialog box in Section 4.3.2.1. Remember to ensure that the **Display frequency tables** box is turned off. Save both the histogram and the output listing.

- **Print the histogram.**

Manipulation of the data set - transforming variables

It is sometimes useful to be able to change the data set in some way. For instance, in the current data set, some people have entered their weight in stones and pounds, and others in kilograms in the current data set. Likewise height has been entered both in feet and inches, and in metres. In order to be able to produce useful data on weight and height, we must use the same units of measurement.

In this exercise we shall adopt metric units (kilograms and metres). Thus we must convert any other measurements into metric measurements.

Do this by using the **Compute** procedure (Section 4.4.2) Once you have clicked on the **Compute** box, type the name of the variable which contains the kilograms' data (*kilos*) into the **Target Variable** box. In the **Numeric Expression** box, enter the conversion factor. Thus you will enter **(stones*14 + pounds) * 0.453** to convert pounds to kilograms using the conversion factor that 1 pound is 0.453 kilograms and remembering to convert stones to pounds by multiplying by 14. Note that formulae in computing must include the symbol * for multiplication. There remains one further problem: what about cases whose weight is already in *kilos* and do not have any values in the *stones* and *pounds* variables? If the formula above were to be immediately applied, these people would finish with no values in the *kilos* column. Thus to convert only the cases with stones and pounds measurements, you must select the **If** box in the **Compute Variable** dialog box, then the **Include if case satisfies condition** box and enter the following expression **(stones > 0)** which tells the program to calculate the kilograms if the entry in *stones* is greater than 0 (we assume that no-one has a weight of less than 1 stone!). Select **Continue** and then **OK**. You will see a message which asks **Change existing variable?**, select the **Yes** option. Now the program will calculate all the missing *kilos* data and enter them in the data set. Check that it has done this.

(It is often regarded as a safer procedure to recode data into a new variable since it allows one to check that the correct recoding procedure has been requested. Note that we have not done this is in the case above because we wanted to preserve the values already present for some cases in *kilos*.)

Save the file, but use the **Save As** option for this, giving the amended file a new name (e.g. *quest2.sav*). This ensures that you still have a copy of the old file, in case you have made any mistakes in calculation and you wish to retrieve the old data at some future time.

Now do a similar conversion for the height data, converting feet and inches to metres. To do this you will need to know that 1 inch is 0.0254 metres. Work out a conversion factor with this in mind. When you have converted the height data, save the file again.

Describing interval data - means of cases categorised by a grouping variable

We can obtain a table of means for one variable relating to cases grouped by categories of another variable or by a combination of other variables.

Use the **Means** procedure described in Section 4.3.2.3 to obtain a two-way table of means for *metres* by *sex*. Then use the same procedure to obtain a three-way table of *kilos* by *sex* by *faculty*. (Look carefully at Section 4.3.2.3 to see how to layer the variables, using the **Next** facility, to produce the three-way table).

- **Print the listing output of this exercise.**

FINISHING THE SESSION

Close down SPSS and any other windows before logging out of the computer.

EXERCISE 6

MORE CHARTS AND GRAPHS

BEFORE YOU START

This exercise shows you how to request various charts and graphs. Restore the data file saved in the previous exercise to the Data Editor window.

CHARTS AND GRAPHS

Stem-and-leaf plot and boxplot

It is often useful to present data in graphical form, which is easily read and conveys the information quickly and effectively. Use the **Explore** procedure (Section 4.3.2.4) to produce stem-and-leaf plots and boxplots of *metres* categorised by *sex.*

The **stem-and-leaf plot** provides more information about the original data than does a histogram. As in a histogram, the length of each row corresponds to the number of cases that fall into a particular interval. However, the stem-and-leaf plot represents each case with a numeric value that corresponds to the actual observed value. This is done by dividing observed values into two components - the leading digit or digits, called the **stem**, and a trailing digit, called the **leaf**. For example, the value 64 would have a stem of 6 and a leaf of 4. In the case of heights in metres, the stems are the metres expressed to the first decimal place, the leaves are the second decimal place. Thus the modal height (i.e. the most frequent height) for males is shown with a stem of 17 (1.7 metres), the leaves being the second decimal place. The * and . after the stem are used in some stem-and-leaf plots to split the leaves into two sections: the * row includes the leaves 0 to 4, the . row includes the leaves 5 to 9. In other plots, the leaves are broken down into * (noughts and ones), t (twos and threes), f (fours and fives), s (sixes and sevens), and . (eights and nines).

The **boxplot** is also a complex diagram which is more fully explained in Section 4.3.2.4. The main box spans 50% of the cases and the extensions (whiskers) cover the remaining cases, provided they are not deemed to be outliers (shown as o's) or extremes (shown as asterisks).

- **Print the listing (including the stem-and-leaf plot) and the boxplots. Within the female group, which stem contains the most leaves (cases)?**

Look at the boxplot for males and note the case numbers of the outliers so that you can check their actual heights in the data set.

There is a procedure for locating a specific case in the data set, namely

Data

Go to case

You then enter the required case number, select **Search forward** (or Search backward), and then **OK**.

- **Write down the actual heights of the males denoted by the outliers on the box plots.**

Bar charts

Draw a bar chart of *kilos* and *metres* by *sex* using the **Bar** option within the **Graphs** drop-down menu. Choose

Graphs

Bar

Clustered

and select the radio button for **Summaries of Separate Variables** in the **Data in Chart Are** box.

Click on **Define** and then enter *kilos* and *metres* into the **Bars Represent** box and *sex* into the **Category Axis** box.

- **Study the chart produced. Does this seem a sensible graphic representation of the two variables? If not, why not? You do not need to print the chart, but make a note of why the representation is not appropriate and what would be a better way of displaying the mean heights and weights of subjects split by sex.**

The moral behind this is that you must always consider what your output is likely to be. SPSS will produce the graph that you ask for, but the end result may not be a sensible representation of the data. It is best to draw by hand a rough representation of what you expect the graph to look like before requesting SPSS to do so.

Transposing data on a graph or chart

It is possible to transpose data on graphs and charts which have more than one variable or factor plotted so that the lines or bars are replotted in a transposed manner. This will become clearer with an example.

Plot a new bar chart of the mean number of cigarettes smoked (*npday*) categorised by *sex* and by *faculty*. Do this by choosing

Graphs

Bar

Clustered

and select the radio button for **Summaries for groups of cases** in the **Data in Chart Are** box.

Click on **Define** and then click on **Other summary function** within the **Bars Represent box**. Then enter *npday* into the **Variable** box (it will appear as **MEAN(npday)**), *sex* in the **Category Axis** box, and *faculty* in the **Define Clusters by** box. Deselect **Display groups defined by missing values** as before.

You should then see in the Chart Carousel window a bar chart arranged by sex, with each cluster consisting of bars representing the three Faculties (apparently no-one in the Other category smokes). Suppose, however, that you would rather see a chart with three clusters (Faculties) of two (sex) instead of two clusters (sex) of three (Faculties). This could be done by returning to the dialog box and changing *sex* and *faculty* around, but a quicker method is to use the **Transpose Data** option within the **Series** drop-down menu. This menu becomes accessible after clicking on **Edit**. Select (in the Chart Carousel window)

Edit

Series

Transpose Data

You will now see that the data have been transposed on the chart.

Pie chart

Another way of presenting data is in the form of a pie chart. Draw a pie chart (see Section 4.3.3.6) for *status* and give the chart a title, including your **own** name in the title (e.g. Pie Chart of Status produced by Joe Bloggs).

Edit the chart to show actual percentages for each slice.

You can do this by selecting in the **Chart Carousel** window

Edit

Chart

Options

Percents

OK

Save the chart in the usual manner.

- **Print the pie chart.**

FINISHING THE SESSION

Close down SPSS and any other windows before logging out of the computer.

EXERCISE 7

RECODING DATA; SELECTING CASES; LINE GRAPH

BEFORE YOU START

This exercise shows you how to recode data, select cases, and draw a line graph. Restore the data file saved in the Exercise 5 to the Data Editor window.

RECODING DATA

Sometimes you may wish to recode values or categories within a variable (e.g. combine more than one value or category into a single value or category). Suppose that you are not particularly interested in whether people are doing a MSc degree or a PhD degree, but just want to know whether they are postgrads. You can change the database to give you this information, either within the original variable, *status*, or by creating a new variable containing the recoded information. In this session we are going to do it using a new variable, since this retains the original variable *status* for checking that the recoding has been done correctly. It also maintains the original values in the variable.

Use the **Recode** (Section 4.4.3) procedure to recode the status codes MSc Postgrad and PhD Postgrad (i.e. categories 2 and 3) into a new category 1 and the codes Undergraduate and Other (i.e. categories 1 and 4) into a new category 2. You will need to follow the section carefully. The recode procedure creates a new variable which you are asked to name: we suggest *postgrad.* To do this, you will have to choose the **Recode into Different Variables** option within the **Recode** procedure.

Choose

Transform

    Recode

        Into Different Variables

to open the **Recode into Different Variables** dialog box. Highlight *status* and click on ► to transfer it into the **Input Variable → Output Variable** box. Type *postgrad* in the **Name** box within the **Output Variable** box and click on **Change**. The new variable name *postgrad* will now appear alongside *status*. Click on **Old and New Values** and then fill in the old and new values in pairs (i.e. 1 & 2, 2 & 1, 3 & 1, 4 & 2), clicking on **Add** each time. Finally click on **Continue** and **OK**.

When you have performed this procedure, check that you have the new variable at the far right of your data set. Double-click on the variable name *postgrad* and then click on **Labels** within the **Change Settings** box to label the new categories 1 as Yes and 2 as No. Click on **Continue** and then **OK**. To see whether this has worked, click on the **Value Labels** item within the **Utilities** drop-down menu. This will allow you to relate the new values or categories in the new variable *postgrad* to any other variable. Save the file again.

Next we will use the **Recode** procedure to recode the heights of people as tall, medium or short. Give the new variable the name ***new_ht*** containing the underline, not the hyphen, symbol. This is allowed in a variable name but the hyphen or a space is not.

Use the following table for recoding the heights into values (we shall attach the labels later):

Range	Value	Label
Under 1.7 metres	1	Short
Between 1.7 and 1.8 metres	2	Medium
Over 1.8 metres	3	Tall

You will need to use the **Range Lowest through** facility for short people, the **Range** facility for medium people, and the **Range through highest** facility for tall people, taking particular care to ensure that there is no ambiguity about the group into which a height will be assigned. SPSS recodes values from the smallest upwards. Thus 1.7 will be included in Short unless it is defined as **Lowest thru 1.6999**. Re-read the end of Section 4.4.3 for extra help.

Check your data to make certain that all the data have been classified in the manner that you planned. Note that although you may see only two decimal places in the Data Editor, a value such as 1.70 may in fact be 1.7068. If the value is highlighted, the full value will appear in the Cell Editor box above the variable names.

Once the new variable *new_ht* has been created, double-click on the variable name, click on **Labels** and enter the value labels *short*, *medium* and *tall* for values 1, 2 and 3 respectively. Click on **Continue** and then **OK**. These labels should then appear in the Data Editor window.

Pie chart

Produce a pie chart with a title showing what percentages of the cases are tall, medium or short. Edit the pie chart to show the percentage for each slice using the **Pie Options** dialog box (see Exercise 6 if you need to check how to do this).

- **Print the pie chart.**

SELECT CASES

Another useful facility is being able to select the cases you want to analyse. Suppose you wished to consider only the data relating to females.

Use **Select Cases** (Section 3.12.1) so that only the female cases will be analysed. Remember that since *sex* is a string variable, you will need to enter F in quotes (i.e. sex='F') when filling in the **Select Cases** dialog box.

Supposing now that, since smoking is said to suppress appetite, you wanted to see whether female smokers were lighter in weight than non-smokers. Use the **Compare Means** (Section 4.3.2.3) procedure to do this. Remember the Dependent variable will be *kilos* and the Independent variable *smoker*.

- **Print the table produced. Note that, as a result of the Select Cases procedure you have just performed, this will be for the female population only.**
- **Are there any differences between the smokers and the non-smokers? Comment briefly on any differences you find. (When you think about this, note the difference in size between the smoking and no smoking groups)**

LINE GRAPH

A line graph is suitable when there is a continuous or ordinal scale for one of the variables with not more than about ten values. When the scale is nominal, a bar chart is preferable. Now that we have an ordinal scale of height with three values in the variable *new_ht*, we can draw a line graph of *sex* against *new_ht*.

Firstly, however, the selection of females in the previous section must be reversed by returning to the Select Cases dialog box and clicking on the **All cases** radio button. Then choose

Graphs

Line

Multiple

Summaries for groups of cases

to open the **Define Multiple Line: Summaries for Groups of Cases** dialog box. Then insert the variable *new_ht* into the **Category Axis** box and *sex* into the **Define Lines by** box. Click on **Options** and deselect **Display groups defined by missing values**. Click on **Continue** and then **OK** to plot the lines. A two-line graph should then appear, one line for M and one line for F, with the points on the abscissa labelled Short, Medium and Tall.

Change one of the lines to a discontinuous line using the editing facility (see Section 4.3.3.3) in order to differentiate the sexes when the graph is printed. Click on the **Edit** box, and then click on the selected line to highlight it. Then click on the editing box marked with a dashed line and select a dashed line. Finally click on **Apply** and **Close**.

Save the chart in the usual way.

- **Print out the line graph.**

FINISHING THE SESSION

Close down SPSS and any other windows before logging out of the computer.

EXERCISE 8

DESCRIBING AND SAVING DATA

BEFORE YOU START

The previous exercises have used data from a questionnaire. The next few exercises will be based on data from experiments designed to test experimental hypotheses. In real experiments, of course, a larger number of subjects would have been used.

GETTING INTO SPSS

Using the procedures described in Section 3.4.1, bring to the screen the SPSS **Data Editor** window.

THE PROJECT

An investigation of the effects of a drug upon performance

The data we are going to explore in this exercise might have been produced by the following project. A team of investigators has good reason to believe that a small dosage of a certain drug increases the speed with which people can make decisions. They decide to try to confirm this by carrying out an experiment in which the decision times of 14 people who have ingested the drug are compared with those of a control group of 14 other people who have performed the task under a placebo condition. The experimenters expect that the decision times of the experimental group will tend to be shorter than those of the placebo group. The results are shown in Table 1.

Table 1.

Decision times of the experimental and placebo groups in the drug experiment

DRUG GROUP				PLACEBO GROUP			
Subject	**Time**	**Subject**	**Time**	**Subject**	**Time**	**Subject**	**Time**
1	471	8	425	15	446	22	440
2	494	9	421	16	749	23	471
3	386	10	407	17	599	24	501
4	323	11	386	18	460	25	492
5	660	12	550	19	390	26	392
6	406	13	470	20	477	27	578
7	345	14	393	21	556	28	398

Constructing the SPSS data set

Construct the data set along the lines described in Section 3.3. The first column in the **Data Editor** window will represent the grouping variable (i.e. the type of treatment - drug or placebo) and we shall name it *group*. The second column will represent all the subjects' scores on the dependent variable and will be named *score*. Notice that this column will include the scores for **both** treatments; the first column, which represents the type of treatment, will be used by the computer to distinguish whether a score in the second column belongs to the drug group or to the placebo group.

Define the variables *group* and *score*, and enter the data of Table 1 into the **Data Editor** window in the manner described in Section 3.4. Use the labelling procedure to assign the value labels *drug* and *placebo* to the code numbers *1*, and *2*, respectively. Note that there is no need to enter the subject numbers, since each row of the Data Editor window is numbered automatically. When the data have been entered, save them to a file with a name such as **explore.sav**, from which they can be recalled at a later session.

Exploring the data

The first step is always to examine the data set to see whether it has any odd features.

Means and standard deviations

We shall want a table of means and standard deviations, together with indicators of distribution shape such as stem-and-leaf displays and boxplots. The statistics for the subgroups are most easily obtained with the **Means** procedure, and the plots from the **Explore** procedure. Follow the instructions in Section 4.3.2.3, remembering that the dependent variable name is *score* and the independent variable name is *group*.

- **Write down the values of the means and standard deviations.**

Note that the **Means** procedure requires the presence of a grouping variable in the data set. To obtain the mean and standard deviation of a set of ungrouped data, use the **Descriptives** procedure.

Graphical displays of the data

To draw the plots, proceed as described in Section 4.3.2.4. The output listing begins with the stem-and-leaf displays for the two groups. The boxplots are then drawn in the **Chart Carousel**. They can be brought to the screen either by clicking on the **Carousel** icon or by clicking on the **Window** drop-down menu and selecting **Chart**. When there is a marked discrepancy between the mean and median of a set of scores, it may be because the distribution is skewed or otherwise asymmetrical. Atypical scores, or **outliers** can also pull the value of the mean away from that of the median. Read Section 4.3.2.4 carefully for an explanation of SPSS's stem-and-leaf and boxplot displays.

- **Identify any outliers by means of their row numbers.**

Printing the listing

If you want to print out the listing, follow the procedure described in Section 3.11. The precise details will depend upon your local set-up.

EXERCISE 9

COMPARING THE AVERAGES OF TWO INDEPENDENT SAMPLES

BEFORE YOU START

Before proceeding with this exercise, we suggest you read Chapter 6 carefully. This exercise concerns the **independent samples t-test** described in Section 6.2.4; the next will be concerned with the **paired samples t-test**, which is described in Section 6.2.3.

The data from Exercise 8 will be used again for the present exercise. In that experiment, the subjects were randomly assigned to either the Drug or the Placebo condition. Their scores, therefore, are two independent samples of interval data. Provided the distributions of the scores are appropriate, the independent samples t-test can be used to test the null hypothesis of no difference (in the population) between the means of the Drug and Placebo groups.

The **t-test** is an example of a **parametric** test: that is, it makes certain assumptions about the populations from which the samples have supposedly been drawn. It is assumed, for example, that the populations are normal, and that they have the same variance. When a data set is examined (by the methods of Chapter 4), it is often quite clear that neither the assumption of normality of distribution nor that of homogeneity of variance is tenable. This can mean that the **tail probability**, or **p-value**, given in the t-test output is misleading. One solution to this problem is to use a **nonparametric** test, a method which makes fewer assumptions about the population distributions. Later in this exercise, we shall use a nonparametric text, the **Mann-Whitney** (sometimes called the Wilcoxon test), to compare the medians of the Drug and Placebo groups.

THE INDEPENDENT SAMPLES T-TEST

If you worked through Exercise 8 and stored the data to a file on floppy disk, they can easily be restored to SPSS by using the **Open** procedure. Otherwise, the data of Exercise 8 must be typed into the **Data Editor** window as described in Exercise 8 and then saved.

Exploring the data

Before any formal statistical tests are carried out, it is essential to explore the data distributions. **Outliers** can also be detected at this stage. In this case, however, the data have already been thoroughly explored. In the previous exercise, it was found that both samples had practically identical variances (i.e. their standard deviations had very similar values) and the various plots (boxplots and stem-and-leaf displays) indicated that the distributions were such as to permit the use of a parametric test. The only untoward finding was that one of the subjects in the Placebo group had a score of *749*, which is highly atypical of the group as a whole.

Procedure for an independent samples t-test

Full details of the procedure for the independent samples t test are given in Section 6.2.4. Run the procedure as described in that section.

Output listing for the independent samples t-test

Guidance on how to interpret the listing is given in Section 6.2.4. We suggest you study that section and try to answer the following questions.

- **On the basis of the Levene test p-value, which row of the t-test will you use?**
- **Write down the value of t and its tail probability. Is the p-value evidence against the null hypothesis? Remember that if the result is sufficiently unlikely (i.e. $p < 0.05$) under the null hypothesis, it is regarded as evidence against the null hypothesis and hence in favour of the experimental hypothesis.**
- **Write down your interpretation of the result of the test: has the t-test confirmed the pattern shown by the means of the two groups?**

A NONPARAMETRIC TEST: THE MANN-WHITNEY

When there are serious violations of the distribution assumptions of the t test, a nonparametric test should be considered. When there are two independent samples of scores, the **Mann-Whitney** test can be used to compare the averages of the two groups. It should be noted, however, that whereas in the parametric test the null hypothesis stated that the two population means are equal, the nonparametric test concerns **medians**, not means: in the **Mann-Whitney** test, the null hypothesis states that the population medians are equal.

Procedure for the Mann-Whitney test

The **Mann-Whitney** test procedure is fully described in Section 6.3.2. Run the procedure as described in that section.

Output listing for the Mann-Whitney test

The listing gives the values of the statistics U and W (the W statistic belongs to a test by Wilcoxon which is the exact equivalent of the Mann-Whitney), followed by an exact 2-tailed probability value, and then a standard normal deviate score Z and a 2-tailed probability value corrected for ties. If this p-value is less than 0.05, the null hypothesis can be rejected and the groups declared to differ significantly.

- **Write down the results of the Mann-Whitney test, including the value of U and its p-value. State whether the result is significant and whether the Mann-Whitney test confirms the result of the t-test. In what circumstances would you expect the p-values of U and t to differ?**

EXERCISE 10

COMPARING THE AVERAGES OF TWO SAMPLES: PAIRED DATA

BEFORE YOU START

The methods described in the previous exercise, (the **independent samples t-test** and the **Mann-Whitney** test), are appropriate for data from a between subjects experiment, that is, one with independent samples of subjects in the two groups. Suppose, however, that the data had come from an experiment in which the same subjects had been tested under both the experimental and control conditions. Such a within subjects experiment would yield a set of paired (or related) data. In this exercise, we shall consider some methods for comparing the averages of the scores obtained under the experimental and control conditions when we have a set of paired data (SPSS calls this **paired samples**), rather than independent samples. Before proceeding with this exercise, the reader should review the material in Sections 6.2.2 and 6.2.3.

THE PAIRED SAMPLES T-TEST

An experiment on hemispherical specialisation

In an experiment investigating the relative ease with which words presented in the left and right visual fields were recognised, subjects were instructed to fixate a spot in the centre of the field. They were told that, after a short interval, a word would appear to the left or the right of the spot and they were to press a key as soon as they recognised it. In the trials that followed, each word was presented an equal number of times in each field, though the order of presentation of the words was, of course, randomised. From the results, a table of median decision times was constructed from the subjects' reactions to presentations of 40 words in each of the two visual fields (Table 1).

Do these data support the experimental hypothesis that there is a difference between the response times for words in the left and right visual fields?

Rationale of the paired samples t-test

In the **paired samples t-test**, the strategy is to subtract (consistently) either the first or the second member of each pair of scores from the other, producing a single column of difference scores. If there is, in the population, no difference between the mean scores for the right and left visual fields, the mean difference will be zero. The null hypothesis to be tested states that our 14 difference scores are a sample from a normal population with a mean of zero and a variance which can be estimated from the difference scores in the sample.

If we can assume that the population of differences is normally distributed, the null hypothesis can be tested with the statistic *t*, where

$$t = \frac{\text{mean difference}}{\text{standard error of the difference}}$$

Table 1.
Median decision times for words presented to the right and left visual fields

Subject	Right visual field	Left visual field
s1	323	324
s2	493	512
s3	502	503
s4	376	385
s5	428	453
s6	343	345
s7	523	543
s8	439	442
s9	682	683
s10	703	998
s11	598	600
s12	456	462
s13	653	704
s14	652	653

If there are n pairs of data (i.e. n subjects), this t statistic has (n-1) degrees of freedom. In the present example, df = 13. The **one-sample t-test** presupposes that the difference scores are normally distributed. Should it turn out from preliminary inspection of the data that the differences are far from being normally distributed or that there are huge outliers, the user should beware of the t-test, especially with a small data set such as the present one, and should consider using a test that makes fewer assumptions about the data. For sets of paired data showing contraindications against the use of the related t-test, there are two nonparametric tests, neither of which assumes normality of the population distribution; both, moreover, are robust to the influence of outliers. These tests are:

(1) **Wilcoxon matched pairs test;**

(2) **Sign test.**

The latter is the more resistant to the leverage exerted by outliers; but, provided there are no outliers, the Wilcoxon is the more powerful test. (On the other hand, there are those who would say that if the data are good enough for the Wilcoxon, they are good enough for the paired samples t-test.)

Before proceeding with this exercise, we strongly urge you to read Section 6.2.3, which describes the procedure for a paired samples t-test.

Preparing the SPSS data set

In the data set for the independent samples t-test, one of the variables must be a grouping variable, showing which subjects performed under which conditions. With the paired samples t-test, however, there was only one group and so no coding variable need be constructed. Define two variables: *rvf* with label *Right Visual Field*, and *lvf* with label *Left Visual Field.* Enter the data in the usual way, as described in Section 3.4. The two columns *rvf* and *lvf* are sufficient for SPSS to run a paired samples t-test. As always, however, it is wise to explore the data, rather than pressing ahead with the formal test automatically. Since the null hypothesis concerns only the population of differences (rather than the separate *rvf* and *lvf* populations), we first calculate the differences and see how those are distributed. It is a very simple matter to obtain the differences by using the **Compute** procedure (Section 4.4.2) to create a new variable, *diffs,* containing the (*rvf* - *lvf*) difference for each subject.

Exploring the data

To list the values within *diffs*, click on

Statistics

Summarize

List Cases

to open the **List Cases** dialog box. Click on *diffs* and then on ▶ to paste the name into the **Variable(s)** box. Click on **OK**.

From inspection of the column of differences, it is quite clear that there is a glaring outlier. It is instructive to ascertain the effect of its presence upon the results of the t-test, in comparison with the nonparametric **Wilcoxon** and **Sign** tests. Although, in the paired samples t-test, the interest centres on the column of differences rather than the original scores, it is nevertheless of interest to see the scatterplot of *rvf* against *lvf,* which, ideally, should show an elliptical cloud of points indicating a bivariate normal distribution. Use the procedure in Section 6.2.3 to obtain a scatterplot of *lvf* against *rvf* and notice how the outlier shows up dramatically.

Running the paired samples t-test

Run the **paired samples t-test** by following the procedure described in Section 6.2.3.

Output listing for the paired samples t-test

From the details given in the t-test listing, it is clear that there are contraindications against the use of the paired samples t-test for the data in the present experiment. There is marked discrepancy between the standard deviations of the scores obtained under the *rvf* and *lvf* conditions. This arises from the presence of an outlier, which showed up dramatically in the scatterplot.

- **From the listing, write down the value of *t* and its p-value. Is *t* significant? Write down, in terms of the research hypothesis, the meaning of this result.**

What has happened here? You should find the t-test result paradoxical to say the least. Each of the fourteen pairs of data (one pair from each subject) shows a difference in the same direction: the *rvf* time is always lower than the *lvf* time. Moreover, in the case of the outlying pair of scores, the difference is even greater. Surely this should strengthen the evidence against the null hypothesis? Yet, in fact, the t-test does not show significance. This is because the outlier has exerted more leverage upon the denominator of the t statistic than it has upon the numerator, thus reducing the value of t (see Section 6.2.3).

NONPARAMETRIC ALTERNATIVES TO THE PAIRED SAMPLES T-TEST

The Wilcoxon matched pairs test

Now carry out the **Wilcoxon matched pairs** test, following the procedure described in Section 6.3.1.

- **Write down the value of the statistic and its p-value. Compare the p-value with that for the t-test. Relate the result of the Wilcoxon test to the experimental hypothesis.**

The Sign test

This test is based very simply on how many positive and negative differences there are between pairs of data, assuming that the value of one variable is consistently subtracted from the value of the other. It is a straightforward application of the binomial model to paired data, such as the results of the visual field experiment above. To merely record the signs (rather than the magnitudes) of the differences between the times for the left and right visual fields is certainly to lose a considerable amount of information. Indeed, when paired data show no contraindications, the related t-test is preferable to the Sign test, for to use the latter in such circumstances would be to make a needless sacrifice of power. The great advantage of the Sign test, however, is its robustness to the influence of outliers; moreover, there are no requirements about bivariate normality in the original paired data.

The procedure is very similar to that for the Wilcoxon test except that within the **Test Type** box, the **Wilcoxon** check box should be clicked off and the **Sign** check box clicked on. Click on **OK** to run the procedure.

- **Write down the results of the Sign test, including the p-value. Is the result significant? Compare this with the result of the paired samples t-test and explain any discrepancy.**

You may have noticed that the p-value for the **Sign** test is even smaller than that for the **Wilcoxon** test. This is because, although the Wilcoxon test is less sensitive to the presence of outliers than is the t-test, it is still affected by them to some extent.

ELIMINATING THE OUTLIERS

When there are contraindications for the **paired samples t-test**, the use of a nonparametric test is not the only alternative available. Another approach is to consider the possibility of eliminating some of the data. In the present set of paired data, there is one (*lvf-rvf*) difference which is much larger than all the others. This may have arisen because subject 10 has special difficulty in recognising words in the left visual field. At any rate, that subject's performance is quite atypical of this sample of participants and certainly calls into question the claim that he or she was drawn from the same population as the others. It is instructive to reanalyse the data after excluding the scores of Subject 10. This is done by using the **Select Cases** procedure (Section 3.12.1). Follow the procedure described in that section to eliminate the data from subject 10. (Hint: give the instruction to select cases if ABS(*diffs)* is less than 100; beware of the existence here of negative scores.)

Now re-run the **paired samples t-test**, the **Wilcoxon** and the **Sign** test on the reduced data set. Examine the new listings.

- **Write down the value of t and its tail probability. Write down your interpretation of this new result. Similarly give the statistics and their p-values for the Sign and Wilcoxon tests, commenting on the relative sizes of the p-values.**

Appendix to Exercise 10

SOME NOTES ON ONE-SAMPLE TESTS

So far, we have been concerned with tests of the null hypothesis that, in the population, there is no difference between the averages of two correlated samples of data. There can arise, however, situations where one has a single sample of scores and wishes to test the null hypothesis that the sample has been drawn from a population with a specified mean, which may be other than zero.

The one-sample t-test

Suppose it is known that, over the years, the mean performance on a spelling test of children in a particular class at school is 51. One year, however, following the introduction of a new teaching method, it is hoped that a higher level of performance will be achieved. At the end of the year, it is found that the mean of the children's spelling scores is 60. Is this improvement significant? The null hypothesis that the population mean has value 51 could be tested by defining (in the **Data Editor** window) the variable *scores*, containing the children's marks. Then the **Compute** procedure could be used to define another variable *mean,* containing the constant value *51*. Finally the **paired samples t-test** could be used in the usual way to make the required one-sample test.

To demonstrate this procedure with the hemispherical specialisation data, use the **paired samples t-test** to test the hypothesis that the column *diffs* contains a sample of scores from a population whose mean is zero. Define by the **Compute** procedure the variable *hyp* (for hypothesis) by typing *hyp* in the **Target Variable** box and 0 in the **Numeric Expression** box. Click on **OK**. Then select *diffs* and *hyp* within the **paired samples t-test** dialog box and click on **OK**. You should finish with the same t value as previously.

The binomial test

Underlying the Sign test is the binomial model. There is also an explicit **binomial test** which can be used in situations such as the following. Suppose that a child is presented with a series of 20 pairs of objects, one member of each of which contains a reward. Sometimes the child makes the correct choice; but is this just good luck, or has the rule really been understood?

There are two ways of entering the data for the binomial test:

Method 1. You can decide upon a code for right and wrong guesses (e.g. 1 for a correct answer, 0 for a wrong one), and enter the person's performance as a series such as:

1 1 0 1 1 1 1 0 0 0 1 1 1 0 1 1 1 1 1 1

If we assume that there were only two choices for each question (i.e. the probability of a correct guess is ½ each time), the procedure for the first method is as follows:

Define the variable *guesses*, containing the above sequence of code numbers representing the subject's performance.

Next, choose

Statistics

Nonparametric Tests

Binomial

to open the **Binomial Test** dialog box. Click on *guesses* and on ▶ to transfer the name to the **Test Variable** box. Click on **OK** to run the procedure.

Method 2. Alternatively, the data can be entered as the numbers of correct and incorrect answers produced (in the current example, the child got 15 choices right and 5 wrong in a sequence of 20 trials). The **Weight Cases** procedure (see Section 3.12.2) instructs SPSS to treat the values *15* and *5* as frequencies rather than as scores.

As an exercise, try both methods to assess the child's performance.

So far, the binomial test has assumed the default value of 0.5 for the proportion of cases expected in the first category (i.e. the probability p of a case falling into the first category). In most experimental situations (and multiple-choice examinations), however, there are more than two choices at each trial. We need to be able to cope with situations where p is not 0.5. This is easily dealt with by changing the value of **Test Proportion** in the **Binomial Test** dialog box to whatever value is required. If there were four choices for each question, for example, the value would be 0.25.

EXERCISE 11

THE ANALYSIS OF NOMINAL DATA: THE CHI-SQUARE TEST

BEFORE YOU START

Before you proceed with this practical, we strongly recommend that you read Chapters 5 and 11 (especially Section 11.3.2). Basically there are two applications of chi-square tests to the analysis of nominal data:

(1) For **goodness-of-fit** (when one variable is being studied).

(2) For the presence of an **association** between two variables.

THE CHI-SQUARE TEST OF GOODNESS-OF-FIT

Some nominal data on one qualitative variable

Suppose that a researcher, interested in children's preferences, suspects a spatial response bias towards the right hand side. Thirty children enter a room containing three identically-marked doors: one to the right; another to the left; and a third straight ahead. They are told they can go through any of the three doors. Their choices are shown in Table 1.

Table 1. The choices of one of three exit doors by thirty children		
Door		
Left	Middle	Right
5	8	17

It looks as if there is indeed a preference for the rightmost door, at least among the children sampled. Had the children been choosing at random, we should have expected about 10 in each category: that is, the theoretical, or expected distribution (E), of the tallies is a **uniform** one. The observed frequencies (O), on the other hand, have a distribution which is far from uniform.

Pearson's chi-square test can be used to test the goodness-of-fit of the expected to the observed distribution. Its rationale is lucidly discussed in any good statistics textbook (e.g. Howell, 1997). Here, we shall merely describe the SPSS procedure.

Procedure for the chi-square test of goodness-of-fit

Preparing the SPSS data set

Define the variable *position* for the three positional categories and a second variable *freq* for the numbers of children in the different categories. Use the **Labels** procedure to assign the code numbers *1*, *2* and *3* to the *position* categories *Left*, *Centre* and *Right*, respectively.

Run the Weight Cases procedure

To ensure that SPSS treats the entries in *freq* as frequencies rather than scores, follow the procedure described in Section 3.12.2.

Finding the dialog box

Choose

Statistics

Nonparametric Tests

Chi-Square

to open the **Chi-Square Test** dialog box. Click on *position* (not on *freq*) and on ▶ to transfer *position* to the **Test Variable List** box. Click on **OK** to run the test.

- **Write down the value of the chi-square statistic and its p-value. Does the test show significance, i.e. is the p-value sufficiently small to constitute evidence against the null hypothesis? Write down the implications for the experimenter's research hypothesis.**

Running the goodness-of-fit test on a set of raw data

When the researcher carried out the experiment, the door that each child chose was noted at the time. In terms of the code numbers, their choices might have been:

1 1 3 2 1 1 3 3 3 , ..., and so on.

If the user defines the variable *position*, and enters the 30 (coded) choices that the children made, the chi-square test is then run directly: there is no weighting of cases.

THE CHI-SQUARE TEST OF ASSOCIATION BETWEEN TWO QUALITATIVE VARIABLES

The reader should study Section 11.3.2 before doing this part of the exercise.

An experiment on children's choices

Suppose that a researcher, having watched a number of children enter a room and recorded each child's choice between two objects, wants to know whether there is a tendency for boys and girls to choose different objects. This question concerns two variables: *gender* and *choice*. In statistical terms, the researcher is asking whether they are associated: do more girls than boys choose one of the objects and more boys than girls choose the other object? Suppose that the children's choices are as in Table 2.

Table 2.

Choices by 50 children of one of two objects

Object	Boys	Girls
A	20	5
B	6	19

Procedure for the chi-square test of association between two variables

The use of the **Crosstabs** procedure is fully described in Sections 11.3.2.1 and 11.3.2.2. We recommend the inclusion of the option for obtaining the expected frequencies (using the **Cells...** option) so that you can check for the presence of cells with unacceptably low expected frequencies (see Section 11.3.2.2 for details). Remember to select **Chi-square** and **Phi and Cramér's V** from the **Statistics** option.

Output listing for the chi-square test of association

The listing is discussed in Section 11.3.2.3. First, a crosstabulation table is listed showing the observed and expected frequencies in each cell, along with row and column totals. Second, a table of various chi-square statistics, together with their associated significance levels, is listed. Third, the values of Phi and Cramér's V are given, together with their associated significance levels.

- **Write down the value of the Pearson chi-square and its associated tail probability (p-value). Is it significant? In terms of the experimental hypothesis, what has this test shown?**
- **Write down the value of Phi.**

EXERCISE 12

ONE-FACTOR BETWEEN SUBJECTS ANOVA

BEFORE YOU START

We suggest that you review the material in Chapter 7 before working through this practical exercise.

THE EXERCISE

The purpose of this exercise

In one-factor between subjects ANOVA, the **F ratio** compares the spread among the treatment means with the (supposedly uniform) spread of the scores within groups about their group means. The purpose of this exercise is to help clarify the rationale of the F ratio by showing how its value is affected by various manipulations of some (or all) of the data. Before proceeding with this exercise, we ask you to suppose that a one-factor ANOVA has been carried out upon a set of data and yields an F value of, say, 7.23. Now suppose we were to multiply every score in the experimental results by a constant, say 10. What would happen to the value of F: would it still be 7.23? Or would it increase? Or decrease?

We also invite you to speculate upon the effect that adding a constant (say 10) to all the scores in just one of the groups would have upon F: suppose, for example, we were to add 10 to all the scores in the group with the largest mean. Would F stay the same, increase or decrease in value? Would the effect be the same if the constant were added to the scores of the group with the smallest mean?

As a first approach to answering these questions, we shall carry out a **one-factor ANOVA** on a set of data. Then we shall see what happens to the value of F when the data are transformed as described in the previous paragraphs.

Some data from a completely randomised experiment

Table 1.

Results of a completely randomised experiment on the effects upon recall of logographic characters of different mnemonic systems

Group										
No Mnemonic (10 control subjects	4	6	4	3	5	7	10	4	9	11
Mnemonic 1 (10 subjects trained in Mnemonic 1)	11	9	16	10	12	17	18	16	8	11
Mnemonic 2 (10 subjects trained in Mnemonic 2)	21	16	15	16	18	11	9	12	19	20

Suppose a researcher is interested in how well non-Chinese-speaking students can learn Chinese characters using different kinds of mnemonic. Independent groups of participants are tested under three conditions: *No Mnemonic*, *Mnemonic 1* and *Mnemonic 2*. The dependent variable is the number of Chinese characters that are correctly recalled. The data are shown in Table 1.

Construction of the SPSS data set

Recast the data of Table 1 into a form suitable for analysis by SPSS by following the procedure described in Chapter 3. Save the data set: we shall be using it again in the next exercise.

Exploring the data

As always, we recommend a preliminary exploration of the data set before any formal testing is carried out, in case there are contraindications for the use of the ANOVA. As in Exercise 8, use the **Means** procedure for descriptive statistics and **Explore** for checks on the distributions of the scores within the groups. (**Explore** inundates the user with a surfeit of statistics: the **Means** procedure is therefore preferred.)

- **Examine the output listing for the Means procedure. Do the means appear to differ? Are the standard deviations similar in value?**

The output listing for the **Explore** procedure begins with the stem-and-leaf displays for the three groups. It then plots the boxplots in the **Chart Carousel**: they can be seen on the screen by clicking on the **Carousel** icon or clicking on the **Window** drop-down menu and selecting **Chart**. Further details about the boxplots are given in Section 4.3.2.4.

- **Do the boxplots suggest any anomalies in the distributions of the data in any of the three groups? Write a statement assessing the suitability of the data for ANOVA.**

Procedure for the one-way ANOVA

The procedure for the one-way ANOVA is described in detail in Section 7.2.2.

Output listing for the one-way ANOVA

- **Write down the value of F and its associated p-value. Is F significant? What are the implications of this result for the experimental hypothesis?**

RE-ANALYSIS OF TRANSFORMED DATA SETS

In this section, we return to the question of the effects upon the ANOVA statistics of subjecting the data (or sections of the data) to such operations as multiplying every score by a constant.

1) Multiplying every score by a constant

We recommend that whenever you have occasion to transform the values of a variable in the SPSS data set, you should construct a new target variable, rather than change (perhaps irreversibly) the original data. Use the **Compute** procedure (Section 4.4.2) to multiply each value in the data set by a factor of 10. Follow the instructions in that section, choosing, for the target variable, a mnemonic name such as *allbyten*. Now change the **One-way ANOVA** dialog box so that the dependent variable is *allbyten* instead of *score* and click on **OK** to run the analysis.

Output listing for the one-way ANOVA

- **Write down the value of F and its associated p-value. Is F significant? What are the implications of this result for the experimental hypothesis?**

In the output listing, you will see that both the between groups and within groups variance estimates have increased by a factor of 100. This is not at all surprising, since it is easy to show algebraically that when each of a set of scores is multiplied by a constant, the new variance is the old variance times the square of the constant. Since, however, the factors of 100 in the numerator and denominator of the F ratio cancel out, the value of the F ratio remains unchanged.

2) Adding a constant to the scores in only one group

This time, we want a target variable which contains, for two of the three groups, the original scores; but to the values of the Mnemonic 2 group has been added a constant of +10. First, make a copy of the values in *score* to a new variable *g3plus10* in the **Data Editor** window using the technique described in Section 3.5.4. Second, use the **Compute** procedure to add the value *+10* to the values in this new variable when the grouping variable has the value *3*. In the **Compute** dialog box, type *g3plus10* into the **Target Variable** box, transfer it to the **Numeric Expression** box and add *+10* after the variable name. Click on **If** to open the **Compute Variable: If Cases** dialog box. Transfer the name *group* into the box and add the expression *=3*. Click on **Continue** and then on **OK** to run the procedure. In the **Data Editor** window, check that the values in *g3plus10* for the third group have changed but the rest have their original values. Now re-run the **one-way ANOVA**, using *g3plus10* as the dependent variable.

Output listing for the one-way ANOVA

- **Write down the value of F and its associated p-value. Is F significant? What are the implications of this result for the experimental hypothesis?**

You will see that the effect of adding a constant of *10* to all scores in the *Mnemonic 2* group has no effect at all upon the within groups variance estimate, which is not surprising, since adding the same constant to all the scores in a set has no effect upon the spread of the scores - it merely shifts the mean. The between groups mean square, however, computed from the values of the treatment means alone, has increased its value considerably. The within groups mean square, on the other hand, is the average of the variance estimates of the scores within groups and is quite independent of the spread among the group means. Consequently, it is quite possible to change the value of the former without affecting that of the latter and vice-versa. The effect of increasing the mean of the third group is to increase the spread of the three treatment means and hence the value of the numerator of the F ratio.

POST-HOC COMPARISONS: THE TUKEY TEST

If the ANOVA is significant, you will want to know which pairs of levels differ significantly. We recommend that you read Sections 7.1 and 7.2.3.3. With data from a completely randomised experiment, it is a simple matter to run various multiple comparisons procedures with SPSS, because these can be requested from the **One-way ANOVA** dialog box.

Specifying post-hoc comparisons with the one-way ANOVA

Proceed as for the **one-way ANOVA**, but this time click on the **Post-hoc** button to bring to the screen the **One-Way ANOVA: Post Hoc Multiple Comparisons** dialog box. Mark the check box for **Tukey's honestly significant difference**. Click on **Continue** and then on **OK** to run the ANOVA and the multiple comparisons procedure.

Output listing for post-hoc comparisons

Study the output listing for the multiple comparisons test, noting its presentation of the results.

- **Construct your own table showing clearly which pairs of levels are significantly different and which are not.**

EXERCISE 13

FACTORIAL BETWEEN SUBJECTS ANOVA (TWO-WAY ANOVA)

BEFORE YOU START

Before proceeding with this practical, please read Chapter 8. The following exercise assumes a knowledge of the standard **factorial ANOVA** terminology.

TWO-WAY ANOVA

An experiment on the memories of chess players

'Must have a marvellous memory!'. This is something often said of a good chess player; but do good chess players necessarily have better short-term memories than those who are mediocre? To find out, a psychologist tested chess players at three levels of proficiency on their ability to reconstruct board positions they had just been shown. Some of the positions used were from real games selected from tournaments; but others were merely random placings of the same pieces. The psychologist predicted that whereas the better players would show superior reconstructions of real board positions, this superiority would disappear when they tried to reproduce random placements. The dependent variable in this experiment was a subject's *score* on reconstruction. There were two independent variables (factors):

(1) Competence (Novice, Average, Good).
(2) Position (Real, Random).

An important feature of the design of this experiment was that a different sample of subjects performed under each of the six treatment combinations: that is, each group of players at a given level was subdivided into those reconstructing Real positions and those reconstructing Random positions.

What the psychologist is predicting is that, when performance is averaged over Random and Real positions, the better players will achieve higher performance means; but this will turn out to be because of their superior recall of Real board positions only, and the beginners will be just as good at reconstructing Random positions. The **two-factor ANOVA**, therefore, should show a significant interaction between the factors of Competence and Position, as well as (possibly) a main effect of Competence. The latter might be expected to arise because the better players' much superior performance in reconstructing real board positions pulls up the mean value of their performance over both Real and Random positions, even though they may not excel beginners on the Random task.

The results of the experiment are shown in Table 1.

Table 1.

Results of the experiment on the reconstruction of positions by chess players

Position	Competence														
	Novice					Average					Good				
Real	38	39	42	40	40	65	58	70	61	62	88	97	79	89	89
Random	50	53	40	41	36	50	40	43	37	38	41	40	50	42	41

Procedure for the two-factor between subjects experiment

Before proceeding further, we strongly recommend you to study Section 8.2.

Constructing the SPSS data set

Recast the data of Table 1 into a form suitable for entry into SPSS along the lines of the description in Section 8.2.1. You will need two coding variables, *compet* and *position*, and one dependent variable *score*. As always, save the data set.

Exploring the data

Before proceeding with the ANOVA, it is important to explore the data. Construct a table of means to include the cell means and the marginal means (i.e. row means and column means) by using the **Means** procedure twice, the first time including both *compet* and *position* in the **Independent List** box, the second time **layering** both the independent variables (see Section 8.2.2). The first operation obtains the marginal means, the second obtains the cell means. You should now have a table of cell means, and also the row and column means.

- **From inspection of the marginal means, are there any indications of main effects? Do the cell means give any indication of an interaction?**

Procedure for the two-way ANOVA

Follow the description in Sections 8.2.1 and 8.2.2.

Output listing for the two-way ANOVA

The ANOVA summary table gives F ratios for the main effects of *compet* and *position* and also for the interaction between the two factors.

- **Write down the values of *F* (and the associated p-values) for the main effect and interaction terms. Do these results confirm your predictions from inspection of the output from the Means procedure? Relate these results to the experimental hypothesis about the short-term memory of chess players.**

Obtaining a graph of the cell means

Follow the procedure in Section 8.2.4.2. Inspect the graph and interpret the results of the ANOVA tests accordingly.

Post-hoc comparisons among the marginal and cell means

Follow up the main ANOVA with post-hoc comparisons among the marginal and cell means, as described in Section 8.2.4.3.

- **Construct your own table showing clearly which pairs of levels or cells are significantly different and which are not.**

EXERCISE 14

ONE-FACTOR WITHIN SUBJECTS (REPEATED MEASURES) ANOVA

BEFORE YOU START

Before proceeding with this exercise, we suggest you study Chapter 9.

ONE-FACTOR WITHIN SUBJECTS ANOVA

A comparison of the efficacy of statistical packages

Imagine an experiment which measures the time taken for ten subjects to perform an analysis using three statistical computer packages Pack1, Pack2 and Pack3. During the course of the experiment, each subject uses every package and the order of use is systematically varied across subjects. The results are shown in Table 1.

Table 1.

Times taken by participants to carry out an analysis with different computing packages

Subject	Pack1	Pack2	Pack3	Subject	Pack1	Pack2	Pack3
s1	12	15	18	s6	10	12	14
s2	18	21	19	s7	18	17	21
s3	15	16	15	s8	18	17	21
s4	21	26	32	s9	23	27	30
s5	19	23	22	s10	17	25	21

Preparing the SPSS data set

Prepare the SPSS data set as described in Section 9.4.2. Since there is just one group of subjects, there is no grouping variable.

Exploring the data

Use the methods described in Section 9.4.3 to check for any distribution problems.

Procedure for the within subjects (repeated measures) ANOVA

Follow the procedure described in Section 9.4.4 .

Output listing for the within subjects (repeated measures) ANOVA

Section 9.4.5 offers some guidelines for the interpretation of the output listing. The most important item is the univariate ANOVA summary table for the Package factor.

- **What is the value of the F ratio and its associated p-value (tail probability) for *package*? Is *F* significant? What are the implications for the experimental hypothesis?**

At this point, however, we must issue a word of warning. In Chapter 9, attention was drawn to the fact that the model for repeated measures ANOVA makes an important assumption, over and above the usual requirements of homogeneity of variance and normality of distribution. This is the assumption of **homogeneity of covariance**. Often (indeed, usually) the data sets yielded by psychological repeated measures experiments show marked heterogeneity of covariance. If there is heterogeneity of covariance, the true p-value may be somewhat higher than that given in the ANOVA summary table. If, therefore, the p-value is very small, say, less than 0.01, it is safe enough to say that we have evidence against the null hypothesis. If, however, the p-value is just under 0.05, we need to look at the result more carefully, and consider the possibility of a **conservative F test** (see Howell, 1997; Chapter 14).

GREEN HAUS GUESSER
AUTOMATICALLY
CALCULATED IN (7)

EXERCISE 15

TWO-FACTOR WITHIN SUBJECTS ANOVA

BEFORE YOU START

We suggest that you read Section 9.6 before proceeding. In this exercise, we consider the ANOVA of within subjects factorial experiments, that is, factorial experiments with crossed treatment factors and repeated measures on all factors.

THE TWO-FACTOR WITHIN SUBJECTS ANOVA

A two-factor within subjects experiment

An experiment is carried out to investigate the effects of two factors (independent variables) upon the recognition of symbols briefly presented on a screen, as measured by the number of correct identifications over a fixed number of trials. The factors are Symbol (with levels Digit, Lower Case, Upper Case) and Font (with levels Gothic, Roman). Each of the six subjects in the experiment is tested under all six combinations of the two treatment factors. The results are shown in Table 1.

Preparing the SPSS data set

Enter the data into the **Data Editor** window in the manner described in Section 9.6.2.

Exploring the data

Use the methods described in Section 9.4.3 to check for any distribution problems.

Table 1.

Results of a two-factor within subjects experiment

	Upper case		Digit		Lower case	
	Gothic	Gothic	Roman	Roman	Gothic	Roman
s1	18	2	6	3	20	5
s2	20	4	9	6	18	2
s3	15	3	10	2	21	3
s4	10	1	12	9	30	10
s5	13	5	8	8	20	8
s6	14	6	10	10	16	6

Running the two-factor within subjects ANOVA

To run the ANOVA, follow the procedure described in Section 9.6.3 .

Output listing for the two-factor within subjects experiment

The output listing for the two-factor repeated measures ANOVA is explained in Section 9.6.4 .

- **Examine the present listing and interpret the implications of the results of the tests for main effects and the interaction in terms of the aims of the study.**

EXERCISE 16

MIXED ANOVA (BETWEEN AND WITHIN SUBJECTS FACTORS)

BEFORE YOU BEGIN

Readers should study Chapter 10 carefully before proceeding with this exercise.

THE TWO-FACTOR MIXED ANOVA

Effects of ambient hue and sound on vigilance

In an experiment investigating the effect of the colour of the ambient light upon performance of a vigilance task, subjects were asked to press a button when they thought they could discern a signal against a background of random noise.

Table 1.

The results of a two-factor mixed design experiment

Colour	Subject	Signal		
		Horn	Whistle	Bell
Red	s1	25	18	22
	s2	22	16	21
	s3	26	19	26
	s4	23	21	20
	s5	19	18	19
	s6	27	23	27
Blue	s7	19	12	23
	s8	21	15	19
	s9	23	14	24
	s10	20	16	21
	s11	17	16	20
	s12	21	17	19

The experimenter expected that the ambient colour would have varying effects upon the detection of different kinds of sound. Three types of signal were used: a horn, a whistle and a bell. Each signal was presented 30 times in the course of a one-hour monitoring session, during which the subject sat in a cubicle lit by either red or blue light. The dependent variable was the number of correct presses of the button. For theoretical purposes, it was necessary to use different subjects for the different colour conditions; on the other hand, it was considered that there would be advantages in testing each individual with all three kinds of signal. In this experiment, therefore, the factor of Colour was between subjects; whereas the other factor, Signal, was within subjects.

The results are shown in Table 1.

Preparing the SPSS data set

Recast the data of Table 1 into a form suitable for entry into the **Data Editor**. You will need to define a grouping variable *colour* and three variables for the scores: *horn*, *whistle*, and *bell*. The last three variables will be the three levels of the within-subjects factor *signal*, which is not defined until the ANOVA procedure is actually being run. Follow the procedure described in Section 10.2.3.

Exploring the data set

Since there is a grouping variable, use the **Means** procedure as described in Section 10.2.4.1 to obtain means and standard deviations.

Examine the tables of means. Plot by hand the profiles of cell means against the different signals for those subjects who performed under red and blue illumination.

- **Are there signs of main effects or an interaction?**

Procedure for the two-factor mixed ANOVA

Run the procedure as described in Section 10.2.5.

Output listing for the two-factor mixed ANOVA

The main features of the output are explained in Section 10.2.6.

- **Write down the values of *F* and their associated p-values. Relate these findings to the experimental hypothesis**

EXERCISE 17

MIXED ANOVA: THREE-FACTOR EXPERIMENT

BEFORE YOU START

Before proceeding with this exercise, you should study Section 10.3. From the procedural point of view, the analysis of mixed experiments with three factors is a fairly simple extension of the procedure for two-factor mixed experiments. In general, however, the interpretation of data from factorial experiments becomes increasingly problematic as more factors are added. In particular, where there is a complex design with repeated measures on some factors but not on others, the naming of the factors must be carried out with special care.

A MIXED FACTORIAL A x (B x C) EXPERIMENT

The data

Imagine an experiment investigating the recognition of shapes under sub-optimal conditions on a monitor screen. There are three shapes (shapel, shape2, shape3), each of which can be either Open (outline) or Filled. Each subject in the experiment is tested under all six combinations of these two treatment factors, which can be labelled Shape and Shade. The between subjects factor group is the type of observer used: one group consists of Psychology students, the other of Engineering students. The dependent variable is the number of correct identifications over a fixed series of trials. The results are shown in Table 1.

Table 1.
Three-factor mixed factorial experiment with two within subjects treatment factors

	Shape:	Shape 1		Shape 2		Shape 3	
	Shade:	Open	Filled	Open	Filled	Open	Filled
Group	Subject						
Psychology	s1	2	12	3	1	4	5
	s2	13	22	5	9	6	8
	s3	14	20	8	7	5	7
Engineering	s4	12	1	3	9	6	10
	s5	11	2	8	10	5	9
	s6	12	7	2	4	4	10

Preparing the SPSS data set

Recast the results in Table 1 as described in Section 10.3.1. The data will comprise seven variables: a grouping variable and a variable for each combination of the two treatment factors. Define the variables appropriately, remembering to label the values of the grouping variable. Enter and save the data.

Exploring the data

Use the **Means** procedure to obtain tables of cell and marginal means. In a three-factor experiment, there is the possibility of a three-way interaction among all three factors. A three-way interaction is said to occur when the interaction between two factors is heterogeneous across the levels of a third factor. This definition might suggest that the presence of a three-way interaction might be rather easy to discern in a three-way table of cell means by simply comparing graphs of two-way interactions at the different levels of a third factor. In fact, the interpretation of graphs drawn from the cell means of three-way tables requires considerable practice. This is because, just as two-way tables of means (and their graphs) reflect the presence of main effects as well as the interaction, three-way tables (and their graphs) reflect the presence of two-way interactions as well as any three-way interaction that might be present. To the untrained eye, two-way graphs may look heterogeneous; but this may arise entirely from the presence of two-way interactions.

From the listing from **Means**, graph the two-way interactions between two of the factors at the different levels of the third factor. Do this by drawing two graphs side-by-side, one for *psychologists* and the other for *engineers*. With the three levels of *shape* on each x-axis and the values of the means on the y-axes, mark in the *open* means with dots and the *filled* means with crosses. Connect up the dots and connect up the crosses with lines in each graph.

- **Do the patterns of lines seem similar? If not, a three-way interaction may be present.**

Running the ANOVA procedure

The procedure is merely outlined in Section 10.3.1, but is a straightforward extension of the routine for the two-factor mixed experiment.

Output listing for the A x (B x C) mixed factorial experiment

Look for the table of 'Tests of Between-Subjects Effects' for the factor *group*. For the various 'Tests involving ..... Within-Subject Effect', **Mauchly** tests will appear for factors with more than two levels (i.e. the Shape factor and for the Shape x Shade interaction); check that the p-values are greater than 0.05.

- **Write down the F ratios (and p-values) for the three factors, their two-way interactions and the three-way interaction. Do the values of F confirm the patterns among the treatment means you saw earlier in your graphs?**

As always where there are repeated measures factors, special care is needed when interpreting an F ratio that is significant with a p-value just below 0.05.

EXERCISE 18

THE PEARSON CORRELATION

BEFORE YOU START

Before starting to work through this practical exercise we recommend that you read Chapter 11. The Pearson correlation ***r*** is one of the most widely used (and abused) of statistics. Despite its apparent simplicity and versatility, however, it is only too easy to misinterpret a correlation. The purpose of the present exercise is not only to show you how to use SPSS to obtain correlations, but also to illustrate how misleading a given value for ***r*** can sometimes be.

THE PROJECT

A famous data set

This exercise involves the analysis of four sets of paired data, which were contrived by Anscombe (1973). Each set yields exactly the same value for the **Pearson correlation**. The scatterplots, however, will show that in only one case are the data suitable for a Pearson correlation: in the others, the Pearson correlation gives a highly misleading impression of the relationship between the two variables. Ideally a scatterplot should indicate a **linear relationship** between the variables i.e. that all the points on the scatterplot lie along or near to a diagonal straight line as shown in the two left-hand plots in Chapter 11, Figure 1. Vertical or horizontal lines are not examples of linear relationships.

Table 1.

Anscombe's four data sets

Subject	X1	Y1	Y2	Y3	X2	Y4
s1	10.0	8.04	9.14	7.46	8.0	6.58
s2	8.0	6.95	8.14	6.77	8.0	5.76
s3	13.0	7.58	8.74	12.74	8.0	7.71
s4	9.0	8.81	8.77	7.11	8.0	8.84
s5	11.0	8.33	9.26	7.81	8.0	8.47
s6	14.0	9.96	8.10	8.84	8.0	7.04
s7	6.0	7.24	6.13	6.08	8.0	5.25
s8	4.0	4.26	3.10	5.39	19.0	12.50
s9	12.0	10.84	9.13	8.15	8.0	5.56
s10	7.0	4.82	7.26	6.42	8.0	7.91
s11	5.0	5.68	4.74	5.73	8.0	6.89

The data are presented in Table 1. The four sets we shall examine are *X1* with each of *Y1*, *Y2*, and *Y3*, and finally *X2* with *Y4*.

Preparation of the SPSS data set

Name the variables as shown in the data table above (omit subject numbers), enter the data and then save them in the file **anscombe.sav** (this file will be used again in Exercise 19). If the numeric format does not include decimals, click on the **Type** button and enter *2* into the **Decimal Places** box.

Exploring the data

Obtain scatterplots of the four data sets, as described in Section 11.2.2. The plots can be produced either one at a time by choosing **simple scatterplot** or, more dramatically, by opting for a **matrix scatterplot**, which is a grid of scatterplots normally used when one is plotting all pairwise combinations of several variables. In the present exercise, however, we only want the plots of *Y1*, *Y2* and *Y3* against *X*, and of *Y4* against *X2*. It is best to obtain the plot of *Y4* against *X2* separately.

If the matrix scatterplot is selected and variables *X1*, *Y1*, *Y2* and *Y3* are transferred to the **Matrix Variables** box, only the first column of plots, those with *X1* on the horizontal axis, will be of interest.

- **What do you notice about the scatterplots in the first column? Which one is immediately suitable for a subsequent calculation of a Pearson correlation? What is wrong with each of the others?**

Return to the **Graphs** menu (it might be necessary to click on **Window**, and select the **anscombe.sav** window), and set up a simple scatterplot with *X2* and *Y4* (see Section 4.3.3.7 or 11.2.2).

- **Is the plot suitable for a Pearson correlation?**

The plot of *Y1* against *X1* shows a substantial linear relationship between the variables. The thinness of the ellipse indicates that the **Pearson correlation** is likely to be high. This is the kind of data set for which the Pearson correlation gives an informative and accurate statement of the strength of linear relationship between two variables. The other plots, however, are very different: that of *Y2* against *X1* shows a perfect, but clearly non-linear, relationship; *Y3* against *X1* shows a basically linear relationship, which is marred by a glaring outlier; *Y4* against *X2* shows a column of points with a single outlier up in the top right corner.

Obtaining the Pearson correlations corresponding to the four scatterplots

Using the procedure described in Section 11.2.3, obtain the correlations between *X* and *Y* for the four sets of paired data.

The listing will include, in addition to the correlations of *X1* with the various *Y*s, the correlations among the four *Y* variables. The latter can be ignored.

- **What do you notice about the value of *r* for each of the correlations with *X1*?**

Return to the dialog box, click on the **Reset** box, and select *X2* and *Y4* for the remaining calculation.

- **What do you notice about the value of *r* in comparison with the values of *r* involving *X1*?**

The big surprise is that in all cases, the **Pearson correlation** has the same value (*0.817 or thereabouts*), even in the case where there appears to be no systematic relationship between *X* and *Y* at all! Anscombe's data strikingly illustrate the need to inspect the data carefully to ascertain the suitability of statistics such as the Pearson correlation.

REMOVING THE OUTLIERS

It will be instructive to recalculate the **Pearson correlation** for the data set (*X1*, *Y3*) when the values for Subject 3 have been removed. The outlier is the value *12.74* on the variable *Y3*. Use the **Select Cases** procedure to select cases which do not have a value of *12.74* on *Y3*. Since none of the other values exceed 10, it is simplest to eliminate any cases with a value greater than 10.

Return to the **Scatterplot** and **Bivariate Correlations** dialog boxes for *X1* and *Y3* (ignore the other variables) to re-run these procedures using the selected cases. Check that in the listing, only 10 rather than 11 cases have been used. You should find that the Pearson correlation for *X1* and *Y3* is now +1, which is what we would expect from the appearance of the scatterplot.

CONCLUSION

This exercise has demonstrated the value of exploring the data first before calculating statistics such as the **Pearson correlation**. While it is true that Anscombe's data were contrived to give his message greater force, there have been many misuses of the Pearson correlation with real data sets, where the problems created by the presence of outliers and by basically non-linear relationships are quite common.

EXERCISE 19

OTHER MEASURES OF ASSOCIATION

BEFORE YOU START

Please read Section 11.3 before proceeding with this practical exercise. The **Pearson correlation** was devised to measure a supposed linear association between quantitative variables. There are other kinds of data (ordinal and nominal), to which the Pearson correlation is inapplicable. Moreover, even with interval data, there may be considerations that debar the use of the Pearson correlation. Fortunately, other statistical measures of strength of association have been devised and in this exercise, we shall consider statistics that are applicable to ordinal and to nominal data.

ORDINAL DATA

The Spearman rank correlation

Suppose that two judges each rank ten paintings, A, B, ..., J. Their decisions are shown in Table 1.

Table 1.

The ranks assigned to the same ten objects by two judges

	Best									Worst
First Judge	C	E	F	G	H	I	B	D	D	A
Second Judge	C	E	G	F	J	H	I	A	D	B

It is obvious from this table that the judges generally agree closely in their rankings: at most, the ranks they assign to a painting differ by two ranks. But how can their level of agreement be measured? The information in this table can be expressed in terms of numerical ranks by assigning the counting numbers from 1 to 10 to the paintings in their order of ranking by the first judge, and pairing each of these ranks with the rank that the same painting received from the other judge, as shown in Table 2.

Table 2.

A numerical representation of the orderings by the two judges in Table 1

Painting	**C**	**E**	**F**	**G**	**H**	**J**	**I**	**B**	**D**	**A**
First Judge	1	2	3	4	5	6	7	8	9	10
Second Judge	1	2	4	3	6	5	7	10	9	8

This is not the only way of representing the judgements numerically. It is also possible to list the objects (in any order) and pair the ranks assigned by the two judges to each object, entering two sets of ranks as before. Where the measurement of agreement is concerned, however, the two methods give exactly the same result.

Define two variables, *judge1* and *judge2*, and enter the ranks assigned by the judges into the two columns. Obtain the **Pearson correlation** between the two sets of ranks. This is the value of the **Spearman rank correlation**.

Use of the Spearman rank correlation where there is a monotonic, but non-linear, relationship

Consider a common problem. Table 3 shows a set of paired interval data. On inspecting the scatterplot, we see that there is a **monotonic relationship** between the two variables: that is, as X increases, so does Y. On the other hand, the relationship between X and Y is clearly non-linear, and the use of the **Pearson correlation** is therefore inadvisable.

Table 3.

A set of paired interval data showing a monotonic, but non-linear, relationship

Y	1.00	1.58	2.00	2.32	2.58	2.81	3.00
X	2.0	3.0	4.0	5.0	6.0	7.0	8.0

Enter these values into the **Data Editor**, calculate the **Pearson correlation** and obtain the scatterplot.

- **Describe the shape of the scatterplot and write down the value of the Pearson correlation.**

Since there is a perfect (but non-linear) relationship between X and Y ($Y = \log_2 X$), the degree of association is understated by the Pearson correlation coefficient.

Another approach (and arguably a better one) is to convert X and Y to ranks using the **Rank Cases** procedure within the **Transform** menu (the ranks will appear in new variables called *ranoo1* and *ran 002* respectively). Then calculate the Pearson correlation again using these new variables. Now compare this with your previous value of r.

- **Which value of r is the truer expression of the strength of the relationship between X and Y?**

Kendall's correlation coefficients

The association between variables in paired ordinal (and interval) data sets can also be measured by using one of **Kendall's correlation** coefficients, **tau-a, tau-b** or **tau-c** (see Section 11.3.1.2). (When there are no tied observations, **tau-a** and **tau-b** have the same value.)

With large data sets, **Kendall's** and **Pearson's correlations** give rather similar values and tail probabilities. When the data are scarcer, however, Kendall's statistics are better behaved, especially when there is a substantial proportion of tied observations, and more reliance can be placed upon the Kendall tail probability. Kendall's correlations really come into their own when the data are assignments to predetermined ordered categories (rating scales and so on).

There are two ways of obtaining **Kendall's correlations** in SPSS:

(1) In the **Bivariate Correlations** procedure, mark the **Kendall's tau-b** checkbox.

(2) Use the **Crosstabs** procedure (See Section 11.3.2.2).

Use the **Bivariate Correlations** procedure to obtain **Kendall's tau-a** (there are no ties) for the data in Tables 2 and 3.

- **Write down the values of tau-a and compare them with your previously obtained coefficient values.**

MEASURES OF ASSOCIATION STRENGTH FOR NOMINAL DATA

In an earlier exercise, we considered the use of the **chi-square statistic** to test for the presence of an association between two qualitative variables. Recall that, provided that the data are suitable, the **Pearson correlation** measures the strength of a linear association between two interval variables. In that case, therefore, the same statistic serves both as a test for the presence of an association and as a measure of associative strength. It might be thought that, with nominal data, the chi-square statistic would serve the same dual function. The chi-square statistic, however, cannot serve as a satisfactory measure of associative strength, because its value depends partly upon the total frequency.

To illustrate the calculation of measures of association for two-way contingency tables, we can recall an earlier example, concerning the possibility of a gender difference in the choice of objects by children. The data were as shown in Table 4.

Table 4.

The choices between two objects of 50 children

Object	Boys	Girls
A	20	6
B	5	19

Prepare the data set for the **Crosstabs** procedure and run **Crosstabs** (Section 11.3.2.2). This time, however, select **Phi** and **Cramer's V** within the **Nominal Data** box of the **Crosstabs: Statistics** dialog box.

- **Write down the values of the chosen measures of association between the qualitative variables of Gender and Choice.**

EXERCISE 20

SIMPLE, TWO-VARIABLE REGRESSION

BEFORE YOU START

Before proceeding with this exercise, please read Chapter 12.

THE REGRESSION PROJECT

Purpose of the project

In this exercise, we shall look at some of the pitfalls that await the unwary user of regression techniques; in fact, as we shall see, all the cautions and caveats about the **Pearson correlation** apply with equal force to regression.

In Exercise 18, Anscombe's specially contrived data set (whose columns were named *X1*, *X2*, *Y1*, *Y2*, *Y3*, *Y4*) was saved in a file named **anscombe.sav**. Scatterplots and correlation coefficients were obtained for the pairings (*X1*, *Y1*), (*X1*, *Y2*), (*X1*, *Y3*) and (*X2*, *Y4*). All sets yielded exactly the same value for the Pearson correlation. When the scatterplots were inspected, however, it was seen that the Pearson correlation was appropriate for only one data set: in the other sets, it would give the unwary user a highly misleading impression. One problem with the Pearson correlation is that it is very vulnerable to the leverage exerted by atypical data points, or **outliers** as they are termed. It can also show large values with monotonic but non-linear relationships. All this is equally true of the parameters of the regression equation. In this exercise, we return to Anscombe's data to investigate the statistics of the regression lines for the four sets of paired data.

Preparation of the data set

No preparation should be necessary: simply recall Anscombe's data set in file **anscombe.sav** to the **Data Editor** window.

Running the simple regression procedure

Following the procedure described in Section 12.2, obtain the regression statistics of *Y1*, *Y2* and *Y3* upon *X1* and of *Y4* upon *X2*. Remember that the dependent variable is Y, and the independent variable is X. For present purposes, the plotting of the scatterplot of *ZRESID (**y-axis** box) against *ZPRED (**x-axis** box) should provide illuminating tests of the credibility of the assumption that the data are linear. Full details of preparing the **Linear Regression** dialog box are given in Section 12.2.1.3.

Since we want to carry out regression upon all four (*X*,*Y*) data sets, it will be necessary to prepare the **Regression** dialog box for the first pair to include a scatterplot of *ZRESID against *ZPRED, and then change the variable names on subsequent runs for the remaining three pairs. To return to the **Regression** dialog box after inspecting the scatterplot, click on the **Window** drop-down menu, select *anscombe.sav*, click on the **Statistics** drop-down menu and select **Regression** again. After each run, you should record the value of **R Squared** and the regression equation, and note the appearance of the scatterplot.

Output listing for the simple regression analyses

The main features of the output listing of a simple regression analysis are fully explained in Chapter 12.

- **Compare the regression statistics and scatterplots for all four bivariate data sets. What do you notice about the values of R Squared and the appearances of the scatterplots?**

EXERCISE 21

MULTIPLE REGRESSION

BEFORE YOU START

The reader should study Section 12.3 before proceeding with this exercise.

THE PROJECT

A problem in reading research

Reading comprises many different component skills. A reading researcher hypothesises that certain specific kinds of pre-reading abilities and behaviour can predict later progress in reading, as measured by performance on reading tests taken some years after the child's first formal lessons. Let us, therefore, label the dependent variable (DV) in this study *progress*. While they are still very young indeed, many children evince a considerable grasp of English syntax in their speech. Our researcher devises a measure of their syntactic knowledge, *syntax*, based upon the average length of their uttered sentences. Some researchers, however, argue that an infant's prelinguistic babbling (which we shall label *vocal*) also plays a key role in their later reading performance. At the pre-reading stage, some very young children can acquire a sight vocabulary of several hundreds of words. The ability to pronounce these words on seeing them written down is known as logographic reading; but many authorities do not accept logographic reading. Our researcher, who views the logographic strategy as important, includes a measure of this skill, *logo*, in the study.

Preparing the data set

Fifty children are studied over a period beginning in infancy and extending through their school years. Their scores on the four measures, the DV *progress* (P), and the three IVs *logo* (L), *vocal* (V) and *syntax* (S), are listed in the appendix to this exercise. Since it would be very laborious for you to type in all the data during the exercise, we must hope that your instructor has already stored them in an accessible file. Let us suppose it is called **reading.sav**. The data are also available in WWW (http://www.psyc.abdn.ac.uk/teaching/spss/spssbook.htm).

Exploring the data

The distributions of the variables are most easily explored by using the **Boxplot** option from the **Graphs** drop-down menu. Select **Boxplot**, click on the **Summaries of separate variables** button, and then click on **Define**. Transfer the variable names into the **Boxes Represent** box and click on **OK**. This will plot four boxes side-by-side for easy comparison.

Regression is most effective when each IV is strongly correlated with the DV but uncorrelated with the other IVs. Although the correlation matrix can be listed from within the regression procedure, it is often more useful to scrutinise the matrix before proceeding with a regression analysis in order to make judgements about which variables might be retained and which dropped from the analysis. For example, it might be advisable to make a choice between two variables which are highly correlated with one another.

Use the **Bivariate Correlations** procedure to compute the correlation matrix. The same procedure can conveniently be used for tabulating the means and standard deviations which are available as an option. After transferring the variable names to the **Variables** box, click on **Options** and select **Means and standard deviations** within the **Statistics** choice box. Click on **Continue** and then on **OK**. Notice that the DV *progress* shows substantial correlations with both *logo* and *syntax*. On the other hand, there is no appreciable correlation between *logo* and *syntax*. The remaining variable (*vocal*) shows little association with any of the other variables; although there is a hint of a negative correlation with *logo*.

Running the multiple regression analysis

Run the multiple regression of *progress* upon the three regressors, by following the procedure in Section 12.3. Remember that the **Dependent** variable is what you are predicting (*progress*) and the **Independent** variables are the predictors (*logo, vocal, syntax*). Use both the simultaneous (**Enter**) and stepwise (**Stepwise**) procedures.

Output listing for the multiple regression

The main features of a multiple regression output listing, both for the simultaneous and forward stepwise methods, are explained in Section 12.3 .

- **Do the decisions of the multiple regression procedure about which variables are important agree with your informal observations during the exploratory phase of the data analysis?**
- **Write out the regression equation which you would use to predict progress given a subject's values for logo, vocal and syntax.**

Appendix to Exercise 21 - The data

P	L	V	S	P	L	V	S	P	L	V	S	P	L	V	S
65	75	34	48	46	55	75	32	65	50	75	68	34	32	42	27
58	29	18	67	51	31	50	66	71	65	23	64	54	64	55	32
42	40	43	38	61	69	59	46	60	56	52	44	81	82	60	69
55	55	9	48	45	19	71	59	17	10	64	20	77	66	50	79
68	81	41	54	53	48	44	45	55	41	41	55	57	30	20	54
59	28	72	68	46	45	29	45	69	51	14	62	80	82	65	58
50	39	31	42	25	28	58	28	47	49	46	59	89	51	52	48
50	26	78	56	71	70	51	54	53	14	53	77	50	34	45	60
71	84	46	50	30	55	42	25	50	40	51	31	69	49	72	72
65	71	30	52	62	53	52	57	80	45	59	90	71	69	57	60
34	30	30	20	47	20	78	69	51	18	22	61	39	25	81	49
44	71	79	22	60	46	80	67	79	58	13	82				
47	62	26	30	70	66	40	61	51	43	31	50				

EXERCISE 22
LOGLINEAR ANALYSIS

BEFORE YOU START

Before you proceed with this practical, please read Chapter 13.

THE PROJECT

Helping behaviour: The opposite-sex dyadic hypothesis

In the literature on helping behaviour by (and towards) men and women, there is much interest in three questions:

(1) Are women more likely to receive help?
(2) Are women more likely to give help?
(3) Are people more likely to help members of the opposite sex? (This is known as the **opposite-sex dyadic hypothesis.**)

A male or female confederate of the experimenter approached male and female students who were entering a university library and asked them to participate in a survey. Table 1 shows the incidence of helping in relation to the sex of the confederate and that of the subject.

Table 1.

Results of an experiment to test the opposite-sex dyadic hypothesis

Sex of Confederate	Sex of Subject	Help	
		yes	no
Male	Male	52	35
	Female	21	43
Female	Male	39	40
	Female	23	75

Exploring the data

Before carrying out any formal analysis, however, a brief inspection of the contingency table may prove informative. First of all, we notice that, on the whole, help was more likely to be refused than given; moreover, the females helped less than did the males. In view of the generally lower rate of helping in the female subjects, therefore, there seems to be little support for the hypothesis that females help more. Finally, turning to the third question, although the male subjects did help the male confederate more often, the female subjects tended to be more helpful towards the male confederate. This provides some support for the opposite-sex dyadic hypothesis.

Procedure for a loglinear analysis

In order to answer the three research questions, these results will be subjected to a **hierarchical loglinear analysis** (following the **backward elimination** strategy), with a view to fitting the most parsimonious **unsaturated model**. Prepare the data set exactly as described in Section 13.2.2. There are three variables in the contingency table:

(1) Confederate's Sex (*confsx*).

(2) Subject's Sex (*subjsx*).

(3) Subject's Response (*help*).

Since there must be a coding variable for each of these, plus another variable of cell counts (*count*), the data set will comprise four variables in all. Prepare four columns in the Data Editor window, adding appropriate extended variable names and the value labels of the coding variables. Run the loglinear procedure (ignoring the preliminary Crosstabs operation) as described in Section 13.2.2.

Output listing for the loglinear analysis

The main features of the output listing for a hierarchical loglinear analysis are described in Section 13.2.3. The listing reports tests of models in which one of the two-way interaction terms has been left out. It can be seen that only the interaction between *confsx* and *subjsx* can be removed so that the increment in the **L-R chi-square** has a p-value not less than 0.05. That term, therefore, is dropped from the model. The final model has two interaction terms: *confsx*help* and *subjsx* help*.

- **Note down the p-value of the L-R chi-square along with its p-value associated with the best-fitting model. This is a measure of the success of the model to predict the cell frequencies: the greater the size of the p-value, the better the fit.**

Finally the listing shows a table of 'Observed, Expected Frequencies and Residuals'. Notice how small the residuals are.

Test the hypothesis of total independence of all three variables, using the procedure described in Section 13.2.4.

- **Write down the new value of the L-R chi-square along with its p-value. What do you conclude about the total independence model?**

CONCLUSION

It should be quite clear from the foregoing comparisons that the final loglinear model is a very considerable improvement upon the model of total independence. Loglinear models provide a powerful tool for teasing out the relationships among the variables in multi-way contingency tables.

EXERCISE 23

PREDICTING CATEGORY MEMBERSHIP: DISCRIMINANT ANALYSIS

BEFORE YOU START

Before proceeding with this practical, please read Chapter 14.

THE PROJECT

Prediction of reading success at the school-leaving stage

Just before they leave school, students in the most senior class of a school are regularly tested on their comprehension of a difficult reading passage. Typically, only 50% of students can perform the task. We shall also suppose that, for a substantial number of past pupils, we have available data not only on their performance on the comprehension passage but also on the very same variables that were investigated in the exercise on multiple regression, namely, the reading-related measures that we have referred to as *logo*, *syntax* and *vocal*, all of which were taken in the very earliest stages of the children's education.

The full data set is given in the appendix of this exercise. As with the multiple regression example, we can only hope that the data have already been stored in a file with a name such as **discrim.sav**, the contents of which you can access by using the **Open** procedure. Table 1 shows the first and the last few lines of the data set.

The data are also available on WWW (http://www.psyc.abdn.ac.uk/teaching/spss/spssbook.htm).

Table 1.

Part of the data set

Logo	Syntax	Vocal	Comprehension
10	20	64	1
28	28	58	1
...	...	...	...
82	69	60	2
51	48	52	2

The rightmost variable is a coding variable whose values, *1* and *2*, denote, respectively, *failure* and *success* on the comprehension task.

Exploring the data set

Before moving on to the main analysis, a preliminary exploration of the data will bring out at least some of the important features. For example, if a particular variable is going to be useful in assigning individuals to categories, one might expect that, if its scores are subdivided according to category membership, there should be a substantial difference between the group means; if, on the other hand, there is no such difference, that would suggest that the variable will play a minimal role in the final discriminant function. To investigate these differences, **one-way ANOVAs** can be used to compare the group means on the various independent variables. These tests, however, are requested by options within the **Discriminant** procedure. We shall therefore return to the descriptive statistics when we come to prepare the dialog box.

Since discriminant analysis assumes that the distribution of the independent variables is multivariate normal, we shall also need to look at their empirical distributions to ascertain the credibility of that assumption.

Use the **Graphs** procedure to plot boxplots for the predictor variables as in Exercise 21 by choosing the **Summaries of Separate Variables** option and then defining the variables as *logo syntax vocal*.

- **Study the output and note whether the boxplots reveal any outliers. Do the side-by-side boxplots show anything of interest?**

Procedure for discriminant analysis

Run the discriminant analysis as described in Section 14.2.2.2. There, however, we recommended the **Stepwise** method of minimisation of **Wilks' lambda**. In the present example, because of its simplicity, it is better to use the default method known as **Enter**, in which all the variables are entered simultaneously. Since **Enter** is the default method, there is no need to specify it. Click on **Statistics** in the Discriminant Analysis dialog box to open the Discriminant Analysis: Statistics dialog box. Select **Univariate ANOVAs** and click on **Continue**. Click on **Classify** in the Discriminant Analysis dialog box to open the Discriminant Analysis: Classification dialog box. Select **Combined-groups** button in Plots and **Summary table** in Display. Click on **Continue** and then **OK**.

Output listing for discriminant analysis

The main features of the output for a discriminant analysis are explained in Section 14.2.3, which you should review.

In the present example, the first table shows the number of cases in each of the categories of the variable *comp*. The next table, headed 'Wilks' lambda (U-statistic) and univariate F-ratio', shows the F-ratios (and their associated p-values) for the comparisons between the groups on each of the three independent variables. The value of **Wilks' lambda** given in each of the ANOVAs is equal to one minus the **correlation ratio** (see Section 14.1.1).

- **Which variables have significant F ratios and which do not?**

There now follows the first of the tables showing the output of the discriminant analysis proper. Its title is 'Canonical Discriminant Functions'. Because there are only two groups, there is only one function.

The most important entries in the table are the statistic **lambda**, its **chi-square value** and the associated **p-value**. You will notice immediately that the value of lambda is smaller than the value for any of the three IVs considered separately. That is well and good: the discriminant function *D*, which uses the information in all the IVs should do a better job than any one IV alone. Here there is an obvious parallel with multiple regression, in which the predictive ability of the multiple regression equation cannot be less than the simple regressions of the target variable on any one regressor alone. Just as, in multiple regression, predictions can only improve when more regressors are added, the addition of another variable to the discriminant function can only improve its efficacy (although, in the case of the variable *vocal*, the improvement is negligible). Since, however, two of the IVs can each discriminate reliably between the groups, the result of the chi-square test of lambda in the discriminant analysis table is a foregone conclusion. As expected, the p-value is very small. The discriminant function *D* can indeed discriminate reliably between the two groups on the basis of performance on the independent variables.

Ignore the table of standardized Canonical Discriminant Function Coefficients.

A more useful table is the next one, labelled 'Structure Matrix: Pooled-within-groups correlations between discriminating variables and canonical discriminant functions'.

- **Are the correlations as you expected?**

Examine the 'All-groups stacked histogram' to ascertain the success of the discriminant function in minimising the overlap between the distributions of D in the two groups. Notice that, although the groups are generally well separated, some 2s intrude into the area dominated by the 1s and vice versa. This means that, if category membership is unknown, SPSS will misassign some of the cases to the wrong group.

We have shown that the discriminant function D discriminates between the two groups; but how effectively does it do this? This is shown under the heading: 'Classification Results'.

- **Note down the percentage of grouped cases correctly classified, the percentage of correct group 1 predictions and the percentage of correct group 2 predictions.**

Now try out the discriminant function on some fresh data by adding them at the end of the data file (e.g. enter in the columns for *logo*, *syntax*, *vocal*, the values 50, 50, 50; 10, 10, 10; 80, 80, 80 and any others you wish). Leave the column blank for *compreh*. Then re-run the analysis after selecting **Save** in the **Discriminant Analysis** dialog box, clicking the radio button for **Predicted group membership**, and then clicking **Continue** and **OK**. The predicted memberships will appear in the variable called **dis_1**.

- **Will someone with logo, syntax and vocal scores of 50, 50, 50 respectively be expected to pass or fail the comprehension test?**

CONCLUSION

This exercise is intended to be merely an introduction to the use of a complex and sophisticated statistical technique. Accordingly, we chose an example of the simplest possible application, in which the dependent variable comprises only two categories. The simplicity of our interpretation of a number of statistics such as **Wilks' lambda** breaks down when there are more than two categories in the dependent variable. For a treatment of such cases, see Tabachnick & Fidell (1996).

Appendix to Exercise 23 - The Data

L	S	V	C	L	S	V	C	L	S	V	C	L	S	V	C	L	S	V	C
10	20	64	1	45	45	29	1	43	50	31	1	56	44	52	2	84	50	72	2
28	28	58	1	62	30	26	1	48	45	44	1	69	46	59	2	70	54	51	2
55	25	42	1	20	69	78	1	14	77	53	1	53	57	52	2	65	64	23	2
30	20	30	1	49	59	46	1	64	32	55	1	75	48	34	2	69	60	57	2
32	27	42	1	26	56	78	1	55	48	9	1	71	52	30	2	66	79	50	2
25	49	81	1	39	42	31	1	41	55	41	2	50	68	75	2	58	82	13	2
40	38	43	1	40	31	51	1	30	54	20	2	81	54	41	2	45	90	59	2
71	22	79	1	34	60	45	1	29	67	18	2	51	62	14	2	82	58	65	2
19	59	71	1	31	66	50	1	28	68	72	2	49	72	72	2	82	69	60	2
55	32	75	1	18	61	22	1	46	67	80	2	66	61	40	2	51	48	52	2

EXERCISE 24

FACTOR ANALYSIS

BEFORE YOU START

Before proceeding with this practical, please read Chapter 15.

THE PROJECT

A personality study

Two hundred subjects are given a battery of personality tests, comprising the following items:

Anxiety; Agoraphobia; Arachnophobia; Extraversion; Adventure; Sociability.

Preparing the data set

Although the first step would normally be to enter the data for the 200 subjects into the **Data Editor** window, there is obviously insufficient time for you to do that in this exercise. We shall therefore input a correlation matrix directly. Unfortunately, this cannot be done by using the dialog box interface: instead, **SPSS Syntax** must be used, as described in Section 15.2.3.

The **R matrix** is shown in Table 1.

Table 1.

The R matrix

	Anxiety	Agora	Arachno	Advent	Extrav	Sociab
Anxiety	1.0000	0.8560	0.7845	0.0820	0.0560	0.0995
Agora	0.8560	1.0000	0.8271	0.0564	0.0283	0.0752
Arachno	0.7845	0.8271	1.0000	0.0624	0.0369	0.0795
Advent	0.0820	0.0564	0.0624	1.0000	0.8652	0.8396
Extrav	0.0560	0.0283	0.0369	0.8652	1.0000	0.8560
Sociab	0.0995	0.0752	0.0795	0.8396	0.8560	1.0000

Procedure for the factor analysis

Model your data syntax on the example given in Section 15.2.3.1 by typing into the Syntax Window the following:

- The MATRIX DATA VARIABLES command with the appropriate variable names (including ROWTYPE_)
- A BEGIN DATA command
- Rows of correlation coefficients (each preceded by CORR)
- A row indicating the size of n (preceded by N and then the size of n repeated for as many variables as you have)
- An END DATA command concluding with a period (.)

When the data syntax is complete, run it by dragging the cursor over all the syntax and then clicking on **Run**. You should then see the Data Editor window looking like that in Chapter 15, Figure 12.

If all is well, proceed to prepare the FACTOR command by typing in everything shown in Chapter 15, Figure 13, and running it in the same way as described above. An explanation of the output listing is given in Section 15.2.2.

Output listing for the factor analysis

- **Construct your own table from the rotated factor matrix in the listing, showing the loadings of each of the variables on the two factors that have emerged from the analysis. State clearly whether there is a tendency for different groups of variables to load upon different factors.**

REFERENCES

Anderson, A. J. B. (1989). ***Interpreting data: A first course in statistics.*** London: Chapman and Hall.

Anscombe, F. J. (1973). Graphs in statistical analysis. ***American Statistician, 27,*** 17-21.

Cohen, J., & Cohen, P. (1983). ***Applied multiple regression/correlation analysis for the behavioral sciences.*** (2nd ed.). Hillsdale, N. J.: Lawrence Erlbaum.

Darlington, R. B. (1968). Multiple regression in psychological research and practice. ***Psychological Bulletin, 69,*** 161-182.

Delucchi, K. L. (1983). The use and misuse of chi-square: Lewis and Burke revisited. ***Psychological Bulletin, 94,*** 166-176.

Everitt, B. S. (1977). ***The analysis of contingency tables.*** London: Chapman and Hall.

Gravetter, F. J., & Wallnau, L. B. (1996). ***Statistics for the behavioral sciences: A first course for students of psychology and education.*** (4th ed.). St. Paul: West.

Hartwig, F., & Dearing, B. E. (1979). ***Exploratory data analysis.*** Sage University paper series on quantitative applications in the social sciences, 07-016. Newbury Park, CA: Sage.

Howell, D. C. (1997). ***Statistical methods for psychology.*** (4th ed.). Belmont, CA: Duxbury.

Keppel, G. (1973). ***Design and analysis: A researcher's handbook***. Englewood Cliffs, N.J.:Prentice-Hall.

Kerlinger, F. N. (1986). ***Foundations of behavioral research.*** (3rd ed.). New York: Holt, Rinehart & Winston.

Kim, J., & Mueller, C. W. (1978a). ***Introduction to factor analysis: What it is and how to do it.*** Sage University paper series on quantitative applications in the social sciences, 07-013. Newbury Park, CA: Sage.

Kim, J., & Mueller, C. W. (1978b). ***Factor analysis: Statistical methods and practical issues.*** Sage University paper series on quantitative applications in the social sciences, 07-014. Newbury Park, CA: Sage.

Kinnear, P.R., & Gray, C.D. (1992). ***SPSS/PC+ made simple.*** Hove (UK): Lawrence Erlbaum Associates.

Kirk, R. E. (1982). ***Experimental design: Procedures for the behavioral sciences.*** (2nd ed.). Belmont: Brooks/Cole.

Lewis, D., & Burke, C. J. (1949). The use and misuse of the chi-square test. ***Psychological Bulletin, 46,*** 433-489.

Lovie, P. (1991). Regression diagnostics: A rough guide to safer regression. In P. Lovie & A. D. Lovie, ***New developments in statistics for psychology and the social sciences.*** London and New York: The British Psychological Society and Routledge.

Microsoft (1992). ***Microsoft Windows user's guide and getting started.*** U.S.: Microsoft Corporation.

Neave, H.R. & Worthington, P.L. (1988). ***Distribution-free tests.*** London: Unwin Hyman.

Reynolds, H. T. (1984). ***The analysis of nominal data.*** (2nd ed.). Sage University paper series on quantitative applications in the social sciences, 07-007. Newbury Park, CA: Sage.

Siegel, S., & Castellan, N. J. (1988). ***Nonparametric statistics for the behavioral sciences.*** (2nd ed.). New York: McGraw-Hill.

Tabachnick, B. G., & Fidell, L. S. (1996). ***Using multivariate statistics.*** (3rd ed.). New York: Harper and Row.

Tukey, J.W. (1977). ***Exploratory data analysis.*** Reading, MA: Addison-Wesley.

Upton, G. J. G. (1978). ***The analysis of cross-tabulated data.*** Chichester: John Wiley.

Upton, G. J. G. (1986). Cross-classified data. In A. D. Lovie (ed.), ***New developments in statistics for psychology and the social sciences.*** London and New York: The British Psychological Society and Methuen.

Winer, B. J., Brown, D. R., & Michels, K. M. (1991). ***Statistical principles in experimental design.*** (3rd ed.). New York: McGraw-Hill.

INDEX